studies in jazz

Institute of Jazz Studies
Rutgers—The State University of New Jersey
General Editors: *Dan Morgenstern & Edward Berger*

The *Annual Review of Jazz Studies* is published yearly by Scarecrow Press for the Institute of Jazz Studies at Rutgers, The State University of New Jersey.

Authors should address manuscripts and editorial correspondence to:

The Editors
Annual Review of Jazz Studies
Institute of Jazz Studies
Bradley Hall 135
Rutgers, The State University of New Jersey
Newark, New Jersey 07102

Review copies of books should be sent to this address by publishers and marked to the attention of the Book Review Editor.

Authors preparing manuscripts for consideration should follow *The Chicago Manual of Style.* In particular: (1) manuscripts should be original typed or word-processed copies; (2) except for foreign-language quotations, manuscripts must be in English; (3) *all* material (text, quotations, endnotes, author's biographical note) must be neat, double-spaced, and with adequate margins; (4) notes must be grouped together on separate pages at the end of the manuscript and should be complete references following the samples in *A Manual of Style;* (5) on a separate sheet, authors should provide a one- or two-sentence biographical note, including current affiliation; and (6) musical examples should be on separate sheets in camera-ready form; they must be clear enough to be legible if reduction is required to fit the *ARJS* format.

Authors alone are responsible for the contents of their articles.

ANNUAL REVIEW OF JAZZ STUDIES 6 1993

edited by
Edward Berger
David Cayer
Dan Morgenstern
Lewis Porter

Institute of Jazz Studies
Rutgers—The State University
of New Jersey
and
The Scarecrow Press, Inc.
Metuchen, N.J., & London
1993

British Library Cataloguing-in-Publication data available

ISBN 0-8108-2478-7 (ARJS 5)
ISBN 0-8108-2727-1   82-644466

Copyright © 1993 by Rutgers—The State University of New Jersey
(Rutgers Institute of Jazz Studies, Newark, NJ 07102)
Manufactured in the United States of America
Printed on acid-free paper

CONTENTS

BOOK REVIEWS

PREFACE

The sixth volume of the *Annual Review of Jazz Studies* is the second to appear in a hardcover format and to be published by Scarecrow Press, which is also the publisher of the Studies in Jazz monograph series which, like *ARJS,* is sponsored by the Institute of Jazz Studies, a unit of Rutgers, The State University of New Jersey.

Two articles in this volume represent innovations for *ARJS.* As a frontispiece illustrating our lead article, "Anatomy of a Cover" by Charles H. Waters, Jr., we offer the first full-color illustration ever to appear in *ARJS—Time* magazine's August 20, 1956, cover portrait of Duke Ellington by painter Peter Hurd. Through the courtesy of *Time,* the cover, as well as the article and photographs which accompanied it, are reproduced in full as an appendix to Mr. Waters's article.

William Bauer's detailed analysis of the singing styles of Billie Holiday and Betty Carter is the first *ARJS* article based on research supported in part by a grant from the Morroe Berger-Benny Carter Jazz Research Fund at the Institute of Jazz Studies. The editors and publisher of *ARJS* recognized that Mr. Bauer's transcriptions of each artist's performance of "I Didn't Know What Time It Was" would prove hard to decipher if greatly reduced to our format. Furthermore, spreading the music over many pages would make it difficult to follow his detailed comparisons between the two singers. We have therefore reproduced these transcriptions in a larger format and included them in this volume as inserts which can be removed for easy study and comparison.

The introduction of a photographic gallery in *ARJS 5* proved a popular innovation among both readers and reviewers, and this volume includes a gallery of Mitchell Seidel's photos—formal portraits, performance pictures, and backstage or studio candids.

As always, the range of jazz scholarship in *ARJS* remains diverse, both in methodology and in the styles and artists examined.

The current debate in higher education concerning "canons" in the arts and humanities is extended to jazz by a critic with parallel expertise in film and other genres, while another writer ponders the role of Latin influences in defining jazz styles.

Detailed studies of individual jazz artists include two articles on the seminal guitarist Charlie Christian, one presenting a detailed bibliography of his transcribed solos, the other exploring his legacy of after-hours, noncommercial recordings at Minton's. Other articles are devoted to the music of Ornette Coleman, Arthur Taylor, and a proposed standard method of notating melodic elements of jazz performance which are inadequately represented by standard notation.

This volume's book review section examines recent publications ranging from autobiography and biography (including lives of Benny Goodman and Billie Holiday) to a number of reference works.

Publications submitted for review, or for a forthcoming list of newly published works, should be addressed to:

> Review Editor
> *Annual Review of Jazz Studies*
> Institute of Jazz Studies
> 135 Bradley Hall
> Rutgers, The State University
> Newark, NJ 07102

While an annual publication cannot serve as a medium for general correspondence in the manner of a daily or weekly, the editors invite concise commentary on articles and reviews from readers and will publish, as space permits, appropriate correspondence at their discretion and with permission of the writer.

The Editors

ANATOMY OF A COVER: THE STORY OF DUKE ELLINGTON'S APPEARANCE ON THE COVER OF *TIME* MAGAZINE

By Charles H. Waters, Jr.

INTRODUCTION

In the summer of 1956, the fortunes of the Duke Ellington orchestra underwent a dramatic reversal as the result of two events which have since become benchmarks in its history. On the evening of Saturday, 7 July, the orchestra appeared at the Newport Jazz Festival in Rhode Island. During that appearance, the rendition of "Diminuendo and Crescendo in Blue," featuring an extended solo by Paul Gonsalves on tenor saxophone, caused a widely publicized sensation.[1] Shortly thereafter, Ellington was the subject of the cover story of the 20 August 1956 issue of *Time* magazine.[2] The immediate effect of these two events was a rebirth in popularity for the Ellington orchestra, which had endured a period of eclipse during the first half of the decade. In the long term, their positive effects would remain with and benefit Ellington for the remainder of his life.

In his autobiography, *Music Is My Mistress,*[3] Ellington formalized a position he had long espoused about the relationship of the two events: that the Newport success resulted in the *Time* cover story. Subsequent literature repeated and reinforced the proposition that preparation of the cover story began only after Newport and solely in response to it. However, closer examination of the circumstances has demonstrated that the decision to put Ellington on the cover of *Time* resulted from different and far-reaching considerations. Ellington's publicist, Joe Morgen, began efforts to secure the *Time* cover months before Newport. His work came to fruition through an editorial climate as remarkable as it was receptive.

The cover portrait was painted by the noted Southwestern artist, Peter Hurd. His correspondence clearly established that *Time* began to prepare the Ellington cover story prior to the Newport appearance. The portrait also subsumed a meeting between two great American artists from very different backgrounds, an event so alive with possibilities that it invited separate examination.

THE SIGNIFICANCE OF A TIME COVER APPEARANCE

For any person to appear on the cover of *Time* magazine is a significant event which carries with it extraordinary prestige. These effects result directly from the emphasis placed on the cover story by *Time*'s founder and longtime Editor-in-Chief, Henry R. Luce:

> He had a powerful sense of what people should read, what was good for them to read, and an essential belief worthy of the best journalist, that any subject of importance could be made interesting. Thus, the cover story, the personalizing of issues so that a lay reader could become more interested and more involved in serious reading matter. The cover story alone had a major impact on the journalism of our age.[4]

The practice of naming *Time*'s "Man of the Year' as the year's initial cover story is a continuing manifestation of this historical emphasis. The success of the weekly news magazine concept, originated with *Time,* further enhanced the effect of the cover story on public perception.[5] Raymond Horricks accurately referred to a *Time* cover appearance as representing "the ultimate in American acceptance."[6] The noted jazz author, Stanley Dance, in liner notes to the remastered *Ellington at Newport* recording, wrote that Ellington's cover appearance was "like a national seal of approval."[7] Joseph McLaren summarized the effect and meaning of the Ellington cover:

The most significant event of this rebirth was the appearance of the orchestra at the 1956 Newport Jazz Festival in Rhode Island. This performance was reviewed by *Time* in its August 20 issue that featured Ellington as the cover story, a sign of recognition that also reflected the importance of Ellington and his organization to American musical culture. Although Ellington had previously been the subject of cover stories by certain jazz periodicals of the day, the *Time* cover story was a most impressive accolade for an Afro-American musician who had maintained a big band orchestra for over twenty-nine years without disbanding, a feat which was unequaled by any other practitioner of popular American music and jazz.[8]

The *Time* cover story thus served both to acknowledge Ellington's stature and to confirm the renaissance of his orchestra. In coming years, the effect of Newport, as enhanced by this cover, will assume a significance of its own, as Ellington intended.

THE COVER STORY

The *Time* cover story was both a product and a reflection of the times and circumstances in which it arose. In the spring of 1956, Ellington turned fifty-seven. It was then an appropriate point for his stature, already of the highest magnitude, to be acknowledged in a national publication. Stanley Dance succinctly made this point: "When you consider . . . the stature Duke had acquired over the years, the *Time* cover doesn't seem so surprising now as it may have . . . then."[9]

There were more immediate factors at work. The first half of the decade of the 1950s had been a period of artistic highs and lows for the orchestra. Ellington's tone poem, "Harlem (A Tone Parallel to Harlem)," his last extended single work, premiered in January 1951.[10] He continued to produce any number of minor masterpieces, such as the little-known "Deep Night" (1951)[11] and "Ultra-Deluxe" (1953).[12] "Satin Doll" was another 1953 composition. A critical blow, however, was struck early in 1951 when Johnny Hodges,

Lawrence Brown, and Sonny Greer departed.[13] They were replaced, respectively, by Willie Smith, Juan Tizol, and Louis (Louie) Bellson. Despite a further infusion of talent in 1950 and 1951, which also saw Paul Gonsalves, Britt Woodman, Willie Cook, and Clark Terry join the band, there ensued a period of instability in personnel, particularly manifested in the drummer's chair.[14] The problems are generally considered to have reached their nadir with the Aquacades appearance in the summer of 1955, generally regarded as a debacle.[15] Even by then, however, the turnaround had begun. In January 1955, a new bassist, Jimmy Woode, joined the band. In the summer of 1955, Johnny Hodges returned, accompanied by a new drummer, Sam Woodyard.[16] Ellington's contract with Capitol Records expired at the end of 1955. Early in February 1956, an extended session for Bethlehem Records resulted in two recordings which demonstrated the band to be in outstanding form.[17] Ellington then signed a new contract with Columbia Records. Irving Townsend was assigned as his executive producer, and this association would prove exceptionally fruitful.[18]

The positive developments of this period did not go unnoticed by knowledgeable jazz critics. In the spring of 1956, the *Saturday Review* featured an extended appreciation of Ellington by Whitney Balliett, which could be viewed as a harbinger of the *Time* cover story. Although not biographical as the *Time* story would be (Ellington was not interviewed), the article summarized the history of the band, with emphasis on the recent past and the changing present. An excerpt from this warm and eloquent tribute is the following:

> Again, many listeners have been hypnotized by the trappings that often surround his music: the lushness, the use of the growl, the squatty brass and saxophone slurs, the striding humor, the seemingly insouciant, akimbo attitude of his musicians toward their music. This warm, overlaid picturesqueness is not ostentation, however; it is, rather, the result of a mind that moves through greener, more tangled musical meadows than those of the average journeyman jazzman. Ellington,

indeed, is perhaps the first, and as yet the only, complete jazz artist.[19]

In retrospect, for both long-term and short-term reasons, it was an appropriate point in Ellington's career for him to be accorded recognition other than by jazz critics or in jazz periodicals, as had previously been the case. It remained for two men in the midst of these developments, Joe Morgen and Carter Harman, to act effectively to get Ellington onto the cover of *Time*.

In the latter part of 1955, Ellington's publicist, Joe Morgen, conceived the idea of a *Time* cover story. He elected to approach *Time* both because of the exposure which would result from a cover appearance on the leading weekly news magazine and because his contact there, Carter Harman, shared his views about an Ellington cover story.

The personalities of Morgen and Harman were critical factors in the genesis of the *Time* cover story. Morgen was a Falstaffian character of little formal education or sophistication, with an unkempt appearance and an uncouth manner to match. His effectiveness as a publicist derived from the fact that he had the finesse and persistence of a bulldog. He died in 1981, but his forceful personality is vividly recalled by those who knew him. Stanley Dance has written:

> Joe Morgen was a very persistent publicity man. I wasn't in this country in 1956, but he himself always referred to the *Time* cover and story as one of his major coups. [He] was aggressive and hard to take at times, but he was absolutely loyal and devoted to Duke. He was also a hard worker. He knew all the press people and was always on their backs to give Duke publicity. Sometimes, I know, they did so to get rid of him, but they would not shake him for long.[20]

> It was part of Joe Morgen's job to make and maintain contacts with journalists who could give Duke . . . publicity of one kind or another. He was on good terms with Carter Harman, who wrote the story, and Carter had considerable understanding and affection for Duke's music.[21]

The DETS Newsletter of June/July, 1981, published shortly after Joe Morgen's death, contains this tribute:

> Those of us who knew Joe personally always admired his true sense of loyalty to Duke and his sincere love of the man. Joe was a bachelor, and in a sense, Duke was his mistress. I was proud to have known him these many years.[22]

Finally, we have Ellington's appreciation of Joe Morgen, in words which appear to have been written with the *Time* cover story in mind:

> Joe Morgen, who has been with me the longest—over twenty years—is the kind of p.r. who thinks only in terms of cover stories, full page pictures, and big, important articles in magazines. Maybe I exaggerate a little, for he will stand still for a good word in a column.[23]

Late in 1955, Morgen proposed the idea of an Ellington cover story to Carter Harman, music editor of *Time*. Harman now lives in Carmel, California. He is a 1940 graduate of Princeton University, having majored in music and studied under Roger Sessions. He became music editor of *Time* in 1952, after five years as a music reporter for *The New York Times*.[24] During his tenure as music editor, which extended until 1957, he wrote five cover stories, the subjects of which speak to his catholic taste: Rosemary Clooney,[25] George Balanchine,[26] Dave Brubeck,[27] Duke Ellington, and Maria Callas.[28] Harman first heard Ellington on radio in 1934 and first saw him in person in 1938 at the downtown Cotton Club on 48th Street in New York. He met Ellington briefly at a dance pavilion in New Brunswick, New Jersey, during his undergraduate years and retains to this day a deep love of and respect for Ellington and his music. Harman had known Joe Morgen casually for a number of years, but it was some time after they met before he became aware of Morgen's relationship with Ellington.

Morgen also did publicity work for the Hickory House, a steak restaurant on 52nd Street, which featured first-rate jazz

Carter Harman
Photograph by John Urban, Boston, Massachusetts

and was one of Ellington's favorite places to eat.[29] Much of what followed was planned and implemented there. It was through Morgen that Harman was again to meet Ellington and become involved in the cover story.

The first result of Morgen's efforts was an article which appeared in *Time* in January 1956.[30] In it, the band's resurgence is noted, and Sam Woodyard, whose picture appears, is the subject of high praise.[31] Carter Harman has said: "I wrote this article to keep Joe Morgen quiet. It didn't work and I knew it wouldn't."[32] This article was in fact far short of what Joe Morgen had in mind, and he continued into the spring of 1956 to promote Ellington as the subject of a *Time* cover story.

Morgen's dogged persistence and Harman's sympathetic ear would not have brought about the cover story had not responsible editors at *Time,* who never heard of or from Morgen, believed of their own accord that Ellington was a proper cover subject. Fortunately, a favorable editorial climate existed, both about jazz in general and Ellington in particular. For many years, the editorial thinking at *Time* had been that jazz was an American art form which deserved recognition as such. The Armstrong[33] and Brubeck[34] cover stories were manifestations of this editorial commitment to jazz.[35] Given the interval since the Brubeck story in November 1954, *Time* was seeking to reaffirm that commitment with a jazz cover. Given his stature, both in an absolute sense and in comparison to that of the jazz musicians who had previously graced *Time*'s cover, Ellington was clearly the logical subject. Robert Manning, senior editor, to whom Carter Harman reported, actively supported the idea of an Ellington cover. Otto Fuerbringer, assistant managing editor, who would make the definitive cover story recommendation, was also supportive, as was Roy Alexander, managing editor, who would ultimately approve that recommendation.[36]

In the spring of 1956, the efforts of Morgen and Harman, together with *Time*'s receptive editorial climate, began to produce results. From 10 May through 6 June 1956, Ellington had an extended engagement at the Flamingo Hotel in Las Vegas.[37] *Time*'s commitment to proceed with the Ellington cover was first manifested during this engagement. On 20

Otto Fuerbringer
Photograph by Bob Capazzo, Greenwich, Connecticut

May 1956, Otto Fuerbringer sent a telegram to Peter Hurd, inquiring whether Hurd would be interested in painting the cover portrait.[38] During the week of 27 May,[39] Harman flew from New York to Las Vegas, lived with Ellington in a rented house for three or four days, and gathered the background material for the cover story.[40] Morgen accompanied him, keeping a watchful eye on his favorite project. The day after the Flamingo appearance concluded, 7 June 1956, the band travelled to San Francisco to begin a ten-day engagement at the Macumba Club, during which the cover portrait was painted. Thus, by late June 1956, the cover story had been researched, although not yet written, and the cover portrait had been completed. At this point, publication of the Ellington cover story essentially became a reality. On infrequent occasions, cover stories for which portraits had been painted were not published, but Ellington's stature and his acceptance at all editorial levels of *Time* as the leading jazz figure of the period virtually assured that this story would be. A final editorial decision remained: when to publish. That decision would, for all practical purposes, be made by *Time*'s assistant managing editor, Otto Fuerbringer.

Fuerbringer now lives in retirement in Greenwich, Connecticut.[41] Early in 1960, he was named by Henry R. Luce to succeed Roy Alexander as managing editor. Hedley Donovan, who in 1964 would succeed Luce as editor-in chief of *Time,* wrote of this selection:

> Fuerbringer was an excellent choice, imaginative, energetic, as well organized as *Time* itself, as well informed about everything as *Time* sought to make its mythical cover-to-cover reader. His news antennae were beautifully tuned. He was alert to trends in show business, education, the arts, theology—all the "back of the book" departments that some readers who hated *Time*'s politics found indispensable. He had something of Luce's gift for latching onto a scrap of conversation or an obscure item in the paper and seeing a *Time* story in it.[42]

In 1956, one of Fuerbringer's principal responsibilities as assistant managing editor was to chair the weekly cover conference. Representatives of various departments of the magazine attended this conference, each prepared to advocate a cover story subject. Recommendations were developed concerning cover subjects for the ensuing several months. These recommendations were forwarded to Managing Editor Roy Alexander and, given the collegial journalism practiced within *Time,* were invariably followed.

These cover story recommendations necessarily took into consideration a number of editorial parameters intrinsic to *Time* as a weekly news magazine. The majority of its covers and stories dealt with events of the immediate past, or with anticipated future events, in national and world affairs. Periodically, *Time* also featured cover stories about topical matters, such as developments in the arts or sciences. These stories were referred to within the magazine as "back-of-the-book" stories, because their subject matter came from departments which appeared in the second part of the magazine, the first part being devoted to national and world affairs. Back-of-the-book stories were inherently of continuing interest, and were, in that sense, not date-sensitive. Nevertheless, these stories had to have a "news peg," some relationship to current events, even though that relationship need not be direct. The existence of this relationship was critical. The Ellington cover story, as it then stood, did not fit within these parameters because it had no relationship to any discrete current event. Although *Time* was firmly committed to publishing the Ellington cover story at some point, the story was in a posture to be postponed to await a news peg. Suddenly and unexpectedly, one appeared—Ellington's sensational appearance at the Newport Jazz Festival on 7 July.

Morgen recognized that Newport might provide the impetus to publish the *Time* cover story and saw an opportunity to make the point. Harman recalled the occasion vividly. On the evening of Saturday, 28 July 1956, Ellington appeared at the Connecticut Jazz Festival.[43] He returned to New York after the performance to attend an all-night party at the apartment of his longtime friend and onetime colleague, jazz writer Leonard Feather. Morgen invited Harman to the party and there advocated Newport as the current event needed to induce publication of the Ellington cover story. Harman thought Newport weak in this regard because of its increasing remoteness in time. Three weeks had passed since Newport: additional time would be required to write the story and edit it for publication. Nevertheless, he also recognized that Newport might be sufficient as a news peg. He presented the Newport concept to Senior Editor Robert Manning. A preliminary story conference for portions of the back-of-the-book part of the magazine, including music, was held in *Time*'s offices on the morning of Sunday, 29 July 1956. Manning, who chaired that conference, there agreed to active consideration of the Ellington story on the basis that the Newport success provided the necessary current event relationship. The final decision to proceed with the Ellington cover was made at the cover conference, chaired by Fuerbringer, held on the following Thursday, 2 August 1956.

The covers Fuerbringer had under consideration for the next several week all involved hard news. It was his judgement that reader interest would be enhanced by varying the fare of this succession of current events covers with a back-of-the-book cover.[44] An opening for the Ellington cover story was created.[45] Harman was then authorized to write the story, which he did during the remainder of the first week of August.

Fuerbringer and Harman described two particular aspects of the writing of the story. Speaking retrospectively to the current event requirement, Fuerbringer emphasized that by the date of his decision to go forward with the Ellington cover story, he considered Newport sufficient only for the purpose of providing a dramatic introduction to it. Had the story been further delayed, Newport's value as a lead-in would have diminished, and it would have been accorded a less prominent place in the cover story. Moreover, back-of-the-book stories were subject to preemption by events of appropriate magnitude in national or world affairs. Given the fortuitous and waning status of Newport, the Ellington cover story was somewhat vulnerable in this regard. Perhaps more than anyone realized at the time, the cover story on Ellington was nearly postponed, to await the occurrence of some other event which would bring him into the news.

The other aspect of the writing of the story related to a personal matter. Ellington, aware that the story was being written, expressed to Harman the concern that a literal portrayal of his relationships with his wife, Edna, and with his longtime companion, Beatrice (Evie) Ellis, would be embarrassing to all concerned. The details of these relationships would be published three years later in an article in *Ebony* magazine,[46] an event which infuriated Ellington. This section of the story was then rewritten to mention the matter only in passing:

> Before long he had a house, a car, a wife and a son, Mercer. But his musical friends then moved to New York, where the jazz was hot. Duke followed in 1922, though it meant a fresh start, many penniless months, and a separation from his wife that became permanent.[47]

The 20 August 1956 issue of *Time,* featuring Duke Ellington as the subject of its cover story, appeared on the newsstands on Monday, 13 August 1956.

THE HISTORY OF THE COVER STORY

Once printed, the *Time* cover story passed into the lore of Ellingtonia. A perception quickly developed concerning the relationship between the *Time* cover story and Newport. Harman described what occurred:

> Once we had decided to go ahead, everybody happily swallowed the idea that it was Newport that sparked the story and no evidence ever appeared to the contrary. It only would have weakened the story's credibility and nobody wanted that.[48]

Moreover, the Newport-*Time* linkage possessed a certain superficial but compelling logic. The sequence and timing of the events naturally followed one another, and the proposition was attractive in its simplicity. The fiction of the relationship, once advanced, thus acquired a rather vigorous life of its own. When the Ellington literature began to develop some fifteen years later, the treatment accorded the relationship of Newport to the *Time* cover was consistent with that which had gone before.[49]

In *Music Is My Mistress,* Ellington twice mentions the *Time* cover. In the chronological narrative portion of the book, the following appears:

> Nineteen fifty-six was an important year. The performance of *Diminuendo and Crescendo in Blue* (originally written in 1937) at the Newport Jazz Festival, with an epic ride by Paul Gonsalves on tenor saxophone, brought us renewed attention and the cover of *Time* magazine. It was another of those major intersections in my career.[50]

Ellington concludes his appreciation of Joe Morgen, quoted earlier, with these words:

> He was the one who engineered the *Time* cover story in 1956 after our success at the Newport Jazz Festival.[51]

Ellington's characterization of Newport as "another of those major intersections" in his career is reinforced by subsequent tributes in *Music Is My Mistress* to others who had prominent roles in the Newport success—Jo Jones,[52] Sam Woodyard[53] and Jimmy Woode.[54]

Stanley Dance refers to the *Time* cover in *The World of Duke Ellington,* in a brief chronology of Ellington's career which appears as an appendix:

> 1956–Triumph at Newport Jazz Festival, following performance of "Diminuendo and Crescendo in Blue," which featured Paul Gonsalves extensively, resulted in Ellington's appearance on cover of *Time* magazine.[55]

Derek Jewell concludes his discussion of Newport in *Duke: A Portrait of Duke Ellington,* which the following:

> The music, in a sense, wasn't the point. This was an event, a turning point, what Duke called "another of

Paul Gonsalves
Photograph: Rutgers Institute of Jazz Studies

those major intersections" in his career. *Time* magazine
put him on its cover, and splashed his achievement over
several pages. Ellington was back with a vengeance,
and the world knew it.[56]

Mercer Ellington, in *Duke Ellington in Person: An
Intimate Memoir,* relates the two events:

> Paul [Gonsalves] played twenty-seven choruses [of
> "Diminuendo and Crescendo in Blue"], the band was
> really swinging behind him, and together they broke it
> up as nobody else ever had at Newport, before or since.
> There were scenes of the wildest enthusiasm, it was a
> big news item from coast to coast, and Pop's picture
> [*sic*] was on the cover of *Time* shortly afterward.[57]

Arnold Shaw makes reference in passing to the *Time* cover
in *Black Popular Music in America:*

> In 1956, Ellington made the cover of *Time* magazine
> after a "comeback" appearance at the Newport Jazz
> Festival.[58]

James Lincoln Collier cites two references to the *Time*
cover in his biography of Ellington:

> Rapidly, the word went out from Newport: Duke
> Ellington was back. And within weeks Ellington's
> picture was on the cover of *Time*. The record of the
> Newport concert sold in the hundreds of thousands and
> became Ellington's biggest seller.[59]

> The wave of enthusiasm for Ellington that followed the
> Newport success did not immediately ebb. . . . Elling-
> ton was on the cover of the August 20 issue of *Time,*
> whose story said, in part, "The event last month
> marked not only the turning point of the concert, it
> confirmed a turning point in a career."[60]

The *Time* cover story is also mentioned in numerous
secondary sources and in the liner notes to a number of
Ellington recordings.[61] The common denominator of both

primary and secondary sources is the explicitly stated or clearly implied proposition that *Time* began preparation of a cover story on Ellington only subsequent to and solely as a result of Newport. The facts now available simply do not support this proposition. How did it begin and why has it been perpetuated?

The most significant factor in the origination and perpetuation of the Newport-*Time* concept was Ellington's strongly held and frequently stated belief about the effect of Newport on his career.

> Whenever he was asked how old he was in the 1960s, Duke Ellington tended to give a mock scowl and say: "That's a dangerous question. I was born in 1956 at the Newport Festival."[62]

Patricia Willard echoed this characterization. She reiterated Ellington's feeling that he was "born at Newport" and that afterwards it was "Newport up." He expressed to her the feeling that his career prior to Newport was only of historical interest.[63] Ellington, of course, did not mean this in a literal sense. He consistently expressed the conviction that he preferred in all things to look to the future rather than to identify with the past.

In the two-part PBS series *A Duke Named Ellington,* Leonard Feather accurately summarized Ellington's view of Newport in a context which again emphasized and reinforced the connection with the *Time* cover. He concluded an extended interview about Newport with these words, spoken as the *Time* cover was strikingly displayed against a black background:

> And before you knew it Duke was on the cover of *Time* magazine. It represented a sort of renaissance for the orchestra and ever after that Duke would say "I was born at the Newport Jazz Festival on such-and-such a date in 1956."[64]

The text and physical arrangement of the cover story make it conspicuously amenable to the concept that it was prepared after and in response to Newport. The first three paragraphs are a graphic description of the festival appearance.[65] The second page features a page-width photograph captioned "Jazz Buffs Digging Ellington at Newport Festival."[66]

The critical importance Ellington attached to Newport leads to the conclusion that his recollection of all circumstances surrounding it would not have dimmed. To infer otherwise would be to ascribe to Ellington a forgetfulness and inattention to detail in lieu of the astute business practices he had acquired early in his career.[67] Ellington knew the sequence and timing of events, and knew that the *Time* cover story had been in preparation months prior to Newport. His treatment of the Newport-*Time* relationship in *Music Is My Mistress* was the written expression of a position he had taken since 1956—that Newport caused *Time* to prepare the cover story. Ellington's statements that Newport "brought us . . . the cover of *Time* magazine" and that the cover story had been "engineered . . . after our success at the Newport Jazz Festival" may therefore properly be viewed only in the larger context of his extraordinarily strong feelings about the effect of Newport. Through a subtle play on words, Newport and the *Time* cover were indelibly linked by a harmless but very effective fiction. It suited Ellington's purposes to characterize their relationship as one of cause and effect, and thereafter to promote it as such. From 1956 on he did so, and he knew exactly what he was doing.

THE COVER PAINTING

The letter written by the cover artist, Peter Hurd, confirms that *Time* began to prepare the Ellington cover story prior to Newport. On Tuesday, 5 June 1956, Peter Hurd wrote to his lifelong friend, the distinguished author Paul Horgan: "I will be off to San Francisco to paint a portrait of Duke Ellington on Thursday. . . ."[68] The Thursday referred to was 7 June 1956, exactly one month before Newport. San Francisco was agreed upon because of Ellington's engagement at the Macumba Club, which began on 8 June and extended through 17 June.[69]

Peter Hurd had come to paint cover portraits for *Time*

Peter Hurd
Photograph: *Houston Chronicle*

through the efforts of Otto Fuerbringer, who selected the cover artists. In 1953, when he assumed responsibility for covers, Fuerbringer embarked upon a project of his own creation to add a new dimension to cover art. *Time* covers in those years invariably featured portraits of persons painted from photographs by one of a number of artists on retainer.[70] Fuerbringer determined that henceforth, to the extent practical, cover portraits would be painted from life by recognized artists.[71] The resulting portraits, of which the Ellington portrait was one, would enhance an already outstanding body of cover art.[72] In the years to come, such notable artists as Henry Koerner, Marc Chagall, and Andrew Wyeth would paint cover portraits from life. Peter Hurd, a rancher and horseman from New Mexico, had come to the attention of Fuerbringer not only because of his stature as an artist and his ability to paint portraits, but also because he was Andrew Wyeth's brother-in-law.

Peter Hurd was born in Roswell, New Mexico, in 1904, and grew up in its frontier atmosphere. In 1921, he entered the United States Military Academy at West Point, New York, where he studied for two years and sold his first sketches. Recognizing his talent, he resigned from West Point in 1923 and studied art at Haverford College for one year. He then studied for two years in Chadd's Ford, Pennsylvania, under N.C. Wyeth. During this period, he met and courted the woman he would later marry, N.C. Wyeth's daughter, Henriette, and formed a lifelong personal and artistic relationship with Henriette's brother, Andrew.[73] Andrew Wyeth would later influence Peter Hurd's use of watercolors, and in turn would be introduced to the tempera-on-panel technique which Peter Hurd had perfected and which would be the medium for the Ellington cover.

In the 1930s Peter Hurd established his permanent residence in San Patricio, New Mexico, about 50 miles west of Roswell, at a home he called Sentinel Ranch. He spent the majority of his time there, except when on assignment. During World War II, he served two tours overseas as an artist-correspondent for *Life* magazine. He had a long, successful, and artistically productive career, and was the recipient of many honors, honorary degrees, and awards. He once wrote: "My credo is a simple one. It is to live just as intensely as possible, to keep my perceptions at a peak of sensitivity, and to try to realize to the fullest every moment of consciousness." He died in 1984 in Roswell, at the age of 80.[74]

Within these basic biographical facts lie a number of intriguing parallels between the lives of Peter Hurd and Duke Ellington. They were contemporaries in life: their lives overlapped by seven decades. Both evidenced talent as artists early in life. Both underwent a career change at about the same point in life: Peter Hurd from military service to artist; Ellington from commercial artist to professional musician.[75] Both enjoyed a mutually enhancing association with another artist in the same field: Peter Hurd's relationship with his brother-in-law, Andrew Wyeth, had many similarities to that of Ellington and Billy Strayhorn. Both had encounters at the White House in the 1960s.[76] Finally, they had an encounter with one other.

An account of the meeting between Peter Hurd and Ellington appears on the masthead page of the 20 August 1956 issue of *Time*. Appearing over the signature of Publisher James Linen, it is written in a delightfully tongue-in-cheek style, and accurately creates the impression that the artist was somewhat bemused by his encounter with the musician:

> The portrait of Duke Ellington is the first *Time* cover by one of the West's most distinguished artists, New Mexico's Peter Hurd. A *Life* correspondent during World War II, Hurd has painted on all five continents, but the people and scenes he likes best to portray are the ranch folk, the sun-blazed desert and the bare mountains near his New Mexican ranch. His precise tempera paintings of the U.S. Southwest are owned by such leading museums as New York City's Metropolitan, Kansas City's William Rockhill Nelson and the National Gallery in Edinburgh.
>
> For Hurd, a classical music fan, the Ellington assignment was his first brush with the world of jazz. He caught up with the Duke in San Francisco and spent the first two days trying to corner the elusive but affable

musician. "Hi, Hurd. You're the portrait man. Well, fine. Excuse me, I have to see that cat over there," Ellington would say and fade away. But once the portrait was started, Ellington liked to pose as he held court for his innumerable friends in the artist's hotel room.

Said Hurd: "It was an interesting assignment. As they say here 'I wouldn't have taken for the experience!' "[77]

Another description of the meeting between Duke Ellington and Peter Hurd exists in a handwritten letter from Hurd to Fuerbringer. The letter is reproduced below, with idiosyncrasies in style and punctuation intact:

SENTINEL RANCH SAN PATRICIO NEW MEXICO

[COPY FROM TIME INC. ARCHIVES] [6/21/56]

Dear Otto.

The Ellington episode was most interesting and the Duke, once he was badgered and harried enough by his agent posed patiently each afternoon for four days. I think he even enjoyed it for he stayed much longer the final day than was necessary for the completion of the portrait.

There was a more or less steady stream of phone calls and visitors to the hotel room where we worked and though I had known for years that California is over its quota in strange individuals I was amazed at the numbers and variety that turned up in my quarters to pay homage (of a sort) to the Duke. I was delighted for they serve to entertain him and keep his expression animated during the sittings.

Nights I spent listening to the orchestra and making pen sketches at the Macumba Club for at one time I considered putting some of the musicians in the orchestra in the background along with the Duke; finally abandoned this in favor of the simpler statement which you will see.

I made friends with many of the musicians and with Al Celley the manager who was invaluable to me. On

my last night in San Francisco I was invited by the Duke
to a party he was giving after the concert at a place
called Jimbo's Bop City. This was great fun—a party I'll
never forget: we sat eating roast turkey followed by
watermelon until 6:30 a.m. while a frenzied six piece
colored orchestra seemed to pound my eardrums to
ribbons—Say man, this Cat really has had it!

Hope you like the painting, Otto—it leaves air
express today as I remember you are in somewhat of a
hurry for it—

With warm regards to you I am

June 21st   Sincerely
1956
                   Peter

The portrait was received by *Time* on 23 June,[78] and
Fuerbringer praised it highly:

The Ellington portrait is wonderful. I kept looking at it,
seeing more and more nuances in his face, imagining
more and more explosive expressions emanating from
his mouth. The background is simple, direct and very
convincing. I think it should reproduce very well.[79]

Many years later, in his unpublished autobiography,[80]
Peter Hurd warmly recalled the occasion of his meeting with
Duke Ellington. These reminiscences, written in his characteristic clear and precise prose, are reproduced below, again
with idiosyncrasies in spelling and punctuation intact:

TIME COVER ADVENTURES

Duke Ellington 1956

Al Celli, Duke Ellington's manager, met me at my
digs in San Francisco arranged for me by Time. Inc., in
the Huntington Hotel. It would be best, he suggested,
for me to hang around a few days getting the background material and watching Mr. Ellington and the
band at the Mocambo, a night spot on Grant Street.
This I agreed to do and immediately engaged a table

there. I met Mr. Ellington the first evening; he was cordial but seemed a little remote—not really interested in posing for a Time cover by me. After three evenings of watching the show and making notes for the background I realized I was getting nowhere with Mr. Ellington who continued in our brief meetings elegantly courteous but definitely elusive. I was worried, for the deadline for delivery of the portrait was approaching. I decided to move to the hotel where Ellington and most of his band were staying. Much less elegant than the Huntington, it was on Grant Street and near the Mocambo. I went to Celli with my problem, saying that I could go home and complete a painting using photos but I felt this would not be nearly as successful in its outcome as it would be if my subject could give me some posing time.

"I will fix it", said Celli. "Leave it to me."

But nothing happened. I decided I'd better tackle my victim before he escaped.

"Mr. Ellington, do you know what an advertisement in color on the back cover of Time magazine costs?" I mentioned an astronomical figure, taken out of the blue. "Do you know what the front cover would cost?" I quoted another figure, larger. "Mr. Ellington, you are being offered the Front Cover—free. That's the number one slot and not for sale. You're getting it free. They can use a photograph of you, sure, but they've sent me out here to paint you. This is in a way a tribute to you."

I made my point; but it was born of desperation—and shameless on my part.

So it was arranged that my sittings would begin promptly at 2:00 next day. Paints all mixed (I decided on egg tempera), gesso panel cut to the proportion of Time's cover, I awaited my subject's arrival. Two o'clock came and passed, 2:05, 2:10, 2:15—while I impatiently waited. At 2:20 I called Al.

"What? Hasn't he come yet? I'll get him."

Five minutes later Al called.

"Pete, he wants you to go up to his room. He just woke up."

Not at all confident of the promptness of the elevator service in our hotel—the Beverly Plaza whose name implied a tone of posh elegance, unfortunately nonexistent—I decided to try the back stairs. Upward I leapt, two steps at a time, to reach Ellington's room as quickly as possible. My first knock brought no answer although I could hear someone moving around inside. A second knock with more imperative authority brought a sleepy answer, "All right, wait a minute." At the next sound of the voice I walked in to see Mr. Ellington's long frame stretched out in bed. He was wearing a silk kerchief of olive green wound around his head which gave the immediate impression of some royal personage out of the Middle East.

Mr. Ellington after a brief apology, still very sleepy, suggested that I step into the anteroom while he dressed. I had just settled myself there when the telephone rang. At the third ring I called through the door to ask if I should answer it.

"Yes, would you please?"

I picked up the receiver and before I could say a word an urgent female voice said,

"Duke, Oh Duke. It's me. It's Jennie. I'm down stairs. I've got the baby."

"Just one minute" I said.

Speaking through the closed door I reported the situation to Mr. Ellington. There was a long silence, followed by a deep groan.

"O.K., tell her to come up."

The reader no doubt will guess what was running through my mind at this point as to what sort of dramatic meeting was about to take place. No such thing. Jennie was one of his vast host of admiring fans and it seems her marriage of two years had not been blessed with a child. She and her husband had decided to adopt a son. Mr. Ellington was the epitomy of courtliness. "My dear, you are even more beautiful than the last time I saw you", he said—a phrase I heard many times repeated to other ladies during the next few days.

This was the beginning of a procession of Ellington's fans that trooped through my room as I worked on the portrait. Again he reminded me of a story book king, this time receiving his subjects in an informal levee.

Duke Ellington is a delightful person and proved to

be a patient and enduring model as he sat for me in my room. As I recall there were five afternoon sittings and on the fifth day at about 3:30 I announced to Duke and the dozen or so of the ardent admirers then present that the work was complete. I felt I could not improve it; anything more might result in harm. But the Duke looking like a benign maharajah continued the durbar until we all went out to dine at a Chinese restaurant farther down Grant Street.

Toward the end of the sittings I was invited to a wonderful party given by Duke. "Peter, bring along any friends you like and meet us at eight o'clock at. . . It will be a dinner dance." This was a great occasion—unforgettable in its *joie de vivre.* I had invited a doctor and his wife whom I had known during their tour of duty at Walker Air Force Base, and as it turned out, we were the only people of our race there. Most members of the orchestra were present—they and the entire group of guests were beautifully attired, handsome people.

All my travels as a "head hunter" for Time have yielded me rich dividends in the experiences I have had. But becoming well acquainted with Duke Ellington was one of the best and most rewarding of the entire twelve. We seldom meet these days and then always by chance—never with enough time.

I remember a call I had from Chicago on Christmas morning, 1956, the year I painted Ellington. At first I did not recognize the deep, rich voice that spoke to me, until I heard, "Peter, just wanted to say Merry Christmas and tell you how much I liked your cover portrait. Also a distinct rise in Capitol record sales I attribute to the Time cover story."

Since beginning this biography he has died. And I continue to mourn his passing.[81]

The original painting is today part of the collection of the National Portrait Gallery, Smithsonian Institution, Washington, D.C. It is there because *Time* has a longstanding agreement with the Smithsonian Institution to donate its cover art. It will come as no surprise that this agreement was initiated by Otto Fuerbringer.

THE COVER FILM—A STRANGE INTERLUDE

There is in circulation among collectors a five-minute film of Ellington which relates to the *Time* cover. The film begins with an announcer introducing Ellington as "an exciting person to read about in this week's issue of *Time* magazine." Ellington appears on screen, seated at a piano, and proceeds to tell fanciful allegories about how he came to compose and title "Mood Indigo," "Caravan," "Sophisticated Lady," and "Satin Doll," each of which he plays in abbreviated form. This is ostensibly done because these songs are to be mentioned in the *Time* story, although, of the four, only "Mood Indigo" and "Sophisticated Lady" are mentioned and then only in passing. A proof of the *Time* cover appears briefly on screen.[82] The film is obviously unfinished, has no titles or credits and is mentioned in only one source in jazz literature.[83] The purpose and medium for which it was intended remain uncertain. In all likelihood, the film was produced by *Time*'s promotions department for a use or purpose which was abandoned or did not come to fruition.[84]

CONCLUSIONS

Promotion of the *Time* cover as resulting from Newport, and the ensuing concomitant treatment of the cover in jazz literature, served Ellington's purposes admirably. To state that the *Time* cover resulted from Newport was to ascribe a tangible result—a cover appearance on the leading weekly news magazine—to the otherwise intangible effects of the festival appearance. "Success," "rebirth," "triumph" were now manifest in a vivid color portrait and a feature-length story. Newport and the *Time* cover, thus linked, were events which emphasized and enhanced one another. The effect of this linkage has been to consign the *Time* cover to a diminished and subordinate role, and thus to obscure the true nature of the actions taken by those responsible for it.

    Months before Newport, Joe Morgen conceived the idea of an Ellington *Time* cover and set into motion the events which brought it about. His partner in this enterprise, Carter Harman, produced a story which, thirty-five years later, remains the definitive statement about an orchestra once again on the verge of greatness. Otto Fuerbringer, in furtherance of an editorial commitment to jazz which had been implemented during a period of turmoil and uncertainty, made the decisions to commence preparation of the cover story and to publish it.

The extraordinary prescience of the cover story, written only a month after Newport, is best exemplified in this striking paragraph:

> The event last month marked not only the turning point in one concert; it confirmed a turning point in a career. The big news was something that the whole jazz world had long hoped to hear: the Ellington band was once again the most exciting thing in the business, Ellington himself had emerged from a long period of quiescence and was once again bursting with ideas and inspiration.[85]

Newport was a "turning point" for Ellington, one of those "major intersections" as he confirmed seventeen years later in *Music Is My Mistress*. The favorable and widespread attention resulting from it brought him renewed commercial success and thrust him back into lasting prominence. In the years to follow, his "ideas and inspiration" would lead him to compose *Such Sweet Thunder, The Queen's Suite, Idiom '59, Suite Thursday, The Virgin Islands Suite, The Far East Suite, The New Orleans Suite, The UWIS Suite, the Goutelas Suite, The Latin American Suite, The Afro-Eurasian Eclipse,* and *The Togo Brava Suite.*[86] In 1957, Ellington's allegorical history of jazz, *A Drum Is a Woman,* was presented on national television.[87] He composed the background music for a television series, *The Asphalt Jungle,*[88] and the score for a ballet, *The River.*[89] He wrote the scores for the films *Anatomy of a Murder* (1959), *Paris Blues* (1961), *Assault on a Queen* (1966), and the obscure *Change of Mind* (1969). This period of unparalleled creativity culminated in the First,[90] Second[91] and Third[92] Concerts of Sacred Music.

Viewed in its proper perspective, the *Time* cover story can now be seen for what it is and always has been: at once a history of a pivotal time for the Ellington orchestra and a prologue to its future, conceived by an aggressive and effective publicist, crafted by a writer with knowledge of and sensitivity to Ellington's music, and published under the aegis of a visionary editor. Newport, when it inevitably occurred, merely confirmed their judgment.

NOTES

1. Leonard Feather described what occurred:

> Another unforgettable occasion was the chaotic scene at Newport, Rhode Island, during the three-day jazz festival in July 1956. Performing an extended and revitalized version of a fast blues entitled "Diminuendo and Crescendo in Blue," first recorded in 1938 [sic] and lengthened on this occasion to fourteen minutes and fifty-nine choruses, Ellington and his band (with particular help from the frenetic tenor sax of Paul Gonsalves) whipped the audience into such a furor that elder jazz statesmen could recall no comparable scene since the riots in the aisles of New York's Paramount Theater two decades earlier, during Benny Goodman's first wave of glory.

Leonard Feather, *From Satchmo to Miles* (New York: Da Capo, 1972), 54. The recording of the 1956 Newport concert remains in print: *Ellington at Newport,* Columbia Jazz Masterpieces CJ 40587 (LP); CK 40587 (CD).

The proposition that the artistic merit of a performance is inversely related to its popular success led to criticism of the Newport performance of "Diminuendo and Crescendo in Blue," particularly in comparison to the original version. Max Harrison, "Reflections on Some of Duke Ellington's Longer Works," in Max Harrison, *A Jazz Retrospect* (New York: Crescendo, 1977), 121–28.

2. Carter Harman, "Mood Indigo & Beyond," *Time*, 20 August 1956, 54.

3. Edward Kennedy "Duke" Ellington, *Music Is My Mistress* (New York: Doubleday, 1973) (hereinafter cited as "MIMM").

4. David Halberstram, *The Powers That Be* (New York: Knopf, 1979), 48. The influence of a *Time* cover appearance on the careers of Adlai Stevenson, Lyndon B. Johnson, Philip L. Graham, and Leon Jaworski, and on the perception of such events as Vietnam and the Watergate affair, is discussed throughout the book.

5. *Time* began publication on 3 March 1923. It was the first weekly magazine to present news of the previous week in an organized and departmentalized format. The development of this concept, and the rapid increase in circulation which followed, are chronicled in Edwin Emery and Henry Ladd Smith, *The Press in America* (New York: Prentice-Hall, 1954), 643–45; John Tebbel, *The American Magazine: A Compact History* (New York: Hawthorn, 1969), 227–30; and Sidney Kobre, *Development of American Journalism* (Dubuque: Brown, 1969), 722. There also exists a monumental history of Time, Inc. Robert T. Elson, *Time, Inc.—The Intimate History of a Publishing Enterprise, 1923–1941* (New York: Atheneum, 1968); Robert T. Elson, *The World of Time, Inc.—The Intimate History of a Publishing Enterprise,* Vol. 2, 1941–1960 (New York: Atheneum, 1973); Curtis Prendergast with Geoffrey Colvin, *The World of Time, Inc.—The Intimate History of a Changing Enterprise,* Vol. 3, 1960–1980 (New York: Atheneum, 1986).

6. Raymond Horricks, *The Jazzmen of Our Time* (London: Gollancz, 1959), 173. The reference is to the 8 November 1954 *Time* cover story on Dave Brubeck.

7. Stanley Dance, jacket notes, *Ellington at Newport,* Columbia Jazz Masterpieces CJ 40587 (LP).

8. Joseph McLaren, "Edward Kennedy (Duke) Ellington and Langston Hughes: Perspectives on their Contributions to American Culture, 1920–1966" (Ph.D. diss., Brown Univ., 1980), 195–96.

9. Stanley Dance, letter to author, 8 November 1989.

10. Luciano Massagli, Liborio Pusateri and Giovanni Volonte, comps., *Duke Ellington's Story on Records,* 16 vols. (Milan: Cartotecnica Bolzoni, 1966–1983), 265 (hereinafter cited as "DESOR"); W.E. Timner, *Ellingtonia: The Recorded Music of Duke Ellington and His Sidemen,* 3d ed. (Metuchen: Scarecrow, 1988), 117 (hereinafter cited as "Timner"). "Harlem" is discussed and analyzed in Jules Edmund Rowell, "An

Analysis of the Extended Orchestral Works of Duke Ellington Circa 1931 to 1972" (Master's thesis, San Francisco State Univ., 1983), 175–94.
11. Of "Deep Night" it has been written:

> What is certain is that Duke's mastery of the short composition remained; beautiful examples like "Deep Night," an exploration of trombone sonorities from 1951 when the band was apparently in some disarray, are clear evidence.

Andy Hamilton, "The Short and the Suite," *The Wire,* April, 1989, 33.
12. Ultra-Deluxe" is the subject of a vivid, if slightly flawed, description:

> In 1952, there slipped almost unnoticed from the barrage of commercial drivel Duke recorded for Capitol the mystical "Ultra-Deluxe," a remarkable creation slowly expanding from Gonslaves's opening tenor phrase. In the great surges of harmony and color rising from the orchestra we sense the thoughts of the most profound of jazz musicians; the original form of the blues is distorted, its rich spirit recreated in shades of orange and deep red.

Vic Bellerby, "Duke Ellington," in *The Art of Jazz: Essays in the Nature and Development of Jazz,* ed. Martin Williams (New York: Oxford Univ. Press, 1959), 157. "Ultra-Deluxe" was recorded in 1953, and the opening phrase is played by Harry Carney on baritone saxophone. DESOR, 329; Timner, 139.
13. Johnny Hodges had been with the band since 1928. He returned in August 1955 and remained until his death on 11 May 1970. Biographical portraits of him are found in Stanley Dance, *The World of Duke Ellington* (New York: Scribner's, 1970; New York: Da Capo, 1981), 91–102; Burnett James, *Essays on Jazz* (London: Sidgwick and Jackson, 1961; New York: Da Capo, 1990), 144–62; Whitney Balliett, *Dinosaurs in the Morning* (Philadelphia: Lippincott, 1962; Westport: Greenwood, 1978), 123–28; Humphrey Lyttleton, *The Best of Jazz II—Enter the Giants, 1931–1944* (New York: Taplinger,

1982), 132–56; and Max Jones, *Talking Jazz* (New York: Norton, 1988), 58–61.

Lawrence Brown had been with the band since 1932. He returned in 1960 and remained until he retired in 1970. His playing with the Ellington orchestra is analyzed in detail in Kurt Robert Dietrich, "Joe 'Tricky Sam' Nanton, Juan Tizol and Lawrence Brown: Duke Ellington's Great Trombonists, 1926–1951" (D.M.A. diss., Univ. of Wisconsin–Madison, 1989), 86–161. An interview of Lawrence Brown in retirement appears in Lowell D. Holmes and John W. Thompson, *Jazz Greats—Getting Better With Age* (New York: Holmes & Meier, 1986), 107–13.

William Alexander "Sonny" Greer had been Ellington's drummer since 1920. Frank Dutton, "Birth of a Band," *Storyville* 80 (December 1978–January 1979): 44–53. He returned for appearances with the band, or members of it, on single occasions in 1958, 1961, 1962, and 1972. His work with Ellington is discussed briefly in Theodore Dennis Brown, "A History and Analysis of Jazz Drumming to 1942" (Ph.D. diss., Univ. of Michigan, 1976), 421–24, and in Burt Korall, *Drummin' Men: The Heartbeat of Jazz—The Swing Era* (New York: Schirmer, 1990), 307–10.

14. This unsettled period is explored in depth in an aptly titled chapter, "1951–1959 Swing Low, Swing High," in Derek Jewell, *Duke: A Portrait of Duke Ellington* (New York: Norton, 1977), 110–37. Personnel changes within the band during this period are also summarized and discussed in Alun Morgan and Raymond Horricks, *Modern Jazz—A Survey of Developments Since 1939* (London: Gollancz, 1956), 183–90.

15. Ellington appeared in the "Aquacades" show at Flushing Meadow, Long Island, New York, from 22 June through 2 August 1955. Band regulars Paul Gonsalves, Willie Cook, Britt Woodman, Dave Black, and Rick Henderson did not appear because of union card problems. The band was augmented by an extra pianist, a string section, and two harpists. Alun Morgan, "Duke Ellington on Record—The Nineteen-Fifties," in *Duke Ellington: His Life and Music,* ed. Peter Gammond (London: Phoenix House, 1958; New York: Da Capo, 1977), 114.

16. Johnny Hodges and Sam Woodyard are said to have arrived on the same day. Mercer Ellington with Stanley Dance, *Duke*

Ellington in Person: An Intimate Memoir (Boston: Houghton, 1978), 109. Another source has spoken to the impact of their arrival:

> After four years as leader of his own small group, the nonpareil Johnny Hodges came back to him. And on the same day a great new drummer, Sam Woodyard, entered the band. It is not too much to say that the effect of these two men on the group's morale was comparable to that of Ben Webster and Jimmy Blanton fifteen years before. They were certainly an inspiration to Ellington himself and within a year, at the Newport Jazz Festival, he had scored the greatest single triumph of his career.

Stanley Dance, jacket notes, *The Private Collection, Volume One—Studio Sessions, Chicago, 1956,* LMR CD 83000 (CD).

A succession of drummers—Bill Clark, Charlie Smith, Louis (Louie) Bellson, Butch Ballard and Dave Black—had followed in the wake of Sonny Greer's departure. Sam Woodyard was Ellington's drummer from August 1955 through the spring of 1968, with minor breaks. He returned to the band for brief interludes in 1973.

17. *Historically Speaking—The Duke,* Bethlehem BCP-60 and *Duke Ellington Presents,* Bethlehem BCP-6005, recorded in Chicago, Illinois, 7 & 8 February 1956. DESOR, 363–67; Timner, 149. The title of the first album accurately reflects the historical nature of its contents."East St. Louis Toodle-o" (1926), "Creole Love Call" (1927), and "Stompy Jones" (1934) were featured, along with three songs from the extraordinary year of 1940—"Jack the Bear," "Ko-Ko," and "In a Mellotone." Other numbers became history: "Stomp, Look and Listen" would not again be recorded and the record contains the only commercially recorded performance of the intriguing "Lonesome Lullaby." The second album featured two additional songs from 1940, "Cotton Tail" and "Day Dream," together with non-Ellington numbers such as "Summertime," "Laura," "Deep Purple," and "Indian Summer."

18. Columbia released twenty-four long playing records by Ellington during the six-year period from 1956 through 1962. Much of the unissued material recorded during these years later appeared in a five-record, three-album compilation issued by

Columbia in Europe on the CBS France/Holland label. Duke Ellington, *"Duke 56/62",* Vol. 1, CBS 88653; Vol. 2, CBS 88654; Vol. 3, CBS 23606.

19. Whitney Balliett, "Celebration for the Duke," *Saturday Review,* 12 May 1956, 30–31.
20. Stanley Dance, letter to author, 8 November 1989.
21. Stanley Dance, letter to author, 30 November 1989.
22. Jerry Valburn, ed., *D.E.T.S. Newsletter,* Vol. One, No. Three, June/July 1981, privately published by Marlor Productions, Hicksville, New York, in connection with issuance of the *Duke Ellington Treasury Series* of recordings.
23. MIMM, 435. These pointed recollections of Joe Morgen's aggressive character and pervasive presence invite speculation as to his role in the *Saturday Review* story. Carter Harman, for one, believes he was involved. "My guess is that Joe was there, lurking heavily among the shadows." Carter Harman, letter to author, 7 May 1990.
24. James A. Linen, "A Letter from the Publisher," *Time,* 19 October 1953, 18, contains a profile of Carter Harman.
25. Carter Harman, "Girl in the Groove," *Time,* 23 February 1953, 54.
26. Carter Harman, "Ballet's Fundamentalist," *Time,* 25 January 1954, 66.
27. Carter Harman, "The Man on Cloud No. 7" *Time,* 8 November 1954, 67.
28. Carter Harman, "The Prima Donna," *Time,* 29 October 1956, 60.
29. The Hickory House is mentioned twice in MIMM, 211, 400. Its atmosphere is affectionately recalled in Marian McPartland, *All in Good Time* (New York: Oxford Univ. Press, 1987), 19–28. Not coincidentally, the first manifestation of the collaboration between Morgen and Harman was an article on Marian McPartland, whose trio was a fixture at the Hickory House for many years. Carter Harman, "Post-Dixieland Piano," *Time,* 21 September 1953, 65.
30. Carter Harman, "The Duke Rides Again," *Time,* 23 January 1956, 53. Harman had previously written one other article on Ellington. "Duke's Anniversary," *Time,* 3 November 1952, 85.
31. The tribute to Sam Woodyard reads:

> But the chief reason for all the internal excitement
> is the Duke's new drummer, Sam Woodyard. He
> sits, lean and still, behind his battery, neatly

punctuating every phrase, coming as close as any man could to playing a tune on his four side drums and three cymbals (he actually squeezes pitch changes out of one drum by leaning on it with an elbow), while keeping a rhythm as solid as Gibraltar. When the band appeared bored with a number, he seemed to get under and shove—and the band came alive.

Time, 23 January 1956, 53.
32. Carter Harman, interview with author, Carmel, California, 20 January 1990 (hereinafter cited as "Harman Interview").
33. "Louis the First," *Time,* 21 February 1949, 52. *Time* articles during these years carried no bylines. Articles by Carter Harman are so cited because he is known to be the writer. *Time* articles are today credited to the writer or writers.
34. Carter Harman, "The Man on Cloud No. 7," *Time,* 8 November 1954, 67. Oscar Peterson had been considered as an alternative to Brubeck as a cover subject. Brubeck was thought to play jazz more consistently, and Peterson's Canadian citizenship was at odds with *Time's* conception of jazz as an American art form. Harman Interview; Carter Harman, letter to author, 10 October 1990. The interest shown in Peterson by *Time,* and the resulting story by Harman, are detailed in Gene Lees, *Oscar Peterson: The Will to Swing* (Rocklin: Prima, 1990), 83–99.
35. *Time's* commitment to jazz continues. Wynton Marsalis is the subject of a 1990 cover story. Thomas Sancton, "Horns of Plenty," *Time,* 22 October 1990, 64.
36. Harman Interview.
37. Joe Igo, comp., "The Duke Ellington Chronicle," unpublished ms., Gordon R. Ewing, ed., a comprehensive itinerary of Ellington's appearances begun by the late Joe Igo, presently on deposit with the Duke Ellington Collection, National Museum of American History, Smithsonian Institution, Washington, D.C. (hereinafter cited as "Igo Itinerary").
38. The telegram reads as follows:

Peter Hurd   1956 May 20 PM 5 07
Boswell, NMex [sic]

We are going to do a cover on Duke Ellington. He is currently playing at Las Vegas and will be there through June 7. Would you be interested in painting him? Best regards =

Otto Fuerbringer Time Inc =

Otto Fuerbringer to Peter Hurd, telegram, 20 May 1956, *Peter Hurd Papers,* Hurd-La Rinconada Gallery, San Patricio, New Mexico (hereinafter cited as "Hurd Papers"). Documents from the Hurd Papers were provided by Ms. Teresa Curry of the Hurd-La Rinconada Gallery through the courtesy of Mr. Michael Hurd, who kindly gave permission to use them.

39. This time period is established by a letter dated Friday, 1 June 1956, from Otto Fuerbringer to Peter Hurd, forwarding recent photographs of Ellington to aid in painting the cover portrait. The letter reads, in part:

> Carter Harman, our music writer, saw the Duke in Las Vegas early this week, found him fascinating, and reports that he will cooperate fully.

Otto Fuerbringer to Peter Hurd, letter, 1 June 1956, Hurd Papers.

40. Harman Interview. It was unusual for an editor to research a story. This task was customarily performed by the editorial researcher for the subject area, in this instance Dorothea Bourne, assisted by *Time*'s network of correspondents and stringers, as necessary. Harman's musical background, together with his friendship with Ellington and knowledge of Ellington's music, made it appropriate for him to research the story personally.

The relationship developed with Ellington in connection with the cover story led, some years later, to Harman being engaged as Ellington's biographer. Research began with approximately twenty hours of tape-recorded interviews, accomplished at various locations during 1964. The project ended when it became obvious that author and subject were at loggerheads over the tenor of what was to be written. Harman planned a literal biography, one which would supplant the novelistic one of Barry Ulanov, then almost twenty years old. Barry Ulanov, *Duke Ellington* (New York: Creative Age, 1946). Ellington, ever protective of his private self, desired the product to be a replication of his public persona. Ellington's view prevailed, the eventual result being MIMM. Carter Harman, "The Duke Speaks Out," Ellington Study Group Conference, Los Angeles, California, 15 June 1991 (hereinafter cited as "Harman Presentation").

41. The summary of the cover story decisional process which follows was developed during numerous telephone interviews of Fuerbringer by the author during 1989–1992 (hereinafter cited as "Fuerbringer Interviews").

42. Hedley Donovan, *Right Places, Right Times—Forty Years in Journalism Not Counting My Paper Route* (New York: Holt, 1989), 193.

43. Igo Itinerary; DESOR, 383–84; Timner, 152. Ellington was still riding the wave of the Newport success when he appeared three weeks later at the Connecticut Jazz Festival at Fairfield University, Fairfield, Connecticut, on Saturday, 28 July 1956. On the program with him were pianists Willie "The Lion" Smith and Hank Jones, trumpeter Buck Clayton, bassist Walter Page, and drummer Art Trappier. "Diminuendo and Crescendo in Blue" was again featured, with an interlude of thirty-seven choruses by Paul Gonsalves. This performance appears on *Jazz Festival Jazz*, Queen Disc Q-044 (LP) and on *Diminuendo and Crescendo in Blue*, Koala AW 14165 (LP). Excerpts from the remainder of the festival appear on *Duke Ellington, His Orchestra and Friends at the First Annual Connecticut Jazz Festival*, IAJRC 45 (LP). A photograph of Ellington at Fairfield University appears in the cover story. *Time*, 20 August 1956, 55.

44. Fuerbringer Interviews. A number of newsworthy events occurred in the summer of 1956, all of which were reflected on *Time*'s cover. There was a major steel strike in the United States, repercussions from the Suez Canal crisis continued, the Democratic and Republican national conventions were held, and *My Fair Lady* opened on Broadway. The Ellington cover story appeared among cover stories relating to these events. The covers immediately preceding it depicted Prime Minister Jawaharlal Nehru of India (31 July), Greek shipping magnate Stavros Niarchos (6 August) and former President Harry S. Truman (13 August); those immediately following depicted President Gamal Abdel Nasser of Egypt (27 August) and Governor Arthur B. Langlie of Washington (3 September).

45. This would not be the last occasion on which Mr. Fuerbringer would demonstrate his ability to recognize artistic achievement in the midst of current chaos:

> And even his critics felt his sense of timing on cover stories was exquisite. Indeed, it was one of the ironies of his tour that though he was probably most remembered within the shop and within the profession for his dogmatic views on Vietnam, it was his idea to put the Beatles on the cover as 1965's Men of the Year.

Halberstram, *The Powers That Be,* 457. In this instance, however, current events prevailed. General William C. Westmoreland was named *Time*'s Man of the Year for 1965.

46. Marc Crawford, "A Visit with Mrs. Duke Ellington," *Ebony,* March 1959, 132–36. Discussions of these relationships are found in Jewell, *Duke: A Portrait of Duke Ellington,* notably at 30–31 and 225–27. Ellington's private life with Evie Ellis is recalled in Leonard Feather, *The Jazz Years: Earwitness to an Era* (New York: Da Capo, 1987), 62–70.

47. *Time,* 20 August 1956, 56. A representative from *Time*'s Washington, D.C., bureau had interviewed Edna Ellington in connection with the cover story. This led to the insertion into a draft of the story of an "unforgivably brusque" account of Ellington's marriage. Carter Harman, letter to author, 2 November 1990. The account was so at variance with Ellington's expressed desires that Harman took the extreme step of threatening to resign if it were not rewritten. Harman Interview; Harman Presentation.

48. Carter Harman, letter to author, 10 October 1990.

49. Two major works about Ellington contain discussions of Newport but make no mention of the *Time* cover. Peter Gammond, ed., *Duke Ellington: His Life and Music* (London: Phoenix House, 1958); G.E. Lambert, *Duke Ellington* (London: Cassell, 1959).

50. MIMM, 191.

51. MIMM, 435.

52. MIMM, 241.

53. MIMM, 227.

54. MIMM, 226.

55. Dance, *The World of Duke Ellington,* 297.

56. Jewell, *Duke: A Portrait of Duke Ellington,* 122.

57. M. Ellington with Dance, *Duke Ellington in Person,* 112. The Chico Hamilton Quintet, which preceded the Ellington orchestra on stage that night, had a similar experience with its rendition of "Blue Sands." Buddy Collette, reedman for the group, recalled the occasion:

> And we played for about ten minutes, giving it our best shot. And at the end, as we'd do, we just tapered off, and everything just stopped. And for eight or ten seconds nobody moved, and then they jumped up and screamed; they went wild, and it went on and on . . . Later, as we were moving off stage and Duke's band was setting up, we passed Duke on the stairs and he smiled and said, "Well, you sure made it hot for me."

Robert Gordon, *Jazz West Coast: The Los Angeles Jazz Scene of the 1950s* (London: Quartet, 1986), 139. The Chico Hamilton Quintet also appeared with Ellington at the Connecticut Jazz Festival three weeks later. See n. 43.

58. Arnold Shaw, *Black Popular Music in America—From the Spirituals, Minstrels, and Ragtime to Soul, Disco, and Hip-Hop* (New York: Schirmer, 1986), 151.

59. James Lincoln Collier, *Duke Ellington* (New York: Oxford Univ. Press, 1987), 264.

60. Ibid., 268. *See also* James Lincoln Collier, *The Making of Jazz: A Comprehensive History* (Boston: Houghton, 1978), 247:

> Then, at the 1956 Newport Jazz Festival, Paul Gonsalves, tenor soloist with the band, played a long, fervid solo on "Diminuendo and Crescendo in Blue" that left the audiences roaring. Suddenly the band was in the news again: Ellington even made the cover of *Time*.

61. Examples of jacket notes containing mention of the *Time* cover are those to *Duke Ellington—All Star Road Band,* Doctor Jazz W2X39137 (LP) and to *Ellington at Newport,* Columbia Jazz Masterpieces CJ 40587 (LP). *See also* Benny Aasland, ed., *DEMS Bulletin,* 1984/2:3, privately published by the Duke Ellington Music Society, Jarfalla, Sweden (hereinafter cited as "DEMS Bulletin").

62. Jewell, *Duke: A Portrait of Duke Ellington,* 110.

63. Patricia Willard, telephone interview, 7 August 1989. Ms. Willard was associated with Ellington for twenty-five years in research, editing, and public relations capacities. She is a former columnist for *Jazz Times* magazine and a former contributing editor of *Down Beat*. She recently completed two years as a member of the staff of the Duke Ellington

Collection, National Museum of American History, Smithsonian Institution, Washington, D.C.
64. "A Duke Named Ellington," narr., prod., and dir. Terry Carter, *American Masters Series*. Exec. prod. Susan Lacy, PBS, WNET, New York, 18 & 25 July 1988.
65. *Time,* 20 August 1956, 54.
66. Ibid., 55.
67. The sensation created at Newport by Paul Gonsalves's solo in "Diminuendo and Crescendo in Blue" was in itself another illustration of Ellington's acumen in the business of music. Gordon Ewing has explained how it came about:

> Bobby Boyd, who was a band boy and later road manager for Duke from 1951 to 1966, spent several days with me and provided some valuable information: One account, which you may already know, concerned the famous 1956 Newport Jazz Festival. Bobby said that before the concert, George Wein kept after Duke to let him know what he was going to play and offered a number of selections which Bobby said "went in one ear and out the other." Duke would tell him that he didn't know but would have something. Before that on 30 April 1956 the band was playing a dance in Durham, NC [North Carolina]. In the middle of the gig Duke suddenly called out 107–108 (Diminuendo and Crescendo in Blue) which the band hadn't played for years. The men shuffled through their music while Duke played a number of choruses and then the band fumbled around for several more before they got into the groove. Bobby said at that point they were really swinging and Paul Gonslaves, that night, didn't play 27 choruses, he played 36 and the crowd went wild. For the next two months the band played the number only once, at a concert, and Duke gave no indication to the men in the band that he was going to play it at Newport nor did any one else know ahead of time. This account is a little different from Mercer-Dance but so are a number of other stories in Mercer's book.

DEMS Bulletin, 1990/1:5–6 (Letter from Gordon Ewing). "Diminuendo and Crescendo in Blue," again featuring a Paul

Gonsalves solo, was also performed at a concert in Pasadena, California, on 30 March 1953. DEMS Bulletin, 1990/1:6 (Letter from Sjef Hoefsmit).

The account of Newport in Mercer Ellington's book incorrectly implies that "Diminuendo and Crescendo in Blue" was last performed during a Birdland engagement "[s]ome time previously." M. Ellington with Dance, *Duke Ellington in Person,* 112. The performance at Birdland was on 30 June 1951 and featured twenty-six choruses by Paul Gonsalves.

DESOR, 277–79; Timner, 122. The Durham and Pasadena concerts appear in the Igo Itinerary, but not in either DESOR or Timner, which cite no performances of "Diminuendo" between Birdland in 1951 and Newport in 1956. The remaining intervening performance, in May or June 1956, has not been documented.

These circumstances suggest that Ellington's decision to perform "Diminuendo and Crescendo in Blue" at Newport was made at the last moment, based upon his experience in Durham two months before, and possibly upon his recollection of similar experiences in Pasadena and at Birdland. The response of the audience to the Chico Hamilton Quintet which immediately preceeded him certainly must have been a factor. See n. 57.

A summary of the interludes between "Diminuendo in Blue" and "Crescendo in Blue" for the period from 20 September 1937 through 28 July 1956 appears as an appendix.

68. Robert Metzger, ed., *My Land Is the Southwest–Peter Hurd Letters and Journals* (College Station: Texas A & M Univ. Press, 1983), 376.
69. Igo Itinerary.
70. The extensive use of these talented retainer artists is illustrated by the fact that one of them, Boris Artzybasheff, painted 219 covers for *Time* over the 24-year period from 1942 to 1966. Included among these were the cover portraits of Louis Armstrong (21 February 1949) and Dave Brubeck (8 November 1954). Other artists whose paintings frequently appeared on covers were Robert Vickery, Bernard Safran, James Chapin, and Boris Chaliapin. Their paintings represent the golden age of *Time* covers, and are a unique chronicle of the times. The reader is commended to a perusal of this

body of American art, particularly the covers of Boris Artzybasheff.

71. Although there were exceptional cases, it was generally true that the painting of a cover portrait from life was a time-consuming process which could only be accomplished infrequently. A cover assignment had to be completed on relatively short notice, but the artists were in demand and their schedules could not always be adjusted. Travel to the location of the subject was usually required. Finally, the subjects were frequently persons who had neither the time nor the inclination to sit for several days while a portrait was painted. Fuerbringer Interviews.

72. Improvement of the magazine in an artistic sense was a continuing theme of Fuerbringer's tenure as managing editor:

> Fuerbringer greatly invigorated the appearance of the magazine. *Time* moved away from the slightly fusty look of the 1950s and, without reducing its text content, began using photography with almost as much verve as *Life* and *Sports Illustrated*. More liberal use of color in takeouts on foreign countries and in stories on art, architecture, and the performing arts gave many pages of the magazine something its most ardent admirers had never before claimed for it: beauty.

Donovan, *Right Places, Right Times,* 193.

73. Andrew Wyeth painted a cover portrait of President Dwight D. Eisenhower for the 7 September 1959 issue of *Time*. He was, in turn, the subject of *Time*'s 27 December 1963 cover story, the portrait being painted by his sister, Henriette Wyeth Hurd. The extraordinary Wyeths are profiled in Richard Meryman, "American Visions—The Wyeth Family," *National Geographic,* July 1991, 78–109.

74. This summary was derived from Metzger, ed., *My Land Is the Southwest*. This book remains the definitive study of the life and work of Peter Hurd. The author is grateful to Professor Metzger for permission to use this material.

75. Ellington's brief but successful career as an artist is chronicled in Mark Thomas Tucker, "The Early Years of Edward Kennedy 'Duke' Ellington, 1899–1927" (Ph.D. diss., Univ. of Michigan, 1986), 135–37. This dissertation has been published in book form under the title *Ellington—The Early Years* (Urbana: Univ. of Illinois Press, 1990).

76. Ellington's 70th birthday was celebrated at the White House on 29 April 1969. He was a guest there on numerous other occasions, beginning during the Truman administration. MIMM, 424–33. In 1965, Peter Hurd was commissioned by the White House Historical Association to paint the official portrait of President Lyndon B. Johnson. The portrait was completed from photographs, since only one sitting was accorded, and was finished in 1966. President Johnson rejected it as "the ugliest thing I ever saw." Hurd returned his $6,000 fee and donated the painting to the National Portrait Gallery, where it remains. The resulting notoriety plagued him for the reminder of his life, much to his dismay. Metzger, ed., *My Land Is the Southwest,* 389–90.

77. James A. Linen, "Publisher's Letter," *Time,* 20 August 1956, 7.

78. Receipt was acknowledged by the following:

> Peter Hurd   1956 June 23 PM 3 24
> Roswell NMex
>
> Swell cover. Letter follows. All best = Otto Fuerbringer Time Inc New York =

Otto Fuerbringer to Peter Hurd, telegram, 23 June 1956, Hurd Papers.

79. Otto Fuerbringer to Peter Hurd, letter, 24 June 1956, Hurd Papers.

80. Professor Metzger writes of Peter Hurd's autobiography:

> On his return to New Mexico in July, 1944, Hurd wrote several essays on his experiences overseas, and years later incorporated them into a draft of his autobiography, which many persons had asked for, and which he began writing in 1970. . . . He knew that the autobiography would take away from the time and concentration he needed for painting; nevertheless, he applied himself to it with wholehearted, though intermittent, effort. But failing health caused him to cease working entirely, and the manuscript was never completed.

Metzger, ed., *My Land Is the Southwest,* xi–xii.

81. Peter Hurd, unpublished ms., c. 1970–1975, Hurd Papers.

The Beverly-Plaza Hotel was located on the southeast corner of the intersection of Bush Street and Grant Avenue. It is today called the Triton Hotel. The Macumba Club was located at 453 Grant Avenue, on the first block across Bush Street from the hotel. This site has been rebuilt in the intervening years, and the address 453 Grant Avenue no longer exists.

82. Fuerbringer confirmed that *Time*'s promotions department had access to cover portraits upon arrival for preparation of promotional materials. Fuerbringer Interviews. This would date the film no earlier than late June 1956, when the portrait arrived. Given the film's unfinished status and intended promotional use in connection with the cover story, a sufficient interval prior to the 13 August newsstand date would have been required for editing, thus making production in August unlikely. These facts suggest that the film was probably made in July. Possible dates are 9, 24 or 29 July, when Ellington is known to have been in New York State or New York City. Igo Itinerary.

83. Klaus Stratemann, *Duke Ellington Day By Day and Film By Film* (Copenhagen: JazzMedia ApS, 1992), 365–68.

84. Klaus Stratemann, letters to author, 25 June 1989, 15 January 1990, 1 March 1992. The author is indebted to Dr. Stratemann for his extensive and enlightening insights into the Ellington–*Time* film.

85. *Time,* 20 August 1956, 54.

86. The compositions listed represent a partial compilation of Ellington's post-1956 extended works. Many of these are discussed in Harrison, *A Jazz Retrospect,* supra, and in Rowell, "An Analysis of the Extended Orchestral Works," supra. A comprehensive listing of Ellington's compositions is found in Erik Wiedemann, "Duke Ellington: The Composer," *Annual Review of Jazz Studies* 5 (1991): 37–64, and reveals an extraordinary period of copyright activity by Ellington subsequent to 1956. Ellington's musical interpretations of literature, particularly as manifested in *Such Sweet Thunder* and *Suite Thursday,* and in his scores for the plays *Timon of Athens* and *Turcaret,* are explored in Theodore R. Hudson, "Duke Ellington's Literary Sources," *American Music* 9.1 (1991): 20. An excellent capsule history of the background of Ellington's extended works appears in Stanley Dance, jacket notes, *The Private Collection, Volume Ten—Studio Sessions New York & Chicago 1965, 1966, 1971,* SAJA 91234-2 (CD).

87. The work was presented on the United States Steel Hour, 8 May 1957. It was the first color production in the series, and the first

nationally broadcast one hour program featuring an all-black cast. Ellington always considered it one of his favorites. Jewell, *Duke: A Portrait of Duke Ellington,* 123. It received mixed reviews at the time, however, as reflected by the favorable and unfavorable reports published simultaneously in a leading jazz publication. Leonard Feather and Barry Ulanov, "Two Thumps on 'A Drum,' " *Down Beat,* 27 June 1957, 18.

88. Ellington's music was certainly the most memorable aspect of this short-lived series, which appeared weekly from 2 April through 24 September 1961. Tim Brooks and Earle Marsh, *The Complete Directory to Prime Time Network TV Shows, 1946–Present,* 5th ed. (New York: Ballantine, 1992), 56. "Asphalt Jungle Theme" remained in the band's book through early 1963.

89. *The River* was commissioned by the American Ballet Theater, choreographed by Alvin Ailey and premiered at the New York State Theater on 25 June 1970. Ellington's interpretation of its various sections appears in MIMM, 201–02.

90. This work premiered at Grace Cathedral, San Francisco, California, on 16 September 1965. DESOR, 726; Timner, 247.

91. This work premiered at the Cathedral of St. John the Divine, New York, New York, on 19 January 1968. DESOR, 852; Timner, 295.

92. The Third Concert of Sacred Music was performed only twice in its entirety. It premiered in Westminster Abbey, London, England, on 24 October 1973. DESOR, 1142–43; Timner, 389–90. Moving descriptions of the circumstances surrounding this performance appear in Jewell, *Duke: A Portrait of Duke Ellington,* 217–34, and in M. Ellington with Dance, *Duke Ellington in Person,* 192–97. Its second and final performance was in St. Augustine Presbyterian Church, Harlem, New York, New York, on 23 December 1973. Jewell, 226. Portions of the Westminster Abbey performance were issued by RCA Victor; the second performance appears not to have survived in recorded form. The Third Concert of Sacred Music was Ellington's last testament. The date of its first performance was seven months to the day prior to his death.

ACKNOWLEDGEMENTS

The interest and assistance of many people made this study possible. Edward L. Jamieson, Richard Woodbury, and

Elaine Felsher of *Time* provided access to otherwise inaccessible resources. Marian Powers and Reneé Mancini of *Time*'s Editorial Rights division facilitated reproduction of the cover and cover story. Carol Diehl, curator of *Time*'s cover art, located the Peter Hurd letter. The contributions of Stanley Dance, Gordon Ewing, Joseph McLaren, Robert Metzger, Klaus Stratemann, Jerry Valburn, and Patricia Willard are manifest throughout. Sjef Hoefsmit's encyclopedic knowledge of Ellingtonia is reflected in the text and in many footnotes. Willard H. Rosegay provided special insight into the geography of San Francisco. Staff members of the Houston Public Library and the libraries of Rice University and the University of Houston were most helpful. The Hurd Papers were made available by Teresa Curry of the Hurd-La Rinconada Gallery, with the kind permission of the artist's son, Michael Hurd.

Otto Fuerbringer and Carter Harman gave unselfishly of their valuable time to inform, comment, correct, and enhance. Helen Ruth Kuenstler, many years ago, established standards of excellence to which this writer's work can only be asymptotic. Theodore R. Hudson provided constant encouragement and valuable guidance. Melanie M. Theiss reviewed the manuscript and made many astute comments. Particular gratitude is extended to Rob L. Wiley, scholar, colleague, and friend, for his advice, knowledge, and inspiration. Finally, my wife, Saundra Carson Waters, endured the hours of work inherent in this project. She, too, made valuable suggestions to make this essay more readable. My deepest thanks go to her.

SUMMARY OF INTERLUDES BETWEEN "DIMINUENDO IN BLUE" AND "CRESCENDO IN BLUE" AS PLAYED BY THE DUKE ELLINGTON ORCHESTRA 20 SEPTEMBER 1937–28 JULY 1956

INTRODUCTION

The summary which follows lists all documented perfor-mances of "Diminuendo in Blue," "Crescendo in Blue," and the various interludes used to join them for the period from initial recording on 20 September 1937 through the first performance after Newport, that of 28 July 1956.

Performance of "Diminuendo" and "Crescendo," or either of them, together with an extended solo by Paul Gonsalves, inevitably became a staple of Ellington's post-Newport concert and club date repertoire. DESOR and Timner list some ninety performances of various combinations of these works from 28 July 1956 through 2 November 1973. As before Newport, presentation occurred in a variety of formats, all of which showcased Gonsalves's improvisational resourcefulness. Initial performances were simply a reprise of Newport: complete versions of "Diminuendo" and "Crescendo," joined by Gon-salves interludes of varying length. Later performances were sometimes shortened to consist only of "Diminuendo" fol-lowed by a Gonsalves solo which eventually acquired the almost onomotopaeic title "Wailing Interval." On other occasions, only "Crescendo" was played, but featuring an extended Gonsalves introduction. Ultimately, this latter vari-ant became known as "Blow By Blow."

Although the documented performances of these works number over one hundred, the existence of numerous undocumented performances, both before and after New-port, is strongly suspected.

Reflected throughout this summary and the accompanying notes are the contributions of Dan Morgenstern, Sjef Hoefsmit, and Gordon Ewing, to each of whom the author expresses sincerest gratitude.

SUMMARY OF INTERLUDES BETWEEN "DIMINUENDO IN BLUE" AND "CRESCENDO IN BLUE" AS PLAYED BY THE DUKE ELLINGTON ORCHESTRA
20 SEPTEMBER 1937 - 28 JULY 1956

DATE	INTERLUDE (VOCALIST)	DESOR	TIMER	RECORDING	LOCATION	REMARKS
20 SEP 37	NONE	158 d - g	26-27	CBS 88210	NEW YORK, NY	FIRST RECORDING; DESOR 158d & f ISSUED ON BRUNSWICK 8004
29 MAY 38	NONE	NONE	NONE	NONE KNOWN	RANDALL'S ISLAND NEW YORK, NY	NOTE 1
9 JUN 45	"ROCKS IN MY BED" (ME)	357 i - n	71	DETS 9	PARAMOUNT THEATER TOLEDO, OHIO	TREASURY BROADCAST INTRODUCED AS "THE BLUES CLUSTER"
7 JUL 45	"CARNEGIE BLUES"	342 e - o	73	DETS 13	RADIO CITY STUDIO 6B NEW YORK, NY	TREASURY BROADCAST INTRODUCED AS "TRIO IN BLUE"
21 SEP 45	"ROCKS IN MY BED" (JB)	1946 p.LXV	79	JOYCE 1066	CLUB ZANZIBAR NEW YORK, NY	
13 OCT 45	"I GOT IT BAD" (AH)	364 k - m	82	DETS 26	RADIO CITY STUDIO 6B NEW YORK, NY	TREASURY BROADCAST INTRODUCED AS "THREE TUNES IN THE BLUE MOOD"
4 JAN 46	"TRANSBLUCENCY" (KD)	NONE	87	PRESTIGE 24074	CARNEGIE HALL NEW YORK, NY	PREMIERE OF "TRANSBLUCENCY"
20 JAN 46 (AFTERNOON)	"TRANSBLUCENCY" (KD)	NONE	NONE	UNISSUED	CIVIC OPERA HOUSE CHICAGO, IL	
20 JAN 46 (EVENING)	"TRANSBLUCENCY" (KD)	378 i - k	88	DETS 33	CIVIC OPERA HOUSE CHICAGO, IL	AFRS BROADCAST
4 MAY 46	"TRANSBLUCENCY" (KD)	383 f - h	90	DETS 36	DARTMOUTH COLLEGE HANOVER, NH	TREASURY BROADCAST

	"TRANSLUCENCY" (KD)	393 e - g	93	DETS 42	GOLDEN STATE THEATER SAN FRANCISCO, CA	TREASURY BROADCAST
3 AUG 46	"TRANSLUCENCY" (KD)	393 e - g	93	DETS 42	GOLDEN STATE THEATER SAN FRANCISCO, CA	TREASURY BROADCAST
23 OCT 46	NONE	405 e	96	PRESTIGE 24029	NEW YORK, NY	NOTE 2
19 APR 47	ELLINGTON SOLO	416 d, e	99	STARDUST 204	BAILEY HALL CORNELL UNIV. ITHACA, NY	NOTE 3
31 AUG 47	"TRANSLUCENCY" (KD)	426	102 - 103	UNIQUE JAZZ UJ 001	HOLLYWOOD BOWL HOLLYWOOD, CA	NOTE 4
30 JUN 51	GONSALVES SOLO	492 m, n	122	JAZZ ANTHOLOGY STARDUST 202	BIRDLAND NEW YORK, NY	NOTE 5
30 MAR 53	GONSALVES SOLO	NONE	NONE	GNP CRESCENDO 9045	CIVIC AUDITORIUM PASADENA, CA	NOTE 6
30 APR 56	GONSALVES SOLO	NONE	NONE	NONE KNOWN	DURHAM, NC	
MAY OR JUN 56	GONSALVES SOLO	NONE	NONE	NONE KNOWN	UNKNOWN	SEE ENDNOTE 67
7 JUL 56	GONSALVES SOLO	618 j	150	COLUMBIA CL40587 (LP) CK40587 (CD)	NEWPORT, RI	NEWPORT JAZZ FESTIVAL SEE ENDNOTE 67
28 JUL 56	GONSALVES SOLO	604 i	152	QUEEN DISC Q-044 KOALA AW 14165	FAIRFIELD UNIV. FAIRFIELD, CT	CONNECTICUT JAZZ FESTIVAL SEE ENDNOTE 43

<u>VOCALISTS</u>: ME - MARIE ELLINGTON; JS - JOYA SHERILL; AH - AL HIBBLER; KD - KAY DAVIS

NOTES TO SUMMARY OF INTERLUDES

NOTE 1

Previously undocumented performances of "Diminuendo in Blue" and "Crescendo in Blue," discovered by Dan Morgenstern, confirm the power of these works from an early date to cause a crowd to respond. On Sunday, 29 May 1938, the Ellington orchestra appeared as part of a six-hour "Carnival of Swing" organized by broadcaster Martin Block and held at the outdoor auditorium on Randall's Island, New York, New York. Some 25,000 spectators were treated to a program featuring 25 separate orchestra units, including the bands of Woody Herman, Count Basie, Chick Webb, and Gene Krupa. The concert was the subject of a comprehensive review in the British weekly, *Melody Maker,* in which Ellington's appearance was reported in detail by New York correspondent Al Brackman:

> The first exciting moment of the occasion and the biggest thrill was the riotous reaction to Duke Ellington's Band.
>
> Martin Block announced Ellington's recent compositions, *Diminuendo and Crescendo in Blue.* During the first portion, which begins *fortissimo* and recedes to *pianissimo,* the crowd began to clap hands and stamp feet in rhythmic unison. In the second portion, which starts *pianissimo* and builds to *double fortissimo,* the riot started.
>
> ABOUT TEN PERSONS JUMPED FROM THE GRANDSTANDS ONTO THE FIELD, AND TAKING THIS CUE, THREE THOUSAND OTHER ENTHUSIASTS SWARMED THE FIELD FROM THE TIER SEATS IN AN EFFORT TO GET NEAR THE STAGE, CREATING TURBULENT HAVOC WITH THE FIELD ATTENDANTS.
>
> At the conclusion of the selection, with hundreds more pouring from the stands, Martin Block announced that unless order was restored and people returned to their seats the concert would be concluded immediately. A call was put in for extra policemen and the session was delayed about ten minutes.

When order was restored, Ellington and the band continued with inspired performances, so overwhelmed were the boys with the demonstration. Cootie Williams was featured in his familiar concerto, the band played *Rockin' in Rhythm, I Let A Song Go Out of My Heart,* and concluding with a new *St. Louis Blues* arrangement which gave Ivy Anderson an opportunity to sing her wares.

Following this rendition, W.C. Handy was brought forth and introduced to the assemblage.

Al Brackman, "25,000 American Swing Fans Go Crazy To Music Of Duke And Other Jazz Aces," *Melody Maker and British Metronome,* 11 June 1938, 9.

NOTE 2

The recordings of Musicraft Records, made during five sessions in the latter part of 1946, are available on *Happy-Go-Lucky Local,* Musicraft MVSCD-52 (CD). At the first session, on 23 October, four takes each of "Diminuendo in Blue" and "Magenta Haze" were recorded, take four of "Diminuendo" being issued. The prevailing practice, firmly established that year, was to join "Diminuendo" and "Crescendo" with the "Transblucency" interlude featuring Kay Davis, who is not present at this first session. She appears only in the third session, on 5 December, to sing the wordless vocal in "The Beautiful Indians—Part 2 (Minnehaha)." These circumstances may be viewed as either the cause of the anomalous recording of "Diminuendo" alone or the result of a decision to record only that work. As Jerry Valburn observes in the liner notes to the compact disc: "No one around today can recall why Duke recorded only the first part of this work."

DESOR, Prestige 24029, the compact disc and the Igo Itinerary correctly list the date of the first Musicraft session as 23 October 1946. Timner and DEMS Bulletin, 1984/5: 1 list the date of this session as 26 October 1946. No recordings were made on that date.

NOTE 3

Substantially all of the Cornell University concert was preserved on a numbered series of acetates privately issued by the Cornell Rhythm Club ("CRC"). The numbering of these acetates belies the fact that the sequence of performance of the entire concert has not been established, those set out in DESOR and Timner notwithstanding. Much of what was recorded was not of commercially acceptable quality. Accordingly, significant portions of this concert have not been generally available, the most extensive representation appearing on Stardust 204 (LP). "Diminuendo in Blue," the Ellington piano interlude and "Crescendo in Blue" appear on CRC 1204 and on Stardust 204. "Transblucency," also performed at this concert, appears on CRC 1001, but remains unissued on LP. "Transblucency" was performed in its full length, including Kay Davis's wordless vocal and Lawrence Brown's extended trombone solo. Applause heard after the performance confirms that it was played as a discrete number, and not as an interlude between parts of "The Beautiful Indians," as indicated in DESOR (from which the usual breakdown is curiously omitted) and in Timner.

DESOR incorrectly lists the location and date of this concert as being at Dartmouth College, Hanover, New Hampshire, on 30 April 1947. DEMS Bulletin, 1986/1: 3.

NOTE 4

The listing for this performance in DESOR is incomplete, and does not include "Diminuendo in Blue," "Transblucency" or "Crescendo in Blue."

NOTE 5

A description of the circumstances surrounding this performance is found in Mercer Ellington with Stanley Dance, *Duke Ellington in Person—An Intimate Memoir* (Boston: Houghton, 1978), 112.

NOTE 6

DEMS Bulletin, 1990/1:6 (Letter from Sjef Hoefsmit). The Pasadena concert also appears on *Duke Ellington–The 1953 Pasadena Concert,* Vogue 600105 (CD) and *Duke Ellington—Take the "A" Train,* Vogue 670208 (CD). On the LP and both CDs, Paul Gonsalves's solo appears to have been shortened. DEMS Bulletin, 1988/4: 3; 1988/5:1.

MUSIC

Mood Indigo & Beyond
(See Cover)

The chill of a moonless July midnight was in the air, and some of the 11,000 jazz buffs in Newport, R.I.'s Freebody Park drifted towards the gate. In the tented area behind the bandstand, musicians who had finished playing for the final night of Newport's third jazz festival were packing their instruments and saying goodbye. The festival was just about over. But onstage famed Bandleader Duke Ellington, a trace of coldness rimming his urbanity, refused to recognize the fact. He announced one of his 1938 compositions, *Diminuendo in Blue and Crescendo in Blue*. A strange, spasmodic air, that carried memories of wilderness and city, rose through the salt-scented night air like a fire on a beach. Minutes passed. People turned back from the exits; snoozers woke up. All at once the promise of new excitement revived the dying evening.

At that magic moment Ellington's Paul Gonsalves was ripping off a fast but insinuating solo on his tenor saxophone, his fancies dandled by a bounding beat on

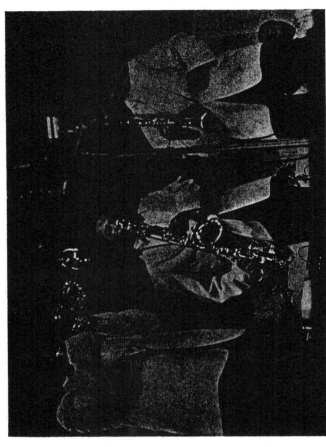

Robert Parent

SIDEMEN TERRY, GONSALVES, HAMILTON

Reproduced from *Time*, August 20, 1956. Copyright 1956 Time Warner Inc. Reprinted by permission.

bass and drums (Jimmy Woode and Sam Woodyard). The Duke himself tweaked an occasional fragment on the high piano. Gradually, the beat began to ricochet from the audience as more and more fans began to clap hands on the offbeats until the crowd was one vast, rhythmic chorus, yelling its approval. There were howls of "More! More!" and there was dancing in the aisles. One young woman broke loose from her escort and rioted solo around the field, while a young man encouraged her by shouting, "Go, go, go!" Festival officials began to fear that something like a rock 'n' roll riot was taking place. One of them was pleading with beaming Bandleader Ellington to stop. When the fellow's entreaties got too emphatic, Duke wagged a soothing finger at him and said mildly, "Don't be rude to the artists."

The event last month marked not only the turning point in one concert; it confirmed a turning point in a career. The big news was something that the whole jazz world had long hoped to hear: the Ellington band was once again the most exciting thing in the business, Ellington himself had emerged from a long period of quiescence and was once again bursting with ideas and inspiration.

At 57, Edward Kennedy Ellington, jazzman, composer, and beyond question one of America's topflight musicians, is a magic name to two generations of Americans. His *Mood Indigo, Sophisticated Lady, Solitude,* and countless other dreamy tunes have become as familiar as any other songs since Stephen Foster. As jazz composer he is beyond categorizing—there is hardly a musician in the field who has not been influenced by the Ellington style. His style contains the succinctness of concert music and the excitement of jazz. His revival comes at a time when most bandleaders who thrived in the golden '30s are partly or completely out of business,* and few have risen to replace them.

Last week Bandleader Ellington returned to New York from a four-night swing through New England and spent his first 24 hours in the company of his arranger, Billy Strayhorn, poring over a

* Benny Goodman plays occasional weekend dates, Tommy and Jimmy Dorsey have combined their bands, Artie Shaw is out of the music business, Cab Calloway is appearing as a solo singing act. Such sweet-music bandleaders as Guy Lombardo and Sammy Kaye, however, are still going strong.

pad of hot score paper. Next night the band met to record the four new songs they had written, while wives and friends looked on. At midnight the whole crew got on the bus and left for Buffalo, where the next night they played for a Negro fraternity meeting. The affair lasted till 4 a.m. Back in New York Duke stayed up late (noon) and got up early (2 p.m.) in order to keep appointments with TV crews and the press. At week's end he was off for a handful of one-night stands before settling down for one of his periodic long runs: a fortnight's engagement in Chicago's Blue Note Café.

Hot Licks. Although Ellington's outfit is the only big band that has never been disbanded in its 29 years, its character has changed over the decades as death or a yen for adventure changed its roster. Yet the Ellington sound is as distinctive today as it ever was. Apart from the Duke himself, its dominant personality is provided by two men who have been with it longest: Harry Carney and the hoarse, jovial tone of his big baritone saxophone, Johnny Hodges and the refined, almost brutally sensual whine of his alto. The other characteristic sounds are the tantrum-tempered groans and howls

JAZZ BUFFS DIGGING ELLINGTON AT NEWPORT FESTIVAL

Robert Parent

of the growl brasses with plunger mute,* an effect originally discovered by the late Trumpeter Bubber Miley, now played on trombone by Quentin ("Butter") Jackson and on trumpet by Ray Nance.

When the saxophones play together, their tone is tinted by one of Duke's innovations, the split harmony, which hauntingly inflects the whole quality of a chord. They seem to play with a fierce joy which is stimulated by the rude sting of the trumpets—or by their melting pleasure—and the short-tempered, but softhearted bleats of the trombones. The sound combinations are already fairly routine in almost any band of today. But in the Ellington band such background licks take on the coherence of speech and frequently turn into lively conversation. In *My Funny Valentine*, for instance, the blue mood of its start turns black in the second chorus; the dialogue becomes desperate and reaches a violent climax before tranquillity is restored.

Fickle Tricks. The man who is responsible for this remarkable musical idiom is a

* Actually, the business end of a "plumber's helper."

tall (6 ft. 1 in.), rangy (185 lbs.) fellow whose newfound trimness parallels his rediscovered energies. His habitual expression combines curiosity, mockery and humor. In his pleasant Harlem apartment or in his dressing room, he usually goes about in his shorts, possibly to preserve the creases in his 100-plus suits of clothes. His public personality resembles his public appearance, which is fastidious to the point of frivolity; few are the people who get a glimpse of the man beneath this polished exterior. "You gotta be older," he explains, "to realize that many of the people you meet are mediocrities. You have to let them run off you like water off a duck's back. Otherwise, they drag you down." Even his close friends say he never exposes himself to unpleasantness if he can help it. Says one: "He likes pretty pictures and pretty melodies."

Often, his efforts to avoid unpleasantness take the form of hypochondria—as he puts it, "I'm a doctor freak." Although his doctor says he is an unusually healthy specimen, Duke tends to mistrust his ability to stay well: if his pulse rate seems slow to him in Las Vegas, it means a call to New York for his doctor to take the next plane out. He will not tolerate air conditioning—"You know, I'm delicate. My hair gets wet, the air conditioning hits it, and I get a sharp pain right down the middle of my back." His personal vanity extends to his feet, which he exercises against the wall at odd moments during his busy days and nights.

Even the Duke himself has trouble fathoming the hidden truths of his personality, although he likes to try. "I may be a heel," he will say, "but I hate for people to think so." Or, "I always take the easy way." Perhaps his best estimate of his life and career is a self-deprecating one: "I'm so damned fickle," he says. "I never could stick with what I was doing—always wanted to try something new. I never accumulated any money, so I always had to keep working."

At Last, Clicks. When Edward Ellington was born in Washington, D.C. in 1899, the capital was jigging to the insolent rhythms of ragtime pianists. Farther west Buddy Bolden's fabulous cornet was shaking New Orleans' levees, and such young idolaters as Joe ("King") Oliver and Sidney Bechet were soon to hammer out the rudiments of instrumental jazz. Washington jazz tended to strings—pianos, banjos, violins—but it had the same

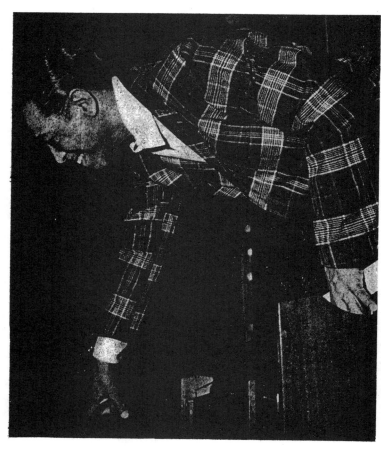

CONDUCTOR ELLINGTON (AT FAIRFIELD, CONN. CONCERT)

ancestry: the sophisticated rhythms of African drums, which later took on a more succinct and sensuous character as they drifted through the Caribbean islands, gradually infiltrated the U.S. via New Orleans and the East Coast. The East Coast variety, with its own flavors added, eventually became the ragtime of Duke's childhood.

"Man, those were two-fisted piano players," he recalls. "Men like Sticky Mack and Doc Perry and James P. Johnson and Willie 'The Lion' Smith. With their left hand, they'd play big chords for the bass note, and just as big ones for the offbeat, and they really swang. The right hand played real pretty. They did things technically you wouldn't believe."

Ellington's father was first a butler, then a caterer, and eventually a blue-print technician, and he provided well for his family. Duke had art lessons, at which he did extremely well, and piano lessons, which he never mastered. He felt they cramped his style. He worked in a soda fountain after school, and spent his hours at home working out his own method of playing the piano. By the time he was 14, he had started a piece called *Soda Fountain Rag*, and he played it so many

After that he never had to split his fees. Before long he had a house, a car, a wife and a son, Mercer. But his musical friends all moved to New York, where the jazz was hot. Duke followed in 1922, though it meant a fresh start, many penniless months, and a separation from his wife that became permanent.

Lucky Six. "A pal and I used to go see Willie The Lion at his club—the Capitol Palace—and Fats Waller at the Orient, and they'd let us sit in and cut in on the tips," Duke recalls. "Every day we'd go play pool until we made $2. With $2 we'd get a pair of 75¢ steaks, beer for a quarter, and have a quarter left for tomorrow." He did his own housework, including mending and pressing his tailor-made suits, always impeccably kept. Periodically, there was work for his five-man combo—Arthur Whetsel on trumpet, Otto Hardwick on bass and alto, Sonny Greer on drums and Elmer Snowden on banjo—but the real break came in 1927. "You know, I'm lucky," says Duke. "I'm lucky because I like pretty music—some people don't—and can write it down. And I was lucky when we auditioned for the Cotton Club job. Six other bands auditioned, and they were all on time. We were late, but the big boss was late too,

WITH COTTON CLUB DANCERS IN 1930
Willie The Lion let him sit in.

Max P. Haas—European

different ways that people thought it was several compositions.

Soon Duke and his friends were playing for private affairs and dances at Washington's True Reformers Hall. A musical contractor arranged bookings in return for half of the fees. Duke noticed that the contractor got his business from a small ad in the classified phone book, so the boy took an ad himself, and he clicked.

and he heard us and he never heard the others." Duke enlarged his band to eleven pieces and stayed at the Cotton Club on Harlem's Lenox Avenue for five years.

As soon as he got on his feet, Duke sent for his mother. "I was never out of her sight until I was eight," he says. "She and my father even used to take me to dances and set me on the bandstand while they danced." He bought her furs and a big diamond ring, and sought her advice constantly. When he toured, she would follow him around the country. When she died, Duke wept in his sister's arms. As for his father, Duke had long since made him road manager of his band.

Every man in the early Ellington band —as in today's—was a soloist, and the music they played was unlike anything anyone had ever heard. Recalls a friend: "One time at the Cotton Club the entire brass section arose and delivered such an intricate and unbelievably integrated chorus that Eddy Duchin, who was in the audience, literally rolled on the floor under his table—in ecstasy." Says Ellington: "We didn't think of it as jazz; we thought of it as Negro music."

It was, indeed, full of thudding tom-toms, sizzling cymbals and gongs. Much of it had an undulating, tropical beat that might have emerged from Africa, and its saxes wailed and its brasses growled in cheerful ill temper. The titles, themselves an important part of the magical atmosphere, were such things as *East St. Louis Toodle-oo*, *The Mooche*, *Creole Love Call* and *Black and Tan Fantasy*. By that time, Composer Ellington was already making some of his important innovations; *e.g.*, the use of a wordless soprano as if she were a musical instrument, and compositions of unusual length for a jazz band (his *Reminiscing in Tempo* was spread over four record sides).

Duke Ellington really started to get around. Recalls one of Duke's former managers: "I've traveled all over with him. I've seen Duke between a real duke and lady-so-and-so, and when he's dressed in those tails, he's as fine a gentleman as England could produce.

"Duke and his band played in England during the Economic Conference, in 1933. They were playing in Lord Beaverbrook's tremendous palace at a party. Jack Hylton's band played waltzes till midnight, and Duke took over at midnight. This mob, they'd never heard music like that. I was standing with Beaverbrook and Lady Mountbatten. We were watching all of these dignitaries, all diamonds and medals and what not. Beaverbrook was so taken with the music, and he said the mob was like a bunch of kids. He asked me questions about the band. I explained this was swing music. The Duke has the type of rhythm that more or less gets into your veins when you're dancing. Beaverbrook wrote an editorial about us."*

Quick Fix. In those days Negroes were still segregated on Broadway. Duke recalls going to work at a nightclub called the Hurricane, which he found a good spot until he began getting complaints from his Harlem friends; not one of them had been able to get in. Ellington spoke to the owner, and it was not long before the doors were opened. Duke is not a militant foe of segregation. He plays for segregated audiences on his annual swings through the South—"everybody does"—and feels lucky that there has never been an incident.

In 1926 Duke met an agent and lyric writer named Irving Mills, and Mills be-

* In the London *Daily Express*, advocating colored colonial Members of Parliament, Press Lord Beaverbrook took Ellington as a fine example of his race, described him as "a genius of Negro music. He sat by the side of his host, modest, dignified, delighting all the company with his gay mind and splendid bearing."

came manager of the band as well as Ellington's personal representative and partner. Out of this relationship came Duke's most successful years as a composer and bandleader, almost in spite of himself. "Oh yes," Mills would say, offhandedly, waving his fat cigar. "We've got a recording date tomorrow. Four new songs." Or, "Oh yes. We're going to introduce a new big work next week." *Creole Rhapsody*, Duke's first composition of greater than pop-tune dimensions (1932), came about after one of Manager Mills's press conferences. At that time *Creole Rhapsody* was just another little tune. A reporter wanted to know how come it was called "rhapsody," and Mills offhandedly said that it was "part of a larger work." And Duke Ellington, too proud to let his manager down, and unwilling to let such a whopper stand, produced the music on time——or almost on time.

Ellington, who seems to derive inspiration from being on the move, wrote many of the tunes in a taxi on the way to the studio, or even in the studio. Sometimes he would jump out of bed in the middle of the night, grunt a tune that had just come to him and play it on the piano. It made little difference, since all new numbers had to be worked out anyhow. "You play

this," Duke would say to one musician at a time, while noodling out a tune on the piano. As soon as they heard a phrase, the musicians learned it, and then toyed with it until they made it sound as if they had invented it themselves.

Even accidents were turned to advantage. One day, when only half the band arrived for a recording session, a new distribution of voices was evolved on the spot to make the few sound richer. The tune was *Mood Indigo*, and the broad-spaced trio at the start became one of Duke's sound trademarks. Other tunes lay fallow in the band's books until somebody set words to them and they caught on, e.g., *Never No Lament (Don't Get Around Much Any More)*, *Concerto for Cootie (Do Nothin' 'Til You Hear from Me)*. Ellington is accustomed to hearing his ideas unexpectedly used by other songwriters, and is resigned to it.

Counting Chicks. Duke's fertile mind continued to turn out songs, even when there were no recording deadlines to meet. The band could now play a week's worth of dances and never repeat itself or play any composer except Ellington. During the early years, Ellington found that one hit tune a year was enough to keep the band popular. What kind of music did he think

he was writing? Mostly, he thinks it was folk music. In any case, he says, his songs are "all about women," and almost any

WITH MANAGER MILLS IN PARIS
The Beaver wrote an editorial.

one who listens receptively will agree. Duke is well qualified to discourse musically—or any other way—on the chicks, as he calls them. He has made a long and continuing study of the subject, and is himself the object of study by his subjects. As soon as he appears on a Harlem sidewalk, the street becomes crowded with chicks. The young ones merely ask for his autograph; older ones pass with glittering, sidelong glances beneath lowered lashes.

In 1939 Musician Ellington and Manager Mills agreed to go separate ways (Mills has since become a successful music publisher). One of Duke's subsequent adventures was *Jump for Joy*, which he wrote and produced with a group of Hollywood artists. It was a revue designed to fight Uncle Tomism in the entertainment world, and the show folded after twelve weeks of backstage wrangling. As usual, Duke had written for his own band, and the band was in the pit. "We stayed out there for a while, just barely keeping our heads above water," he says. "But there were not enough people clamoring to buy at our price. So we put the price up. We gave a concert in Carnegie Hall."

Bop Kicks. It was about the same time that Duke got what he calls "the check." Things were very black. There was a recording ban on,* which meant no extra fees, and the band was taking a $500 loss a week just to play at a club with a "wire," *i.e.*, a radio hookup. "I was short of cash," he says, "so I went into the William Morris office to negotiate a small loan. While I was standing around, a boy came through with the mail, and handed me a letter from Victor records. I glanced at it. It was a check for $2,250. I slid it back into the envelope quick. Just what I needed, I thought. Two thousand, two-hundred-and-fifty dollars would do me nicely. But maybe I had misread it. Probably it was $22.50. I opened it again. It was $2,250, royalties for *Don't Get Around Much Any More*. I went out of there like a shot, and nobody saw me for two months."

During the '40s, Duke turned out several large jazz tone poems, notably *Black, Brown and Beige*, which has to do with states of mind rather than skin colors; *Tattooed Bride*, a humorous episode; *Harlem*, with its smooth changes of pace from nimble to noble; *Liberian Suite*, written on commission for the Liberian government centennial.

Despite the fame of these works, things continued strictly blue for the Ellington gang. Most of the original band members had either quit or died, and with their replacements, Composer Ellington seemed to have trouble writing new songs as distinctive as the old. The jazz world was getting its kicks from bop, but when Ellington tried to go along with the new style, he seemed to be regressing: he had been using their tricks for years. On the fringes of show business, men became reputable critics overnight simply by writing attacks on Ellington

The Clock Ticks. But the attraction of the Ellington band never faded among musicians. And today, joining him means both musical glory and financial security. "You hear the band, when you're not in it," says Butter Jackson, "and you like the way it sounds. You think you'd like to be playing that." Once in, every man is tempered by the fire of 14 other men's alert ears. There is no other discipline. Says Duke: "I told those guys in 1927 they were never going to drive me to the nuthouse. 'We may all go there,' I said, 'but I'm going to be driving the wagon.'"

* Instituted by Music Czar James C. Petrillo in a campaign to force radio stations, bars and restaurants to employ members of the American Federation of Musicians.

He can't remember ever firing anybody, but he has driven some to quit. One man regularly arrived tight and got drunker as the evening wore on. At the worst moment Duke would schedule the fellow's solo in racing tempo, so fast that he could not play the notes, and he eventually quit in humiliation.

Mercer Ellington (who is now in the recording business) well remembers the days when he was working his way up through the ranks of the band as baggage boy. "We got to Cleveland about 8 or 9 o'clock one morning," he says. "I complained that I was hungry. 'What!' said my father. 'Didn't you just eat yesterday?'" Today, things are different. The Ellington band, back on top, asks a tidy $2,500 a night for a dance, plus about half of the net gate receipts. The fee is $3,500 for a college concert-and-prom. Altogether, Duke Ellington, Inc. grosses between $500,000 and $700,000 a year. Part of the reason for the band's durability is the fact that, unlike most bands, it plays everything—concerts, proms, dances, theaters, nightclubs, hotel dining rooms, and even rock 'n' roll hops. Most of its time is devoted to living "on the other side of the clock" while playing one-night

George Rowen

THE DUKE (CENTER) & FAMILY*
Mostly on the other side of the clock.

* From left: Mercer Ellington and wife Evelyn, Duke, his sister Ruth, Arranger Strayhorn.

stands. The band packs up its instruments between 1 and 4 a.m., gets aboard the big bus with "Mr. Hi-Fi of 1956" on the fluted sides, and rides, argues and snores its way to the next town (favorite topics: chicks, music, food, geography). The arrival may be at dawn or dusk, depending on the distance. One musician described the rest of the process: "You go to the hotel, take a long look at the bed, go play the date, take another look at the bed and get on the bus." Such a life seems to agree with the Ellington bandsmen, who are cushioned against some of life's jolts by getting the highest pay in the business ($200-$500 a week).

Duke travels by car or train these days. He never flies, and has serious reservations about steamships. But when he hits New York between tours, his rounds of lawyers, music publishers, recording studios, photographers and tailors are fairly ducal. He likes to play the patriarch of his family which includes his sister, his son Mercer, 37, his three grandchildren and (by virtual adoption) his doctor and his arranger, Billy Strayhorn.

Ellington's second wind has been felt in the music business for months, and the major record companies have been bidding for his remarkable signature:

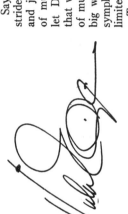

This week he plans to sign (with Columbia) a contract designed to give him the broadest possible scope. He will have time to write more big works, both instrumental and dramatic. Planned for the immediate future: a musical on the history of jazz, specifically composed for records. Ellington began work on this score 15 years ago in Hollywood, on a commission from Orson Welles, but he soon put it aside. "I wrote a piece of music . . . just 28 bars," he wrote later. "It was a gasser —real great, I confess it. And I lost it. I always said, and I say to this day, that it was the greatest thing I ever wrote. . . . I got the money, but they never got the 28 bars." Now, Duke is determined to go on with the project despite the missing 28 bars.

Says a friend: "Duke hasn't hit his stride yet. If he retired for a few years and just wrote, he would leave a wealth of music. The record companies should let Duke write tremendous symphonies that would represent America and a style of music. He should be allowed to write big works, to write and record with big symphony orchestras. He shouldn't be limited to 14 or 15 men."

To which Edward Kennedy Ellington replies: "We're not worried about writing for posterity. We just want it to sound good right now!"

THE JAZZ CANON AND ITS CONSEQUENCES

By Krin Gabbard

Jazz talk is becoming jazz discourse. Scholars at major universities are now granted the Ph.D. primarily on the basis of their contributions to jazz scholarship. The institutionalization of jazz in higher education would be consistent with current demystifications of the distinctions between high and low culture, with the growing trend toward multiculturalism in university curricula, and with the postmodernist cachet now enjoyed by marginal arts and artists. Signs of jazz's ascendancy can be found in such periacademic phenomena as the proliferation of jazz titles now being published by university presses, the birth of jazz repertory orchestras, and the new jazz division at New York's Lincoln Center. For several years Lincoln Center has also run a series of "Classical Jazz" concerts under the artistic directorship of Wynton Marsalis, himself an eminent symbol of jazz's new legitimacy.

Even television commercials testify to the music's rising cultural capital. In an advertisement a few years ago, a well-heeled white gentleman cited a Mozart concerto as the sound most appropriate for the total appreciation of his Mercedes-Benz; more recently, a cool, Milesian trumpet performed a similar function by providing elegant background music in a commercial for the Infiniti, a new luxury car. Concurrent with the Infiniti spot a faithful recreation of the Duke Ellington Orchestra's 1941 recording of "Chelsea Bridge" played behind a scene of casual affluence in a commercial for the American Express card; and at the time of this writing, Benny Goodman's 1952 recording of "How Am I to Know?" graces a series of spots for the Chase Manhattan Bank. Advertisers no longer use jazz to connote the night life and slumming that can be purchased along with their products—jazz can now signify refinement and upper class status, once the exclusive province of classical music.[1]

This new parity of jazz with classical music in the sign systems of popular media is an important breakthrough. Because jazz has historically been treated as a stepchild of "serious" music, the music's value is usually established with appeals to standards developed for classical music. The project is explicit, for example, in the title of Grover Sales's book, *Jazz: America's Classical Music.*[2] All jazz writers are richly aware of the various strains of prejudice that place classical music in a loftier position in the cultural hierarchy. A great deal of jazz writing implicitly or explicitly expresses the demand that jazz musicians be given the same legitimacy as practitioners of the canonical arts. When the arbiters of taste finally understand that the intrinsic value of jazz is unrelated to its exile from the Eurocentric canon, jazz will ascend to its rightful place in American culture as well as in the university, where jazz scholarship will flourish.

Or will it? The hypothetical ascension of jazz studies would take place at a peculiar moment in the history of academic institutions. Conditions that appear to bode well for jazz scholarship also conceal difficulties for the discipline. The canonization of jazz—or more precisely, the canonization of certain jazz artists and styles—would seem to be inescapable if the music is to claim its place within the academy, where an array of organizations such as grant-giving institutions support and further legitimize subjects of research and teaching. At the same time, however, humanistic disciplines are being re-canonized if not de-canonized while the entire process by which texts come under scrutiny is itself being scrutinized. And in spite of the occasional jazz group that called itself an "orchestra" or the jazz writer who composed a "fantasy," the music has almost from the beginning placed itself at odds with the canonizing language of high culture. The entry of jazz discourse into the dialogues of the university can only result in the transformation of that discourse. Scott DeVeaux has suggested that the term "jazz concert" once ran the risk of being an oxymoron.[3] Much the same can now be said for "the jazz canon."

My argument in this paper is arranged around two themes that complicate the attempt to establishment a jazz canon: (1) the resistance of jazz writing to the protocols of contemporary theory that follow canon-building wherever it takes place, and (2) the conviction on the part of many theorists that ideological forces masquerade as disinterested aesthetics in the discourse around *all* canonical works. I will make regular references to debates within other disciplines—film studies, most prominently—that offer instructive models for the imminent institutionalization of jazz. The creation of a jazz canon, I will argue, is as self-defeating as it is inevitable, especially as jazz studies move towards professionalization and autonomy.

CANONICAL STATUS

Although people inside and outside academia are now less inclined than ever to subscribe to the concept of the "masterpiece," canonical works of Western literature, classical music, and European painting still bear traces of the Benjaminian aura. Likewise, the term "canon" still carries the marks of its religious origins: the Oxford English Dictionary defines *canon* as "The collection or list of books of the bible as accepted by the Christian Church as genuine and inspired . . . . Any set of sacred books."[4] Although the sacral antecedents of canons are usually ignored in discussions of great art, music, and literature, those works that appear to have endured for centuries possess a mystifying sense of inevitability, as if they had been handed down by God. Like the books of the Bible, "great" works of art are "universal" and "timeless."

In stark contrast to the sacral haze that surrounds canonical texts, the actual path a work takes to "masterpiece" status has little to do with religion. In fact, canonization is usually determined by the likes and dislikes of the last few generations of university professors.[5] If nothing else, professors are more comfortable teaching the material once inflicted upon them in graduate school, if not in college and high school. Teachers can become self-conscious about the hidden politics of canon formation and cease referring to works as immortal masterpieces, even choosing to teach them anticanonically. Still, texts that are repeatedly inscribed in course syllabi possess a largely unquestioned claim upon the attention of scholars and students. This aura of inevitability masks the often tortuous paths such texts may have taken on their way to canonization. Lawrence Levine's account of Shakespeare's fortunes in mid-nineteenth century America provides a particularly revealing example of how texts can be wrested from a popular canon and sequestered within the academy for an educated elite.[6] But at least in part because English professors seldom teach history of reception, Shakespeare is widely regarded as an eternally stable fixture of the high art canon. We can also chart the ups and downs of novelists, painters, sculptors, and composers who now occupy equally unquestioned positions in our cultural hierarchies. In spite of the Infiniti and Chase Manhattan Bank commercials, few Americans today regard anything in jazz history as the auratic equal of Faulkner, Copland, or Wyeth. Consequently, the disciplines that attend to these works carry a legitimacy that jazz studies lack, if only because the music has not been around long enough to acquire real canonical status.

FILM STUDIES AS A MODEL

The progress of a youthful discipline such as film studies may offer a better model for contemplating the future of jazz studies. Cinema stood just outside the classroom door in the early 1960s, a position not unlike the one currently occupied by jazz. Colleges and universities had for many years provided meeting places for film societies and buffs, just as "hot record societies" and student jazz bands have long been fixtures at universities. Amidst the clutter of fanzines, a bare handful of journals published scholarly articles on movies; a few intellectuals had begun writing on the history and aesthetics of the cinema, in the case of the German-born psychiatrist Hugo Münsterberg as early as 1916.[7] Serious jazz criticism has historically lagged behind film criticism; although jazz was already a popular topic in newspapers and magazines by the second decade of the century, thoughtful jazz articles did not begin to appear in the United States and Europe until the 1930s.[8] In the academy, many universities developed professional schools for filmmakers; in the case of film history and criticism, some faculty members showed feature films in their classrooms to supplement more conventional pedagogical tools, and at a few schools, students could even take a course devoted entirely to cinema. Such courses, however, were usually ghettoized in departments of English or theatre. Much the same can be said for jazz today: while there are a number of schools that train young musicians to play the music (Berklee College, William Paterson College, North Texas State, etc.), these must be distinguished from schools where jazz is most often taught by musicologists more secure with Eurocentric forms or by a lone jazz musician retreating to the security of academia after several years of paying dues on the road. Institutes and archives such as those at Rutgers and Tulane are much more the exception than the rule.

Cinema, on the other hand, as been more successful in gaining acceptance at American colleges and universities. The first Ph.D. in film studies was granted by New York University in 1971. According to the latest survey by the American Film Institute, over 300 colleges and universities offered degrees in film study in 1980.[9] The number has surely grown since. By contrast, as late as 1990, only 100 colleges and universities in the United States offered degree programs in jazz, almost all of them undergraduate.[10] The success of cinema in becoming a recognized academic discipline might be attributed in part to the importation from France of *la politique des auteurs* in the 1960s. Andrew Sarris deserves substantial credit for Americanizing an auteur theory of cinema that identifies the director as the true author of a film.[11] The more romantic auteurists created an agonistic model of filmmaking, casting the director as a serious artist imprinting a unique vision on his films in spite of the arbitrary demands of studio bosses, star egos, and the Production Code. Anything that was aesthetically weak or unsavory in a film could be blamed on someone else so long

as the auteur's signature was visible in the film's "privileged
moments."

By authorizing the reading of a film around a single artist's
work, auteurism gave a new aesthetic legitimacy to movies.
In universities, films "by" Ford and Welles or Bergman and
Antonioni could be collected and interpreted according to
many of the same methods developed for, say, the novels of
Henry James. Evidence of order and thematic unity, once
the sole possession of high culture, was also found in works of
cinematic auteurs, and canonized filmmakers were said to
possess transcendent artistic visions that spoke to all humanity.[12] As the university was being transformed by the sea
changes of the 1960s, auteurism helped clear room in the
university for film study, bringing with it an aesthetics and a
canonical list of director/authors. Sarris eventually became a
professor of film studies at Columbia University in spite of
his lack of conventional academic credentials.

Auteurism still has force today, even among the filmgoing
public who now recognize a large variety of brand-name
directors—Spike Lee and David Lynch as well as Steven
Spielberg and Woody Allen. In academic film studies any
number of theories from the 1970s and 1980s can be cited as
refutations, revisions, or rethinkings of auteurism. In general, the mainstreams of the discipline have moved away
from extolling the transcendent vision of a director and
towards what Paul Ricoeur has called "a hermeneutics of
suspicion."[13] Film theoreticians now rely on Marxist, psychoanalytic, semiotic, and poststructuralist methodologies to
connect forces outside the text with meanings that lie
beneath the film's smooth narrative surface. These meanings
are usually uncovered through techniques of demystification
developed by critics such as Roland Barthes who see
bourgeois ideology passing itself off as nature. Canonical
directors are still the subject of some research, but many
scholars have found that the ideological workings of a film
are more accessible to analysis when the director is relatively
obscure and the film is more "typical" of the industry's
production. As befits a discipline moving rapidly towards
professionalization, film scholars have adopted a language
that is notoriously remote. Most jazz scholars, for better or

worse, still speak a language drawn from other disciplines and/or journalism.

As in the more established disciplines, the dominant canons of cinema study have been radically questioned by previously excluded groups, most prominently by women. Recently, however, feminist critics have become concerned that their critique of traditional male canons is equally applicable to the emerging feminist canons. Virginia Wright Wexman's essay on the various interpretations of Alfred Hitchcock's *Vertigo* (1958) is exemplary of a feminism that recognizes its own investment in an institutional dialectic of power that feminism itself has sought to expose.[14] *Vertigo* was singled out by Laura Mulvey in what is undoubtedly the single most influential essay in early feminist film theory.[15] Far from labeling the film a work of genius, Mulvey sees *Vertigo* as a convincing illustration of Hollywood's submission of female characters to the sadistic gaze of the male characters, who function as stand-ins for the men in the audience. Wexman suggests that many feminists—who promote a theory that may be illustrated most completely by the obsessive gaze directed at Kim Novak by James Stewart in *Vertigo*—have effectively secured their place in the discipline by helping to place Hitchcock's film on key lists that define the canons of film study.[16]

Wexman observes that canon formation is essential to the political prestige of groups and subgroups in the academy. Following Gramsci, Wexman distinguishes between "traditional intellectuals," who perpetuate and rationalize the values of a society, and "organic intellectuals," who advocate new value systems, in essence theorizing themselves into the society's structures of power.[17] Institutionally established critics have insisted that *Vertigo* is a work of "pure cinema," and, by extension, that as a work of art it transcends commerce. For Wexman, the interpretations of these traditional intellectuals promote bourgeois notions of the autonomy of art. She debunks these readings of the film by demonstrating that large portions of *Vertigo* are endorsements for the touristic delights of San Francisco as well as for the classical beauty of its star, Kim Novak. Wexman also finds alternatives to readings of *Vertigo* by certain feminist critics, "organic intellectuals" who have advanced their own cause by holding up the film as an important document for which they offer the most compelling interpretation. By laying claim to a film such as *Vertigo,* feminist scholars have hastened that film's rise to canonical status at the same time that they have rationalized their own ascent in American universities.[18] In much the same way, Sarris promoted himself by creating a pantheon of exclusively male auteur/directors in the 1960s.

The history of film studies suggests that a postcanonical study such as Wexman's is possible only after the discipline has built a foundation around key works. The current demystification and deconstruction of cinematic texts by film theorists might not have become so prominent without canonizing discourses to oppose. The concept of authorship, in both film and literary studies, has been under assault for some years now, most notably in the works of Barthes and Michel Foucault.[19] Coincidental with the collapse of the author has been the ascent of the critic. No longer required to pay tribute to infallible creators, critics gain autonomy and authority of their own. The privileged position of Jacques Derrida in today's critical canon is surely related to his liberation of the critic from subordination to literary texts. Critics establish autonomy most effectively by creating a metalanguage and a series of methodologies that close out the amateur. Anyone can engage in evaluation and express an opinion about a book, a play, or a film. Only a professional can speak a language and brandish a paradigm understood only by a small coterie of specialists with mastery over the same language and paradigm.[20]

AN EMERGING JAZZ CANON?

Turning at last to jazz studies, I would argue that the discipline has for a long time been in a phase comparable to the auteurist era of film studies in the 1960s and 1970s: ever since the first serious writings about jazz appeared, critics have sought to become organic intellectuals, who would theorize themselves and the music into positions of importance. Although a number of writers have ascended to stations with some power, they have not yet been able to carve their canon into the granite of American culture or to install their discipline in the structure of the university. If I am right that jazz may follow the path of film studies in becoming a stable fixture in constantly mutating university curricula, a number of its scholars will become more self-conscious about the problematic nature of canon formation even as they continue to write about the key artists of their discipline.[21] It is also likely that jazz scholars will develop a professional discourse that may at first draw upon the vocabularies of musicology, sociology, critical theory, and other disciplines but that ultimately will be unique to jazz studies.

In doing so, jazz scholars run the risk of losing touch with a group of critics who do not have conventional academic credentials but who nevertheless play a large role in the professional life of the discipline by reading grant proposals and evaluating manuscripts for university presses. In addition, the new metalanguage of the field may strike most jazz enthusiasts as impenetrable. This is the trade-off that professionals in other disciplines have accepted as they have gradually but inexorably separated themselves from the general public. For some time now, the vast majority of poetry lovers have *not* consulted *PMLA* and *Modern Philology* to supplement their enjoyment, just as few movie buffs today expend the effort necessary to read the articles in *Cinema Journal* and *Camera Obscura*. Most academics regret this situation; some of the most eminent among them even bemoan their isolation in speeches at plenary sessions during professional conferences.[22] Tenure, promotion, and job mobility, however, are based not on professors' fortunes with general readers but on their reputations among a handful of professional colleagues. Similarly, as the work of jazz studies expands, something more than the straightforward celebration of canonical artists is required if the field is to stand alongside established disciplines that have long since ceased making appeals to outsiders.

The actual development of a jazz canon—not to mention the critic's role in the process—is complex and multidetermined, caught in a complicated web of changing conditions. In the 1920s, for example, the entry of Louis Armstrong's recording of "West End Blues" into a jazz artist's canon can be documented at least in part by a King Oliver recording of the tune that appeared six months after Armstrong's version: on Oliver's record of "West End Blues," trumpeter Louis Metcalf attempted a note-for-note recreation of Armstrong's opening cadenza.[23] There are a number of reasons why Metcalf may have chosen to duplicate Armstrong's solo, just as Oliver—who in fact wrote "West End Blues" and considered Armstrong his protégé—may have had reasons of his own for directing Metcalf to recreate the difficult solo. We might also interrogate the processes that brought Armstrong and later Oliver into the recording studio as well as those forces that made their records available to large audiences. Basically, however, we have a case of canon formation through a somewhat uncomplicated process of communication by phonograph record. Today, this kind of homage to one artist by another is only one among numerous phenomena that contribute to the creation of a jazz canon: a partial list would include grant-giving agencies, recording contracts and sales, collections issued by mail order companies and the Book-of-the-Month Club, public appearances by artists, academic appointments, the political structures of universities, roles for jazz musicians in movies (Dexter Gordon in *Round Midnight,* for example), record reviews, "ten best lists" in the popular press, promotion by disc jockeys, Grammy awards, film scores, and faces on postage stamps.

In the academy, however, canonizers are more likely to adopt the strategy of romanticizing the artist. The improvising jazz artist is, after all, a composer as well as a performer, not unlike the mythologized composer/performers of the Romantic Era such as Liszt and Paganini who improvised on well-known works. Although this equation is seldom explicit in jazz writings, its traces can usually be found, hinting at why a music associated with prostitution and drug addiction is as valid as the music associated with landed gentry in premodern Europe. A disproportionate amount of jazz scholarship is and has been devoted to finding the most effective means for identifying and exalting favored artists.

DISCOGRAPHY AND CANON-BUILDING

Consider, for example, jazz discography. The practice has long been the almost sole province of an international network of devoted record collectors, largely uninterested in profits and often with careers outside of music.[24] From the beginning, discographers have been intimately and unavoidably involved with the work of canon-building. When Charles Delaunay published his first *Hot Discography* in 1938, he created a guidebook for those who agreed with him that the music had more than ephemeral value.[25] He was also committing an act of exclusion, declining to catalogue certain performers from "race records," blues, ragtime, and dance music whom he considered to be outside the charmed circle of jazz. Like the auteurists of cinema studies, he built the discography on a model that centered on great artists: Delaunay would combine, for example, all the recordings of Armstrong in one section of his book even when titles had not been recorded under Armstrong's name or when the trumpeter was only a sideperson at someone else's recording session. Delaunay did the same with Bix Beiderbecke, even less likely to be listed as leader during his recording history. Just as auteurist critics attributed an entire film to the director rather than to the producer, the screenwriter, the cinematographer, the stars, or some combination of coworkers, Delaunay in effect credited Armstrong or Beiderbecke with a recording even when the trumpeter was essentially an accompanist.[26] For Delaunay, the centrality of Armstrong and Beiderbecke was more consistent with an idealized jazz history than were the pedestrian blues singers and sweet dance bands with whom the two trumpeters had recorded. His view of jazz history was reflected in the very arrangement of his discography.

Delaunay's catalogue laid the groundwork for several generations of discographers who fall into two broad catego-

ries: (1) single artist discographers who fetishize the recordings of specific musicians, almost always to the point of
detailing those sessions in which the artist is present but
undetectable in a large ensemble; (2) Orin Blackstone, Dave
Carey, Brian Rust, Jorgen Jepsen, Walter Bruyninckx, Erik
Raben, and Tom Lord who have, like Delaunay, inventoried
the music in large historical sweeps that inevitably repress
artists who do not play in appropriate styles. While the
discographers in the first category might be considered
inclusionists, tracking down every recorded scrap of specific
artists, those in the second are primarily exclusionists.[27]
Walter Bruyninckx, surely the most catholic of all jazz
cataloguers, provides a good illustration of the exclusionist at
work. His regularly updated discography, currently known as
Seventy Years of Recorded Jazz, is an international inventory
of jazz as well as gospel, blues, and jazz-inflected pop that
fills several feet of shelf space. Nevertheless, even Bruyninckx is likely to truncate the listings for an artist if he
believes that at some moment the recordings cease to have
jazz content. He also frequently writes statements such as the
following: "Although negroid in origin this group recorded
mainly for the white audiences and their recordings have very
little of the sincerity and enthusiasm that is to be found in
other negro recordings of religious oriented music."[28] Bruyninckx's candor becomes him well, but his didactic criterion
for banishing one group instead of another is characteristic of
any and all enterprises that seek to sort out the real from the
ersatz. Discographers such as Bruyninckx unavoidably par-
ticipate in the formation of a jazz canon, a project that is
scarcely value free. Single artist discographies appear because a cataloguer has responded to a variety of forces that
make an artist worthy of complete documentation. The
methodologies operating in the larger, exclusionary discographies are invariably grounded in critically sanctioned
judgments that discographers are seldom interested in
interrogating. For example, Erik Raben, one of the more
recent exclusionists, devotes two sentences to the issue:

> In many cases it has been difficult to decide where the
> boundaries to blues, R&B, dance-oriented big band

music, pop-vocal music, jazz/rock fusion music and
Latin music should be drawn. In some cases non-jazz
recordings are included to "complete" the discography
of a musician or a group/band.[29]

Like his predecessors, Raben does not reveal how he drew
the boundaries between jazz and nonjazz.

The canonization of jazz artists has almost always been the
major thrust of jazz scholarship, regardless of whether the
writers take their methodology from traditional musicology
or from social science. Two articles from the Austrian
journal *Jazzforschung/Jazz Research* provide extreme examples of both approaches. An essay on Clifford Brown begins
with the following paragraph:

> It is now twenty-two years since the passing of Clifford
> Brown, yet his loss is felt today almost as much as it was
> in the late summer of 1956. Musicians and fans alike,
> some of them too young to have heard him in person,
> pay tribute to this creative person. For many people,
> there is something amazing about the way that beauti-
> fully developed musical structures flowed from his horn
> with ease and joy. There is something phenomenal
> about the way that his improvisations are understood
> and appreciated even by those who ordinarily are not
> jazz lovers. Clifford Brown was possibly the rare
> musician who comes along only once in a generation.[30]

The body of the essay, however, is devoted to a highly
technical, Schenkerian analysis of Brown's improvisations,
devoid of the adulatory tone that opens the essay. Here is a
representative sample: "The middleground structure of the
original piece includes the neighbornate, b^1, which serves to
prolong a^1, and the movement d^1 in measure 8 which serves
to provide acoustical support for a^1 by virtue of the fifth
relationship" (136). At this point, the rhetoric of jazz studies
is indistinguishable from that of academic music theory.

An article on Lester Young, also published in *Jazz-
forschung,* grafts the history of racist violence against
African-American people onto a biographical sketch of
Young. Here is the conclusion of the article:

The sensibilities of Lester Young and other Black
artists assume even more impressive significance when
compared to the callow, materialistic, and often violent
nature of the world they inhabited. Young's humanistic, benevolent, and non-materialistic values set him
apart from both businessmen and conformist consum-
ers. He represents an ideal example of the qualities
allegedly treasured by the people whose actions suggested the very opposite.[31]

Without in any way rejecting the judgments of these two
writers, I would point out that both insist on the value of their
subjects even when it means speaking with two voices: each
scholar writes almost entirely in the professional language of
a canonical discipline, but at the beginning or end of his
piece, he switches to the vocabulary of the fan and the record
collector. Their praise for jazz artists is not and cannot be
documented with traditional scholarly apparatus. Footnotes
and musical examples disappear when the scholar becomes
essentially indistinguishable from the fan. The collapsing of
these two categories has run through a great deal of jazz
writing ever since the appearance of the first books that dealt
with the music.

By contrast, scholarly writing today in literature, music,
and art is increasingly less likely to be built around the
unequivocal glorification of the artist or the bald valorizing of
one artist over another. In literary studies, Northrop Frye
was calling such evaluative criticism "debaucheries of judi-
ciousness" in the 1950s.[32] Hyperbolic praise for the auteur
has been largely abandoned by film scholars during the past
two decades—it is now left almost entirely to critics in the
popular press. If a discipline can be considered "profession-
alized" when it develops its own metalanguage and a
self-consciousness about its canon, then jazz study is still in
its infancy. The discipline's lingering preprofessionalism is
especially evident in Gunther Schuller's *The Swing Era,*
doubtlessly one of the most important jazz texts in recent
years.[33] Schuller brings impressive credentials to this and his
already canonical study of early jazz.[34] In both books,
however, he rejects scholarly prose in favor of journalistic

terms such as "truly magnificent," "totally unredeemable," and "heartrendingly moving." Because Schuller is also devoted to the myth of jazz's autonomy, he seldom considers the music's contextual and historical relationships.[35] His consistent reluctance in *The Swing Era* to press his analyses beyond his own impressions is most explicit when he states, for example, that Billie Holiday's talent is "in the deepest sense inexplicable" (528), or when he writes of Ben Webster, "as with most truly great art, Webster's cannot be fully explained" (590), or when, after a few words on Lester Young's mastery of understatement, he calls Young "The Gandhi of American jazz" (562). These passages are likely to become increasingly uncharacteristic of jazz writing as the subject advances into the academy. No assistant professor in any discipline is tenured today for declaring a phenomenon to be "in the deepest sense inexplicable" (unless that professor is a deconstructionist, and Schuller is no deconstructionist).

AN AESTHETIC OF UNITY AND COHERENCE

Even when jazz writers perform close analysis on the music, they engage in a kind of canon-building based in paradigms that have been radically questioned in other disciplines. One historically prominent strategy for canonizing the jazz artist is based in an aesthetic of unity and coherence. Few writers employed this strategy as persuasively as Martin Williams, who studied the New Criticism in the 1950s while working on a graduate degree in English at Columbia University. A striking but not atypical example of William's application of formalist literary principles to jazz is his discussion of Charlie Parker's 1946 improvisation on the first take of "Embraceable You":

> In his one-chorus improvisation on "Embraceable You," Parker barely glances at Gershwin's melody. He begins with an interesting six-note phrase which he then uses five times in a row, pronouncing it variously and moving it around to fit the harmonic contours of

Gershwin's piece. On its fifth appearance the six-note motive forms the beginning of a delicate thrust of melody which dances along, pauses momentarily, resumes, and finally comes to rest balanced at the end with a variant of that same six-note phrase . . . [I]t is the core of his improvisation, and, speaking personally, I have seldom listened to this chorus without realizing how ingeniously that phrase is echoed in Parker's remarkable melody.[36]

As many theorists have pointed out, a work's value is not simply a function of how well its artist understands internalist principles of unity and coherence. Jonathan Culler has written, "The notion that the task of criticism is to reveal thematic unity is a post-Romantic concept, whose roots in the theory of organic form are, at the very least, ambiguous."[37] Parker's work might just as easily be discussed in terms of how he *destroys* the illusion of organic unity in his solos by inserting easily recognizable fragments from other musical traditions such as the Habenera from Bizet's *Carmen,* "The Campbells Are Coming," and Alphonse Picou's clarinet solo from "High Society."[38] Williams overlooked the ways in which Parker resisted recuperation into a Eurocentric aesthetic by in fact "Signifyin(g)" upon it, as Henry Louis Gates, Jr., might suggest.[39]

Because of the music's youth, jazz writers have gone about the business of canon-building without having to look over their shoulders at those who would demand alternative canons. The infamous battle between "the ancients and the moderns" in the 1940s was easily resolved by making room in the canon for bebop alongside older forms associated with New Orleans and Chicago. No legitimate history of jazz today can afford to omit either one.[40] In other disciplines, however, canons have faced powerful challenges from women, minorities, and those working with various poststructuralisms (and more recently from resurgent white males such as Allan Bloom, William Bennett, and Roger Kimball). The progress of various teaching anthologies is a good index to canon struggles in literature departments. In the 1970s, newly acquired female and minority editors began to effect the contents of W.W. Norton Company's well established anthologies of English and world literature. For some time Norton had invested in the belief that single, two-volume anthologies could present coherent canons for an entire discipline. Other presses subscribed to the same proposition and published their own one- and two-volume selections from the canon. Today, however, in addition to more pluralistic anthologies of English and world literatures, Norton has published an anthology of women writers, and Henry Louis Gates, Jr., perhaps the single most articulate critic of the old canon, is currently editing a Norton anthology of African-American literature.[41] Although Gates is clearly ambivalent about his new role as canonizer,[42] he has taken the original step of including in the anthology a sound recording of African-American writers reading from their work. Not only has Gates emphasized the performative dimensions of a great deal of black literature; he has also changed the rules for canon formation. By contrast, *The Smithsonian Collection of Classic Jazz,* now in its second edition and available on compact discs, stills stands as the only major listening text for an introductory course in jazz history. Many critics have second-guessed Martin Williams's choices for what ought to be included in the box, but as of this writing, no one has undertaken to replace it with a comparable anthology of favored recordings.[43]

PITFALLS OF CANON FORMATION

Although jazz scholars may need a canon to establish their legitimacy, there are other consequences of acquiring one. Like feminists who have found themselves in the uncomfortable position of deploying an institutional politics not unlike the one which had once been used to exclude women, jazz canonizers may find it difficult to be true to the full range of jazz culture at the same time that they rely upon Eurocentric traditions. Bernard Gendron has broached the subject of what is at stake as the discipline solidifies around a canon.[44] In discussing André Hodeir's preference of Igor Stravinsky's appropriation of jazz over that of Darius Milhaud, Gendron refers to Hodeir's "inadmissibly essentialist construction of 'authentic' jazz" (13). Milhaud most likely understood jazz as anything influenced by the rhythms of African-American music. Gendron argues that Hodeir and other historians have defined jazz more narrowly as an art music with specific qualities that they have then "read back" into earlier, amorphous forms of the music.

> We can understand this exclusionary re-reading of history as part of a decades-old struggle to establish jazz as a genuine art music, indeed as "America's classical music." Recent histories of jazz have bypassed those early types of nominal jazz which do not fit into the trajectory leading to modern jazz or give sense to its aesthetics; it is not that they have succeeded in separating the genuine from the counterfeit. . . . Much of what [Milhaud] called "jazz" is no longer part of the canon of jazz history. (14)

The tendency of jazz historians to search for predecessors of the more ambitious modernists may in part explain the inordinate amount of attention afforded Jelly Roll Morton, whose 1920s recordings are said to anticipate the "orchestral" aspects of swing and modern jazz. Schuller has called him "The First Great Composer."[45] The centrality of Morton in many jazz histories is consistent with a "masterpieces only" approach that tends to create a series of museum pieces alleged to possess universal meanings that travel with the work beyond its time and place.

The exclusion of anything not consistent with the "art" of jazz is complemented by the somewhat opposite phenomenon of celebrating the down-and-out, subcultural appeal of a repressed artform. This tradition in jazz criticism dates back at least to the various critical uproars in the 1930s and 1940s that accompanied each stage in Duke Ellington's progress towards concert music and away from his titillating "jungle music." Ellington perfected his jungle style in the late 1920s while his band was in residence at the Cotton Club playing behind gyrating, light-skinned, African-American female dancers.[46] A comparable fascination with the sordid aspects of substance abuse and mental illness has surely enhanced the charisma of artists such as Beiderbecke, Holiday, Young,

Parker, Chet Baker, and Bud Powell (and perhaps detracted from the amount of attention devoted to the clean-living Clifford Brown). The trend has culminated most recently in documentary and fiction films, such as *Round Midnight* (1988), *Bird* (1989), and *Let's Get Lost* (1989), that center on the broken lives of jazz artists.[47] In the academy, however, the ideology of jazz criticism has tended away from pathobiography and towards explicit or implicit connections between jazz and canonical aesthetics. Although a jazz musicologist influenced by André Hodeir may not overtly argue that Duke Ellington is the equal of Brahms, his use of analytical methods designed for Brahms makes the argument all the same.

In this context, few jazz scholars have yet to grapple with the critique of canons that has become central in many humanistic disciplines.[48] A consensus is now emerging that canon formation is a discourse of power, reinforcing the values of the canonizers. Groups that have been marginalized by generations of Eurocentric, mostly male academics can legitimately question the claim that certain works speak to us across the ages and possess universal truths. Barbara Herrnstein Smith has argued that any value attributed to a work of art

> is radically contingent, being neither a fixed attribute, an inherent quality, or an objective property of things but, rather, an effect of multiple, continuously changing, and continuously interacting variables or, to put this another way, the product of the dynamics of a system, specifically an *economic* system.[49]

Smith does not adopt a vulgar Marxist concept of an economic system driven by monopolistic forces, urging instead that we understand how certain works perform desired or desirable functions for certain groups at certain moments in history. A work that continues to provide these functions through extended periods of time becomes amenable to new generations with new economies largely because it has been carefully transmitted and preserved and is thus most easily discovered by a new generation searching for its

central texts. Once canonized, a work need not answer to all
the demands of a newer culture because its guardians will
find reasons why objectionable features—Smith lists "inci-
dents or sentiments of brutality, bigotry, and racial, sexual,
or national chauvinism" (49)—ought to be overlooked in
favor of other features, usually those that accommodate
themselves comfortably to humanist ideologies. Those people in whose economy the canonical authors of the West have
little or no value are frequently characterized as primitive or
culturally deprived by canonizers who are reluctant to
acknowledge that other cultures find value in activities
bearing little resemblance to Western conceptions of art.

Smith goes to special lengths to rebut the "axiological
logic" of writers such as Hume and Kant who have explicitly
argued that aesthetic judgments can have objective value.[50]
In deconstructing the prose of Hume, Smith finds a pattern
of qualifications and hedges that ultimately undermines his
claim for universal standards of judgment:

> Hume's claim is that there is empirical, factual evidence
> for a natural norm of taste. When restated with the
> conceded qualifications, however, the foundation of
> that norm, the alleged fact that some objects, by the
> very structure of the mind, are naturally calculated to
> please and others to displease, becomes the limp
> truism, *some objects tend to please or displease some
> people under some conditions. . . . (63)*

Kant's argument for the objective validity of some judgments
is rooted in the premise that we are capable of putting aside
all stimuli that distract from a direct appreciation of "the
beautiful." Once subjects achieve this uncontaminated state,
they will, according to Kant, invariably arrive at the same
judgments. Smith points out that Kant's list of what one must
put aside in order to become uncontaminated amounts to the
sum total of one's humanness.

> Contrary to the key requirements of Kant's analysis,
> then, our interactions with our environments are always
> and inevitably multiply contingent and highly individu-
> ated for every subject: our "sensations" and "percep-

tions" of "forms" or of anything else are inseparable from—or, as it might be said, thoroughly contaminated by—exactly who we are, where we are, and all that has already happened to us, and there is therefore nothing in any aspect of our experience of anything that could ever be, in the required sense, pure. (69)

I have quoted Smith at length because her work is especially persuasive and systematic in refuting the notion that one work of art can be declared intrinsically superior to another. By appropriating her work, jazz scholars need no longer argue with those who find classical music more valuable, more beautiful, or—as a colleague of mine once phrased it—"more interesting" than jazz. Although Smith bases her work in rigorously philosophical procedures, she is nevertheless working within the hermeneutics of suspicion that has yet to cast a significant shadow over jazz studies. Once jazz scholars have followed out her arguments in order to dispose of the assertion that Brahms is intrinsically superior to Ellington, they must then face up to equally valid proposition that Ellington is not necessarily superior to Brahms, nor for that matter that Ellington is necessarily superior to Jimi Hendrix or even to Kenny G. They must also confront the possibility that a solo by a canonical jazz artist in no way communicates universal emotions but rather communicates to both the initiated and uninitiated listener through highly mediated complexes of cultural forces. Jazz studies will come of age only when these cultural forces have been thoroughly investigated.

Of course, jazz scholars may choose to resist Smith's gambit and continue to build their canon with preprofessional professions of faith in the transcendent value of favored artists. Ironically, the impulses that have driven jazz writers to avoid a rhetoric based in suspicion share many of the same radical aspects that have led to the recent transformation of other disciplines. Literary critics today who *attack* the old white canon for marginalizing minority authors have a good deal in common with jazz critics who *defend* what could soon become the old canon in their discipline. Since the vocation of the jazz scholar is intimately bound up with highly charged issues of

race, a large group of scholars has almost always shied away
from positions that might in some way suggest white-against-
black racism. A white critic, for example, may feel more
secure in simply praising the achievements of an African-
American artist than in coming to terms with the forces that
may have affected what the artist played and how that playing
was received. Any number of jazz writers have continued to
write laudatory interpretive criticism even after musicians such
as Archie Shepp and critics such as Frank Kofsky have accused
the critics of paternalism and of pretending to speak for black
artists.[51]

The need to find tortuous paths around and/or through the
currents of racism is only one factor that inhibits a thorough
interrogation of canonizing traditions in the study of jazz.[52]
A hermeneutics of suspicion has much less raw material
when the subject is music. Catherine Clément and Carolyn
Abbate have both written feminist critiques of opera,[53] but
the uncovering of sexism and racism or the deconstruction of
false binarisms is substantially more difficult when the music
is attached to no program or literary text. Perhaps as a result,
traditional musicology has only recently begun to develop
feminist, ideological, and metacritical practices.[54]

ELEMENTS OF RESISTANCE
TO CRITICAL THEORY

There may also be a psychological dimension to musicology's
resistance to contemporary critical theory. In an argument
that can be applied to the work of musicologists, Donald
Kuspit has offered reasons why many art historians react
negatively to the introduction of structuralist and poststructuralist theories into their discipline.[55] He lists four assumptions that account for what he calls "the peculiarly hermetic,
cult-like character of so-called traditional art history" (346):
(1) the artwork possesses a sacral quality that distinguishes it
from ordinary objects and that induces the critic to explain
why it is special; (2) the visual is closer to the "madness of
inner life" than the verbal—to reduce the visual artwork to a

series of linguistic gestures is to repress its sensual, libidinous, and/or transgressive character; (3) correlatively, the visual has more to do with "bodiliness," the gut feelings that effect the spectator more profoundly than can anything expressed in words; (4) and finally, the activity of the critic is secondary to the activity of the artist—to suggest otherwise is to embrace the profane over the sacred.

Most of what Kuspit says about "traditional art history" can be adapted to jazz studies in particular and to musicology in general. Like almost everyone else, disciples of jazz respond to the sensual, libidinous dimensions of their music. If jazz has few conventionally sacral dimensions, it may have an even greater agonistic appeal as its advocates resist the class and racial prejudices that regularly stigmatize their work. With jazz in particular, strong emotional attachments of youth can persist throughout the devotee's life, especially when that attachment signifies a crucial developmental moment such as the willful rejection of bourgeois values. In addition, what Kuspit calls the "bodiliness" of the visual may have its equivalent in the gut feelings of jazz that seem to render words impotent: "If you have to ask, you'll never know." The jazz writer's corresponding discomfort with words takes many forms. One is the critical trope of privileging the experience of musicians—even when unarticulated—over any written statement by outsiders, i.e., other writers and critics.[56]

Popular music, meanwhile, has quickly followed cinema in acquiring a theoretically sophisticated body of scholarship. Like cinema, rock 'n' roll involves a huge industry and a highly conventionalized sign system and thus becomes especially accessible to critics skilled in the theories of Barthes, Foucault, Louis Althusser, Raymond Williams, and the Frankfurt School.[57] And because rock critics, unlike their jazz counterparts, have seldom laid claim to the formalist aesthetics developed for classical music, they have been more attentive to the contexts of the music. Lawrence Grossberg has suggested a useful model for writing about rock and roll, conceptualizing it as what Foucault calls "an apparatus."[58]

> The rock and roll apparatus includes not only musical
> texts and practices but also economic determinations,
> technological possibilities, images (of performers and
> fans), social relations, aesthetic conventions, styles of
> language, movement, appearance and dance, media
> practices, ideological commitments and media repre-
> sentations of the apparatus itself. The apparatus de-
> scribes 'cartographies of taste' which are both syn-
> chronic and diachronic and which encompass both
> musical and non-musical registers of everyday life.
> (236)

As I have pointed out, many jazz writers tend to ignore the
extramusical aspects of the music by conceptualizing it as a
safely autonomous domain. In doing so, however, they close
themselves off from the kind of work undertaken by
Grossberg and the more sophisticated commentators on pop
music.[59] Although theoretically informed studies of canonical artists have already been written and should continue to
be written, there still seems to be a vacuum in the academic
literature of jazz relating to fusion and the more commercial-
ized forms of jazz. Gary Tomlinson's evocative and erudite
defense of Miles Davis's post-1969 recordings is one of the
more promising signs of a new turn in jazz writing.[60]

CONCLUSION

I must make it clear that I am not unequivocally valorizing
terms such as "theory" and "professionalism" in this essay. I
have no illusions about the jargon-mongering that passes
itself off as theory in many quarters of academia today. I am
also ambivalent about the trade-offs that seem to be
necessary as disciplines move away from public concerns and
into a sequestered world of professionalism. As DeVeaux
has suggested, it may be a little unfair to deconstruct a
canonical view of jazz history so soon after it has been
constructed.[61] My goal has been to take a long view of jazz
studies as it makes its way along the arduous path to
institutionalization. I would hope to see more analyses
consistent with Grossberg's "apparatus" model that address

the actual function of jazz within culture rather than a disciplinary teleology of jazz's equality with classical music. Whether or not such projects prove to be compatible with the current and future place of jazz within academic political structures remains to be seen.

I conclude by returning once again to the paradigm of film studies to conceptualize the course of jazz studies. The late Charles Eckert, a film theorist of some prescience, wrote in 1974 of the new methods entering his discipline: "there is a stiff, cold wind blowing against partial, outmoded, or theoretically unsound forms of film criticism—and it just might blow many of them away."[62] Having boarded up the windows against the winds for some time now, jazz scholarship now faces two significant choices: it may continue developing and protecting its canon, or it may take the consequences of letting in some fresh, if chilling, air.

NOTES

I am extremely grateful to the following colleagues who commented on earlier drafts of this paper: Burton W. Peretti, Ronald M. Radano, Lewis Porter, Vera Micznik, Steven Elworth, Michele Bogart, William Howland Kenney III, John L. Fell, John Hasse, and Dan Morgenstern.

1. Since I will be attributing a number of qualities to "jazz" throughout this essay, I feel obliged to offer a definition of the term that distinguishes it from "classical music." Realizing that numerous artists complicate any such distinction (James Reese Europe, Duke Ellington, Benny Goodman, John Lewis, Anthony Davis, John Zorn, Anthony Braxton, Willem Breuker, and many others), I would define jazz as a music that is rooted primarily in the confrontation between African-American traditions and European music, involving some improvisation and syncopation, and performed more often in night clubs and dance halls than in concert halls. The music has changed too quickly throughout its history to accommodate a more precise definition. I am convinced that any attempt to arrive at such a definition must be based in a socio-cultural analysis of jazz rather than in its internal aesthetics. In this

sense, I am in almost total disagreement with assumptions underlying the otherwise convincing essay by Lee B. Brown, "The Theory of Jazz Music: 'It Don't Mean a Thing . . .'," *Journal of Aesthetics and Art Criticism* 49 (1991): 115–27. In his rigorous analysis of André Hodeir's writings, Brown never questions the purely formalist criteria that Hodeir and others employ in their attempts to define jazz. Nowhere does he ask crucial questions about who is listening, what the listener expects, or under what conditions the listening is taking place. Nor does Brown ask what cultural and ideological forces lay behind Hodeir's decision to write a definition of jazz in France in the 1950s.

2. Grover Sales, *Jazz: America's Classical Music* (Englewood Cliffs, N.J., 1984); also see Billy Taylor, "Jazz—America's Classical Music," *Black Perspective in Music* 14, no. 1 (1986): 21–25. On the other hand, a number of critics have made claims for jazz as the *antithesis* of classical music, most notably Hugues Panassié. In *The Real Jazz,* trans. Anne Sorelle Williams (New York, 1942), Panassié effectively redefines music in order to privilege jazz and to reverse the familiar musical hierarchies: "For music is, above all, the cry of the heart, the natural spontaneous song expressing what man feels within himself" (6). He is thus in a strong position to denigrate the environment in which classical music is consumed: "Likewise many feel that it is ridiculous for Negroes to clap their hands, dance in their seats, sing and cry when listening to an orchestra . . . But to me the most ridiculous spectacle is the sight of a concert hall filled with hundreds of spectators who sit statue-like in their seats listening with a lugubrious expression to solemn music which is served up to them in massive doses" (29).

3. Scott DeVeaux, "The Emergence of the Jazz Concert, 1935–1945," *American Music* 7 (1989): 7.

4. *Oxford English Dictionary,* s.v. "canon, 4." In addition, canon is a rule, law or decree from the church or from the Pope, as in canonical law. The portion of the Catholic Mass between the Preface and the *Pater,* containing the words of the consecration, is also known as the canon. Finally, a canon is a clergyman or anyone living a canonical life, that is, one devoted to the canons of the church.

5. "The problem of the canon is a problem of syllabus and curriculum, the institutional forms by which works are preserved as *great* works. One might contrast this institutional

function of the school with the function of the library, where ideally *everything* is preserved and where the system of preservation makes no distinction at all between good books and bad." From John Guillory, "Canon," in Frank Lentricchia and Thomas McLaughlin, eds., *Critical Terms for Literary Study* (Chicago, 1990), 240.

6. Lawrence W. Levine, *Highbrow/Lowbrow: The Emergence of Cultural Hierarchy in America* (Cambridge, Mass., 1988).

7. Hugo Münsterberg, *The Film: A Psychological Study* (1916; rpt. New York, 1970).

8. For a good deal of original research on the earliest jazz criticism, see James Lincoln Collier, *The Reception of Jazz in America: A New View,* I.S.A.M. Monographs, no. 27 (Brooklyn, 1988). Also see Ron Welburn, "The American Jazz Writer/Critic of the 1930s: A Profile," *Jazzforschung/ Jazz Research* 21 (1989): 83–94.

9. Charles Granada, Jr., ed., *American Film Institute Guide to College Courses in Film and Television,* 7th ed. (Princeton, 1980).

10. Susanna L. Miller, "Classroom Gigs—Funding for Musician/ Clinicians," *Down Beat* 57, no. 6 (June 1990): 56.

11. Sarris's seminal essay, "Notes on the Auteur Theory in 1962," first appeared in *Film Culture* (Winter 1962–63). It is collected along with responses by Peter Wollen and Pauline Kael in Gerald Mast and Marshall Cohen, eds., *Film Theory and Criticism,* 3rd ed. (New York, 1985), 527–62. The bible of American auteurism is still Sarris's *The American Cinema: Directors and Directions, 1929–1968* (New York, 1968).

12. Janet Staiger, "The Politics of Film Canons," *Cinema Journal* 24, no. (Spring 1985):4–23.

13. Paul Ricoeur, *Freud and Philosophy* (New Haven, 1970), 29–33.

14. Virginia Wright Wexman, "The Critic as Consumer," *Film Quarterly* 39, no. 3 (1986): 32–41.

15. Laura Mulvey, "Visual Pleasure and Narrative Cinema," *Screen* 16, no. 3 (Autumn 1975): 6–18, rpt. with afterthoughts in Mulvey's *Visual and Other Pleasures* (Bloomington, Ind., 1989).

16. Perhaps the best place to look for a scholar's film canon is the ten-best list published every decade—to considerable media attention—in the British journal *Sight and Sound.* Although *Vertigo* did not appear on previous editions of the list, it appeared in 1982, the prime time of a Mulveyian method of

feminist analysis. For the 1982 list, published alongside the previous three lists, see *Sight and Sound* 51, no. 4 (Autumn 1982): 243. Significantly, *Vertigo* is also on the first list of 25 protected American films established by the Librarian of Congress in 1989.

17. Wexman references Antonio Gramsci, *Selections from the Prison Notebooks,* ed. and trans. Quintin Hore and Geoffrey Nowell-Smith (New York, 1971).

18. Wexman has not had the last word on the feminist canonization of *Vertigo.* Susan White, an eminent feminist film theorist in her own right, has responded to Wexman's assertion that feminists have been "blind" to the vested interests of their critical positions on key films. In "Allegory and Referentiality: *Vertigo* and Feminist Criticism," *MLN* 106, no. 5 (1991): 910–32, White asks first "how it is that Wexman, a white, feminist, academic critic, is *not* blinded by her own position" (923). Employing a strategy developed by Paul de Man, White then deconstructs the opposition "blindness/insight," suggesting that blindness is in fact what makes insight possible. She concludes by arguing against the claim that *Vertigo* or any other text can be read "from a single, dominating reality that knows itself, knows its priority, comes from a position that knows no blindness and seems to have no vested interest . . ." (931).

19. Roland Barthes's "The Death of the Author" and Michel Foucault's "What Is an Author?" are collected with other relevant material in *Theories of Authorship: A Reader,* ed. and trans. John Caughie (London, 1981).

20. Brian McCrea has written an extended critique of "the professional" in English studies, *Addison and Steele Are Dead: The English Department, Its Canon, and the Professionalization of Literary Criticism* (Newark, N.J., 1990), esp. chapters 7 and 8. For a more polemical but compatible argument, see Leslie A. Fiedler, "Literature as an Institution: The View From 1980," in Leslie A. Fiedler and Houston A. Baker, Jr., eds. *English Literature: Opening Up the Canon,* Selected Papers from the English Institute, 1979 (Baltimore, 1981), 73–91.

21. Scott DeVeaux has recently published an extensive and well-argued article that confronts many of these issues. In "Constructing the Jazz Tradition: Jazz Historiography," *Black American Literature Forum* 25, no. 3 (Fall 1991): 525–60, DeVeaux addresses problems in jazz writing such as a chronic insistence upon the music's autonomy from social praxis, the

"romance" paradigms promoted by its historians, and the need for canonical figures. Ultimately he calls for "an approach that is less invested in the ideology of jazz as aesthetic object and more responsive to issues of historical particularity" (553).

22. In *Addision and Steele Are Dead,* McCrea describes the typical presidential address at the annual meeting of the Modern Language Association as

> the address in which a man or a woman who has achieved eminence on the basis of publications and holds an endowed chair at a major research university laments our failure to pay enough attention to introductory classes and the task of bringing undergraduates to know the joys of studying literature. (147)

McCrea, however, observes that "all such talk is nostalgic and largely empty" (147). The demands of professionalism take precedence over goals expressed in the official rhetoric.

23. Louis Armstrong, "West End Blues," rec. 28 June 1928, *Louis Armstrong, Vol. IV: Armstrong and Earl Hines* (Columbia CK 45142); King Oliver, "West End Blues," rec. 16 Jan. 1929, *King Oliver and His orchestra 1928–1930* (Classics 607). There is also a 1929 recording by a territory band, Zach Whyte's Chocolate Beau Brummels, that includes a passage for two unison trumpets and rhythm based on Armstrong's cadenza in "West End Blues."

24. Recently, however, discography has begun to move into the academy. The Institute of Jazz Studies in Newark has begun publishing exhaustive discographies of artists such as Benny Carter, Duke Ellington, Art Tatum, Erroll Garner, James P. Johnson, and Benny Goodman. As a participant in this project, Ed Berger has written on the problems of compiling a complete listing for Benny Carter, who has recorded as a multi-instrumentalist and an arranger in conventional jazz formats but also as the composer and arranger of movie scores and television soundtracks: "Benny Carter: A Discographical Approach," *Journal of Jazz Studies* 4, no. 1 (1976): 47–64. In fact, the *Journal of Jazz Studies* itself was effectively inaugurated by the single issue of *Studies in Jazz Discography* (1971), also published by the Institute of Jazz Studies and with the same cover design as *JJS*.

25. Charles Delaunay, *Hot Discography* (Paris, 1938).
26. The work of Gary Giddins, who regularly reviews movies as well as jazz, provides an equally revealing parallel between cinema auteurism and jazz criticism. Auteurist critics transformed previously neglected films into significant texts if they happened to appear in the filmography of a "pantheon" director such as John Ford or Orson Welles. In particular, the late works of the auteur were extolled in spite of previously received notions of his decline. Similarly, Giddins has responded to negative judgments of aging jazz artists (in the writings of André Hodeir, most prominently) by celebrating the later phases of their work. In his book on Louis Armstrong, for example, Giddins confronts critical commonplaces about the trumpeter's decline by bestowing praise on Armstrong's recording of "Hello Dolly" (1963) as well as on his 1968 album of Disney Songs. See Giddins, *Satchmo* (New York, 1988), 191, 203.
27. The label discographies of Michel Ruppli ought to be considered inclusionist rather than exclusionist. Ruppli's inventories of canonical jazz labels such as Blue Note, Prestige, Savoy, Chess, and Clef/Verve are meant to be complete, even when this necessitates the inclusion of whatever blues, folk, pop, or comedy acts the labels recorded along with the jazz material.
28. Walter Bruyninckx, *Seventy Years of Recorded Jazz, 1917–1987* (Mechelen, Belgium, 1978–1990), F110a. The group is "Fiske [sic] Jubilee Singers."
29. Erik Raben, *Jazz Records 1942–80: A Discography,* Vol. 1: A–Ba (Copenhagen, n.d., issued in 1989), iii.
30. Milton L. Stewart, "Some Characteristics of Clifford Brown's Improvisational Style," *Jazzforschung/Jazz Research* 11 (1979): 135–164.
31. Douglas Henry Daniels, "History, Racism, and Jazz: The Case of Lester Young," *Jazzforschung/Jazz Research* 16 (1984): 87–103.
32. Northrop Frye, "Polemical Introduction," *Anatomy of Criticism* (Princeton, 1957), 18.
33. Gunther Schuller, *The Swing Era: The Development of Jazz, 1930–1945* (New York, 1989). Further references to this book will be included in the text.
34. Schuller, *Early Jazz: Its Roots and Musical Development* (New York, 1968).
35. In "Constructing the Jazz Tradition," DeVeaux calls Schuller's work "a monument to the ideal of jazz as an

autonomous art" (542). For a thorough analysis of *The Swing Era* and the problems it raises, see Lewis Porter's review in *Annual Review of Jazz Studies* 5 (1991): 183–200.

36. Martin Williams, *The Jazz Tradition*, rev. ed. (New York, 1983), 137. The passage appeared with the exact same wording in the first edition of *The Jazz Tradition* (1970).

37. Jonathan Culler, *Structuralist Poetics: Structuralism, Linguistics, and the Study of Literature* (Ithaca, N.Y., 1975), 119.

38. See my essay, "The Quoter and His Culture," in Reginald T. Buckner and Steven Weiland, eds. *Jazz in Mind: Essays on the History and Meanings of Jazz* (Detroit, 1991), 92–111.

39. Gates, *The Signifying Monkey: A Theory of Afro-American Literary Criticism* (New York, 1988).

40. DeVeaux has identified the notion that jazz has undergone an *organic* growth process as the legitimating force behind the eventual reconciliation between bebop and older forms: "In the long run, it proved as much in the interests of the modernists to have their music legitimated as the latest phase of a (now) long and distinguished tradition, as it was in the interests of the proponents of earlier jazz styles (whether New Orleans jazz or swing) not to be swept aside as merely antiquarian" (DeVeaux, "Constructing the Jazz Tradition," 539).

41. Gates, "Canon-Formation, Literary History, and the Afro-American Tradition: From the Seen to the Told," in Houston A. Baker, Jr., and Patricia Redmond, eds., *Afro-American Literary Study in the 1990s* (Chicago, 1989), 14–39. Gates's most important transformation of the literary canon is surely his multi-volume edition of African-American woman writers.

42. See Gates's *Loose Canons: Notes on the Culture Wars* (New York, 1992).

43. For a survey of anthologies of jazz recordings that *preceded* the *Smithsonian Collection,* see John Hasse, "The Smithsonian Collection of Classic Jazz: A Review-Essay," *Journal of Jazz Studies* 3, no. 1 (Fall 1975): 66–71. Creating real competition for the *Smithsonian Collection* has always been complicated by legal issues related to acquiring permissions from a wide variety of record companies. Now that the major jazz catalogues are owned by Japanese (Columbia, Decca) and European (RCA, Verve) corporations, the opportunities for a competing anthology may be even more diminished.

44. Bernard Gendron, "Jamming at Le Boeuf: Jazz and the Paris Avant-Garde," *Discourse* 12, no. 1 (Fall-Winter 1989–90):

3–27. Further references to this work will be included in the text.

45. Schuller, *Early Jazz,* 134.

46. James Lincoln Collier is especially sensitive to the tension between Ellington and his critics in *Duke Ellington* (New York, 1987).

47. Self-destructive artists are not, of course, the sole province of jazz history. Americans are especially fond of crash-and-burn legends among their poets (Lowell, Berryman, Plath), painters (Rothko, Pollock) and rock stars (Joplin, Hendrix, Morrison). Spike Lee has claimed that his film *Mo' Better Blues* (1990) corrected the myth of the doomed jazz artist promoted in *Bird* and *Round Midnight.* I have argued to the contrary that, although the trumpeter-hero of Lee's film is not a drug addict or an alcoholic, he can only be "saved" when at the end he gives up the jazz life with its attendant dangers. See my article, "Signifyin(g) the Phallus: *Mo' Better Blues* and Representations of the Jazz Trumpet," *Cinema Journal* 32, no. 1 (1992): 43–62.

48. See, for example, the papers published in various issues of *Critical Inquiry* and collected as Robert von Hallberg, ed., *Canons* (Chicago, 1984).

49. Barbara Herrnstein Smith, *Contingencies of Value* (Cambridge, Mass., 1988), 30. Further reference to this book will be included in the text.

50. The crucial texts here are Hume's "Of the Standard of Taste" and Kant's *Critique of Judgment.*

51. Ronald M. Radano's forthcoming book on Anthony Braxton (Chicago, 1993) has much to say about the artist's struggle to make himself heard above the voices of critics, many of them well intentioned and supportive if ultimately unhelpful.

52. The many African Americans writing about jazz and related subjects (Stanley Crouch, Albert Murray, Amiri Baraka, Gates, Houston Baker, etc.) will undoubtedly continue to have much to say about jazz canons in years to come. In a personal communication, Burton W. Peretti has suggested that jazz is most likely to be grouped with other black musics and with the study of African-American oral traditions as it moves into the academy: Gates and Baker in particular have regularly made implicit and explicit arguments for the inseparability of jazz from African-American traditions that long preceded its emergence.

53. Catherine Clément, *Opera, or the Undoing of Women,* trans. Betsy Wing (Minneapolis, 1988); Carolyn Abbate, *Unsung Voices: Opera and Musical Narrative in the Nineteenth Century* (Princeton, 1991).
54. The most widely heard call for a new hermeneutics in musicology is probably that of Joseph Kerman, *Contemplating Music: Challenges to Musicology* (Cambridge, Mass., 1985). The several books that have responded at least in part to that call include Leo Treitler, *Music and the Historical Imagination* (Cambridge, Mass., 1989); Susan McClary, *Feminine Endings: Music, Gender, and Sexuality* (Minneapolis, 1990); Katherine Bergeron and Philip V. Bohlman, eds., *Disciplining Music: Musicology and Its Canons,* (Chicago, 1992); and Steven Paul Sher, ed., *Music and Text: Critical Inquiries* (Cambridge, 1992).
55. Donald Kuspit, "Traditional Art History's Complaint Against the Linguistic Analysis of Visual Art," *Journal of Aesthetics and Art Criticism* 45, no. 4 (1987): 345–49. Further references to this article will be included in the text.
56. See, for example, Stephan Palmié, "Jazz Culture in the Thirties: 'Kansas City, Here I Come!' " *Jazzforschung/Jazz Research* 16 (1984): 43–85, in which Palmié scorns those writers who claim to be "more knowledgeable than the musicians themselves" (43). Ira Gitler and Stanley Dance are two of the most prominent critics who have for decades uncritically reported the utterances of jazz artists.
57. A full account of how these various authors and schools have come together in the study of mass culture appears in the editors' introduction to James Naremore and Patrick Brantlinger, eds., *Modernity and Mass Culture,* (Bloomington, Ind., 1991), 1–23.
58. Lawrence Grossberg, "Another Boring Day in Paradise: Rock and Roll and the Empowerment of Everyday Life," Richard Middleton and David Horn, eds., *Popular Music,* Vol. 4 (London, 1984): 225–58.
59. Also see Simon Frith and Howard Horne, *Art Into Pop* (London and New York, 1987); Greil Marcus, *Lipstick Traces: A Secret History of the Twentieth Century* (Cambridge, Mass., 1989); and the several essays in the "Rock & Roll Culture" issue of *South Atlantic Quarterly* (90, no. 4 [1991]).
60. Gary Tomlinson, "Cultural Dialogics and Jazz: A White Historian Signifies" in Bergeron and Bohlman, *Disciplining*

Music. Also see Robert Walser, " 'Out of Notes': Signification, Interpretation, and the Problem of Miles Davis" (forthcoming).

61. DeVeaux, "Constructing the Jazz Tradition," 553.

62. Charles Eckert, "Shall We Deport Lévi-Strauss?" *Film Quarterly* 27 (1974): 63–65, rpt. in Bill Nichols, ed., *Movies and Methods, Vol. II,* (Berkeley, Cal., 1985), 426–29.

1

("X" indicates rhythmic placement of final consonant)

BILLIE HOLIDAY AND BETTY CARTER: EMOTION AND STYLE IN THE JAZZ VOCAL LINE[1]

By William R. Bauer

I

One of the many pleasures of listening to jazz may be found in the way a performer plays around with what we know to be "the song." In the process of weaving variations from a standard tune, the player dances fluently between literal quotation and liberal elaboration. No mere game, however, this process serves as a means of exegesis through which a performer subjectively colors her rendition with personal responses to the tune. Regardless of the degree to which she improvises, a jazz performer contributes her own perspective to the materials.[2]

At the risk of oversimplification, we may contrast this approach with that of the classical musician, for whom adherence to the written score usually precedes and informs the making of an interpretation. While the classical musician holds up the making of a personal statement as the ultimate achievement, even a mediocre jazz performer must produce some form of personal statement. The difference in the two approaches may hinge upon whether the listener hears the emotion expressed in the performance as the composer's or the performer's. In the classical world, the work embodies the composer's feelings, and we perceive the performer as someone who recreates and communicates these feelings. In the jazz world, however, no clear boundary separates composer, arranger, and performer, and thus the song can function as a vehicle for the performer's own personal expression. While such expression may take root in the emotions suggested by the performer's material, the performance must ultimately grow into a full blown revelation of the performer's feelings in order for it to exist *as jazz*.

Manipulating given materials has its risks and its limits, however, especially when these materials consist of well-known favorites. Thus a musician's alterations of a standard tune can easily slip from playful modifications into full-scale distortions that threaten the listener's ability to recognize the tune.[3] The degree to which a listener will accept the manipulation of familiar material depends upon many factors, including the style of the performer. When paraphrasing a standard, some jazz musicians make an expressive point via barely noticeable digressions from the original, while others will use crossing the threshold of recognizability itself as an expressive tool.

The relationship between emotional expression and personal style in music tends to resist analysis. One obstacle to such analysis lies in the abstract nature of sound. We can identify elements in an instrumental performance that act as general stylistic features, but we cannot consistently or precisely articulate what elements of a performance result from and indicate the performer's emotional contribution to it. However, by using words, vocalists communicate concrete meanings in sound. Thus by examining the work of singers we can gain a better understanding of how the specific meanings of words interact with musical expression to shape individual style. For this reason the work of singers provides the basis for this study.

In a jazz vocal performance, lyrics provide concrete images for the nonverbal meanings suggested by the music, and therefore play a significant role in the singer's response to the song. Furthermore, by providing grammatical structure (words functioning in different roles as parts of speech, their inflection, and their syntax), lexical meaning (or, semantics) and phonetic content (vowel length, accent, and rhyme), the lyrics also affect how a singer approaches her musical decisions, especially if she wants the listener to understand the words.[4] In responding to the emotional and linguistic contents of the lyrics, and in making her musical choices grow out of her response, the singer brands the reading of a song with her personality. An examination of a singer's rendering of a song's lyrics, and specifically how she alters the song's melody in order to accommodate linguistic features, will therefore help us to identify how stylization occurs.

The works of Billie Holiday and Betty Carter, two of music's greatest stylists, offer ample opportunity to study the process of stylization. Distinguished from one another by important temperamental differences, both singers nonetheless share two traits which intensify this process: a strong commitment to improvisation and an equally strong commitment to communicating the lyrics. In sharing these traits, both singers stand apart from many other jazz vocalists.[5] A fluid approach to what constitutes the tune may at first seem incompatible with an emphasis upon intelligibility. Yet both singers' improvisational decisions actually enhance our understanding of the words, by revealing personal meanings that the words hold for each singer. Thus we may most readily observe the process of stylization when singers have the freedom and the inclination to allow verbal meanings in the lyrics to interact with nonverbal meanings in the music.

In order to identify how the interaction of verbal and nonverbal meanings enables each of these singers to make a song distinctively hers, we will analyze Billie Holiday's and Betty Carter's performances of the Rodgers and Hart song "I Didn't Know What Time It Was." A musical transcription will serve as a means of referring to specific moments in each singer's performance. We will also need to differentiate among the registers of language each singer uses: phonetic, semantic, and syntactic, and to understand how these distinct registers interact with musical elements of the performances. Thus, in addition to describing the musical features of each performance, these transcriptions also must describe phonetic features. I use the modified Trager-Smith phonetic notation found in the *American Heritage Dictionary*[6] to identify specific speech sounds produced by each singer and to relate them to corresponding moments in the vocal line. Phonetic relationships within the lyrics, such as rhyme, also emerge more clearly without the incongruities of traditional spelling. Table 1 presents the song's lyrics respelled phonetically, based upon standard American pronunciation.

Table 1: American Pronunciation of the Lyrics to "I Didn't Know What Time It Was," Spelled Phonetically Using the Trager-Smith System (Underlined Syllables Receive Accents)

I didn't know what time it was,
/ay/<u>did</u>n/now/wə t/taym/it/wə z/

Then I met you.
/ðen/ay/met/yuw/

Oh, what a lovely time it was,
/ow/wə d/ə /<u>lə v</u>liy/taym/it/wə z/

How sublime it was too!
/hæw/sə <u>blaym</u>/it/wə z/tuw/

I didn't know what day it was.
/ay/<u>did</u>n/now/wə t/dey/it/wə z/

You held my hand,
/yuw/held/may/hænd/

Warm like the month of May it was
/wohrm/layk/ðə /mə nθ/ə v/mey/it/wə z/

And I'll say it was grand.
/ænd/ayl/sey/it/wə z/grænd/

Grand to be alive,   to be young,   to be mad,   to be yours alone!
/grænd/tuw/biy/ə layv/tuw/biy/yəŋ /tuw/biy/mæd/tuw/biy/yohrz/ə lown/

Grand to see your face, feel your touch, hear your voice say I'm all your
/grænd/tuw/siy/yohr/feys/fiyl/yohr/təč /hihr/yohr/voys/sey/aym/ohl/yohr/

own!
own/

I didn't know what year it was.
/ay/didn/now/wə t/yihr/it/wə z/

Life was no prize.
/layf/wə z/now/prayz/

I wanted love and here it was
/ay/want id/ləv/ænd/hihr/it/wə z/

Shining out of your eyes,
/šayniŋ /æwt/ə v/yohr/ayz/

I'm wise and I know what time it is now!
aym/wayz/ænd/ay/now/wət/taym/it/iz/næw/

We see that traditional spelling does not adequately represent the generally connected quality of speech sounds. However, singers exploit this connected quality in order to produce a flowing vocal line. The table does not show how certain words receive more emphasis within sentence, because each performance may emphasize different words.

An initial examination of each singer's performance reveals that while certain linguistic features of the song remain relatively constant between the two versions, the dramatic implications of the lyrics as they unfold in each singer's treatment vary considerably, due to different musical choices made by each singer. (Transcriptions of their performances appear as Examples 1 and 2, published as inserts to this volume to facilitate comparison and reference in reading the analysis which follows.)

Comparison of the performances also reveals slight differences in pronunciation, but as these differences do not strongly affect the analysis they will receive little attention. One obvious way that the transcriptions reflect the interaction between musical and textual elements of each performance becomes apparent when we look at and listen to the ends of phrases. The "x" in the melodic line which indicates the rhythmic placement of final consonants reveals that both singers end words and phrases with careful regard to the beat.

Before we make any further comparisons between the two singers, we must first hear how the text influences each individual singer's approach to the tune, and in turn, how each singer's rendition influences the way we hear the text.

II

Richard Rodgers cast the song "I Didn't Know What Time It Was" (see Example 3) in a standard thirty-two-bar AABA form with a not-so-standard four-bar coda.[7] The song's division into four-bar phrases results from several related factors: motivic parallelism, the placement of long rhythmic values every fourth measure, the rhyme scheme, and the closure of sense units in the text. Furthermore, in each A

Example 3

section, the song's harmonic progression combines with additional motivic parallelisms, internal rhymes, and the partial closure of sense units to further articulate these phrases into two-bar subgroupings.

While this regularity of phrase articulation lends rhythmic

⌐ for reincarnation
⌐h uniform marching
⌐cceeds in holding our
⌐l design, which counter-
⌐g's phrase structure. In its
⌐ on either the major form of
⌐or, the harmony weaves a
⌐l path and keeps us wondering
⌐ether or not the song's ending will
⌐n. The tonal design also explains
⌐nexpected and logical. Each eight-bar
sec⌐ ⌐ dominant, which leaves all of them,
inclua⌐ ⌐onally unresolved. Thus in order to satisfy
the need ⌐ sure created by the tonal design, the song
requires extr⌐ measures. The coda restates the melody from
the opening two measures, with new harmonies.

Hart's lyrics render the chiaroscuro of Rodgers's unsettled
tonality through the voice of a narrator that vacillates
between past and present, pain and pleasure, loneliness and
love. As each successive A section nearly duplicates its
antecedent musically, so too does each begin with the textual
formula "I didn't know what X it was."[8] The song's high
degree of rhythmic, melodic, and textual redundancy thus
presents an ideal backdrop against which the relationship
between a song's lyrics and a jazz singer's phrasing may
emerge.

Comparison of each of the A section's opening measures,
as sung by Billie Holiday in her first chorus (see Example 4),
reveals an important difference between Holiday's and
Rodgers's approach to melodic form: for Holiday, each A
section differs from the one that precedes it via subtle
rhythmic alterations. To begin, we notice that each time the
word "I" recurs, it falls earlier in the measure. It also gets
progressively longer at each recurrence, in order that
"know" will fall on the downbeat. Later we shall consider a
consequence of increasingly emphasizing the pronoun "I."

In the tune as written (see Example 3), each occurrence of
the words "time it was," at m. 2 and at m. 6, receives a
similar treatment rhythmically. In Holiday's reading, however, each new context produces a different rhythmic

Example 4

treatment and a shift in emphasis. Hear how in m. 2 she delays these words slightly, partly in order to enunciate the repeated consonant between "what" and "time." (In the later A statements at m. 10 and m. 26 the substitution of "day" and "year" respectively after the word "what" eliminates the repeated consonant, and hence the delay.) Further back in m. 2 we discover that the delay begins even earlier, when Holiday expands the word "know" beyond the second beat, deferring what follows. That "know" occurs with a relatively long rhythmic value on the downbeat intensifies its metric accent, and shorter values on the preceding upbeat further strengthen this accent by leading "didn't" agogically to "know." Thus in the opening statement of the tune, Holiday has shifted the focus of the phrase from the word "I" to the word "know," accomplishing this mainly via rhythmic means.

With regard to pitch, Holiday waits until the words "time it was" to depart from Rogers's version, and the resulting changes in the melody, while subtle, nonetheless affect the words' accentuation. Despite a change in pitch at the word "it," Rodgers's original melody deemphasizes this word, by giving it a short rhythmic value, and the resulting "escape-tone" places emphasis on the word "was" by leaping down to it. In contrast, Holiday's melodic changes use the ascending move to create emphasis; she anticipates the ascent by one note, which shifts it to the word "time," and she gives it a longer note value. The rhythmic break after the word "what" further draws our attention to this ascent. As in Rodgers's melody, "it" receives a short rhythmic value, but because it now falls on a passing tone between "time" and "was," it receives even less emphasis than in the original, in spite of its falling *on* the beat, rather than after it.

Significantly, Holiday retains Rodgers's pitch on the downbeat of m. 2. By obscuring the harmonic motion to the relative minor with the uneasy arrival on a dissonant eleventh, Rodgers's melody literally undermines the verb "know." This musical gesture is so integral to the sound and emotion of the song that most performers retain it, even when dramatically reshaping many other elements.[9]

Contrast the above description with the recurrence of the words "time it was" in m. 6 (see Example 5). We immediately notice that Holiday does not delay it (see arrows); in fact, she anticipates it. The long vowel /iy/ of the preceding word, "lovely," allows her to move the rhythm forward to the word "time" by affording a smooth transition to the /t/ sound; and Holiday exploits the phonetic environment here by giving the word "lovely" shorter note values than in the original tune. Increased rhythmic activity on the downbeat weakens metric stress on the adjective "lovely," and sets it in motion to its goal—the noun "time." In addition to placing an agogic accent on "time," Holiday's rhythm speeds its arrival.

Example 5

Keeping Rodgers's melodic shape here, which does not change pitch on "time," further smooths the transition through the word "lovely." Notice in m. 6 that the word "it" falls on the beat, rather than between beats. Recall that in m. 2 "it" likewise falls on the beat, in this case the fourth beat of the measure. On paper both instances seem to accent an unaccented word; to the ear, however, Holiday's syncopations, as well as her dynamic inflections, conform to the prosody. A later examination of these syncopations will reveal how they help to produce Holiday's swing.

In response both to the meaning and the sound of the word "lovely," and to a lesser degree the melodic (but not harmonic) arrival on the tonic, Holiday anticipates and then stretches out the words "time it was." In so doing she evokes the sensation of rushing to a lover and then lingering there, a gesture which echoes warmly against the hesitations of the opening line. Although her changes of Rodgers's melody undermine the musical parallelism between these two passages, Holiday deepens their connection by allowing the speech rhythms and the emotional development of the words to reshape the music; by making musical choices which differentiate the sense units and the meaning of each passage, she helps us to understand their meaning. To see how truly effective and expressive are Holiday's subtle digressions from the original, we need only reverse the two settings (see Example 6). Phonetic similarity between two passages does not necessarily generate a new rhythmic

treatment, despite a change in meaning. For example, m. 2
("know what") and m. 5 ("Oh, what") both share the sounds
/owhwət/ (see Example 5). Yet in spite of a difference in
meaning the durations are comparable. The recurrences of
these sounds, at m. 10 and again at m. 26 (see Example 4),
with their corresponding rhythmic parallels suggest that the
long-short vowel sequence usually generates long-short
rhythmic values accordingly, unless overriding factors pre-
vail (when a short vowel occurs on the final syllable of a
phrase, for example). Listening to similar sequences in
Holiday's performance reveals a general consistency, regardless of whether the short vowel falls on or off the beat. Her
respect for this aspect of prosody contributes to the intelligibility of her performance.

Holiday modifies Rodgers's motivic parallelism between
mm. 9–10 and mm. 13–14, in order to accommodate
important linguistic differences at these places in the lyrics
(see Example 7). Consider the several factors which distinguish these two passages. In m. 9 the word "I" receives a
single, sustained pitch, as it did previously; but in m. 13
Holiday capitalizes on the voiced /r/ of the word "warm," by
giving it a descending slide.[10] Holiday lingers on this word,
too; so much, in fact, that she rhythmically displaces what
immediately follows. Compared to m. 9, where Holiday
retained the anacrucic quality of the word "didn't," in m. 13
she delays the word "like," which in turn makes "the" fall on
the downbeat and form a dissonant ninth with the harmony.
In addition, although the words "like the" and the word

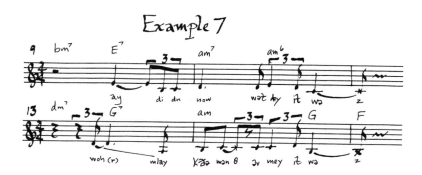

Example 7

"didn't" both consist of two syllables, the sounds /laykɜə/ are more complex phonetically than the sounds /didn/, and therefore require more time to sing. Note that, as in m. 1 and later in m. 25 (see Example 4), Holiday simplifies "didn't," clipping off the final /t/ so it elides with the /n/ of "know," thereby allowing even greater flow through this word.

At first glance Holiday's rhythm in mm. 13–14 seems to damage the prosody by giving "the" a metric accent. The metric accent is weakened, however, by the melodic shape, in which "the" functions as a passing tone; by the rhythm, in which "like the" leads agogically to "month"; and by the dynamic nuancing, with which "the" is uninflected. One important result of this approach is to bring her barline (on the word "month") into direct conflict with the band's. We will come back to this. Notice, finally, that the sliding and lingering on the word "warm" produce a highly expressive touch of word-coloring, which increases her identification with the song's narrator.

Other rhythmic accommodations to phonetic content may be found in Example 7, by comparing m. 10 to m. 14. Whereas the long /ow/ sound of "know" dictates the word's rhythmic elongation m. 10, at the corresponding moment in m. 14, the short /ə/ vowel of "month" shortens its rhythmic value. As in m. 2, the word "know" flows smoothly into "what," because of the shared /w/ (/nowwət/), which provides a transitional rounding between the two words. In contrast, the caesura after "month" groups the fricative ending, /Ө/, with what precedes it (/mən/) and articulates it from what follows (/əv/), thus averting the possibility of hearing the non-sensical /mən/ - /Өəv/. As one might expect, the internal rhymes "day it was" and "May it was" receive nearly identical treatment. Nevertheless, "what" is slightly longer than "of." Holiday does this in order to accommodate the unvoiced alveolar cluster between "what" and "day" (/td/) in m. 10; the /vm/ between "of" and "may" requires less time to enunciate, because both of the voiced elements, /v/ and /m/, are produced at the lips.

The two analogous passages at mm. 25–26 and mm. 29–30 resemble each other more than other passages we have heard (see Example 8). Holiday's virtually identical rhythmic,

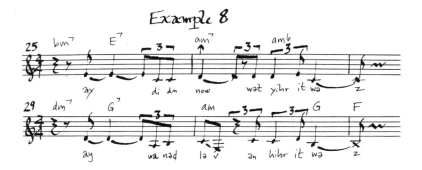

Example 8

metric, and motivic treatment of these two passages combines with the rhyme scheme to create the strongest moment
of musical parallelism in her performance, yet even here
there are subtle differences which underline her interpretation. A slight upward bending of pitch on the word "know"
in m. 26 intensifies the third statement of the lyric's "hook"
by lending this word a yearning quality. What a different
effect the sudden, almost disdainful falling-off of pitch on the
word "love" creates in m. 30, an effect we will consider
again. If we recall how the sound /ə/ in the syllable /lʌv/ at m.
6 (see the word "lovely" in Example 5) helped to quicken the
rhythmic activity on the downbeat of that measure, then the
way this same sound in m. 30 (see Example 8) acts to truncate
the syllable will come as no surprise. The way Holiday treats
the same sound in the syllable /wəz/ throughout the song,
however, lengthening the vowel at phrase endings, and
quickening it within phrases, suggests that her main purpose
in abandoning the word "love" almost as soon as it begins in
m. 30 is to color it with irony.

    After members of the band solo on the tune, Holiday sings
the song a second time. Her second "chorus" reveals that she
improvises only in a narrow sense, for the two choruses differ
only in the subtlest ways (see Example 1). Nevertheless,
certain details in the second chorus suggest that she intends
for it to build upon the emotion of her first chorus. In
Example 9, we hear one such detail, with which Holiday sets
the final statement of the A material apart from all previous
A sections. At m. 26[II] (a roman numeral "II" after the

measure number indicates that the measure is located in the second chorus), she uses the words "know," "what," "year," and "was" to stress each beat of the measure, contrasting significantly with the way Holiday has woven her rhythms around the beat earlier in the song; the word "didn't" stands out because of its fresh pitch shape; the word "year" rises yearnfully to an f-natural, creating a cross relation with the f-sharp in the am6 chord. Holiday keeps the falling major-third that extends from "I" to "was," but because she replaces the intervening d-natural that occurred previously on "know" in all of the preceding A sections, with an insistent e-natural, the fall to c-natural happens suddenly, at the final two words. All of these features conspire to make this last statement of the A material the most expressive.

The general trend of increasing variation and intensity with each statement of A over the period of two choruses suggests that Holiday sought to extend the formal shape of her performance beyond the confines of a single chorus. Her use of the song's verse as an introduction (excluded in Example 1 and Example 3) contributes to this effect, and two other factors add to this impression.

First, unlike the sheet music, which closes all but the first A section with the fifth scale degree, Holiday closes only the very last A section in the second chorus with the fifth scale degree (see Example 1). In doing so, she delays the effect of a rising line, e-f-g-a, that Rodgers concealed in the song, starting at the first note of the song and proceeding through the endings of the first two A sections, to the beginning of the bridge (see Example 3).[11] Holiday's change sacrifices the

formal integrity and melodic development of the song, as
Rodgers intended it. Instead she saves the g-natural for the
crucial moments in the song's form at the end of the bridge
and at the close of the final statement of A. In the former
case, which occurs in both choruses, she immediately slides
down from it, which weakens its impact. It figures more
prominently at the end of the second chorus, when she
compresses the ascent e-(f-)g into the last A section. The
pitch variations at the beginning of the final A section (see
Example 9) may now be heard as preparatory to this
sustained g-natural, lending a climactic quality to the entire
eight-measure section from m. 25[II] to m. 32[II], and giving
a destination to the entire performance. By touching upon
this important pitch in the second coda, Holiday effects a
summary of the performance's defining vocal compass (see
Example 10).

Second, the coda of the second chorus creates a greater
feeling of closure than does the coda of the first chorus.
Holiday creates partial closure in the first coda by singing the
tonic on the downbeat of the third measure of the phrase, a
rhythmic location that his hitherto received no emphasis. In
effect this phrase closes two measures too soon, leaving
vacant a full measure and a half of established phrase time in
the vocal line. The vocal line's disappearance here acts as the
traditional "break" before the next chorus, which makes way
for the coming horn solos. By disrupting the established
phrasing and by dropping out early in the four-bar time span

Example 10

Holiday signals that more will follow. Thus Holiday's phrasing prepares the listener for the instrumental chorus to come, and contributes to the coda's incomplete quality.

Contrast the above with the second coda. A different chord progression, an increased vocal range, and a new rhythmic placement for the melodic line within the four-bar time span, which emphasizes the last measure of the phrase (m. 36[II]), all create a stronger feeling of closure this time, and precipitate the arrangement's codetta (not included in the example). Listeners who know Holiday's other performances will recognize the final two notes of the second chorus (a 2-1 appoggiatura) as her signature ending. Thus, through her approach to the successive A sections and to the two codas, Holiday achieves a compelling design to her entire performance. Despite intervening solos, her subtle variations act to increase consistently the emotional intensity throughout both choruses and to keep the listener attuned to her every nuance of expression.

The musical gesture Holiday employs to color the word "love" in the last A section of both choruses, discussed above (see Example 8, m.30) reflects the general character of this rendition. Holiday's overall air of detachment lends the performance an almost cynical tinge. In *The Swing Era,*[12] Gunther Schuller mentions Holiday's unsentimental delivery, and here it conditions our perception of the narrator's persona, by enabling her to amplify the nostalgic quality of the song without inviting pity. The casually withdrawn mood, due partly to the choice of tempo, is broken only occasionally by flashes of expression which stand in direct relief against the hard-edged backdrop. These nuances betray an emotional undercurrent which is all the more intense because it lies scarcely beneath the surface.

As mentioned before, Holiday's treatment of the word "I" takes on added significance as her performance unfolds; because this word is embedded in the textual formula discussed earlier, it occurs frequently in the lyrics. Holiday emphasizes it and keeps it fresh each time it occurs by increasing its duration and by changing its placement within the measure. She further stresses the word by syncopating many of its entrances, thereby setting them against the

metric backdrop of the supporting ensemble. The synco-
pated entrances stand out all the more because the song and
each successive A section begin with it.

Example 11 presents another instance of the word "I," and
we notice that Holiday inverts the original rhythmic relationship between the words "then" and "I" in m. 3. Little
surprise that the short-long rhythmic design here conforms to
the vowel length. Contrasting this passage to the same
passage in the sheet music further demonstrates Holiday's
focus on the "I" word.[13]

Holiday's tendency to emphasize the word "I" over the
course of the song has a two-fold effect: it lends a self-
absorbed persona to the song's narrator, and it heightens
Holiday's identification with her material, making the song
seem autobiographical. Lorenz Hart built the narrator's
persona into the song by his choice of words and by their
placement in the melody, but Rodgers's tune does not allow
for many nuances in the dramatic development of this
feature, because of the strict formal demands of the AABA
song-form; the persona therefore remains somewhat static
throughout the song. Here Holiday's unique musical contribution steps in to create the singer's personal identification
with the song's narrator, lending the song a confessional
quality that several of her performances share. The impression that "Holiday doesn't sing a song; she lives it," which
echoes throughout the writings about Holiday, grows from
just such musical choices, which act to turn a song into a
personal testimony. Her choice of this particular song may

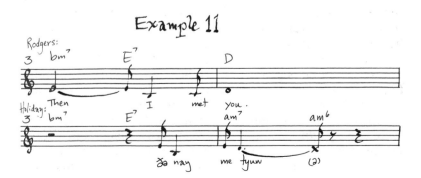

Example 11

not have grown directly from the song's existentialist narrative, but she exploits its intimate revelations to maximum dramatic effect.

A performer's stylization of a song derives as much from her limitations as her assets, but the best performers use even their weaknesses to good effect. While Holiday's choice of key, for example, puts the song comfortably within her low range, transposing the song thus also darkens the general timbre of the song and lends the lowest pitches a "growly" quality. Her choice of material and key suits her dark tone color well, and although "I Didn't Know What Time It Was" (insert, Example 1) ends on an affirmative note, Holiday's vocal timbre gently shades the song with sadness throughout.

Lack of adequate breath support also poses a problem for Holiday; yet instead of spoiling her phrasing in this song, her shortness of breath somehow enhances it, creating gaps in the line which set each thought in relief against the steady pulse and harmonic support of the band. By "airing" out the phrases in this way she also allows the obbligato lines of the horn players to be heard. Her complex approach to beat and meter is the source of her swing, and it requires that the clear rhythmic foundation provided by the supporting ensemble emerge distinctly. This is accomplished superbly by her approach to phrasing, which also is the key to her dramatic timing.

The coda (see Example 10) provides a wonderful moment when phrasing and dramatic timing coalesce. Earlier we noted the striking absence of harmonic and melodic closure in the final measure of the last A section (just before the coda), a moment which typically serves to close an AABA song form. This moment underscores the narrator's indecisiveness and precipitates the coda musically. In addition, unlike any other phrase in the song, Rodgers's coda begins with an upbeat, and, as though provoked by the new rhythmic impulse, the narrator changes from past to present tense. The mood also switches from one of recollection to one of action. The change in grammatical tense points to the transformation in the narrator's outlook and serves as the turning point of the text. The fact that Rodgers reharmonizes the coda's melodic reference to the beginning of the song (see mm. 33–4 in Example 1) now takes on extramusical significance.

Like Rodgers, Holiday waits until the coda to change to an anacrucic rhythmic impulse, but the change impresses us all the more now, because we have heard each A section begin with a delayed entrance. Her approach to the phrase structure also spares us the tedium of hearing e-natural persistently fall on the downbeat beginning all three A sections, and keeps it fresh for the downbeat beginning the coda.

Compare the rhythm of the words "(I) know what time it (is now)" as they appear in the coda with the broken rhythm of their earlier appearance, "(I didn't) know what time it (was)" (see Example 4). The change in feeling at the coda motivates a smoother delivery, which sacrifices the enunciation of the repeated /t/. This suggests that while Holiday may capitalize upon specific phonetic elements in order to amplify the word's expression, she is willing to dispense with them when rhythmic factors accomplish this expression better.

Holiday's swing, while less overtly dramatic than her phrasing, fills no less essential a place in her style. Her willingness to use speech accents to contradict the song's regular meter produces a delightful interplay between the rhythms of the vocal line and the meter as stated by the band. Example 12 shows the beginning of Holiday's vocal line, rebarred so the barlines fall on textual downbeats (i.e. before "I," "know," "then," and "you"). In the original line the textual downbeats correspond to the metric downbeats, yet in her performance they often contradict them, creating wonderfully complex polymeters. The resulting measures in the vocal line consist of a variable number of beats, expanding and contracting according to where the singer wishes to place emphasis. Holiday's swing results from superimposing these unequal measures over the regular metric template generated by the supporting ensemble. Hear in m. 4 how the agogic stress of the word "you" sets up a downbeat in the vocal line which conflicts with the metric downbeat, while the shorter value of "met" weakens the metric downbeat by leading agogically to "you." We noted other instances of this phenomenon back in m. 2 and m. 6 (see Example 5) and in mm. 13–14 (see Example 7). To

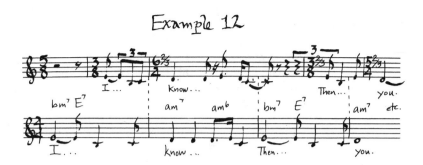

Example 12

listeners who know the song in its original form, as Holiday's audience members undoubtedly did, and who focus their attention almost exclusively on the melody and the words, the effect of these variable measures is to accelerate and retard the song, creating fulfillment and suspense.

Hear in Example 12 how freely the additive measures[14] of irregular length in the vocal line float above the regular metric foundation of the accompaniment, unhindered by the accompaniment's vertical regularity of downbeats. While Holiday relates her rhythmic designs to the accompaniment by referring to the band's tempo, beat, and subdivisions, only one of her four downbeats shown in Example 12 corresponds to the band's downbeats. In the vocal line's relationship to and independence from the meter we may hear the meeting of two rhythmic worlds.

Holiday's swing arises from the linguistic impulse of the lyrics, which acts in turn to stall or propel the melodic line in order to suspend or fulfill the meaning of each sense unit in the text. The additive meter of the vocal line amplifies the effect of agogic accents, which work in conjunction with speech accent to produce syncopations (see note 4). Holiday's swing liberates the rhythms of her vocal line from reinforcing the vertical template of the meter. The resulting horizontal flow makes her vocal line a remarkably effective vehicle for the setting of English prosody.[15]

Holiday's swing, phrasing, vocal compass and tone color, formal and melodic judgment, and diction all contribute to project her characteristic reading of the text, and brand the performance as hers. To be sure, the stylization of a single Holiday performance cannot be fully understood without reference to her other performances, which would indicate her musical style in a larger sense, and to the performances of other jazz singers, which would establish those traits shared by the community within which she creates. Questions remain as to whether she made certain musical decisions for reasons specific to that performance or on larger stylistic grounds. Nevertheless, while patterns that emerge from a single performance can only hint at some of her distinguishing habits, we may begin to approach a sense of how distinctively Billie Holiday communicates her image of a song by hearing how differently Better Carter handles the same material.[16]

III

Betty Carter's version of "I Didn't Know What Time it Was" (insert, Example 2) bears little resemblance to Billie Holiday's. We know that each singer's performance takes the same song by Rodgers and Hart as its point of departure, mainly due to the obvious similarities both in text and chord changes that each has to the original; yet the two performances differ from each other in so many other respects, in tempo and rhythmic feel,[17] in supporting ensemble, in melodic design, and in overall form, that only by some considerable stretch of the imagination can we hear them in relation to one another.[18] Carter's bold departure from the original standard assumes that at least a few members of the audience already know the tune in some form, and, judging from their grateful response to the first measures of her singing, she assumes correctly. As we consider how Carter's response to the lyrics influenced her musical choices, and how these choices in turn effect the text's delivery, we will begin to hear important relationships between the two performances.

On first hearing, each appearance of the song's hook reveals striking rhythmic departures from the original (see Example 13). Perhaps more striking still, Carter departs from Rodgers's tune nearly as much melodically as she does rhythmically. Instead of approaching the word "know" from

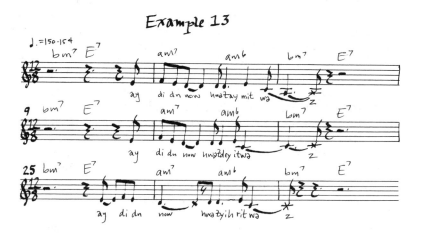

below, as the original tune does (see Example 3), Carter inverts the melodic direction of the first four pitches. Studying the example carefully reveals that she retains the pitch motion from e-natural, through d-natural to c-natural, around which the original hook is built; however, her elaborations disrupt our immediate sense of the connection between the original tune and her performance, especially when we rely solely upon our ears.

The low a-natural she sings at the end of the hook's first occurrence, in m. 4, further undermines the connection between the two versions, partly because we now hear the preceding c-natural as an elaboration of this new note, rather than as the structural ending of the phrase. By singing the word "was" on the root of a tonicized a-minor chord, Carter strengthens the word's tonal stability, and gives the song's opening statement greater definition. We immediately identify Carter's narrator as an altogether different character from Holiday's: one who projects a sense of assurance in her convictions.

As in Holiday's version, subtle rhythmic alterations distinguish each A section from the one that preceded it. The words "know" and "was," both verbs, receive agogic accents that get amplified in different ways with each recurrence.

Carter syncopates "know" against the beat the first two times we hear it, and lengthens it the third time; she always syncopates "was" across the barline, whether she begins it on the fourth beat, as in m. 10, or after it, as in m. 2 and m. 26; and her slurring of the word "was" going into m. 3 further accents it. The noun substitutions "time," "day," and "year" also get agogic stresses, but to a lesser degree; and despite surrounding rhythmic displacements she consistently sings these nouns on the third beat of the measure, as if to anchor each phrase to them.

Coming off the bridge (at m. 25) Carter sings the word "I" a beat earlier in the measure. She also lengthens this word slightly, but not enough to keep the word "didn't" from advancing into this measure now, and enhancing the anacrucis to the downbeat of m. 26. In so doing she keeps the word "I" rhythmically connected to "didn't know." Shortly we will hear how this connection contrasts with the effect Rodgers's melody has on Hart's lyrics.

Almost as a response to the subtle emphasis Carter gives to the word "I" this last time, she lengthens the word "know" too. These metric displacements cause the word "know" to fall on the ensemble's downbeat, and its greater length strengthens the metric accent in this measure. If we recall that the rhythmic activity on the downbeats of m. 2 and m. 10 tended to weaken the metric stress in those measures, then we become aware that the ways in which the last A section of the first chorus differs from its earlier counterparts amplify the urgency in the narrator's reminiscence, especially in light of what she has revealed in the bridge.

Notwithstanding the effect of the rhythm on the word "didn't," the slight rise in pitch and volume on each occurrence of this word does produce a gentle stress. In Rodgers's melody this word also receives an accent (see Example 3), but Carter's accentuation differs significantly, both in method and effect. Instead of assertively leaping down a fourth to a syncopation, which, in conjunction with the long note that preceded it, acts to disconnect "didn't" from "I," Carter gently leans on the word "didn't" by an expressive half-step, linking it to the word "I" with shorter rhythmic values. The fast tempo enhances the linking effect of these short values. Thus, by altering the original tune, both through changes in pitch and in rhythm, Carter regroups Hart's words, now binding them more closely together with quicker rhythmic values and stepwise melodic movement, at other times separating them with durations, silences and leaps; new relationships unfold among the words with each alteration.

Carter's driving tempo invests the song's phonetics with even greater effect on the rhythmic propulsion and articulation than they had in Holiday's performance. Compare the noun substitutions in Example 13. In m. 2 the rhythmic value of the words "time it" exceeds the rhythmic value of their counterparts in m. 10 and m. 26 (at the words "day it" and "year it"). In the first instance longer rhythmic values allow time for the voiced consonant /m/ to resonate. In each of the latter two cases, however, the semi-vowel glides (/y/ and /r/, respectively) generate a smoother rhythmic flow and hence require shorter rhythmic values. Because of the faster tempo, Carter also has less time to enunciate as carefully, or in as mannered a fashion, as Holiday. Thus, moments in the song that Holiday articulates, such as between the words "what" and "time," in m. 2, Carter tends to connect.

Each A section's second half offers more striking examples of Carter's melodic freedom (see Example 14). While we

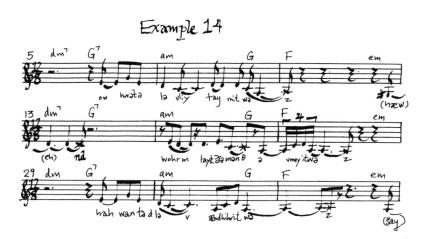

Example 14

could still faintly discern elements of Rodgers' melody in the first two measures of each A section (see Example 13), albeit with the mnemonic aid of the transcription, we can barely hear the passages represented by Example 14 in relation to the same passages in the original tune, even when looking closely at the notes. In the fifth and sixth measures of each A section, Carter completely recomposes Rodgers's tune. In so doing, she not only weakens her version's association with the original but also weakens the parallel function these measures once had in relation to one another and to other passages in the song. Nevertheless, Carter's motivation for such freedom is not arbitrary, nor is it strictly musical.

Recall that Rodgers repeats the opening motive a step lower in each of these passages. While this descending sequence creates a melodic parallelism with the beginning of each A section, it also produces a subtle drop in energy. As we noticed earlier regarding Holiday's rendition (see Example 5 and Example 6), however, the lyrics continue a dramatic development that goes against this musical effect. Not content to adapt the lyrics to Rodgers's melody via rhythmic adjustments (as Holiday does in her performance), Carter allows the lyrics' development to distort Rodgers's line, even at the expense of his melodic parallelism. As a result, she not only redirects the emphasis of the song but also entirely transforms its emotional thrust.

By rising a third on the second word of the phrase beginning in m. 5, for example, she places a tonic accent on the word "what," thus echoing and exceeding the stress placed on the corresponding word, "didn't," at m. 1 (see Example 15). Also, the appoggiatura on "lovely" and the drawing out of its second syllable (/liy/) combine to add weight and expressiveness to this adjective. Significantly, despite the similarities between Carter's singing of the words "time it was" in both phrases, the second phrase has a feeling of growth, due largely to the different way Carter approaches these words.

The way Carter obliterates the parallel relationship mm. 14–15 had to mm. 5–6 (see Example 14), by almost completely inverting the earlier phrase's melodic shape and by delaying the whole passage nearly half a measure,

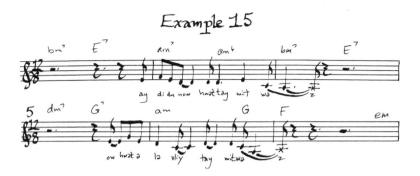

damages the original song's formal design even more overtly.
Carter makes the former change in order to shift the word
accents from the second word of the phrase, "like," to the
first word of the phrase, "warm." With this shift she again
emphasizes the adjective, despite its new location in the line.

In order to understand the deeper motivation for such
extreme changes, however, we need to contrast the duration
of each syllable in m. 14 with each corresponding syllable in
the parallel measure from the preceding phrase, at m. 10 (see
Example 16). By listening closely to how Carter sings each
syllable, we can hear now that she draws out the rhythm at
the words "warm like the month" to make room for the
many and complex phonetic sounds they contain. The words
"I didn't know" in m. 10 required less time to sing, so for
them Carter used quick rhythmic values. In addition,
separating the words "like the month of May it was" slightly
from the word "warm" clarifies their grammatical function.
In the original tune (see Example 3) the leap down and the
rhythmic delay made an even greater separation here, and
this may explain why, despite strong rhythmic and melodic
disparities between them, Carter's pitch shape in m. 14
approaches the original tune's more closely (at m. 13) than
other analogous passages in the song. We will hear Carter
amplify this separation considerably in the second chorus.
Like Holiday, Carter wishes to expressively color the word
"warm," and she too allows the word's expressiveness to
influence what follows, but to a far greater degree.

Example 16

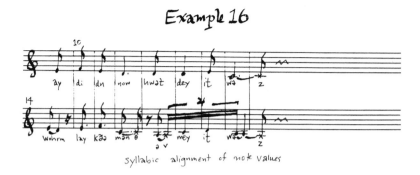

Syllabic alignment of note values

Combined with the delay mentioned above, for example, the longer rhythmic values at the beginning of the phrase in m. 14 force her to squeeze the words "of May it was" into rhythmic values that are significantly shorter than their rhyming counterpart in m. 10. Comparing m. 14 to m. 6 and m. 30 (see Example 14) we learn that the phonetic structure of the words "May it was," which hinges on the semi-vowel glide /y/ makes this transformation possible, and thus allows for the effect of an accelerando.[19] The phonetics in the parallel passages before and after are not conducive to the rapid delivery of text demanded by such an acceleration. Here in m. 14 the lyrics' sound and meaning conspire to provoke Carter's extreme musical changes.

While Carter's rhythmic nuances may stem from a sense of dramatic timing that prompts her to savor certain words and animate others, they have a significant impact on the song's musical development as well. Her delaying of the phrase beginning in m. 14, for example, causes the phrase that follows, "and I'll swear it was grand," to extend into the beginning of the bridge at m. 17 (see Example 17). A unique formal tension gets generated by the overlapping here, owing to the clash between two different kinds of phrases: vocal phrases that result from the rhythmic cohesion Carter gives the lyrics' sense units, and formal divisions such as the one that marks the bridge's beginning, which result from the song's chord changes. This formal tension reveals how much Carter understands Holiday's swing and how far she has gone

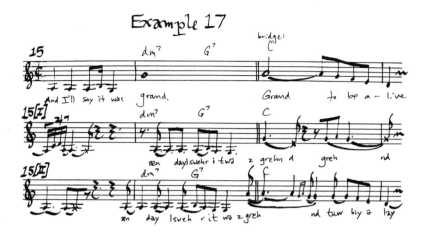

Example 17

beyond it—far past the rhythmic level of beat and measure, to the level of phrase itself. Carter's swing allows whole vocal phrases to come into direct conflict with the song's formal divisions, thereby exploiting the song's stable phrase structure in order to create a volatile rhythmic dynamic that is nonetheless formally coherent.

Due to the phrase overlap here at mm. 16–17, the time between the last word of the phrase and its echo at the beginning of the next phrase gets concentrated, with both now happening in the course of a single measure. On a grander scale, this concentration prepares the listener for the fuller expression that the word will receive in the second chorus (see Example 17), where its echo collapses into a single climactic statement and where two vocal phrases dramatically merge into one. The performance's climax in the second chorus most vividly demonstrates how Carter uses her swing as a powerful expressive tool, a tool with which she often propels her material well beyond the limits of recognizability. Ironically, her second-chorus bridge quotes Rodgers's melody more closely than any other moment in the song; yet because of the way she disrupts rhythm, phrase, and section, and their interrelation, we no longer hear these pitches in relation to the original tune.

Going back to the first chorus, notice how Carter gives the

adjective, "grand," a prominent position in the measure and in the phrase, by singing it on the first downbeat of the bridge (see m. 17 in Example 2). She further draws our attention to this moment by singing the words that come before, "and I'll swear it was," as an extended anacrucis to "grand." Furthermore, for the very first time in the song, a downbeat in the vocal line marks the beginning of a formal division. Carter will use the same approach to phrasing in both codas as well. Recall that Holiday reserved this phrasing technique solely for each of her codas, where it highlighted the song's turning point. Future investigations of jazz vocalism might consider whether either of the singers in question, or other singers as well, use the technique of singing "behind the beat," and indeed behind the phrase, as a means of establishing a rhythmic foil, against which the singing of a song's climax, or crucial moments in the text, may stand out. Jazz writers generally assume that this technique of "airing out" phrases serves a strictly musical/stylistic function, but some jazz singers may also be using it to rhythmically punctuate certain passages, by establishing a backdrop of silences against which they set these moments in relief.

Carter also sets certain pitches in relief, by saving them for crucial moments in the song's overall form. Recall that Rodgers embeds a stepwise melodic line in the first half of the song that travels from the starting note, e-natural, through the final pitch of each A section, f-natural and g-natural, to arrive at the song's highest point, the a-natural that begins the bridge (see Example 3 and note 11). Until the coda, Carter avoided emphasizing a-natural, only using it to coyly elaborate the g-natural that serves as the first-chorus's uppermost limit. She carefully reserves the a-natural for three important moments in her performance, moments in when she gives the pitch special weight: at the first-chorus coda, where it serves to introduce the transition to her upper register (see Example 2); in the second chorus at the end of the first A section (mm. 8–9 [II]), where it elides with the beginning of the second A section, and thus sustains the intensity of the second chorus while preparing us for the disrupted phrasing of the bridge; and at the song's climax in the second-chorus bridge, where the emotion of the entire performance crystallizes.

In terms of short term formal factors, Carter's transition to her upper register in the coda of the first chorus acts to deny the coda its function as the song's ending. Carter's treatment of the coda's lyrics, her shift of register, her phrasing and her dynamics all lend the beginning of second chorus the character of an interruption; and because it has the character of an emotional outburst, Carter's second chorus goes even further to disrupt Rodgers's melodic line (see Example 18). She begins the opening phrase of the second chorus on the highest pitch we've heard so far, and within two measures drops to the lowest, she picks up the tempo and has the bass "walk," she intensifies accents and increases the general dynamic level. She also replaces the subtle tonic accent and slight metric shift we heard earlier on "didn't" (see Example 13), with an agogic accent, upon which she heavily leans. The verb "know" now falls squarely on the downbeat of m. 2 [II], with a longer duration than it had earlier; instead of the eleventh of the chord resolving to the tenth, the ninth now resolves to the root. These factors generate a feeling of urgency and yearning which distinguishes this chorus dramatically from the one before it.

Example 18 reveals some of the ways that Carter steadily increases the energy level of the second chorus up to the bridge and then decreases the energy level after it: she gives the first sections of this chorus greater weight and breadth by drawing each phrase out; on the downbeat of m. 10 [II] she amplifies the metric accent of the word "know" with a tonic accent, lengthening the c-natural here, and slurring it to b-natural to give greater feeling to the word than it received m. 2; she also curtails the lyric here to "I didn't know the day." Only until m. 25 does she begin to draw back from the emotion of this chorus, reversing the process by decreasing the dynamic level, shortening the phrases and putting the word "know" on a lower pitch. Nevertheless, the slightly flattened fifth degree of a-minor on "know" and the curtailed lyric "I didn't know the year" help to accomplish a smooth transition to the ending by preventing the intensity from

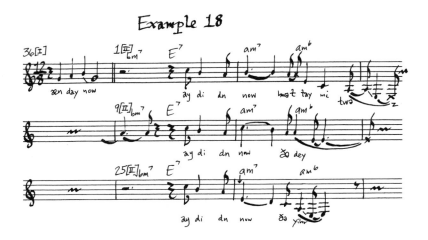

Example 18

dropping too suddenly. The interested reader can find other examples of how Carter shapes the energy of the second chorus in Example 2 (insert).

Carter's shaping of the song's formal development over two choruses owes something to the place these choruses fill in the overall form of the performance, which, as it turns out, includes more than this one standard: the second-chorus coda segues directly into another standard, "All The Things You Are," and the performance ultimately ends with the standard "If They Asked Me, I Could Write A Book," thus rounding out a medley of compositions by Richard Rodgers. The jazz listener generally does not expect a typical performance to exceed the presentation of a single tune. With this medley, Carter challenges that expectation, so that the listener will hear each successive song as a response to the one that preceded it. Medleys such as this one have served throughout her career as one of several ways in which she has sought to exceed the expressive scope of the jazz standard, and deal with questions of long-term form. While such an approach in itself breaks no new ground, Carter goes beyond the typical arbitrary approach to medleys.

Carter has yoked these particular songs together for dramatic reasons. Their juxtaposition, and especially the relationship between the first two, amplifies the shift in the narrator's perspective that occurred in the coda(s) of the first song, from the negative to the positive, and from the past to the present. The second song continues the dramatic trajectory begun in the first by maintaining the present tense and positive tone that the coda initiated, while shifting from first to second person (from "I Didn't Know" to "You Are"). Thus, although the climax of her performance of the song "I Didn't Know What Time It Was" occurred at the second-chorus bridge, the dramatic turning point for the entire medley occurs at the second-chorus coda.

The way that the second-chorus coda resonates against our memory of the first-chorus coda reveals that Carter intended the first coda to do more than avoid short-term closure. In addition to the function it served in relation to what immediately followed it, we can now hear that she also meant for the first-chorus coda to prepare us for the role the coda has in effecting the song's nonclosure at the end of the second chorus. By having the first-chorus coda refer rhythmically to the way she began the bridge, Carter had already hinted at the role this first coda will play in the song's larger form.

Recall how the silence after the words "I'm wise" in mm. 34–5 (see Example 2) hung uncertainly when the clarifying rejoinder "and I know (what time it is now)" did not immediately follow. At the end of the second chorus, the words "I'm wise" are now put in closer relation to the words "and I know," suggesting that we may yet hear the full realization of the title's transformation "I know what time it is now," which was denied us the first time around; but after singing this phrase (twice this time) Carter again interrupts the line, not with another chorus now, but with another standard. As in the first chorus, the second-chorus coda accomplishes nonclosure textually, by deleting the words "what time it is now" from the final line of lyrics. Carter reinforces the coda's lack of closure this time by substituting a dominant pedal for the standard changes. In recalling the tune's brief introduction, this dominant pedal pulls both choruses together, and places them within the medley's larger framework.

Carter also uses her vocal compass to help create the performance's larger form, and, as we discussed earlier, she gives certain pitches a specific role in the development of her melodic ideas. She limits the vocal compass of the first chorus to the major ninth from g-natural to a-natural; but especially in the A sections, most of her singing sits within the fifth between a-natural and e-natural, which acts to reinforce the minor tonality in the song. In Example 19 we may hear the pitches Carter uses to organize her vocal line placed within the vocal compass of each chorus. (The single occurrence in mm. 7–8 of g-sharp does not stand out beyond its ornamental function.) Carter generally sings the pitches above f-natural with either short rhythmic values, or a descending slide, both of which tend to de-emphasize their occurrence. The pitch b' occurs at the very end of the first chorus, exceeding this range, but because Carter delays its occurrence until the last measure of the coda, after a two-measure pause in the vocal line, we tend to hear it more in relation to the second chorus than the first. This seems appropriate, as it helps to accomplish the registral shift into the second chorus.

The range expands dramatically in the second chorus to a minor thirteenth, from e to c", and the pitch collection expands to include f-sharp, g-sharp, b-flat, and a-flat. Although the chromatic pitches receive slightly more prominence than the g-sharp did in the first chorus, they still serve an ornamental function, with none of them receiving substantial duration. (The instability of the pitches in mm. 27–8[II] does lend the words "life was no prize" a touch of irony.) The pitch b' receives special emphasis in the second

Example 19

Betty Carter's Pitch Materials for
"I Didn't Know What Time It Was"

chorus. Where the first-chorus coda led upwards from this pitch, we now hear the second-chorus bridge as a downward resolution of this pitch; and where the first chorus gently elaborated the e'-d'-c' tessitura, the second emphasizes the c"-b'-a' tessitura, each in their own way dramatizing the song's inherent tonal suspense.

Carter's melodic approach over both choruses increases the importance of the a-minor tonality, by giving it more melodic stability. This would lend the coda's resolution of the song's tonal ambiguity even greater surprise value than it had in Rodgers's version if Carter allowed the coda to bring resolution. As we discussed earlier, she does not, and thus she provides a musical equivalent for her truncation of the lyric's closing sentiment. This approach weakens the structural importance of the coda, which allows Carter to shift the formal weight to the second chorus bridge.

The simplified pitch collection of the melodic line begins essentially as a pentatonic one ([g];a;c';d';e';g';[a']), with a minor second, f-natural, above the fifth scale degree of a-minor, and a minor second, b-natural, below the tonic degree of c-major. While the f-natural takes on slightly more melodic importance in the bridge, in general the tones used to elaborate the pentatonic collection help to create the tonal anticipation for a-minor and c-major resolutions. The a-minor/c-major polarity of this song make this malleable pitch collection especially appropriate, since either pitch of the major second pair g-natural/a-natural is available both at the bottom and at the top of the compass, and depending upon the harmonic context may be used as a structural tone (fifth degree of c-major/tonic of a-minor).

Carter makes effective use of this feature in the first bridge, where she ornaments the g-natural as a fifth degree to c-major, first in its upper form at parallel locations, m. 17 and m. 21, and then in its lower form to close the bridge. Unlike the original, which ends the bridge with an ascent to the upper g-natural (see m. 24 in Example 3), Carter keeps this pitch and register fresh by taking this moment down into the bottom of this chorus's compass. Significantly the descent here produces a greater feeling of closure than most of her other phrase endings. The counterpart to this passage in the second chorus elaborates the upper g-natural with pitches borrowed from the parallel minor. In sum, a close examination to Carter's treatment of pitch reveals her extreme sensitivity to the harmonic and expressive possibilities of the tone/semitone distinction.

Given how much Carter digresses from the original tune's pitches, the ones she does choose to retain warrant attention. We have already noted how much the beginning of the second-chorus bridge resembles the bridge in the original. At key moments in the first chorus Carter refers to specific shapes from the original, distilling these shapes into momentary allusions to Rodgers's melody (see Example 3). For example, the beginning of each A section refers to the falling major third (e'-c') with emphasis on the intervening d-natural (see Example 13). Like Holiday she simplifies the third and fourth measures of each of Rodgers's A sections to an e'-d' descent (see Example 2). The fifth and sixth measures of each A section seem the most transformed, but when we approach the end of each A section, Carter reconnects with the original pitches. Similarly, while the first four measures merely hint at the original melody, the bridge's second half bears a stronger resemblance to it. Recall that the rising minor seventh (g-f') at the end of the first A section, which prepared us for the return of the e-natural that begins the next A section, was elevated to motivic importance in Holiday's version. Carter sings it once, in m. 8, and thereafter dispenses with it.

By destroying many of the melodic parallelisms within the original, Carter gives her performance the character of a through-composed line, in the manner of a recitative or chant. Eliminating the "jingle" produced by many of the rhymes contributes to this character. In the absence of the original melody's rather extreme formal logic, we may wonder what holds her performance together.

On one level, Carter's melodic simplifications may be interpreted as a way of allowing the flow of speech rhythms to direct the melodic line. In this respect they shift our attention from the music to the words, and they give the lyrics more importance in shaping the music's development. On another level her melodic approach, which emphasizes the repetition and variation of little pitch shapes, recalls the melodic approach of Sonny Rollins. The accumulation and development of these fragments replace the periodic, and somewhat static, coherence of the original with a less predictable, more flexible organization. Carter's unpredictable melodic approach makes her performance seem spontaneous, which lends greater immediacy to her delivery of the song's lyrics, but comparison with her earlier performance of this song (see discography) reveals that a very detailed plan lies behind the the apparent freedom of her performance.

When we listen closely to Carter's performance, we become aware that its apparent freedom conceals a formal logic that keeps Carter's melodic choices from seeming arbitrary. For example, despite the fact that the pitch choices in m. 14, at the words "warm like the month" contrast strongly with mm. 5–6, as well as with other phrase beginnings in the performance, we may understand them in terms of what we heard earlier, in m. 10 at the words "day it was" (Example 13 and Example 14), and in terms of the general role of the descending second, e′-d′ as a melodic point of reference (see note 13). At mm. 29–30 (see Example 14) Carter combines melodic elements from the beginning of mm. 5–6 and the ending of the mm. 13–14, this time emphasizing the word "love," and to a slightly lesser degree, the word "want."

By comparing the second chorus to the first (see Example 20) we may further understand how Carter's formal logic works. In the bridge the persistent minor third, g′-e′, that Carter sang in mm. 19–20[I] to the adjectives "young" and "mad" becomes in mm. 18–19[II] a descending second that gets increasingly higher, a motivic transformation that contributes powerfully to the climactic character of the bridge. In the first chorus, the word "love" in m. 30[I] echoed the word "lovely" in m. 6[I] (see Example 14). In the second chorus (see Example 2), Carter reiterates the d′-c′ appoggiatura at m. 6[II]; but the echo occurs sooner this time, at m. 13[II] where the word "warm" now gets placed more prominently in the phrase. At m. 28[II] Carter now substitutes lower pitches, in part because the expressive potential of this motive has been exhausted. From these

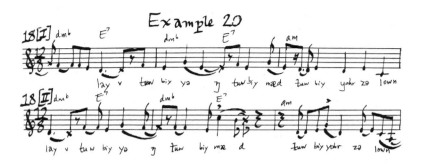

examples and others we can hear how Carter builds her two-chorus solo by taking a melodic fragment, and expanding upon it rhythmically and melodically, in order to transform its expressive function. In fact, Carter embeds enough of the first chorus in the second, that we may hear the second chorus as an intensified paraphrase of the first. In the closing measures of the second chorus (see Example 2), Carter refers to the motive e-g-e-d-c which has provided a point of reference for the entire performance, having occurred in both choruses at mm. 5–6 and mm. 29–30. This choice reveals the consistency of Carter's formal logic; by ending her rendition of this standard with the two passages that most violently distort Rodgers's melody, she makes it truly hers.[20]

Carter's approach to the overall form of the two choruses now emerges more clearly. The reader will recall that back in mm. 25–32 of the first chorus she began an intensification that grew out of the first chorus's bridge. At that point, one felt the music's formal character begin to evolve, changing from an expository to a developmental nature. The intensification, begun so subtly then, continued through the first coda, and into the second chorus to culminate in the bridge of the second chorus. In the course of this progression, the mood grew from an urgency that had its roots in the tempo Carter has chosen to a desperation that gets revealed in the increased dynamic and higher pitch. Before resolving the emotion of this song into the calm determination that characterizes her rendition of "All The Things You Are,"

Carter draws back in the final A section of the second chorus, starting at m. 25 [II]. The way she sings "I wanted love" the second time, in m. 29[II], now eliminating the expressive appoggiatura from before, modulates the energy of the motive from the first chorus to a lower level. Carter does this to prepare us for the second inconclusive coda that now serves as a transition to "All The Things You Are."

If we consider Carter's use of vocal register and dynamics to communicate her emotions as the song's narrator, we may then hear the overall shape of her performance as a direct product of modes of nonverbal expression. Thus, Carter's emotional response to the lyrics generates not only the many nuances of expression that color every word, but the performance's entire formal design as well.

In this light, Carter's interpretation of Rodgers and Hart's song seems unrelated to the meaning intended by its authors. By reducing the song's persistent emphasis on the word "I," for example, she minimizes the narrator's self-absorbed quality, so strongly implied by the lyrics. Carter also replaces the wistful tempo marking in the sheet music with a lively one that lends the narrator's persona a vitality and involvement with the moment that the original narrator lacks. In the process of reinterpreting this tune, she exposes an irony in the authors' original conception: that although the text is about the awakening of a person by the power of love, the emotional state suggested by the original version seems to derive from before the narrator's transformation.

IV

A stylistic gulf separates the two performances of "I Didn't Know What Time It Was" under consideration. Besides the obvious difference in tempo, the two performances generate an entirely different rhythmic feel. While both singers replace the two-step feel of the original version's cut time (see Example 3) with a steady four-to-the-bar, Billie Holiday's line grows out of a predominantly binary subdivision of the beat (or two eighth notes to the beat), whereas in Betty Carter's line a ternary subdivision (or three eighth notes to the beat) prevails (see note 17). Unlike many of their differences, this one does not come from their individual responses to the lyrics, but results mainly from each singer's participation in a different jazz tradition. While Holiday's swing-era roots influence the rhythmic feel of her arrangement, Carter's approach owes its feel to the bebop tradition.

We may also attribute other differences between Holiday's and Carter's arrangements, such as choice of ensemble and the use of chord substitutions and extensions, largely to each singer's allegiance to different jazz styles. The way Holiday uses the horns, for example, and the character of her harmonic support grow directly out of the swing era approach to making a small ensemble vocal arrangement. On the other hand, Carter's trio consists of players schooled in hard bop and bop styles. Significantly, Carter feels no need for horns, as her line has effectively replaced a solo horn line.

We may not conclude from these general stylistic factors that textual considerations do not influence a jazz singer's arrangement. Only upon examining a singer's repeated performances of the same song, accompanied by a new ensemble each time, may we discover the role of a song's text upon a singer's arrangement. As Holiday did not record this song before or after the performance currently under discussion, in her case the question will await further inquiry. Carter did record this tune within a year before the performance discussed here, but the supporting ensemble and the arrangement were identical. The minor differences between these performances reveal a lot about Carter's approach to improvisation, but they do not indicate to what extent the arrangement originates in her reading of the lyrics. The analysis undertaken here has thus been limited to each singer's vocal line and to how the line relates to the accompaniment.

The most revealing dissimilarity between the two different approaches is the way they diverge from one another in their interpretation of the formal and dramatic weight of the coda and the bridge. While Holiday's approach makes her rendition turn upon the song's coda, Carter's transitional coda shifts the emphasis of the lyrics to the bridge of the second chorus, where her performance climaxes. In the bridge, verbs about sensing predominate ("to be," "to see," "to touch" and "to hear"), and by climaxing here Carter reinforces the emotional intensity and vividness of the narrator's character. Another instance of this reinterpretation may be found in the importance Carter gives to adjectives, which gives more weight to the narrator's response to her past than to her description of it.

While the performances display a strong conflict in approaches, both singers nevertheless agree upon some values. If only on this basis alone, these areas of concurrence deserve consideration. The most obvious consensus lies in the way they break the line: both singers agree that musical phrases should generally segment the text into grammatical units. Because of this overall agreement, the few passages in which they break the line differently have relevance to the study of each singer's personal style.

As Hart's lyrics unfold in the second half of the bridge, at mm. 21–24, ambiguity emerges about how the narrator will continue the thought "(it was) Grand to . . . hear your voice" (see Example 3). This ambiguity results in part because of the way the bridge grows out of the lyrics "and I'll say it was grand," and because of the way it refers back to them. In addition, the phrase "hear your voice" parallels the phrases "see your face" and "feel your touch," and the expectation created by this parallelism sets up a sense of completeness. Yet in m. 23 we are also vaguely aware that the thought remains unfinished, if only because the song's rhyme scheme and phrase lengths lead us to expect a rhyme in m. 24 for the word "alone" in m. 20. When the bridge ends, fulfilling this formal expectation, we realize that the thought "(it was) Grand . . . to hear your voice say: I'm all your own," has also emerged. The extended meaning turns on the verb "say," which frames the words that follow, as though they were in quotation marks. Each singer has a distinctive way of handling this complex grammatical structure.

Turning to their performances, we notice that during the first chorus each singer breaks the line differently at the words "hear your voice say I'm all your own," in m. 23 (see Example 21). At this point Holiday breaks the line before the verb "say," while Carter breaks the line after it. As we

Example 21

observed in the original song, Hart used this verb to connect two thoughts by defining the grammatical function of the words that ensue. Holiday's way of breaking the line tends to weaken the relationship between the verb and the words that precede the verb, by grouping the verb with the words that follow it. In the entire passage above, Holiday emphasizes the nouns "face," "touch," and "voice," and deemphasizes the verb, "say." Sung in this fashion, the words "hear your voice" reinforce the parallelism, and the melodic repetition of the preceding phrases "see your face" and "feel your touch," and therefore serve mainly a musical purpose. Her approach is so musical, in fact, that we don't even notice the resulting damage it causes to the sentence's structure and to its logic.

In contrast, Carter accents the verb, and groups it with the words that precede it. The accent stands out all the more precisely because she so eagerly disrupts the parallelism that Holiday strives to reinforce. By doing this she sets apart the words that follow, thereby clarifying their grammatical function. In her second chorus, the significance of Carter's approach takes on greater proportions. By singing this same passage in even note values, thus eliminating the line break altogether, and to the tune of an ascending scale, Carter further communicates the words' complex inter-connections and the sense of excitement the narrator feels.

In each of the singer's first chorus A sections, the procedure for articulating the grammatical units is to delay the beginning of each two-measure phrase, producing gaps between phrases of roughly two beats in length. Carter lays back more than Holiday to provide a foil for her second chorus, where the gaps are shortened. She also relates the bridge to the coda by beginning both on the downbeat of the four-bar section and by accenting both downbeats with a descending slide. As mentioned earlier, Holiday reserves this phrasing solely for the coda.

In the second chorus, Carter alters line breaks from before, in order to increase the emotional intensity to the climax. She makes a rhythmic and registral break after the phrase "how sublime it was," at the word "too" (meaning "also") in m. 8[II], making it almost sound as if she means "too" (meaning "excessively"). The separation here, and the word's rhythmic placement, cause it to sound like an anticipated downbeat at the beginning of the next phrase. These factors combine with the word's pitch to cause this passage to anticipate the performance's climax. In m. 13[II] the word "warm" now occurs much earlier in the phrase and gets connected to what preceded it, "you held my hand," so that we now associate the warmth more directly with the lover's hand. The phrase structure of Carter's first chorus weakened this association, and perpetuated a vagueness inherent in the original song's break in the line (between "hand" and "warm"). Despite Carter's greater freedom with phrase articulations, varying them substantially in her second chorus to express the development in the narrator's emotional state, she never damages the sentence structure.

Both singers share certain phonetic habits. They generally respect the prosody, by assigning short-long rhythmic values to short-long vowel lengths. More specifically, a comparison of the way each singer differentiates m. 10 from m. 14 (see Example 7 and Example 16) reveals that they both allow the consonant's placement in the front or back of the mouth to affect the rhythmic articulation and flow. The tiny break after the word "month" in m. 14, provides another example of this phenomenon. Compare the way Holiday and Carter both give the fricative, /Ө/, a moment to resonate (see Example 7 and Example 14). A corresponding moment in m. 2 (see Example 7 and Example 13) required no such articulation, owing to the semi-vowel glide /w/ which connected "know" and "what." The moments that both singers vary in the second chorus display the same responsiveness to the phonetic demands of the text, regardless of the degree of variation. In addition, both singers use final consonants to articulate the beat (as indicated by the x that appears at the end of many words and all phrases notated in the transcriptions).

Both singers agree upon the importance of giving the performance an overall shape, and both agree that the second chorus provides an opportunity for growth. Holiday makes fewer overt changes in her second chorus, partly because she must work within the limitations of the swing-era style. Nevertheless, her more static conception of the narrator's persona requires less development during the course of her two choruses. For Carter, the first chorus lays the foundation for the second, providing the basis upon which she will expand upon the first motivically, registrally, dynamically, rhythmically, and emotionally. Neither chorus would make sense without the other. In addition, both singers transpose the tune down a fifth. Among other effects, this change places the song in each singer's chest voice, which gives the song a mature, voice-of-experience quality.

Finally, within a framework that makes syncopation the norm, both singers emphasize the beat to build intensity. For Holiday, the strongest example of this may be found in the final statement of A (see Example 9); for Carter, it occurs throughout the second chorus. Because Carter "airs out" the phrases less in the second chorus than in the first, references to the beat in the vocal line keep her rhythms explicitly grounded in the band's support. That both singers choose to delay the entry of the phrases in the first chorus can be seen as a mechanism of swing, and not as a textually motivated decision.

The phenomenon of swing lends the jazz vocal line a

melodic freedom most appropriate to the setting of American English, enabling the singer to duplicate the flow and articulation of speech in her rhythmic choices. As used by both Holiday and Carter, speech accent becomes an ideal vehicle for the musical cross-accentuation essential to swing. On the other hand, because consonants and vowels define the envelope of each pitch, the more the jazz singer concerns herself with intelligibility, the more the sounds of the language will influence the melodic line. Gerald Abraham stated in *The Tradition of Western Music:*

> . . . owing to the hybrid nature of our language, ambiguities remain, and the result of this hybridism has perhaps been to deprive the language of any obvious positive formative influence on English and American music, though it offers a rich variety of phonetic raw materials.[21]

At least in the case of American popular song this description does not apply, especially in light of the performance practice of jazz singers. Analysis of this repertoire must account for the improvisations of jazz singers and the new vocal lines that result from these improvisations, if it seeks to reflect the musical results accurately. Clearly, the jazz vocal lines in these two performances bear the distinct mark of having evolved in direct response to the demands of linguistic factors. The implications of this fact may extend beyond vocal music, for some jazz instrumentalists, such as Lester Young, have stressed the importance of knowing the words to the tune, and many of them, including Louis Armstrong and Jack Teagarden, gained recognition as singers in their own right. An examination of the actual performances of other genres of English and American music may reveal that native speech inflections have played more of a "formative" role than Abraham suspects.

Nevertheless, the way the jazz vocal line balances textual values against musical ones sets jazz singing apart from other genres of music. We owe this to the subtle play in a jazz singer's performance between improvisation and paraphrase, a play which enables a singer's own speech rhythms and inflections to shape the vocal line even while she performs it. The musical-verbal balance that each jazz singer arrives at must therefore be counted among her stylistic features, for it can do much to reveal her personal conception of a song. Jazz singing appears in this light as a richly layered process, in which the sounds of the text color the musical line as it emerges, while the musical line, in turn, colors the meaning of the text as it unfolds. Music's subtle degrees of accentual differentiation afford the singer a means to lend the words greater nonverbal implications than speech itself allows; and the rhythms and timbres of the text give the singer/improviser a unique means to set her line in relief against the many levels of rhythm which constitute her backdrop.

What is more, even the large-scale form may be affected by nonverbal considerations. Betty Carter literally "raises her voice" in her second chorus. From the panic and urgency that develops in her voice we may infer the desperation of a woman begging her lover not to leave her, trying to convince him that she's different now, that she's changed. From an actor's standpoint, which Carter claims to adopt,[22] Carter's nonverbal expression projects a subtext, or hidden motivation "to grasp," or "to hold onto at any cost," and from her persistent emphasis on verbs and adjectives we sense the intense vitality and powerful sensuality of the character she plays in this rendition. Holiday's version has a wholly different meaning, one which has less overt drama but no less impact. Even the fact that she refuses to "raise her voice" has its roots in the nonverbal expression of withheld emotion and irony that characterize her rendition. While her version conveys a quality of resignation or withdrawal, ultimately she exposes less overt emotion than Carter.

Thus do we listen to the performance of a jazz standard through the filter of personality. From examining Holiday's and Carter's idiosyncratic approaches to one song, we have determined that the ways in which a song varies from one performer to the next result at least as much from what a singer wishes to say about the text as from any of her musical/stylistic attributes. Future research will reveal if patterns of interpretation and technique may emerge from the application of these analytic methods to a larger body of jazz vocal performances. Nevertheless, this study demonstrates that we arrive at a deeper understanding of a how a jazz singer realizes her intentions by confronting how the singer's emotional response to the text and her musical decisions resonate against one another.

NOTES

1. The research for this paper was partly supported by an award from the Carter-Berger Fund at the Institute of Jazz Studies, Rutgers University. This article benefited from the helpful suggestions of Lewis Porter. Comments by Howard Brofsky, Leo Treitler, and my wife, Marge, have also guided the paper's revisions. I would also like to thank the staff of the Institute of Jazz Studies for their assistance.
2. Cases in which improvisation ultimately proves absent show that some performers may work out arrangements in advance, performing them from memory; for those who analyze jazz performances from a formulaic standpoint, improvisation itself proves less spontaneous than it seems on first hearing. Nevertheless, even within a style that maintains very clearly defined stylistic constraints both in vocabulary and syntax (e.g., when playing bop), a jazz player's execution inevitably warrants less attention than her ideas.
3. King Oliver acknowledged this threat when he discouraged Louis Armstrong from straying too far from the melody. At the other end of the spectrum, Miles Davis's famous Philharmonic Hall performance of "My Funny Valentine" from 1964 challenges us with extreme distortion. Davis seems to paraphrase the tune at times, but he consistently blurs the line between paraphrase and improvisation. This results in part because he omits a formal "head," or complete paraphrase of the tune. Classical musicians cannot allow their personal styles to distort a work this much; accusations of self-indulgence at the expense of the composer would follow.
4. Of the phonetic elements given above, accent shares musical and linguistic functions, a fact which comes into play later in this paper. In music, accent heightens expression; in the English language accent conveys meaning (for example, distinguishing the verb "[to] perfect" from the adjective "[it's] perfect"). Yet we achieve accent in language via the musical

means of pitch, duration, and dynamics. Thus by using these musical means to define the specific nature of the accent at any given point in the text, the musical setting of words fixes their nonverbal content into the vocal line to create a stylized reading of the lyrics.

5. For example, when Ella Fitzgerald retains the lyrics to a standard and improvises a new melodic line, she sometimes will sacrifice intelligibility, placing musical concerns above textual ones. On the other hand, her paraphrases sometimes quote the tune more faithfully than one might expect. (For an example of this last point listen to her rendition of the tune discussed below, done with the Buddy Bregman Orchestra in 1956. This recording also warrants attention because Billie Holiday's recording falls roughly nine months later.) Like Holiday and Carter, Lorez Alexandria respects the song's lyrics when generating new melodic lines (see discography). This paper continues the sad neglect of her remarkable work, solely for space considerations.

6. A phonetic chart of the Trager-Smith phonetic symbols appears in the Appendix.

7. Richard Rodgers and Lorenz Hart. From "Too Many Girls," New York, N.Y. (Chappel & Co., 1939). I have transposed the tune from its original key of G-major for the sake of comparison.

8. Hart employs this lyricist's tool, often called a "hook," in many of the lyrics he wrote. The construction "Grand to . . ." in the bridge of this song serves a similar function, unifying the lyrics within the bridge and relating the bridge lyrically to what precedes it. Note that the customary approach of most songwriters at the time involved writing the lyrics *after* the music was composed. (See Oscar Hammerstein II, *Lyrics,* Hal Leonard Books (Milwaukee, 1985, p. 5.)

9. See discography for other important performances.

10. The term "voiced" refers to a consonant's ability to carry pitch.

11. Alec Wilder gets the credit for observing this hidden ascent. See *American Popular Song,* p. 213.

12. Gunther Schuller. *The Swing Era.* New York, N.Y. (Oxford University Press, 1989), pp. 530 and 543. Schuller's discussion of Billie Holiday (pp. 527–547) warrants reading.

13. In m. 4 (see Example 11), and later, in m. 12 and m. 28 (see insert, Example 1), Holiday replaces Rodgers's passing-tone c-natural with a return to the e-natural. That she does this

consistently throughout both choruses, despite differences in phonetic content, strongly suggests that her reasons are musical and not motivated by the lyrics. If we relate her pitch changes in m. 2 and m. 10 to this phrase ending, we may hear the new line's persistent repetition of the e'-d' descent as a tendency to reduce Rodgers's original melody to something akin to a reciting tone with occasional melodic extensions, at least at these key moments in the song. This explanation may also help us to understand her elimination of the chromatic descent in m. 20, on the words "yours alone" (see Example 1), which allows her to hearken back to the descending major third e-c that serves as a point of reference for much of the song.

14. As opposed to proportional meter, in which measures divide into equal, regularly occurring beats, additive meter results from the accumulation, and regrouping of the shortest rhythmic value into beats and measures of irregular size. Examples include Eastern European folk music, Indian *talas,* and the music of Bartok and Stravinsky. Because Holiday derives the smallest rhythmic unit for regrouping from the subdivision of the beat, her additive measures sometimes include fractions of the beat. To describe this phenomenon, I suggest the term "irrational measures." Lewis Porter has drawn my attention to another perspective on the rhythmic conflict between a jazz vocal line and its accompaniment, which places them each in different tempi. I have not been able to locate a copy of the paper that Hao and Rachel Huang delivered at the 1987 National Conference of the College Music Society in New Orleans, which presents this approach.

15. Significantly, the flowering of seventeenth century English song occurred in the context of a premetric rhythmic vocabulary which gave the prosody room to flow forward according to the demands of phonetic and metric considerations. See Elise Bickford Jorgens, *The Well Tun'd Word.*

16. This author's Ph.D. dissertation in progress, *Betty Carter: Style and Expression in the Jazz Singer's Art,* treats the subject more thoroughly.

17. I have transcribed Carter's line in $\frac{12}{8}$ because of this, even though the band clearly feels *four* beats to the measure. She so consistently uses a ternary subdivision of the beat, and so frequently regroups these subdivisions to form longer values that the standard approach of using triplets would have done more to obscure than to reveal her rhythmic approach. Notice,

for example, in mm. 22–4[II], how she introduces a new metric feel in each measure (see insert, Example 2). Specifically she changes from feeling four dotted quarter notes to the measure in m. 22[II] to six quarter notes to the measure in m. 23[II] to three half notes to the measure in m. 24[II]. I entertained the notion of using different time signatures in measures such as these, where she changes from the original metric feel. I chose the $\frac{12}{8}$ approach, however, because she still feels the original four-to-the-bar as well. However, standard jazz notation (which uses swung eight notes) cannot capture these metric transformations (which happen throughout Carter's performance) without looking unnecessarily complicated. On the other hand, Holiday does not consistently swing her eighth notes and sometimes performs them evenly. Therefore the distinction between triplet and eighth note in my transcription truly reflects her rhythmic approach. Again, standard jazz notation does not distinguish between even and swung eighths very well. The notational difference in the two transcriptions thus articulates in tangible form the difference between the singers rhythmically.

18. Leo Treitler has raised important questions on the relationship between the performance of Gregorian chant and its notation, and on how chant singers generated melodic variants. Some of his observations seem relevant to jazz singing because they address questions about improvisation. Treitler's work hints at some of the difficulties inherent in trying to learn what significance the sheet music may have for jazz singers, specifically with regard to the making of their own distinctive renditions. How much other singers' versions of the same song influence them (even versions from which they learned the tune) will also remain hard to ascertain. These difficulties become even more apparent when we try to account for other elements such as chord extensions and substitutions, and the bass line, which may further distance the singer's arrangement from one suggested by the sheet music. Thus, instead of considering a jazz vocal performance as an attempt to realize the notated version of a song, hearing it as merely one instance of a conceptual model's manifold expressions may provide a more useful understanding. Listening to Billie Holiday struggle to produce a composer-approved take of Bernstein's "Big Stuff," supports the notion that Holiday generally did not want simply to realize the song's notation. The previously unissued rehearsals have recently become available on *Billie Holiday:*

The Complete Decca Recordings, MCA Records, (NY, NY: 1991).

Keep in mind that transcriptions may mislead us, because without our noticing, we can easily begin to think of them in the same way we often think of sheet music (i.e. synoptically). Unless one is attempting to recreate a jazz performance literally, however, its transcription serves a purely descriptive function. To adapt an image of Jan LaRue's, it traces the path left behind by the unfolding of the music. On the other hand, the sheet music prescribes and hence remains incomplete until someone realizes it in some way. It acts as a blueprint for the sounds that we are to make and as such has served as a point of reference for this study.

What importance may we give, then, to the observation that the transcription of Carter's performance bears less overt a resemblance to the sheet music than the transcription of Holiday's performance? Given the extreme difference in function between the sheet music and the transcription, we can more fruitfully compare apples and oranges than these superficially similar musical notations. Don't we mean, rather, that we hear Holiday's performance in relation to a literal realization of the sheet music, such as the ones produced by the swing band singers (for examples of the latter see the discography) more easily than we do Betty Carter's? As noted earlier, however, in the context of jazz performance, literal realizations have no inherent value as jazz. The matter awaits fuller consideration.

19. Imagine the difficulty of singing the words "time it was" in this rhythmic configuration.
20. This motive consists of the closing pitches of Holiday's performance. Could Carter be paying homage to one of her self-proclaimed models?
21. Gerald Abraham. *The Tradition of Western Music.* Oxford University Press. California: 1974, p. 79.
22. Carter has emphasized the dramatic implications of her job in numerous published interviews and several conversations with me.

DISCOGRAPHY

(Bold face indicates recordings discussed in this article.)

Bob Eberle (with Jimmy Dorsey), Decca, NY 7/16/39

Louise Tobin (with Benny Goodman), Jazum 41; Tax m-8021, NY 9/13/39

Louise Tobin (with Benny Goodman), Phontastic 7606, NY 9/13/39

Mildred Bailey (with Benny Goodman), unreleased air check, "Camel Caravan" NBC Radio Network, NY 11/4/39

Helen Forrest (with Artie Shaw), Bluebird; Montgomery Ward; His Master's Voice, NY 11/9/39

[Charlie Parker (instrumental with strings), Verve 833268-2; 837141-2; NY 11/30/49]

Ella Fitzgerald (with Buddy Bregman), Verve MGV 4002-2; MGV 4023, Verve 821580 LA 8/29/56

Billie Holiday, Verve MGV 8257; Verve 817.359-1, Verve 513.859 (complete Verve set) LA 1/4/57
Produced by Norman Granz
Personnel: Harry "Sweets" Edison, trumpet
               Ben Webster, tenor saxophone
               Jimmy Rowles, piano
               Barney Kessel, guitar
               Red Mitchell, bass
               Alvin Stoller, drums

Frank Sinatra (with M-G-M studio orchestra), Capitol W912, LA 9/25/57

Lorez, Alexandria, King LP676, Chicago 1959

Betty Carter, "Finally," Roulette SR5000, at Judson Hall, NY 12/6/69 (Stuart Nicholson gives this date in the CD notes to the 1991 EMI reissue, which draw upon a discussion he had with Ms.

Carter. According to Nicholson, Betty Carter recorded the next entry, "Betty Carter," "just a few days later.")

Betty Carter, "Betty Carter," Bet-Car MK 1001, NY 1970
Recorded live at the Vanguard, possibly on Ms. Carter's Birthday, May 16, or in December 1969, (see above entry) Same trio as on "Finally."
Personnel: Norman Simmons, piano
              Lisle Atkinson, bass
              Al Harewood, drums

Sarah Vaughan (with Joe Pass), Pablo Today 2312137, Hollywood 3/1-2/82

Ernestine Anderson (with Hank Jones), Concord CJ214, San Francisco 2/83

Cassandra Wilson (with Mulgrew Miller), JMT 834419-1, NY 2/88

APPENDIX

Modified Trager-Smith phonemes

VOWELS

short
pit /i/   put /u/
pet /e/   cut /ə/   Paul[1] /oh/
pat /æ/   pale[2] /eh/   pot /a/

long
beat /iy/   boot /uw/
bait /ey/   dispute /yuw/   boat /ow/
bite /ay/   boy /oy/   about /æw/

SEMI-VOWELS

yes /y/   hat /h/   with /w/

CONSONANTS

pop /p/   tight[3] /t/   kick[4] /k/
Bob /b/   did /d/   gag /g/
                                                church /č/
                                                judge /j/
               fife[5] /f/   thin /θ/   sass /s/   shush /š/
               valve /v/   this /ð/   zebra[6] /z/   measure /ž/
mum /m/   nun /n/   sing /ŋ/
                               lull /l/   rear /r/

The above layout of consonants indicates their vocal placement; those on the left of the chart get produced toward the front of the mouth, and those on the right of the chart get produced toward the back of the mouth.

---

[1] Also paw

[2] Trager-Smith notation does not account for this vowel sound, except before /r/, as in the word "where."

[3] Also stopped

[4] Also cat and pique

[5] Also phase and rough

[6] Also xylem

AN ANNOTATED BIBLIOGRAPHY OF NOTATED CHARLIE CHRISTIAN SOLOS

By Clive G. Downs

INTRODUCTION

My aim in this paper is to give details of all publications containing notated solos of Charlie Christian, and to identify every solo included in them. Several authors have already listed published transcriptions, for example Summerfield (1978), Voigt (1978), Koger (1985), Kernfeld (1989), and Hitchcock et al. (1986), but all are incomplete, and are not intended to be comprehensive. Most list only five or so sources.

As a discography lists deleted records, so this bibliography gives details of out-of-print books and periodicals. This will be of value for those who study Christian's music. Christian recorded several versions of certain compositions, and some records contain solos spliced from different performances or takes. Most published transcriptions do not give full discographical data, so the aim here is to provide that information, so each notation can be readily identified.

There are few bibliographies of solo transcriptions; Koger (1985) lists solos published in *Down Beat* from 1939 to 1985; Downs (1986) is an earlier attempt to document Christian solos; and Downs (1989) deals with Eric Dolphy solos. A related genre, the solography, which gives discographical information and discusses all solos by a specific artist (but does not list published notations), was pioneered by Jan Evensmo, and Evensmo (c. 1976) documents all known Christian solos.

As Kernfeld (1989) points out, it is accepted that jazz

musicians use solo transcriptions to develop their art, yet there is little discussion of the history or process in the literature. Notated solos began to be published in the 1920s and more frequently in the 1930s in such journals as *Melody Maker* and *Down Beat,* and in the 1940s collected albums of transcriptions appeared; jazz education flourished in the 1970s and 1980s, and with it the number of published transcriptions increased.

Charlie Christian played, it is reported, in a number of local bands during his youth, but was never recorded then. It is said he was heard by the impresario John Hammond, who in 1939 arranged for him to audition with Benny Goodman, with whom he then played until his hospitalization in 1941, shortly followed by his death from tuberculosis in 1942.

His brief recording career, from 1939 to 1941, comprises mainly tunes with the Goodman small groups, where Christian usually plays short solos of one chorus or less. He recorded also with Lionel Hampton and Edmond Hall; further recordings with Jerry Jerome and at Minton's have more extended solos. He is generally acknowledged to be a major influence on jazz guitar playing ever since.

METHOD USED TO COMPILE BIBLIOGRAPHY

My personal collection was the starting point for the bibliography, supplemented by inquiries to many publishers, periodicals, libraries, correspondence with jazz educators, and checking of reference books. In addition, I learned of some sources through responses to my earlier published bibliography, which included a request for information.

PUBLICATIONS CONTAINING SOLO TRANSCRIPTIONS

Each publication is followed by a summary of the notated solos it contains, in alphabetical order of title. Some sources contain photographic reproductions of previously published notations, and these are indicated. In some cases, sources include notations which have been transcribed from previous publications, and these too are identified where possible. In order to avoid undue repetition in this section, only such comments that apply to *all* notations in a compilation are noted. For publications consisting of a single solo notation, or where only *some* solos in a compilation are not original transcriptions, this fact is noted in the next section, a listing of notations in alphabetical order of solo title.

Some publications do not acknowledge that notations have been copied from previous sources, and in such cases they have been compared with other transcriptions and a judgment formed of the most likely source.

Details of each solo are followed by brief discographical information showing where it was issued. Wherever possible, the most recent US issue on CD (or CD available in the USA as an import) is cited, except where notations are clearly transcribed from particular LP issues with tracks containing solos spliced from various master takes. If a track has not been issued on CD, details of a representative LP issue are provided, or if never issued on LP, the 78 catalog number.

Almo (1978a). *World's Greatest Jazz Solos: Flute.* Hollywood: Almo,

(———) (1978b). *World's Greatest Jazz Solos: Guitar.* Hollywood: Almo,

(———) (1978c). *World's Greatest Jazz Solos: Saxophone.* Hollywood: Almo,

(———) (1978d). *World's Greatest Jazz Solos: Trumpet.* Hollywood: Almo.

Note: All the above publications notate the same solo, transposed for the instrument in question.

Solo Flight March 4 1941 Columbia CL652

Antonich, Mark E. (1982). *The Jazz Style and Analysis of the Music of Charlie Christian.* Thesis, Duquesne University.

Note: All notations in this thesis are transcribed from previously published sources.

Air Mail Special March 13 1941 Columbia CL652
Boy Meets Goy April 16 1940 Columbia CK 40846
Breakfast Feud December 19 1940/January 15 1941 Columbia
   CL652
Guy's Got to Go May 1941 Vogue 600135
I Can't Give You Anything But Love December 19 1940
   Columbia CK 40379
I Found a New Baby *(take 2)* January 15 1941 Columbia
   CG30779
Lip's Flip May 1941 Vogue 600135
Profoundly Blue February 5 1941 Blue Note B-6505
Rose Room October 2 1939 Columbia CK 40846
Seven Come Eleven November 22 1939 Columbia CK 40846
Six Appeal June 20 1940 Columbia CK 40846
A Smo-o-o-oth One March 13 1941 Columbia Co 36099
Solo Flight March 4 1941 Columbia CK 40846
Swing to Bop May 12 1941 Vogue 600135
Till Tom Special February 7 1940 Columbia CK 40846
Up on Teddy's Hill 8 May 1941 Vogue 600135

Ayeroff, Stan (ed.) (1979). *Charlie Christian.* New York: Consolidated Music Publishers.

As Long as I Live November 7 1940 Columbia CG30779
Dinah December 16 1939 Vintage Jazz Classics VJC 1021
Good Morning Blues December 24 1939 Vanguard VCD2-47/48
Guy's Got to Go May 1941 Vogue 600135
Honeysuckle Rose November 22 1939 Columbia CG30779
Honeysuckle Rose December 24 1939 Vanguard VCD2-47/48
Honeysuckle Rose November 19 1940 Vintage Jazz Classics VJC
   1021
I Can't Give You Anything but Love December 19 1940
   Columbia CK 40379
Ida Sweet as Apple Cider April 14 1941 Vintage Jazz Classics
   VJC 1021
I Found a New Baby*(take 1)* January 15 1941 Columbia CK
   40846
I Found a New Baby*(take 2)* January 15 1941 Columbia
   CG30779
I Surrender Dear April 16 1940 Columbia CK 40379

Lip's Flip May 1941 Vogue 600135
Pagin' the Devil December 24 1939 Vanguard VCD2-47/48
The Sheik of Araby April 10 1940 Columbia CK 40379
The Sheik of Araby April 12 1940 Vintage Jazz Classics VJC
   1021
Stardust September 24 1939 Columbia CG30779
Stardust October 2 1939 Columbia CK 40379
Swing to Bop May 12 1941 Vogue 600135
Up on Teddy's Hill 8 May 1941 Vogue 600135

Bell, Anne M. (n.d.). *Styles Lessons: Charlie Christian.* Boston:
Freelance Music.

Note: This publication consists of loose leaf, photocopied sheets.

Air Mail Special March 13 1941 Columbia CG30779
Boy Meets Goy April 16 1940 Columbia CK 40846
Breakfast Feud January 15 1941 Columbia CG30779
Breakfast Feud January 15 1941 Columbia CG30779
I Found a New Baby January 15 1941 Columbia CG30779
I Got Rhythm September 24 1939 Columbia CG30779
On the Alamo January 15 1941 Columbia CK 40379
Stardust September 24 1939 Columbia CG30779
Waitin' for Benny March 13 1941 Columbia CK 40846

Berklee School of Music (n.d.). *Transcriptions Library Archive.*
Boston: Freelance Music.

Note: This source consists of photocopied, loose leaf sheets.

Air Mail Special March 13 1941 Columbia CL652
As Long as I Live November 7 1940 Columbia CG30779
Benny's Bugle November 7 1940 Columbia CK 40846
Boy Meets Goy April 16 1940 Columbia CK 40846
Breakfast Feud December 19 1940/January 15 1941 Columbia
   CL652
Flying Home October 2 1939 Columbia CK 40379
Gone with "What" Wind February 7 1940 Columbia CG30779
Honeysuckle Rose November 22 1939 Columbia CG30779
I Can't Give You Anything but Love December 19 1940
   Columbia CK 40379
I Found a New Baby January 15 1941 Columbia CG30779
I Got Rhythm September 24 1939 Columbia CG30779

I Surrender Dear April 16 1940 Columbia CK 40379
Memories of You*(take -A)* November 22 1939 Columbia CK 40379
Memories of You*(take -B)* November 22 1939 Columbia CG30779
Poor Butterfly April 10 1940 Columbia CK 40379
Profoundly Blue February 5 1941 Blue Note B-6505
Rose Room October 2 1939 Columbia CK 40846
Seven Come Eleven November 22 1939 Columbia CK 40846
The Sheik of Araby April 10 1940 Columbia CK 40379
A Smo-o-o-oth One March 13 1941 Columbia CL652
Solo Flight March 4 1941 Columbia CK 40846
These Foolish Things June 20 1940 Columbia CK 40379
Wholly Cats November 7 1940 Columbia CL652

Birkett, James (transcr.) (1987). *Jazz Guitar*. Woodford Green, England. International Music Publications.

I Got Rhythm September 24 1939 Columbia CG30779

Britt, Stan (1984). *The Jazz Guitarists*. New York: Sterling.

I Can't Give You Anything but Love December 19 1940 Columbia CK 40379

Carter, Rich (1979). *Jazz Guitar Masterpieces*. Flat Five Publishing.

I Found a New Baby January 15 1941 Columbia CG30779

Down Beat (1940, April 15), p. 17. "Charlie Christian's Guitar Get-Offs on 'Flying Home'. "

Flying Home October 2 1939 Columbia CK 40379

(———)(1943, January 15), p. 22. "By the Late Charlie Christian."

Rose Room October 2 1939 Columbia CK 40846

(———)(1950, February 10), p. 16. "Charlie Christian Solo: 'I've Found a New Baby'."

I Found a New Baby January 15 1941 Columbia CK 40846

(————)(1950, August 25), p. 12. "Jazz off the Record," Russo, B., & Lifton, L.

Rose Room October 2 1939 Columbia CK 40846

(————)(1961, July 20), pp. 25–28. "Up beat: Charlie Christian," Berklee School of Music.

Boy Meets Goy April 16 1940 Columbia CK 40846
Honeysuckle Rose November 22 1939 Columbia CG30779
I Found a New Baby January 15 1941 Columbia CK 40846
On the Alamo January 15 1941 Columbia CK 40379
Profoundly Blue February 5 1941 Blue Note B-6505
A Smo-o-o-oth One March 13 1941 Columbia Co 36099

(————)(1968, October 31), pp. 36–37. "Gone with What Wind."

Gone with "What" Wind February 7 1940 Columbia CG30779

(————)(1969, July 10). "Charlie Christian Solo on Rose Room."

Rose Room October 2 1939 Columbia CK 40846

(————)(1970, June 11), p. 36. "A Charlie Christian Blues Solo."

Boy Meets Goy April 16 1940 Columbia CK 40846

(————)(1991, May), pp. 56–57. "Charlie Christian's Solo on 'I Got Rhythm'."

I Got Rhythm September 24 1939 Columbia CG30779

Duchossoir, René (1987). *Jazz Guitar True Notes. Vol 1.* Paris: Behar.

Stardust October 2 1939 Columbia CK 40379

Edmonds, Hank, and Prince, Bob (transcr.) (1958). *The Swingingest Charley Christian.* New York: Charles Colin.

Guy's Got to Go May 1941 Vogue 600135
Lips Flips May 1941 Vogue 600135
Swing to Bop May 12 1941 Vogue 600135
Up on Teddy's Hill May 8 1941 Vogue 600135

Feather, Leonard (1957). *The Book of Jazz.* New York: Horizon.

Up on Teddy's Hill May 8 1941 Vogue 600135

Fox, Dan (ed.) (1964). *The Art of the Jazz Guitar: Charley Christian.* New York: Regent Music. [reprinted, 1988].

Air Mail Special March 13 1941 Columbia CL652
Benny's Bugle November 7 1940 Columbia CK 40846
Boy Meets Goy April 16 1940 Columbia CK 40846
Breakfast Feud December 19 1940/January 15 1941 Columbia CL652
Gone with "What" Wind February 7 1940 Columbia CG30779
Seven Come Eleven November 22 1939 Columbia CK 40846
Shivers December 20 1939 Columbia CK 40379
Six Appeal June 20 1940 Columbia CK 40846
A Smo-o-o-oth One March 13 1941 Columbia CL652
Solo Flight March 4 1941 Columbia CK 40846
Till Tom Special February 7 1940 Columbia CK 40846
Wholly Cats November 7 1940 Columbia CL652

Guitar Extra (1990, Summer), p. 15. "Analyzing Charlie Christian."

Seven Come Eleven November 22 1939 Columbia CK 40846

Guitar Player (1982, March), pp. 56–57. "Charlie Christian's Solo Style: 'Honeysuckle Rose'," Obrecht, Jas.

Honeysuckle Rose November 22 1939 Columbia CG30779

Guitar World (1982, January), p. 73. "Charlie Christian Takes Off." Dave Steen (transcr.)

Breakfast Feud January 15 1941 Columbia CG30779

Hitchcock, H. Wiley, & Sadie, Stanley (eds.) (1986). *The New Grove Dictionary of American Music, Vol. 1.* New York: Macmillan. (Thomas Owens, "Charlie Christian.")

Breakfast Feud December 19 1940/January 15 1941 Columbia CL652

Ingram, Adrian (1980). *Modern Jazz Guitar Technique.* Northampton, England: Hampton.

Boy Meets Goy April 16 1940 Columbia CK 40846
I Found a New Baby January 15 1941 Columbia CG30779

Jazz Educators Journal (1979, Dec./Jan.), p. 38.

Seven Come Eleven November 22 1939 Columbia CK 40846

Jazz Hot (1972, May), p. 283. "Charlie Christian: From Swing to Bop."

Swing to Bop May 12 1941 Vogue 600135

Kernfeld, Barry (ed.) (1989). *The New Grove Dictionary of Jazz.* New York: Macmillan. (Thomas Owens, "Charlie Christian.")

Breakfast Feud December 19 1940/January 15 1941 Columbia CL652

Mairants, Ivor (1988). *Famous Jazz Guitar Solos 2.* London: International Music Publications.

Flying Home [unidentified date]
Solo Flight March 4 1941 Columbia CK 40846

Martin, Henry (1986). *Enjoying Jazz.* New York: Schirmer.

I Found A New Baby (take 1) January 15 1941 Columbia CK 40846

Matzner, Antonín, and Wasserberger, Igor (1969). *Jazzové Profily.* Prague: Supraphon.

Up on Teddy's Hill May 8 1941 Vogue 600135

Melody Maker (1947, August 23), p. 3. "Theme—and extemporisation," Mairants, I.

I Surrender Dear April 16 1940 Columbia CK 40379

Mongan, Norman (1983). *The History of the Guitar in Jazz*. New York: Oak Publications.

Swing to Bop May 12 1941 Vogue 600135

Owens, Thomas (see Hitchcock, Kernfeld).

Petersen, Jack (1979). *Jazz Styles & Analysis: Guitar*. Chicago: Down Beat.

Air Mail Special March 13 1941 Columbia CL652
Boy Meets Goy April 16 1940 Columbia CK 40846
Rose Room October 2 1939 Columbia CK 40846
Solo Flight March 4 1941 Columbia CG30779

Polillo, Arrigo (1979). *I Grandi Del Jazz: Gli Stilisti*. Milan: Fabbri.

On the Alamo January 15 1941 Columbia CK 40379

Schiff, Ronny S. (ed.) (1988). *Solos for Jazz Guitar*. New York: Carl Fischer.

Air Mail Special June 20 1940 Columbia CK 40379
Air Mail Special March 13 1941 Columbia CG30779

Schuller, Gunther (1989). *The Swing Era*. New York: Oxford University Press.

Breakfast Feud December 19 1940/January 15 1941 Columbia CG30779
I Found a New Baby January 15 1941 Columbia CK 40846
Memories of You December 24 1939 Vanguard VCD2-47/48
Rose Room October 2 1939 Columbia CK 40846
Stardust October 2 1939 Columbia CK 40379
Stompin' at the Savoy May 12 1941 Vogue 600135

Smith, Earl, & Tharp, Paul (transcr.) (1958). *Hot Jazz Guitar Solos*. Pueblo: Smith Tharp Publishing.

Boy Meets Goy April 16 1940 Columbia CK 40846
Rose Room October 2 1939 Columbia CK 40846
These Foolish Things June 20 1940 Columbia CK 40379

Spaces IV Jazz Fake Book

Note: All notations are transcribed from previously published sources. A notation of "I Got Rhythm" is included that is attributed to Charlie Christian, but it does not appear to correspond to the only known performance of September 24, 1939.

Gone with "What" Wind February 7 1940 Columbia CG30779
Profoundly Blue February 5 1941 Blue Note B-6505
Rose Room October 2 1939 Columbia CK 40846

Spring, Howard A. (1980). "The Improvisational Style of Charlie Christian." MFA Thesis, York University.

AC-DC Current December 2 1939 Vintage Jazz Classics VJC 1021
AC-DC Current June 1940 Vintage Jazz Classics VJC 1021
Ad-Lib Blues October 28 1940 Jazz Document va-7997
Air Mail Special June 20 1940 Columbia CK 40379
Air Mail Special March 13 1941 Columbia CG30779
Air Mail Special March 17 1941 Vintage Jazz Classics VJC 1021
All Star Strut February 7 1940 Columbia CG30779
As Long as I Live November 7 1940 Columbia CG30779
Benny's Bugle November 7 1940 Columbia CK 40846
Benny's Bugle November 19 1940 Vintage Jazz Classics VJC 1021
Benny's Bugle May 28 1941 Vintage Jazz Classics VJC 1021
Boy Meets Goy April 16 1940 Columbia CK 40846
Breakfast Feud December 19 1940 Columbia CL652
Breakfast Feud January 15 1941 Columbia CG30779
Charlie's Dream October 28 1940 Vintage Jazz Classics VJC 1021
Dinah December 16 1939 Vintage Jazz Classics VJC 1021
Flying Home August 10 1939 Jazz Archives JA-23
Flying Home March 10 1941 Vintage Jazz Classics VJC 1021
Gone with "What" Wind February 7 1940 Columbia CG30779
Gone with "What" Wind April 6 1940 Vintage Jazz Classics VJC 1021
Good Morning Blues December 24 1939 Vanguard VCD2-47/48
Guy's Got to Go May 1941 Vogue 600135
Honeysuckle Rose November 22 1939 Columbia CG30779
Honeysuckle Rose November 19 1940 Vintage Jazz Classics VJC 1021

I Can't Give You Anything but Love December 19 1940 Columbia CK 40379

Ida Sweet as Apple Cider April 14 1941 Vintage Jazz Classics VJC 1021

I Found a New Baby January 15 1941 Columbia CG30779

I Got Rhythm September 24 1939 Columbia CG30779

I Never Knew October 28 1940 Vintage Jazz Classics VJC 1021

Lester's Dream October 28 1940 Vintage Jazz Classics VJC 1021

Lips Flips May 1941 Vogue 600135

Memories of You October 23 1939 Vintage Jazz Classics VJC 1021

Memories of You November 22 1939 Columbia CG30779

On the Alamo January 15 1941 Columbia CK 40379

Rose Room October 2 1939 Columbia CK 40846

Rose Room October 9 1939 Vintage Jazz Classics VJC 1021

Royal Garden Blues November 7 1940 Columbia CG30779

Seven Come Eleven November 22 1939 Columbia CK 40846

The Sheik of Araby April 12 1940 Vintage Jazz Classics VJC 1021

Six Appeal June 20 1940 Columbia CK 40846

Six Appeal June 22 1940 Vintage Jazz Classics VJC 1021

Stompin' at the Savoy May 12 1941 Vogue 600135

Till Tom Special December 31 1939 Vintage Jazz Classics VJC 1021

Till Tom Special February 7 1940 Columbia CK 40846

Up on Teddy's Hill May 8 1941 Vogue 600135

Wholly Cats October 28 1940 Vintage Jazz Classics VJC 1021

Wholly Cats*(take 3)* November 7 1940 Columbia CG30779

Wholly Cats*(take 4)* November 7 1940 Columbia CG30779

Wholly Cats November 19 1940 Vintage Jazz Classics VJC 1021

Wholly Cats April 7 1941 Jazz Archives JA-23

(———) (1991). "The Use of Formulas in the Improvisations of Charlie Christian." *Jazz Research/Jazzforschung*, 22, pp. 11–51.

Note: All notations transcribed (some are extracts) from Spring (1980).

Air Mail Special March 13 1941 Columbia CG30779

Air Mail Special March 17 1941 Vintage Jazz Classics VJC 1021

All Star Strut February 7 1940 Columbia CG30779

Benny's Bugle November 7 1940 Columbia CK 40846

Benny's Bugle November 19 1940 Vintage Jazz Classics VJC 1021

Benny's Bugle May 28 1941 Vintage Jazz Classics VJC 1021
Boy Meets Goy April 16 1940 Columbia CK 40846
Breakfast Feud January 15 1941 Columbia CG30779
Dinah December 16 1939 Vintage Jazz Classics VJC 1021
Flying Home August 10 1939 Jazz Archives JA-23
Flying Home March 10 1941 Vintage Jazz Classics VJC 1021
Gone with "What" Wind April 6 1940 Vintage Jazz Classics VJC 1021
Guy's Got to Go May 1941 Vogue 600135
Honeysuckle Rose November 22 1939 Columbia CG30779
Honeysuckle Rose November 19 1940 Vintage Jazz Classics VJC 1021
Lips Flips May 1941 Vogue 600135
Memories of You October 23 1939 Vintage Jazz Classics VJC 1021
Royal Garden Blues November 7 1940 Columbia CG30779
Seven Come Eleven November 22 1939 Columbia CK 40846
The Sheik of Araby April 12 1940 Vintage Jazz Classics VJC 1021
Stompin' at the Savoy May 12 1941 Vogue 600135
Up on Teddy's Hill May 8 1941 Vogue 600135
Wholly Cats October 28 1940 Vintage Jazz Classics VJC 1021
Wholly Cats*(take 3)* November 7 1940 Columbia CG30779
Wholly Cats*(take 4)* November 7 1940 Columbia CG30779
Wholly Cats November 19 1940 Vintage Jazz Classics VJC 1021
Wholly Cats April 7 1941 Jazz Archives JA-23

Takayanagi, Masayuki. (1975). *Charlie Christian Jazz Improvisation.* Tokyo: Nichion.

As Long as I Live November 7 1940 Columbia CG30779
Gone with "What" Wind February 7 1940 Columbia CG30779
Honeysuckle Rose November 22 1939 Columbia CG30779
(*note: complete score*)
I Can't Give You Anything but Love December 19 1940 Columbia CK 40379
I Found a New Baby January 15 1941 Columbia CG30779
I Surrender Dear April 16 1940 Columbia CK 40379
Memories of You *(take -A)* November 22 1939 Columbia CK 40379
Memories of You *(take -B)* November 22 1939 Columbia CG30779
Royal Garden Blues November 7 1940 Columbia CK 40846

The Sheik of Araby April 10 1940 Columbia CK 40379
Stardust September 24 1939 Columbia CG30779
Stardust October 6 1939 Collectors' Classics CC18

Tempo (1947, March), p. 8. "By the Late Charlie Christian."

Rose Room October 2 1939 Columbia CK 40846

Wise (1987a). *Jazz Transcriptions for the Alto Saxophone*. New York: Wise Publications.

I Surrender Dear April 16 1940 Columbia CK 40379

(————) (1987b). *Jazz Transcriptions for the Guitar*. New York: Wise Publications.

Stardust September 24 1939 Columbia CG30779

Gridley (1978) reports that the publisher Giant Steps produced transcriptions of Charlie Christian solos, but it has not been possible to obtain a copy of these. A bibliography of jazz guitar notations published in *Jazz Hot* (1972) lists an item which appears to include Christian material, but this could not be traced; although it is not clear from the bibliography, the publication may also include notations of Barney Kessel, and Chuck Wayne, and appears to be titled *Manuscript series of recorded jazz chorusses* [sic]. No publisher or date of publication is given.

ANALYSIS OF PUBLISHED SOLO TRANSCRIPTIONS

Each recorded solo of Christian for which a transcription is published is listed in alphabetical order of title. The date of recording is noted, and the catalog number of a familiar LP issue. Relevant details of the transcription are noted, such as its completeness, inclusion of annotations, chord symbols, and the key in which it is notated, if there is inconsistency between multiple versions. The format of entries is based on that used in Koger (1985).

AC-DC Current   December 2 1939   Vintage Jazz Classics VJC 1021

Spring (1980). Chords unidentified; notates only 2 solos of 4 bars; annotated.

AC-DC Current   June 1940   Vintage Jazz Classics VJC 1021

Spring (1980). Chords unidentified; complete (3 solos of 4 bars); annotated.

Ad-Lib Blues   October 28 1940   JazzDocument va-7997

Spring (1980). Chords identified; complete (2 choruses); annotated; this includes a 4-bar notation of the false start guitar solo.

Air Mail Special   June 20 1940   Columbia CK 40379.

Schiff (1988). Chords identified; complete; annotated; referred to in text as "Air Mail Special (I)."

Spring (1980). Chords identified; complete; annotated.

Air Mail Special   March 13 1941   Columbia CG30779.

Note: This L.P. issue has two guitar solos spliced from the same takes as Columbia CL652 (see below), except that the second solo has the first 8 bars omitted (details in Callis, 1978, p. 41).

Bell (n.d.). Chords unidentified; notates only the first 13 bars of the first solo; not annotated; referred to in text as "Good Enough to Keep."

Schiff (1988). Chords identified; complete (i.e. first solo of 32 bars, second of 24 bars); annotated; referred to in text as "Air Mail Special (II)."

Spring (1980). Chords identified; complete; annotated.

(———)(1991). *Adapted from Spring (1980);* notates 1st 11 bars of first chorus, then bars 18–25 (i.e. starting at 2nd bar of bridge) of 2nd chorus

Air Mail Special   March 13 1941   Columbia CL652.

Note: This L.P. issue has two guitar solos (each a 32-bar chorus) spliced from separate takes (details in Callis, 1978, p.41).

Antonich (1982). *Transcribed from Fox (1964); annotated.*

Berklee School of Music (n.d.). Chords identified; complete (i.e. both solos); not annotated.

Fox (1964). Chords identified; complete (i.e. both solos); annotated.

Petersen (1979). Chords identified; notates only the second guitar solo; annotated.

Air Mail Special   March 17 1941   Vintage Jazz Classics VJC 1021.

Spring (1980). Chords identified; complete; annotated.

(————)(1991). *Adapted from Spring (1980);* notates from bar 24 to end; annotated.

All Star Strut   February 7 1940   Columbia CG30779.

Spring (1980). Chords identified; complete; annotated.

(————) (1991). *Transcribed from Spring (1980); annotated.*

As Long as I Live   November 7 1940   Columbia CG30779.

Ayeroff (1979). Chords identified; complete; annotated.

Berklee School of Music (n.d.). Chords identified; complete; not annotated.

Spring (1980). Chords identified; complete; annotated.

Takayanagi (1975). Chords identified; complete; annotated (in Japanese).

Benny's Bugle   November 7 1940   Columbia CK 40846.

Berklee School of Music (n.d.). Chords identified; complete; not annotated.

Fox (1964). Chords identified; complete; annotated.

Spring (1980). Chords identified; complete; annotated.

(————) (1991). *Transcribed from Spring (1980); annotated.*

Benny's Bugle   November 19 1940   Vintage Jazz Classics VJC 1021.

Spring (1980). Chords identified; complete; annotated.

(————) (1991). *Transcribed from Spring (1980); annotated.*

Benny's Bugle   May 28 1941   Vintage Jazz Classics VJC 1021

Spring (1980). Chords identified; complete; annotated.

———— (1991). *Transcribed from Spring (1980); annotated.*

Boy Meets Goy   April 16 1940   Columbia CK 40846

Antonich (1982). *Transcribed from Fox (1964); annotated.*

Bell (n.d.). Chords identified; notates first chorus and two bars of second chorus; not annotated; referred to in text as "Goy."

Berklee School of Music (n.d.). Chords identified; complete; not annotated.

Down Beat (1961). Chords identified; complete; annotated.

Down Beat (1970). *Reproduced from Down Beat (1961).*

Fox (1964). Chords identified; complete; annotated.

Ingram (1980). Chords identified; notates only 4 bars from bar 11, first chorus; annotated; untitled in text, transcription 2.

Petersen (1979). Chords identified; complete; annotated.

Smith & Tharp (1958). Chords unidentified; complete; not annotated.

Spring (1980). Chords identified; complete; annotated.

(————) (1991). *Transcribed from Spring (1980); annotated.*

Breakfast Feud

Table 1 shows which takes of the composition "Breakfast Feud," recorded on December 19, 1940 and January 15, 1940, have been notated. Some of the notations were taken from earlier LP issues, which included tracks with solos from different takes, spliced together in various combinations. Full details of this splicing are given in Callis (1978, p. 40), and Evensmo (n.d., p. CC18–20). Principal LPs concerned are Columbia CL 652 and CG30779.

Antonich (1982). *Transcribed from Fox (1964); annotated.*

Bell (n.d.). Chords identified; notates first 12 bars of first spliced solo from take 29512-Y; annotated; referred to in text as "Feud" (page 1).

Table 1:   Notations of "Breakfast Feud" solos

Source	December 19, 1940	January 15, 1941			
Matrix	29259-1	29512-1	29512-2	29512-X	29512-Y
Bell (n.d.)				(2)	(1)
Fox (1964)	(1)		(3)	(2)	
Guitar World (1982)					(1)
Schuller (1989)	(1)	(5)	(4)	(3)	(2)
Spring(1980)	(1)	(4)	(3)	(2)	(1)
Spring(1991)		(4)	(3)	(2)	(1)

Notes:
1. Take numbers are those supplied by Evensmo (c. 1976).
2. Numbers in brackets show the order in which solos are notated in the source.

(————). Chords unidentified; notates 8 bars from start of solo from take 29512-X; not annotated; referred to in text as "Feud" (page 2).

Berklee School of Music (n.d.). Chords identified; not annotated; notation of solos is similar to Fox (1964).

Fox (1964). Chords identified; notates take 29259-1 (sections I and J), then 29512-X (sections K, and first chorus of L), then 29512-2 (sections L (second chorus) and M); annotated.

Guitar World (1982). Chords unidentified; notates take 29512-Y; annotated.

Hitchcock et al. (1986). Chords identified; notates three fragments from take 29259-1; annotated.

Kernfeld (1989). *Reproduced from Hitchcock et al. (1986);* annotated.

Schuller (1989). Chords unidentified; notates take 29259-1 from December 19, 1940, and takes 29512-1, -2, -X, and -Y from January 15, 1941; annotated.

Spring (1980). Chords identified; notates all solos from same takes as transcribed by Schuller (1989); annotated;

(————) (1991). *Adapted from Spring (1980);* notates solos only from January 15, 1941, takes as follows: 29512-Y (complete), -X (first 8 bars), -2 (first 8 bars), -1 (last 12 bars); annotated.

Charlie's Dream   October 28 1940   Vintage Jazz Classics VJC 1021.

Spring (1980). Chords identified; complete; annotated.

Dinah   December 16 1939   Vintage Jazz Classics VJC 1021.

Ayeroff (1979). Chords identified; complete; annotated; key A^b.

Spring (1980). Chords identified; complete; annotated; key B^b.

(————) (1991). *Adapted from Spring (1980);* notates up to bar 23; annotated.

Flying Home   August 10 1939   Jazz Archives JA-23.

Spring (1980). Chords identified; complete; annotated.

(————) (1991). *Transcribed from Spring (1980);* annotated.

Flying Home   October 2 1939   Columbia CK 40379.
(take - A)

Berklee School of Music (n.d.). Chords unidentified; complete; not annotated.

Down Beat (1940). Chords unidentified; complete; not annotated.

Flying Home   March 10 1941   Vintage Jazz Classics VJC 1021.

Spring (1980). Chords identified; complete; annotated.

(————) (1991). *Adapted from Spring (1980);* notates first 11 bars only; annotated.

Flying Home   date unknown

Mairants (1988). Chords identified; annotated; the text suggests this transcription is from the 78 Parlophone Pa R2917, but it does not appear to correspond to the equivalent CD issue (Columbia CK 40379), nor to the alternate take (Nost. 7610), and not to other well known LP issues.

Gone with "What" Wind   February 7 1940   Columbia CG30779.

Berklee School of Music (n.d.). Chords identified; complete; not annotated.

Down Beat (1968). *Reproduced from Fox (1964).*

Fox (1964). Chords identified; complete; annotated.

Spaces IV (n.d.). *Similar to transcription in Fox (1964).*

Spring (1980). Chords identified; complete; annotated.

Takayanagi (1975). Chords identified; complete; annotated (in Japanese).

Gone with "What" Wind   April 6 1940   Vintage Jazz Classics VJC 1021.

Spring (1980). Chords identified; complete; annotated.

(———) (1991). *Transcribed from Spring (1980);* annotated.

Good Morning Blues   December 24 1939   Vanguard VCD2-47/ 48.

Ayeroff (1979). Chords identified; complete; annotated; this solo is attributed to Eddie Durham in the text.

Spring (1980). Chords identified; complete; annotated.

Guy's Got to Go   May 1941   Vogue 600135.

Antonich (1982). *Transcribed from Ayeroff (1979);* annotated.

Ayeroff (1979). Chords identified; complete; annotated.

Edmond & Prince (1958). Chords identified; complete; not annotated.

Spring (1980). Chords identified; complete; annotated.

(———) (1991). *Adapted from Spring (1980);* notates from bar 32 (last bar) of 1st chorus, until 1st bar of middle eight; annotated.

Honeysuckle Rose   November 22 1939   Columbia CG30779.

Ayeroff (1979). Chords identified; annotated; referred to in text as "Honeysuckle Rose (I)."

Berklee School of Music (n.d.). Chords unidentified; complete; not annotated.

Down Beat (1961). Chords unidentified; complete; annotated.

Guitar Player (1982). *Reproduced from Ayeroff (1979).*

Spring (1980). Chords identified; annotated.

(———) (1991). *Adapted from Spring (1980);* notates only first 24 bars; annotated.

Takayanagi (1975). Chords identified; annotated (in Japanese); includes complete score of the arrangement.

Honeysuckle Rose   December 24 1939   Vanguard VCD2-47/48.

Ayeroff (1979). Chords identified; complete; annotated; referred to in text as "Honeysuckle Rose (III)."

Honeysuckle Rose   November 19 1940   Vintage Jazz Classics VJC 1021.

Ayeroff (1979). Chords identified; omits half-bar lead-in; annotated; referred to in text as "Honeysuckle Rose (II)."

Spring (1980). Chords identified; complete; annotated.

(———) (1991). *Adapted from Spring (1980);* notates first 13 bars only; annotated.

I Can't Give You Anything but Love   December 19 1940   Columbia CK 40379.

Antonich (1982). *Transcribed from Ayeroff (1979).*

Ayeroff (1979). Chords identified; complete; annotated.

Berklee School of Music (n.d.). Chords identified; complete; not annotated.

Britt (1984). Chords identified; notates first 8 bars; annotated.

Spring (1980). Chords identified; complete; annotated.

Takayanagi (1975). Chords identified; complete; annotated (in Japanese).

Ida Sweet as Apple Cider   April 14 1941   Vintage Jazz Classics VJC 1021.

Ayeroff (1979). Chords identified; complete; annotated.

Spring (1980). Chords identified; complete; annotated.

I Found a New Baby   January 15 1941   Columbia CK 40846.
(*take -1*)

Ayeroff (1979). Chords identified; complete; annotated; referred to in text as "I've Found a New Baby (I)."

Down Beat (1950). Chords identified; complete; annotated.

(———) (1961). *Reproduced from Down Beat (1950).*

Martin (1986). Chords identified; complete; annotated.

Schuller (1989). Chords unidentified; notates bars 4 to 6, and bar 8; annotated.

I Found a New Baby   January 15 1941   Columbia CG30779. *(take - 2)*

Antonich (1982). *Transcribed from Ayeroff (1979);* annotated.

Ayeroff (1979). Chords identified; complete; annotated; key F; referred to in text as "I've Found a New Baby (II)."

Bell (n.d.). Chords identified; notates only first 12 bars of first chorus; not annotated; key F; referred to in text as "Baby."

Berklee School of Music (n.d.). Chords identified; complete; not annotated; key G^b.

Carter (1979). Chords identified; complete; annotated; key F; untitled in text.

Ingram (1980). Chords identified; notates first 4 bars only; annotated; key F.

Spring (1980). Chords identified; complete; annotated; key F.

Takayanagi (1975). Chords identified; complete; annotated (in Japanese); key G^b.

I Got Rhythm   September 24 1939   Columbia CG30779

Note: This L.P. issue is spliced from separate recordings; details are given in Callis (1978, p. 2).

Bell (n.d.). Chords identified; notates first 8 bars of first chorus only; not annotated; key B; referred to in text as "Rhythm."

Birkett (1987). Chords identified; complete; annotated; key B^b.

Down Beat (1991). Chords identified; notates first chorus, then middle eight of 2nd spliced chorus; annotated; key B^b.

Spring (1980). Chords identified; complete; annotated; key B.

I Never Knew   October 28 1940   Vintage Jazz Classics VJC 1021.

Spring (1980). Chords identified; complete; annotated.

I Surrender Dear   April 16 1940   Columbia CK 40379.

Ayeroff (1979). Chords identified; complete; annotated.

Berklee School of Music (n.d.). Chords identified; complete; annotated.

Melody Maker (1947). Chords identified; complete; annotated.

Takayanagi (1975). Chords identified; complete; annotated (in Japanese).

Wise (1987a). Chords identified; complete; not annotated.

Lester's Dream   October 28 1940   Vintage Jazz Classics VJC 1021.

Spring (1980). Chords identified; complete; annotated.

Lips Flips   May 1941   Vogue 600135.

Antonich (1982). *Transcribed from Ayeroff (1979);* annotated.

Ayeroff (1979). Chords identified; complete; annotated; key D^b.

Edmonds & Prince (1958). Chords identified; complete; not annotated; key C; final 15 bars of notation are not guitar solo.

Spring (1980). Chords identified; complete; annotated; key D^b.

(———) (1991). *Adapted from Spring (1980);* notates 1st chorus, and 1st 16 bars of 2nd chorus; annotated.

Memories of You   October 23 1939   Vintage Jazz Classics VJC 1021.

Spring (1980). Chords identified; complete; annotated; key E.

(———) (1991). *Transcribed from Spring (1980);* annotated.

Memories of You   November 22 1939   Columbia CK 40379.
(take - A)

Berklee School of Music (n.d.). Chords identified; complete; not annotated; key E^b; first item on page.

Takayanagi (1975). Chords identified; complete; annotated (in Japanese); key E^b; p. 16.

Memories of You   November 22 1939   Columbia CG30779
(take - B)

Berklee School of Music (n.d.). Chords identified; complete; not annotated; key E^b; second item on page.

Spring (1980). Chords identified; complete; annotated; key E^b.

Takayanagi (1975). Chords identified; complete; annotated (in Japanese); key E^b; p. 19.

Memories of You   December 24 1939   Vanguard VCD2-47/48.

Schuller (1989). Chords identified; notates only final 4 bars; annotated; key E^b.

On the Alamo   January 15 1941   Columbia CK 40379.

Bell (n.d.). Chords unidentified; complete; annotated; referred to in text as "Alamo."

Down Beat (1961). Chords identified; complete; annotated.

Polillo (1978). Chords unidentified; complete; annotated (in Italian).

Spring (1980). Chords identified; complete; annotated.

Pagin' the Devil   December 24 1939   Vanguard VCD2-47/48.

Ayeroff (1979). Chords identified; complete; annotated; solo attributed to Eddie Durham in text.

Poor Butterfly   April 10 1940   Columbia CK 40379.

Berklee School of Music (n.d.). Chords identified; complete; not annotated.

Profoundly Blue   February 5 1941   Blue Note B-6505.
Note: First take (i.e. not "Profoundly Blue No. 2").

Antonich (1982). *Transcribed from Down Beat (1961);* annotated.

Berklee School of Music (n.d.). Chords identified; complete; not annotated; key F; referred to in text as "Profoundly Blue #1."

Down Beat (1961). Chords unidentified; complete; annotated; key E^b.

Spaces IV (n.d.). *Similar to transcription in Berklee (n.d.)*

Rose Room   October 2 1939   Columbia CK 40846.

Antonich (1982). *Transcribed from Spaces IV (n.d.);* annotated.

Berklee School of Music (n.d.). Chords identified; complete; not annotated; key A^b.

Down Beat (1943). Chords identified; complete; not annotated; key A^b.

(———) (1950). *Transcribed from Down Beat (1943).*

(———) (1969). *Reproduced from Down Beat (1950).*

Petersen (1979). Chords identified; complete; annotated; key A^b.

Schuller (1989). Chords identified; notates bars 1 to 29 only; annotated; key A^b.

Smith & Tharp (1958). Chords identified; complete; not annotated; key A^b.

Spaces IV (n.d.). *Similar to transcription in Berklee (n.d.).*

Spring (1980). Chords identified; complete; annotated; key A^b.

Tempo (1947). *Reproduced from Down Beat (1943).*

Rose Room   October 9 1939   Vintage Jazz Classics VJC 1021.

Spring (1980). Chords identified; complete; annotated; key B^b.

Royal Garden Blues   November 7 1940   Columbia CK 40846. *(take - 1).*

Takayanagi (1975). Chords identified; complete; annotated (in Japanese).

Royal Garden Blues   November 7 1940   Columbia CG30779. *(alternate take).*

Spring (1980). Chords identified; complete; annotated.

(———) (1991). *Transcribed from Spring (1980);* annotated.

Seven Come Eleven November 22 1939   Columbia CK 40846.

Antonich (1982). *Transcribed from Fox (1964);* annotated.

Berklee School of Music (n.d.). Chords identified; complete; not annotated.

Fox (1964). Chords identified; complete; annotated.

Guitar Extra (1990). Chords identified; complete; annotated.

Jazz Educators Journal (1979). *Reproduced from Fox (1964).*

Spring (1980). Chords identified; complete; annotated.

(———) (1991). *Adapted from Spring (1980);* notates first 24 bars only; annotated.

The Sheik of Araby April 10 1940   CBS CK 40379.

Ayeroff (1979). Chords identified; notates complete solo chorus, omits four bar exchanges; annotated; referred to in text as "The Sheik of Araby (I)."

Berklee School of Music (n.d.). Chords identified; notates complete solo, omits 4-bar exchanges; not annotated.

Takayanagi (1975). Chords identified; complete; annotated (in Japanese).

The Sheik of Araby April 12 1940   Vintage Jazz Classics VJC 1021.

Ayeroff (1979). Chords identified; complete; annotated; referred to in text as "The Sheik of Araby (II)."

Spring (1980). Chords identified; complete; annotated.

(———) (1991). *Adapted from Spring (1980);* notates first 7 bars only; annotated.

Shivers December 20 1939   CBS CK 40379.

Fox (1964). Chords identified; complete; annotated.

Six Appeal June 20 1940   Columbia CK 40846

Antonich (1982). *Transcribed from Fox (1964);* annotated.

Fox (1964). Chords identified; complete; annotated.

Spring (1980). Chords identified; complete; annotated.

Six Appeal June 22 1940 Vintage Jazz Classics VJC 1021

Spring (1980). Chords identified; complete; annotated.

A Smo-o-o-oth One March 13 1941 Columbia CL 652 *(take -1)*.

Berklee School of Music (n.d.). Chords identified; complete; not annotated; key G^b.

Fox (1964). Chords identified; complete; annotated; key G^b.

A Smo-o-o-oth One March 13 1941 Columbia Co 36099 *(take -2)*

Antonich (1982). *Transcribed from Down Beat (1961);* annotated.

Down Beat (1961). Chords identified; complete; annotated; key F.

Solo Flight March 4 1941 Columbia CK 40846. *(take - 1)*

Antonich (1982). *Transcribed from Fox (1964);* (omits non guitar passage, section E).

Berklee School of Music (n.d.). Chords unidentified; follows same pattern as Fox (1964); not annotated; key C.

Fox (1964); Chords identified; complete—from the clarinet solo (E), an earlier section of the solo (almost all of section D) is repeated, and before the final section of the solo is a passage not heard on the record; annotated; key C.

Mairants (1988). Chords identified; notates only the first two 32-bar sections; annotated; key C.

Petersen (1979). Chords identified; complete; annotated; key D^b.

Solo Flight March 4 1941 Columbia CL652 *(take - 2)*

Almo (1978a). Chords identified; complete; annotated; key C.

(———) (1978b). Chords identified; complete; annotated; key C.

(———) (1978c). Chords identified; complete; annotated; key (transposed) A.

(———) (1978d). Chords identified; complete; annotated; key (transposed) D.

Stardust   September 24 1939   Columbia CG30779.

Ayeroff (1979). Chords identified; notates first chorus only; referred to in text as "Stardust (I)."

Bell (n.d.). Chords identified; notates first 12 bars only; annotated; referred to in text as "Dust."

Takayanagi (1975). Chords unidentified; notates first 32 bars only; annotated (in Japanese).

Wise (1987b). *Reproduced from Ayeroff (1979)*.

Stardust   October 2 1939   CBS CK 40379.

Ayeroff (1979). Chords identified; complete; annotated; referred to in text as "Stardust (II)."

Duchossoir (1987). Chords identified; complete; annotated (in French).

Schuller (1989). Chords identified; notates only bars 1 to 25; annotated.

Stardust   October 6 1939   Collectors Classics CC18.

Takayanagi (1975). Chords identified; complete; annotated (in Japanese).

Stompin' at the Savoy   May 12 1941   Vogue 600135.

Schuller (1989). Chords identified; notates only bars 9 to 25 of first chorus of first solo; annotated; untitled.

Spring (1980). Chords identified; complete; annotated.

(———) (1991). *Adapted from Spring (1980);* notates first 5 bars, then first 7 bars of fifth chorus; annotated.

Swing to Bop   May 12 1941   Vogue 600135.

Antonich (1982). *Transcribed from Edmonds & Prince (1958)* (chorus 1 until bridge, transposed to B^b minor), then from *Ayeroff (1979)* (to end); annotated.

Ayeroff (1979). Chords identified; omits first section until first middle eight; annotated; key B^b minor.

Edmonds & Prince (1958). Chords identified; complete; not annotated; key A minor.

Jazz Hot (1972). Chords identified; notates second and third complete choruses only; not annotated; key B^b minor.

Mongan (1983). Chords identified; notates only first three choruses of first solo; annotated; key B^b minor; notates each note as though twice its correct length (e.g. eighth-note as quarter-note).

These Foolish Things   June 20 1940   Columbia CK 40379.

Berklee School of Music (n.d.). Chords identified; complete (includes 4-bar guitar introduction); not annotated.

Smith & Tharp (1958). Chords identified; omits introduction; not annotated.

Till Tom Special   December 31 1939   Vintage Jazz Classics VJC 1021.

Spring (1980). Chords identified; complete; annotated.

Till Tom Special   February 7 1940   Columbia CK 40846.

Antonich (1982). *Transcribed from Fox (1964);* annotated.

Fox (1964). Chords identified; complete; annotated.

Spring (1980). Chords identified; complete; annotated.

Up on Teddy's Hill   May 8 1941   Vogue 600135.

Antonich (1982). *Transcribed from Edmonds & Prince (1958);* (first section until 2 bars before first bridge, transposed to D^b), then from *Ayeroff (1979),* to end; annotated.

Ayeroff (1979). Chords identified; omits first 10 bars of solo; annotated; key D^b.

Edmonds & Prince (1958). Chords identified; complete; not annotated; key C.

Feather (1961). Chords identified; notated from bar 17 to end of third chorus; annotated; key D^b.

Matzner & Wasserberger (1969). *Similar to transcription in Feather (1961);* annotated.

Spring (1980). Chords identified; complete; annotated; key D^b.

(———) (1991). *Adapted from Spring (1980);* notates bar 8 to 17 of first chorus, then bars 19 to end of 3rd chorus, and bars 12 to 17 of fourth chorus; annotated.

Waitin' for Benny   March 13 1941   Columbia CK 40846.

Bell (n.d.). Chords unidentified; notates 12 bars from bar 14 of audible start of solo; not annotated; referred to in text as "Wait'n."

Wholly Cats   October 28 1940   Vintage Jazz Classics VJC 1021.

Spring (1980). Chords identified; complete; annotated.

(———) (1991). *Adapted from Spring (1980);* notates bars 2 to end of second chorus, and entire second chorus; annotated.

Wholly Cats   November 7 1940   Columbia CL652.
(take -1)

Berklee School of Music (n.d.). Chords identified; complete; not annotated.

Fox (1964). Chords identified; complete; annotated.

Wholly Cats   November 7 1940   Columbia CG30779.
(take - 3)

Spring (1980). Chords identified; complete; annotated.

(———) (1991). *Transcribed from Spring (1980);* annotated.

Wholly Cats   November 7 1940   Columbia CG30779.
(take - 4)

Spring (1980). Chords identified; complete; annotated.

(———) (1991). *Adapted from Spring (1980);* notates only first chorus; annotated.

Wholly Cats   November 19 1940   Vintage Jazz Classics VJC 1021.

Spring (1980). Chords identified; complete; annotated.

(———) (1991). *Transcribed from Spring (1980);* annotated.

Wholly Cats   April 7 1941   Jazz Archives JA-23.

Spring (1980). Chords identified; complete; annotated.

(———) (1991). Adapted from Spring (1980); notates first chorus only; annotated.

COMMENTS ON NOTATIONS OF CHRISTIAN PERFORMANCES

Boukas (1977) does not contain any Christian notations, although Voigt (1978) indicates that it does.

An important research question concerns the proportion of Christian's solo performances which have been notated and published. To assess this, the author counted all solo passages that have been issued on commercial recordings, defining "solo passages" to include solo choruses, introductions, obbligatos, and accompaniments. Evensmo's (c. 1976) solography was used as a database, updated to include certain more recent issues. This survey indicated a total of 142 solo passages, as defined above. Of these, published transcriptions are available for 78, just 55 percent.

Not included in this article is a cross-referenced index of all known solos, annotated to show sources of published notations and indicating solos that remain untranscribed. Such an index is useful and has been prepared by the author.

DISCUSSION

In his analysis of Charlie Parker's technique, Owens (1974, p. 271) suggests that the literature of jazz contains little technical discussion of the style of individual performers. For example, it is difficult, Owens notes, to find any documentation of the favorite melodic phrases used by a jazz soloist. Similarly, Spring (1980) observed that there had been no detailed study of the style of Charlie Christian. Certainly there are a number of brief discussions of his improvisational style, including the sleeve notes by Al Avakian and Bob Prince on Columbia CL652, annotations to the transcriptions in Fox (1964), an interesting analysis (mainly of the rhythmic features) of the "Seven Come Eleven" solo by Collier (1981) (but without any notations), and Schuller's (1989) recent analysis. Spring (1980) provides the first extended study of Christian, including the largest single collection of solo transcriptions.

The body of transcriptions identified here is a resource, which may save much of the laborious task of transcribing for future research, and should serve as the basis for further studies of his technique. Some 233 solo notations, and 49 published sources have been identified here. One of the major problems in this task has been in locating material, most of which is published in books or collections of transcriptions and thus cannot be found by computerized literature searches or in most catalogues. This is clearly a significant issue for information scientists and librarians.

Although this study focuses on *published* notations, we should note that Leo Valdes of El Paso, Texas, has transcribed nearly all Charlie Christian's solos, riffs, and introductions. Also, Patrick Zemb of Lorient, France, has notated the bulk of Christian's recorded legacy.

ADDITIONAL REFERENCES

Boukas, R. (1977). *Jazz Riffs for Guitar.* New York: Amsco.

Callis, J. (1978). *Charlie Christian 1939–1941: A Discography.* London: Tony Middleton.

Collier, J. L. (1978). *The Making of Jazz.* Boston: Houghton Mifflin.

Downs, C. G. (1986, Jan.). "Charlie Christian: A guide to published solo transcriptions." *Names & Numbers, 3,* pp. 15–17.

Downs, C. G. (1989). "An Annotated Bibliography of Eric Dolphy Solo Transcriptions." *Jazz Research/Jazzforschung, 21,* pp. 49–54.

Evensmo, J. (c. 1976). *The Guitars of Charlie Christian, Robert Normann, Oscar Aleman.* Oslo: Author.

Gridley, M. C. (1978) *Jazz Styles.* (1st Ed.) Englewood Cliffs: Prentice-Hall.

Jazz Hot (1972, May). "Joe Viera: Bibliographie," p. 81.

Koger, T. S. (1985). "Fifty years of Down Beat solo jazz transcriptions: A register." *Black Music Research Journal,* pp. 43–79.

Owens, T. (1974). *Charlie Parker: Techniques of Improvisation.* Ph.D Dissertation, University of California.

Summerfield, M. J. (1978). *Jazz Guitar: Its Evolution and its Players*. Ashley Mark. Gateshead, England.
Voigt, J. (1978). *Jazz Music in Print*. (2nd ed.). Hornpipe Music. Boston.

COMPACT DISCS

1941 Historical Performances. Vogue 600135.
The Benny Goodman Sextet 1939–1941 Featuring Charlie Christian. Columbia CK 40379.
Charlie Christian: The Genius of the Electric Guitar. Columbia CK 40846.
Solo Flight. Vintage Jazz Classics VJC 1021.
Spirituals to Swing. Vanguard VCD2-47/48.

LP RECORDS

The Alternate Goodman: Vol. II. Nostalgia NOST 7610.
B.G., His Stars and His Guests. Queen-disc Q-016.
Charlie Christian with the Benny Goodman Sextet and Orchestra. Columbia CL652.
Charlie Christian with Benny Goodman and the Sextet (1939–1941). Jazz Archives JA-23.
Jazz Classics: Celestial Express. Blue Note B-6505.
The Rehearsal Sessions: Benny Goodman 1940. JazzDocument va-7997.
Solo Flight—The Genius of Charlie Christian. Columbia CG30779.

ACKNOWLEDGEMENTS

I am grateful to the following people who have been most helpful in supplying information and giving access to certain publications: Judith Barnes, Christopher Beeston, Thierry Bruneau, Gary Carner, Lubomír Dorůžka, Mark Gridley, Nancy Huntress, Wolfram Knauer, Elisabeth Kolleritsch, John Kuzmich Jr., Ivor Mairants, Thomas Owens, Jack Petersen, Howard Spring, Maurice Summerfield, Mike Sutcliffe, Fred Turco, Leo Valdes, Martin Williams, and Patrick Zemb. In particular, I am indebted to Gail L.

Freunsch and the Music Specialist staff of The Library of Congress for their patient assistance and to the staff of Reading Public Libraries for their continued help.

Also I am grateful to my reviewers and to Leo Valdes for their helpful comments and suggestions on earlier drafts of the paper. For her tolerance and support, I am indebted to Maureen Stallard.

FURTHER INFORMATION

I should be most grateful for information on any other published solos not listed in this paper. Please contact me with any details which you have available: 2 Ennerdale Road, Reading, Berks, England RG2 7HH.

CHARLIE CHRISTIAN, BEBOP, AND THE RECORDINGS AT MINTON'S

By Jonathan Finkelman

Charlie Christian (1916–1942) has been acknowledged by his contemporaries as well as by jazz historians as a pivotal figure in the formation of the music that came to be known as "bebop." Yet the fact that he did not live to see the style come into its first maturity, and the fact that nearly his entire recorded legacy lies within the context of Benny Goodman's group (one of the foremost "swing" bands of the time), make it difficult to assess fully the nature and extent of his contribution.

While Christian's recordings with Goodman reveal a tremendously creative and innovative talent, the circumstances under which Christian recorded were severely restrictive. Of the forty or so studio sides on which he played solos with Goodman (not including alternate and composite takes), Christian is given as much as a full chorus on only about half of them, and he takes more than one chorus only on fast 12-bar blues numbers (where he is usually given two choruses). The lone exception is "Solo Flight," a big band recording which features Christian almost all the way through but which is so dense in orchestration that he does not really get a chance to "stretch out." In the "live" airchecks that survive, the soloing formats generally follow those of the studio recordings, with little or no additional solo space added, even in the small group recordings.

As an antidote to this confining situation, Christian began participating regularly in after-hours sessions at Harlem clubs, most notably Minton's, on West 118th Street, and Clark Monroe's Uptown House on West 133rd Street. Minton's and Monroe's were two of the most important venues where experimentation by younger musicians such as Thelonious Monk, Kenny Clarke, Dizzy Gillespie, and Charlie Parker led to the formation of bebop. Jerry Newman, a young jazz enthusiast who recorded Christian and many others on his portable disc recorder in New York in 1941, recalls:

> He [Christian] would bring his guitar and amplifier uptown to sit in at Minton's, where he was treated as a "maestro." Charlie never disappointed his listeners, and if he knew that people were paying attention he really improvised. . . . the paying customers paid tribute by standing still in front of the stand and just listening while Charlie played the same exciting jazz that was driving the whole Goodman band.[1]

Christian began spending more and more time at Minton's, eventually leaving a spare amplifier there so that he could travel uptown quickly and easily after a night with Goodman.[2]

There exist six known recordings of Charlie Christian made by Newman at Minton's and Monroe's (a selected discography is appended to this article.) They capture Christian in loose, after-hours jam sessions far removed from the restrictions of the Goodman band. Three of them feature bop innovators Monk and Clarke, who, along with trumpeter Joe Guy and bassist Nick Fenton, comprised the house band at Minton's. Recorded in May 1941, these are also among the last recordings Christian made. Gunther Schuller describes them as marking "a new stylistic departure" for Christian.[3]

For this essay, I have chosen to focus on two of the Minton's recordings, "Charlie's Choice" (based on the chords of "Topsy" and also issued as "Swing to Bop") and "Stompin' at the Savoy." These recordings feature the most extended Christian solos on record and also represent some of his greatest, most exciting playing.

TRAITS AND INFLUENCES

Ross Russell, in his article "Bebop," writes: "Christian's playing . . . actually foreshadowed bebop line phrasing and harmony."[4] Such assertions are common in jazz histories but are rarely substantiated beyond such general descriptive terms. Hesitancy to go beyond this point in analysis is understandable, since it is difficult to state precisely *how* Christian's playing "foreshadowed bebop." While mature swing and mature bebop are easily distinguishable and the differences between them relatively easily described, a transitional figure like Christian tends to exemplify the commonality and continuity between the styles more than their radical differences (and both commonality and radical differences exist at the same time). Through studying these solos, I hope to be able to describe more precisely what has generally been perceived as Christian's shift towards the emerging bop style. In order to provide a frame of reference for discussion of the recordings at Minton's, it may be helpful to discuss, in a general way, some of Christian's stylistic traits and influences.

Charlie Christian, growing up in the musically rich and varied environment of Oklahoma City, was exposed to many kinds of music, including jazz, southwestern blues, country, western swing, and classical, and he absorbed many of these influences.[5] When asked about specific early musical models, Christian never named any particular musician,[6] but there can be little doubt that one of the most important was Lester Young, whom Christian was said to have heard in Oklahoma City when Young passed through there in 1929 and 1931.[7] In attempting to define Christian's style, particularly in terms of his "modernist" tendencies, it is probably best to begin by looking at Young's influence on Christian. Lewis Porter, in his study of Young, thoroughly documents many aspects of Young's style. His analysis warrants close inspection as it relates to Christian's style.

One important component which defines a player's style is what Porter calls "formulas:"

> A formula—called a "lick" by jazz musicians—is a brief idea that is functional rather than compositional. It is, for example, a pattern that fits a particular chord, chord sequence, or cadence. Formulas recur in similar contexts regardless of the song.[8]

A player's collection of formulas is in large part what makes his style unique and recognizable. At the same time, excessive reliance on those formulas contribute to routine and predictable playing. Several of the formulas cited by Porter as characteristic of Young are also found frequently in Christian's playing.

Of course, Christian used many other formulas which were very much his own. As Schuller points out, Christian's "recurrent use of formulaic motivic figures"[9] are a central component of his style, which would become monotonous without frequent variations and alternating nonformulaic passages. In some of Christian's Goodman recordings (for example, "Shivers" and "Six Appeal"), his use of formulas is so extensive that his playing borders on predictability.

Porter makes other observations about Young's style which bear comparison to Christian's. He points out Young's frequent use of the major sixth scale degree in both major and minor keys.[10] Although the sixth was commonly used in the Swing Era, both Young and Christian used it extensively, often as a repeated, stressed note. A favorite device employed by Young to emphasize the sixth was the repetition of the note using alternate fingerings to vary its timbre.[11] Christian also often accentuated the sixth scale degree, sometimes emulating Young's technique and effect by playing the same note on adjacent strings. According to Porter, Young did not use many ninths in his solos until after 1942.[12] In contrast, Christian used the ninth and other higher chord tones throughout his entire recording career, often as stressed notes.

Porter cites Young's penchant for "long, flowing eighth-note lines."[13] Christian adopted this characteristic and extended it further, as we shall see later. Christian was also one of the first players to incorporate Young's approach to the beat (which divided the quarter note between two eighth notes more evenly than was the norm) into his style. If anything, Christian's eighth notes were sometimes *more* even than Young's. As Schuller suggests, Christian may also have been influenced in this regard by the single-string guitar soloists (such as Leon McAuliffe) of the western swing bands.[14]

Asymmetrical phrasing is another significant feature of Young's style. "Lester's musical thought flowed, not within the accepted confines of two- or four-bar sections, but more freely," writes Ross Russell.[15] Christian's playing exhibits a similar freedom, which developed further as his style evolved.

Then there is the matter of sound. Christian's sound— cool, vibratoless, relaxed, detached (compare it to the fiery, passionate sound of Django Reinhartdt)—is a perfect parallel to Young's distinctive voice on the tenor saxophone. It is perhaps easiest to hear the link between Young and Christian in the area of pure sound.

Many of the above characteristics shared by Young and Christian are those often cited by those who view Young as a forerunner of the bop style: the introduction of stressed nonchord tones or higher chord intervals, the use of relatively even eighth notes, extended eighth-note passages, asymmetrical phrasing, and reduced vibrato. We have seen how Christian adapted these traits and in some cases extended them further. Like Young, when Christian began recording, his style was already fully formed and mature. Since we do not have documentation of his early development, we can only guess at the precise nature of Young's or others' influence. But in terms of Christian's connection to bebop, Young's influence must be considered the most important.

THE MINTON RECORDINGS

I will next examine the recordings at Minton's in the context of the larger body of Christian's recorded work in order to discover how he further developed these "modernistic" tendencies.

From his earliest recorded solos, Christian tended to construct longer, more complex lines over the B section of an AABA 32-bar song form while playing simpler figures over the A sections. Christian's solo on "Seven Come Eleven," recorded November 22, 1939, provides a good early example of this tendency. The A sections consist mainly of short, blues-inflected phrases which are largely diatonic or in the "blues pentatonic" mode. In the bridge (Example 1), Christian plays longer, more flowing eighth-note lines which demonstrate many of the hallmarks of Christian's style: accented chromatic passing tones, harmonic anticipations, and extensive use of upper-chord tones (sometimes dispensing with the root altogether).

Example 1: Seven Come Eleven, mm. 16–25

These characteristics appear more extensively in the bridge sections of "Stompin' at the Savoy" and "Charlie's Choice." For example, while the "Seven Come Eleven" bridge does contain long eighth-note runs, the phrases correspond more or less to the harmonic rhythm; that is, Christian plays two-measure phrases (enlivened by harmonic anticipations) which relate to each chord. This type of phrasing is typical of his playing style with Goodman. In contrast, the first bridge of "Stompin' at the Savoy" consists of an almost unbroken flow of eighth notes (see Example 2). This continuity is achieved by an intensified use of chromatic passing tones in conjunction with a profusion of harmonic anticipations. As a result, the melodic line seems to "float" over the chords. Also, the consistent use of harmonic anticipation leads to a heightened sense of tension between the improvised line and the underlying harmony.

Example 2: Stompin' at the Savoy (1st solo) mm. 17–24

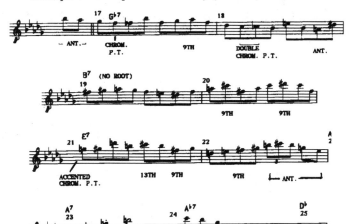

In addition to actual anticipations of chord changes, Christian plays notes which can be heard as functioning in two harmonic areas simultaneously. For example, the B and C# in the triplet figure on the third beat of m. 22 in Example 2 at first sound like the fifth and sixth (or thirteenth) degrees of E. The G-natural which follows on the fourth beat antici-pates the A7 in m. 23. Then in m. 23, the notes of the last half of m. 22 are repeated over the A7 harmony, but now clearly arpeggiating a rootless A9 chord. Thus, in retrospect, we hear the B and C# in m. 22 as the third and ninth of the approaching A7 chord.

The omission of the root (or its placement on a weak part of the beat) during the bridge is pervasive throughout these solos and is another difference between them and Christian's recordings with Goodman. A survey of the bridges of Christian's solos with Goodman reveals that, while Christian often omits the root of a chord or plays it only on the weak part of a beat, many other times he comes down firmly and repeatedly on the root. Emphasis of the root in dominant seventh progressions is much rarer in the Minton's solos, contributing to their feeling of increased harmonic freedom.

Other harmonic devices which appear in earlier solos are expanded upon. In the bridge of "I Found a New Baby" (master take from January 15, 1941), Christian plays the figure in Example 3.

Example 3: I Found a New Baby, mm. 21–23

Here, Christian uses an accented chromatic passing tone (G^b) in conjunction with the following D to imply a momentary interpolation of D-major, the dominant of the underlying chord, which is then immediately "resolved" to G7 by the tritone F-B. This device, used occasionally in Christian's earlier recordings, appears extensively throughout "Charlie's Choice" and "Stompin' at the Savoy." In Example 4, Christian uses this idea to further intensify the sense of increased harmonic activity. Here, he plays three consecutive tritones, implying two descending parallel chromatic lines (A^b—G—G^b; D—D^b—C) which outline the progression B^b7—E^b7—A^b7 (with an eighth-note harmonic anticipation of A^b7).

Example 4: Charlie's Choice (1st solo, 4th chorus), mm. 20–21

In general, chromatic lines appear more frequently in the Minton's recordings than they do previously. The use of tritones to connect dominant seventh chords also becomes more common.

There is, however, another set of recordings in which Christian's playing at times approaches the harmonic and rhythmic adventurousness of the recordings at Minton's. Significantly, these recordings, made with a pickup group in Minneapolis in 1939 or 1940 (the date is disputed),[16] also take place in an informal setting outside of the context of the Goodman band. Here, Christian plays extended solos on "I Got Rhythm," "Stardust," and "Tea for Two." Although Christian's approach to the bridge sections on these recordings is generally comparable to his playing on "Seven Come Eleven" (largely consisting of two-measure phrases which closely follow the underlying harmony), on "I Got Rhythm" he plays one extraordinary bridge (Example 5) which is the equal of any on the Minton's recordings in terms of innovative harmony and phrasing.

Example 5: I Got Rhythm (3rd solo), mm. 17–25

Additionally, on "Tea for Two," Christian plays a three-against-four whole-tone run in augmented triads (Example

6) that is remarkably similar to a Dizzy Gillespie formula which first appears on another 1941 Minton's recording.

Example 6: Tea for Two (last solo), mm. 17–20

Dizzy Gillespie: Kerouac (1941) (2nd solo), mm. 13–15

This pattern was later incorporated into the 1946 Gillespie big band arrangement of "One Bass Hit."

Many motives and formulas which appear in earlier solos recur throughout the Minton's recordings. In some cases, Christian developed them further. Beginning at m.10 of his first solo on "Charlie's Choice," Christian plays a repeated three-note figure. This figure also appeared at the beginning of Christian's solo on the alternate take of "I've Found a New Baby," though here he extends it much further. As he repeats the figure, he shifts its placement, resulting in occasional accented passing tones. The figure is extended in mm. 17–18 and mm. 19–20, and finally expanded further into an even longer figure in mm. 21–23. Christian relates every figure in the entire complex of phrases from m.10 through m.23 by ending each one on an off-beat, accented D^b. Here Christian has created a unified yet varied statement which arises out of the simplest of materials.

Another Christian formula which is transformed on the Minton's recordings is a rootless arpeggiation of a dominant thirteenth chord (Example 7).

Example 7: I Found a New Baby (1/15/41—alternate take), m. 32

Christian plays variations of this formula several times in "Charlie's Choice," each time over the final chord of the bridge (always in a less symmetrical way than in Example 7). In Christian's first use of the figure (Example 8), he places it rhythmically in such a way that he creates a two-beat anticipation of the dominant seventh chord, while the thirteenth, the most harmonically "distant" note, lands on the downbeat of the measure in which the chord actually appears.

Example 8: Charlie's Choice (1st solo, 1st full chorus), m. 23

The next time the figure occurs (Example 9), Christian begins it half a beat later, embellishing it with a descending chromatic run, and ending it with a striking and unusual exposed major seventh leap up to the thirteenth, an uncharacteristic turn for Christian or any other swing player.

Example 9: Charlie's Choice (1st solo, 3rd chorus), m. 24

Christian evidently liked this variation, for he repeats it note for note in the following bridge.

STRUCTURAL ARTICULATION

Due to the sheer length of Christian's solos, we can hear in these recordings an approach to form that could only be hinted at in the Goodman recordings. (Since Christian rarely played more than one chorus with Goodman, he obviously didn't get much of a chance to experiment with form.) On the Minton's recordings, Christian brings the aforementioned contrast between A and B sections of a 32-bar form into even sharper relief and uses it over the course of several choruses to build an effective dramatic structure. Saxophonist James Moody recalls hearing Christian at Minton's:

> I used to remember that tune "Savoy." They used to play it, and I remember Charlie Christian would be playing on it, and he'd start playing, and on the outside of it he would just be going along slowly, and as soon as he came to the difficult part, the bridge, he would tear it up, he would dive in. Now I know that was intentional, it was beautiful.[17]

The third chorus of Christian's second solo on "Charlie's Choice" provides a striking example of this type of structural articulation. Christian repeats a single spare, riff-like motive throughout the A section. This contrasts sharply with the following bridge, which consists of a highly chromatic exploration of the chord changes in continuous eighth notes. The continual contrast between A and B sections provides an overarching structure which builds anticipation and tension through the A sections and finds release in the outbursts of eighth notes at the bridges.

The blurring of form is another characteristic which distinguishes bop from swing. On a localized scale, Christian achieves this through the increased use of harmonic anticipations. On a larger scale, Christian sometimes connects one chorus with another by playing across the "seam" between two choruses (for example, mm. 30–34 of "Stompin' at the Savoy" and mm. 15–18 of "Charlie's Choice").

RHYTHMIC VITALITY

On the Minton's recordings, Christian exhibits a new, aggressive approach to the beat which derives from Young's propulsive, streamlined style, but is more relentless and driving and seems to look forward to the rapid-fire eighth-note feel of bop. Additionally, Christian connects his eighth notes more fluidly, contributing to the sense of forward momentum. This increased legato is also discernible on some of Christian's later Goodman sessions, notably the privately issued March 13, 1941, rehearsal (which fortuitously caught the Goodman sextet warming up while waiting for the leader to arrive).

An important factor in the increased rhythmic vitality of Christian's playing on the Minton's recordings is the presence of Kenny Clarke. Clarke is generally acknowledged to be the founder of bop drumming, and his playing here provides a fascinating glimpse of his style at a transitional stage. In his dissertation on jazz drumming, Theodore Brown includes an extended discussion of Clarke's playing on "Charlie's Choice." According to Brown, Clarke uses a combination of swing and bop techniques, sometimes playing the bass drum on all four beats in the swing style, and at other times using the bass drum for off-beat punctuations (also known as dropping "bombs").[18]

Although Clarke displays these modern tendencies throughout the recordings, his playing with Christian is even more interactive than with the other soloists, as Brown acknowledges:

> It is important to note that Clarke's playing consistently depends upon the ideas presented by Christian, for the interaction between soloist and drummer is an essential part of bop. This type of interaction . . . is an indication of the intense concentration Clarke applied to his playing.[11]

The close rapport between guitar and drums can be heard as Clarke takes up Christian's rhythmic motives and incorporates them into his accompaniment. At one point, this give-and-take results in Clarke and Christian playing the same figure simultaneously (Example 10).[20]

Example 10: Charlie's Choice, last 3 mm. of 1st chorus
and mm. 1–3 of 2nd chorus

The interaction between Clarke and Christian is one of the most exciting aspects of the Minton's recordings and, as Brown indicates, is an important step towards a bop conception. Clarke's role as rhythmic catalyst is crucial, particularly in the increased incidence of asymmetrical phrasing in Christian's solos.

In sum, Christian's playing on the Minton's recordings does not represent a dramatic stylistic departure from the rest of his recorded output. Rather, certain tendencies that were already present are developed more fully. The formulas and patterns that help to define Christian's style are sill there, but in the freer atmosphere of Minton's, and spurred on by the incipient bop rhythm section of Clarke, Monk, and Fenton, they begin to undergo a transformation.

Christian's eighth-note lines become even more elongated, incorporating a greater degree of chromaticism than before. There is an increased use of harmonic anticipations, particularly in the use of tritones to anticipate dominant seventh chords. Tritones are also used to imply interpolated dominant seventh chords. At the same time, a further de-emphasis of the root in dominant seventh progressions contributes to a greater sense of harmonic freedom. Asymmetry is increased through harmonic anticipations and by the blurring of the divisions between choruses. Rhythmically, Christian's eighth notes become more connected, resulting in a more dynamic sense of swing. The presence of Clarke provides a new rhythmic impetus, and the interplay between Clarke and Christian prefigures the spontaneous interaction between soloist and drummer that is typical of bop.

Although many important elements of mature bop are not in place here (for example, chord substitutions, phrasing and syntax, double-time runs), the Minton's recordings provide ample evidence of a bop sensibility emerging from Christian's established style.

NOTES

1. Jerry Newman, liner notes to *The Charlie Christian Memorial Album* (Vox VSP 302).
2. Rudi Blesh, *Combo USA* (Philadelphia: Chilton, 1971), p. 180.
3. Gunther Schuller, *The Swing Era* (New York: Oxford University Press, 1989), p. 577.
4. Ross Russell, "Bebop," in Martin Williams, ed., *The Art of Jazz: Essays on the Nature and Development of Jazz* (New York: Oxford University Press, 1959), p. 193.
5. Schuller, p. 563.
6. Ibid., p. 566.
7. Blesh, p. 171.
8. Lewis Porter, *Lester Young* (Boston: G. K. Hall, 1985), p. 57.
9. Schuller, p. 573.
10. Porter, p. 66.
11. Ibid., p. 68.
12. Ibid., p. 66.
13. Ibid., p. 87.
14. Schuller, p. 564.
15. Russell, p. 209.
16. Bruyninckx (p. C315) dates these sessions "early March 1940," while Jan Evensmo (p. CC3) dates them as either from September 24, 1939, (a date "which has turned up recently") or early March 1940. John Callis (p. 2) leans toward the 1939 date, as Goodman had been in St. Paul the night before, but

says the date is not certain. Schuller (p. 576) does not mention a date, but implies a later date, associating these sessions with the Minton's recordings stylistically.

17. Ira Gitler, *Swing to Bop* (New York: Oxford University Press, 1985), p. 41.
18. Theodore Dennis Brown, "A History and Analysis of Jazz Drumming to 1942." (Ph.D. dissertation, University of Michigan, 1976), p. 489.
19. Ibid., p. 490.
20. Ibid., p. 492.

BIBLIOGRAPHY

Ayeroff, Stan, ed. *Charlie Christian.* Jazz Masters Series. New York: Amsco, 1979 [transcribed solos].

Blesh, Rudi. *Combo USA.* Philadelphia: Chilton, 1971.

Brown, Theodore Dennis. "A History and Analysis of Jazz Drumming to 1942." Ph.D. dissertation, University of Michigan, 1976.

Bruyninckx, W. *Sixty Years of Recorded Jazz, 1917–1977.* Issued in looseleaf form. Belgium: various dates.

Callis, John. *Charlie Christian 1939–41.* Lewisham, London: Middleton, 1977 [discography].

Connor, D. Russell and Warren Hicks. *Benny Goodman on the Record.* New Rochelle, N.Y.: Arlington House, 1969.

DeVeaux, Scott Knowles. "Jazz in Transition: Coleman Hawkins and Howard McGhee 1935–1945." Ph.D. dissertation, University of California at Berkeley, 1985.

Evensmo, Jan. *The Guitars of Charlie Christian, Robert Norman, Oscar Aleman (in Europe).* Jazz Solography Series, no. 4. Oslo: Jan Evensmo, n.d.

Feather, Leonard. *From Satchmo to Miles.* New York: Stein & Day, 1972.

Fox, Dan, ed. *The Art of the Jazz Guitar: Charlie Christian.* New York: Regent Music, 1964 [transcribed solos].

Gitler, Ira. *Swing to Bop.* New York: Oxford University Press, 1985.

Hennessey, Mike. *Klook: The Story of Kenny Clarke.* New York: Quartet Books, 1990.

McKinney, John Francis. "The Pedagogy of Lennie Tristano." Ph.D. dissertation, Farleigh Dickinson University, 1978.

Morgan, Alun and Raymond Horricks. *Modern Jazz: a Survey of Developments Since 1939.* London: Victor Gollancz, 1956.

Porter, Lewis. *Lester Young.* Boston: G. K. Hall, 1985.

Russell, Ross. "Bebop." *The Art of Jazz: Essays on the Nature and Development of Jazz.* Edited by Martin Williams. New York: Oxford University Press, 1959, pp. 187–214.

Schuller, Gunther. *The Swing Era.* New York: Oxford University Press, 1989.

Shapiro, Nat and Nat Hentoff, eds. *Hear Me Talkin' To Ya.* 1955. Reprint: New York: Dover Publications, 1966.

Spring, Howard. "The Use of Formulas in the Improvisations of Charlie Christian." *Jazzforschung* 22 (1990): 11–52.

Stone, Rick, ed. "Stompin' at the Savoy." Unpublished manuscript [transcribed solo].

Strunk, Steven. "The Harmony of Early Bop—A Layered Approach." *Journal of Jazz Studies* 6 (1979): 4–53.

Wang, Richard. "Jazz Circa 1945—A Confluence of Styles." *Musical Quarterly* 59 (1973): 531–546.

SELECTED DISCOGRAPHY

I have tried to list the most recent issues available. The long-playing records may be out of print. Most of the cited recordings have been available on other issues.

Christian, Charlie. *Charlie Christian.* Vols. 1 and 2. Masters of Jazz 3024, 3029 (CD), 1939–1941.

———. *Charlie Christian Live 1939–1941.* Music Memoria 34009 (CD).

———. *Genius of the Electric Guitar.* Sony/CBS 40846 (CD), 1939–1941.

———. *Live Sessions at Minton's.* Accord Jazz 550012 (CD), 1941.

———. *Solo Flight: Charlie Christian with the Benny Goodman Sextet.* Vintage Jazz Classics VJC-1021-2 (CD), 1939–1941.

Goodman, Benny. *The Un-heard Benny Goodman.* Blu-Disc T1006 (LP), 1941. Contains rehearsal of March 13, 1941.

Guy, Joe, and Oran "Hot Lips" Page. *Joe Guy and Hot Lips Page: Trumpet Battle at Minton's.* Xanadu 107 (LP), 1941. Contains one title, "Rhythm-a-ning," with Christian.

LATIN JAZZ, AFRO-CUBAN JAZZ OR JUST PLAIN OL' JAZZ?

By Vernon W. Boggs

In a recent issue of *Latin Beat* magazine, Max Salazar, the writer, mildly rebuked bandleader Ray Barretto for implying that Afro-Cuban jazz does not exist. Salazar noted that Barretto asserted that just because some musicians have played jazz with an accompanying Afro-Cuban rhythm section does not mean that it is no longer purely jazz.[1] To understand this debate fully, we must first conceptualize it musically and then review its history to determine whether the term *Afro-Cuban/Latin jazz* is a misnomer or an accurate statement.

Perhaps the most appropriate musical conceptualization for this genre of music is the one provided by Fernando Ortiz between 1952 and 1956 in his many discussions of Afro-Cuban music: *musical transculturation*.

> . . . The Negro's music first passes on to the dances of the lowest classes of the whites . . . and the *musical transculturation* is begun. Little by little, the exotic dances pass on, undoubtedly with readjustments, to the customs of the underworld . . . and the poor who live together with the Negroes . . .; there comes a time in which, now generalized and naturalized for the common people, the folk, the new dances . . . continue climbing . . . to the highest levels of society . . . (italics added).[2]

Although his emphasis is seemingly on Afro-Cuban dances, Ortiz was addressing the bicultural nature of all Afro-Cuban music. He argued that Cuban popular music stemmed from the "fusion" of Spanish and African roots. In essence, his argument suggests that musical "purity" would not explain

Afro-Cuban musical traditions. This notation of "purity" lies implicitly at the center of the Salazar v. Barretto debate. Therefore, we must turn our attention to the American history of Latin jazz in order to draw an informed conclusion about its nature.

More than thirty years ago, Marshall Stearns's *The Story of Jazz* devoted one chapter to "Afro-Cuban Music":

> The powerful and largely rhythmic influence of Afro-Cuban music on jazz . . . reached a peak in the winter of 1947 when bandleader Dizzy Gillespie hired the Cuban drummer, Chano Pozo, for a Town Hall concert. . . .[3]

Stearns added that Cuban music had had a tremendous influence on American jazz since the late nineteenth century, but "the final blending proceeded at different speeds, in different places, and at different times".

The blending of jazz and Afro-Cuban rhythms was not stable until the 1940s:

> Perhaps the most stable pattern in this blending of blends was established by Machito and his Afro-Cubans. Organized in 1940, this band slowly but surely assimilated the jazz idiom—they grew up in the Cuban idiom—and created a new blend of both. . . . The key to the pattern was Mario Bauza, Machito's brother-in-law, who organized the band, arranged the music, and played lead trumpet.[4]

Stearns felt that, with the exception of Tito Puente's and Machito's efforts, much of what passed for Afro-Cuban jazz was an imperfect blending of two musical genres. But he added:

> . . . Afro-Cuban music brought a large and enthusiastic audience along with it in the process of blending with jazz . . . and it made many jazz [fans convert] to Latin music. The demand was genuine, the support consistent, and the combination self-propelled.[5]

John Storm Roberts further clarified the impact of Cuban music on American jazz:

> . . . the first half of the 1940s saw Latin music become
> an established style and influence within mass popular
> music. During the second half of the decade, two major
> creative movements developed that were to reach
> maturity during the 1950s. One—the mambo—
> belonged to the central core of U.S. Latin music, the
> other—Afro-Cuban jazz, or Cubop—was a fusion style;
> but both were extremely tightly intertwined, especially
> during the 1940s.
>
> Though its impact was sudden and dramatic, Cubop
> did not spring fully armed from anybody's head. It was
> one flowering of a fusion process that had been going on
> ever since the days of the habañera, and has continued
> ever since. Many of the swing bands of the early 1940s
> had dabbled in jazz-Latin fusion. Though most of the
> these were fairly superficial, they were also increasingly
> Latin. . . .[6]

Roberts argued that many of the efforts to "marry" Cuban
rhythmic patterns with jazz harmonies did not work out too
well at first despite the common roots of the two. But in time,
they were successfully merged.

> Though much of the Latin music of the 1940s was
> frankly silly, it was also a decade of enormous creativ-
> ity. Above all, it was the first decade in which Latin
> elements began to move below the surface of U.S.
> music, so to speak, and establish themselves as an
> integral part of it. . . .[7]

Another informed source, Dizzy Gillespie, stated that
collaboration with Chano Pozo "was really the fusion
between Afro-Cuban music and jazz." This required effort
on the part of composers and arrangers because their time
signatures were different, but, more importantly, phrasing
and rhythm were the areas needing great change. And
according to bandleader Alberto Socarras, Gillespie accomplished just that:

> Dizzy did something with the Cuban and the jazz music
> . . . with Chano Pozo . . . called "Manteca." . . . That
> was very effective. And right after that, a whole lot of

American arrangers or orchestra leaders started having bongos, conga drums, [playing] the same rhythm that Cubans have, together with jazz. . . . I mean [making] improvement[s] on the rhythmically poor American music . . . [by] adding the best of the conga drums and things [which] added rhythmically to American music.[8]

This was only one of the first explicit musical fusions between the United States and Cuba. Other Gillespie-led compositions like "Cubano Be, Cubano Bop," "A Night in Tunisia," and "Guarachi Guaro" became models for emulation. Within four decades, this musical fusion had become widely disseminated throughout the world.

The Afro-Cuban/Afro-American musical collaborations among Bauza, Gillespie, Machito, and Pozo left an indelible imprint on Western Europe. When Pozo was murdered, Sabu Martinez, a Puerto Rican percussionist, was selected to replace him. Sabu eventually relocated to Stockholm and, with the help of Wilfredo Stephenson, established "Hot Salsa," the first Latin Jazz band in that city. One needs only to hear the band's fourth LP, *Hot Salsa Meets Swedish Jazz*, to recognize the Pozo/Gillespie legacy. In 1990, Eva Svensson, a Swedish woman who had studied conga-drumming in Cuba, returned to Stockholm and organized a Latin Jazz band called "Hatuey."

Jan Hartong, a Dutch resident of Rotterdam, organized a band in 1982, specializing in a "Latin jazz synthesis." After playing within a salsa dance music mode for several years, the band reverted to its former style and changed its name to the "Nueva Manteca Latin Jazz Septet." Hartong asserted that all of their recordings were dedicated "to the memory of the great Cubop pioneers." This development in the Netherlands gives further proof of the impact of the early musical collaboration that took place between Cubans and Americans in New York City, an impact variously referred to as Cubop, Latin Jazz, and Afro-Cuban jazz.

In concluding, it can be said that although various writers call this genre of music by different names and assert that it is a "mix", "blending," or "fusion", what is actually being discussed is *musical transculturation*. It has seemingly never been compared with a well-defined musical model, an "ideal type," in order to judge its authenticity. At the moment, it is uncritically accepted as a musical fact. This uncritical acceptance lies at the heart of the Barretto-Salazar controversy. While each party to this controversy makes a strong case for his own point of view, the issue of transculturational authenticity is overlooked. Consequently, one is led to ask what indeed are the ideal parameters of an Afro-Cuban/jazz "fusion" and how well does the present-day music by that name measure up to it. When these questions are answered, we will clearly understand whether we are listening to Afro-Cuban Jazz or simply jazz. We will then be able to place a crown on either Salazar's head or that of Barretto's. Until that time, the controversy will simply remain: "Latin Jazz, Afro-Cuban Jazz, or Just Plain Ol' Jazz?"

NOTES

1. Max Salazar, "Afro-Cuban History," *Latin Beat* 2, no. 2: 20–25.
2. Fernando Ortiz, *Los Instrumentos de la Musica Afrocubano* (Havana: Ministerio de Educación, 1952–56).
3. Marshall Stearns, *The Story of Jazz* (New York: Oxford University Press, 1960), p. 173.
4. *Story of Jazz,* p. 179.
5. *Story of Jazz,* p. 182.
6. John Storm Roberts, *The Latin Tinge* (Tivoli, New York: Original Music, 1984), p. 113.
7. *Latin Tinge,* p. 126.
8. Dizzy Gillespie (with Al Fraser), *To Be or Not to Bop* (New York: Da Capo Press, 1979), p. 323.

PHOTO GALLERY:
MITCHELL SEIDEL

Mitchell Seidel began photographing jazz musicians in earnest while a student at New York University in the 1970s. A self-taught photographer, he has more than fifty magazine and album covers to his credit and is regularly published in *Down Beat, Jazz Times,* and *Swing Journal* (Japan). Many other periodicals have published his photos, including the *New York Times, Village Voice, Black Enterprise, Jazz Forum* (Poland), and *Rimshot* (Germany).

Seidel photographs in varied settings: posed portraits, live performances, and backstage or rehearsal candids. He credits a number of earlier lensmen as major influences:

> I remember looking at all those old Impulse albums and seeing Chuck Stewart's name. I was thrilled to finally meet him, and I consider it an honor every time I'm working beside him at a jazz festival.

> Another person I consider an influence is Raymond Ross. Self-taught photographers like me usually gain insight by picking peoples' brains, and Ray has always been generous with knowledge gleaned from years in the business.

> Oddly enough, my favorite book of jazz photographs was produced by Dennis Stock, a man not particularly well known for photographing musicians. However, his 1960 collaboration with Nat Hentoff, *Jazz Street,* remains the standard by which I judge all others.

> Among my contemporaries, I consider W. Patrick Hinely my favorite photographer. He's got a very individual style and a collection of images I wish I had shot myself.

> I'm also grateful to Jack Kleinsinger, a producer who generously allowed me to shoot his concerts at New York University when I was a student, and to Mark

Morganelli, with whom I've worked on countless occasions.

Seidel's photographs have appeared in many exhibits, including shows at Lincoln Center in New York City, the New Jersey State Museum, and two annual "Jazz Photo" exhibits in Europe, one of which toured Poland, the Netherlands, and Switzerland, the other Poland and Germany. His awards include a fellowship from the New Jersey State Council on the Arts; a grand prize at "Jazz Photo 1988" in Europe; and two Outstanding Service awards from the International Association of Jazz Educators.

The photographs on these pages date from the mid-1970s to the late 1980s, most of them taken in the New York area. Seidel usually uses an old model Canon F-1; for some more recent photos he has used a Pentax 645.

Sonny Rollins

Top: Dizzy Gillespie and Buddy Rich
Bottom: Mel Tormé and Buddy Rich

Charlie Rouse

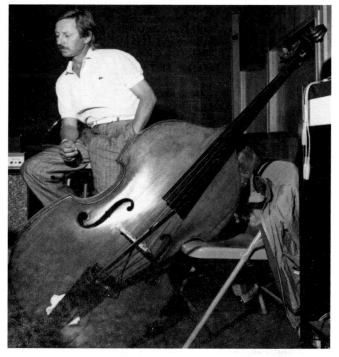

Top: Charlie Haden
Bottom: George Mraz

Gil Evans

Barry Harris

Top: Oscar Peterson
Bottom: Ray Bryant

Top: Gerry Mulligan, Ed Koch, Benny Goodman
Bottom: Alberta Hunter

Joe Williams with Freddie Green and Count Basie

Jon Faddis

Top: Branford Marsalis and family
Bottom: Shelly Manne

Top: Harry "Sweets" Edison, Mel Tormé, Buddy Rich
Bottom: James Moody

Marshall Royal and George Shearing

Richard Davis

Top: Stan Getz
Bottom: Miles Davis

Dexter Gordon and son Benji

ORGANIZED SOUND: PITCH-CLASS RELATIONS IN THE MUSIC OF ORNETTE COLEMAN

By Steven Block

More than 30 years have passed since Ornette Coleman made his historic debut at the Five Spot night club in New York City. Coleman, along with Cecil Taylor and John Coltrane, helped to forge a new era in which the harmonic, rhythmic, and timbral freedoms that emerged changed the nature of jazz in a manner which parallels the great changes in western concert music at the turn of the century. Considering the importance of Coleman's work, however, the number of musical analyses of Coleman compositions or of other composers of "free jazz" are relatively few, and these analyses rarely transcend the initial analytical commentary made by Gunther Schuller, who sponsored Coleman in the 1960s, or by Ekkehard Jost, who in 1974 wrote the seminal work on "free jazz."[1]

The term "free jazz," comes from Ornette Coleman's landmark album of the same title,[2] in which two quartets carried out a 36-minute improvisation utilizing nontonal material with neither the benefit of a fixed meter (though there is a steady beat) nor, in all cases, fixed entries of the ensemble.[3] Unfortunately, the term has become as much a misnomer as the term "atonality" which has been used, often in a deprecatory manner, to describe twentieth century music of the formative period. It is clear that Free Jazz is *not* a music of total freedom, relying on such techniques as developing variation and the derivation of pitch material from pitch-class sets which are *not* necessarily tonal.

Using two compositions by Coleman that were written twelve years apart and in supposedly different stylistic periods, it can be illustrated that Coleman's pitch organization is very sophisticated: an organization that cannot be understood by simply referring to the harmonic underpinnings of more tonal sections or by referring to a process whereby the performer invents motives that are independent of a theme and develops them in a free associative manner.[4]

As in analyses of earlier twentieth century music, set-theoretical tools prove to be very useful in the analysis of free jazz. This is consistent with the fact that jazz evolved from a music based primarily on chords and chord changes, while set-theoretic analysis often involves the classification of pitch structures which may also fall into the category of chords. In Coleman's case, though this is not always true of all free jazz composers, notably Cecil Taylor and Anthony Braxton, the surface of the music is diatonic and a tonal description of the music can sometimes be considered. This duality helped to lead to some of the more vicious criticisms of Coleman, which implied that Coleman could not improvise well or that his improvisations were meaningless.[5] Since the surface of the music contained recognizable diatonic elements which were not functional, it was not surprising that those looking for traditional elements would find the music incomprehensible.

"Lonely Woman' and "Street Woman"[6] were both performed by Ornette Coleman, alto sax; Don Cherry, trumpet; Charlie Haden, bass; and Billy Higgins, drums.

"STREET WOMAN"

The transcription of the theme of "Street Woman," along with some cursory analysis, can be found in Example 1a. (The original key is G-minor. Due to equipment problems, the discussion and examples are in A^b minor.) The theme has been divided into phrase units formed by Coleman's own pauses in the piece, and these are labeled in the example. The most obvious surface characteristic is that of the descending three-note motive whose outside interval spans a minor third, major third, or perfect fourth. This derives from the initial statement where two quick ascending three-note

Example 1a: Street Woman—Theme, Shown with Melodic Pcset Segmentation by Phrase (Originally in G-Minor; transcribed by S. Block)

motives are introduced. Except for phrases 4 through 6, which are sequential, the three-note motive is quite varied in total pitch content since of the seven remaining three-note phrases, six different trichords or three-note chord types are used.

The theme of "Street Woman" is a good example of the way Coleman mixes diatonic and chromatic elements in his music, coupled with the saturation of a few pitch-class sets.

In both this piece and "Lonely woman," larger sets which include chromatic subsets, particularly the chromatic 4-1 tetrachord, come into play.[7] The most important set of this type shown here is the 6z3 set which can be conceived of as a chromatic tetrachord and dyad a whole-tone apart (Example 1b); 6z3 has an important role as a kind of source set for this composition which cannot be found on the surface of the piece.

The total pitch content of the bass line in the theme is this 6z3 set, the main feature being the initial descent from G^b to E^b (mm. 1–4), since this is separated from the rest of the bass line by the alternation in the middle of the theme of an E^b and E-natural pedal before the final descent to C. Clearly, A^b minor is implied by both the opening and the dominant pedal, but at the same time this is undercut by the fact that the bass line descends only to the major third degree, C-natural, rather than C^b and the tonic, A^b, is not strongly enunciated.

The upper voices, alto sax and pocket trumpet, work together in strong harmonic bond. Following the phrasing as marked in the score, the first two phrases form a diatonic subset of the natural minor, scale-degrees 7 through 5, or 6–32, the "diatonic" hexachord. The third phrase features three accidentals, raised third, sixth, and seventh, but the total pitch content of this phrase is still a transposition by a minor third of the 6–32 diatonic set (Example 2a). We can thus analytically describe the first system in the upper voices as being a melodic declaration of a set (phrase 1), followed by a *verticalization* of the same pitch material (phrase 2), followed by a new arrangement of a transposition of the same pitch material (phrase 3). The important distinction here is that the third phrase does not follow directly from the previous phrase in a manner which might be expected from a superficial variation of material such as a chain-association. Its complete motivic derivation can be found only by examining pitch-class transformation, which in turn points to the use of the classic techniques of intervallic manipulation (transposition, retrogression, and inversion) by the improvisors.

While phrases 4–6 in the winds are sequential, they are

only sequential in the sense of pitch-class transposition, and not in the sense of direct pitch transposition (Example 2b). All six melodic lines form the 3–2 trichord, semitone plus whole-tone, and as a tonal unit, each phrase forms the 5–10 pentachord, a chord which is not diatonic and which is a subset of the 6z3 hexachord (the subset is literal in the fifth phrase). This is far from trivial since the exact rendering of the trichord is different from phrase to phrase (the fourth phrase is represented as descending minor second followed by descending major second; the fifth and sixth phrases are represented as descending major second followed by a descending minor second). The harmonic content of the winds in the fourth phrase, then, is a 5–10 pentachord which is followed in the fifth phrase by an inversion of that pentachord, and then a transposition down a minor third of the fifth phrase. The structure thus revealed shows that Coleman uses the same pitch-class operation on both diatonic 6–32 and chromatic 5–10 sets in contiguous passages (T9, down a mi. 3). This implies a way of thinking which is intervallically based and based on pitch-class operations (it is not significant whether the operations are intuitive or improvised). Not only is the same 5–10 set produced harmonically in the winds at each phrase, but across phrases 4–6 (see Example 1, second system), the trumpet and alto sax each form a different linear 5–10 set as well, the alto forming the set whose pitch content is that of the harmonic content of phrase 6 while the trumpet forms the set whose pitch content is that of the harmonic content of phrase 5. Thus, this single five-note chord appears in three different and related versions and saturates three phrases both linearly and harmonically. There can be no question that a choice is being made here by Coleman: if, for instance, Coleman began phrase 5 on F-natural instead of F^b, all the harmonic associations would still be present but the essential linear connection across phrases 4–6 would be destroyed.

The seventh phrase literally reiterates the diatonicism of the opening in that the three-note phrase here, while not exact, certainly implies both by rhythm and pitch, a retrogression of the first part of the second phrase, both units forming the A^b minor seventh chord.

The last three trichord motives are included as a single phrase, phrase 8, because there is an acceleration at this point, with little space between the motives. The entire phrase consists of a chromatic 7–4 set, in which the last six notes form the same 6z3 hexachord that makes up the total content of the bass material for the entire theme (Example 2c). It is important to note the chromatic content of this set because, while it could be construed as tonal in cases where the root, third, and fifth, of a minor or major triad were being chromatically decorated, this is not the case here. The hexachord's outer pitches, too, serve to bring to the ear a sense of aural condensation of the bass line since this hexachord too spans the G^b-C interval.

A brief digression is necessary in order to make one final point about the theme and this 7–4 set; the implications of the following are great for the analysis of free jazz. Henry Martin and Robert Morris[8] have shown that the most common chord progression in tonal jazz, that of the downward circle of fifths, has a function which is equivalent to a chord progression based upon a root movement of a descending chromatic scale. In particular, Morris and Martin both point out that the specific operation of mapping the two circles and transposition by the tritone describes common jazz chord substitutions. If one starts with a bass line whose root movement is a descending fifth, constructs an incomplete dominant seventh above the line, and then has each line similarly move by downward fifth motion, the result, above the bass, is the same as if one starts with a descending chromatic scale and similarly constructs a V7 above it (Example 3a). The same relationship holds true for the construction of the ^{b}9th above a descending chromatic bass or one built on descending fifths. This paradigm helps to explain why the substitution of ^{b}II7 for V7, commonly known as the tritone substitution, is so prevalent in tonal jazz. But, as Morris and Martin also point out, the example also illustrates an operation which has been expounded by Henry Weinberg, Hubert Howe, and many others, as a twelve-tone operation in addition to transposition and inversion. The *multiplicative* operation maps the circle of fifths onto the chromatic scale (or vice versa), sometimes changing the

Example 1b: Chromatic Segmentation of the 6z3 Hexachord

Example 2a: Operation on 6–32 in Phrases 1–3

Example 2b: Operation on 4–10 in Phrases 4–6

Example 2c: 7–4 Chord in Prime Form and
as Played by Coleman in Phrase 7

Example 3a: Chord Substitution: The Mapping of the Circle
of Fifths onto the Chromatic Scale

Example 3b: Multiplication Operations Mapping 7–29 Pitch Content
in Phrase 2 to 7–4 Pitch Content in Phrase 8

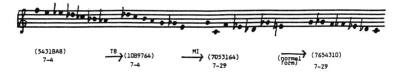

specific intervallic relationships while preserving contour. In tonal jazz, then, there is a specific application of this mapping, the T6MI mapping (multiplication by 7 and transposition by tritone). An additional feature of this operation, which is important in jazz, is the fact that a diatonic pitch-class set will be often be mapped onto a chromatic set.

The last phrase of the theme of Ornette Coleman's "Street Woman" forms a 7–4 chromatic set which is related by this circle-of-fifths mapping to the pitch content of the second phrase without the pickup, a phrase which forms a 7–29 chord and which is specifically related to the final phrase by the T8MI operation, which can be understood as transposition up eight semitones, followed by multiplication by 7 (Example 3b).[9] Thus, there is a neat summing up in the final measures of the theme: the last phrase is directly related to the opening in that a diatonic set is mapped onto a chromatic one, and the same final phrase includes the pitch material of the entire bass line.

The coda is included here to show that though the theme is repeated several times throughout the piece, only the final iteration moves to the clear A^b minor tonality. The final pitch, F-natural, somewhat of a spicy aural surprise, changes the pitch content of the tonic triad with added second to a 5–29 pentachord, one which is a literal subset of the 7–29 chord in the second phrase and an abstract complement (Example 3c).[10] Thus, even the final note, which is analogous to moments in many jazz pieces which end on a dissonance, provides an important structural grounding.

The first two sections of Ornette Coleman's solo in "Street Woman" are excellent examples of how important set relations may exist even within what appears to be a straightforward diatonic language (Example 4). One diffi-

Example 3c: Relationship of Coda to Phrase 2

culty with analysis of this music in the past has been the neglect of the vertical in transcriptions. The vast majority of transcriptions have followed the earlier practice of a music based upon chord changes; often only a single melodic line is transcribed. Some of Coleman's solos, as well as those of other free jazz practitioners like Coltrane, often appear with implied harmonies written above the solo in letter notation. This does a disservice to such music in which there may not be prescribed chord changes. Coleman's performance of "Street Woman," is really not so much a solo as it is two-part counterpoint with the bass. It is therefore necessary to have an entire score at one's disposal in order to understand both pitch structure and the ensemble idea which is such an important part of free jazz.[11]

Viewing the melodic line alone in the first two sections, the tonal implications are quite clear. The key is now the parallel major and no nonharmonic tones are heard in the first section in either saxophone or bass. Ornette projects a clear voice-leading background (see score, Example 4), with the first section of his improvisation centering around a third descent from the mediant to the tonic. The initial C-natural is prolonged through the beginning of the second phrase over an arpeggiation of the tonic triad, then locally descends in m. 4 to B^b when the motion of the dotted rhythmic figure speeds up, and the descent to B^b is accompanied by an octave span. B^b returns in the original register in m. 7 and this time the descent is that of a sixth to D^b, D^b in turn answered an octave above in the opening register and as an upper neighbor resolving to C in m. 10. A local descent to A^b then occurs before the final descent at the end of the chorus.

This description of a voice-leading middleground suffices to describe a simple strategy that may underly Coleman's solo. Yet here, too, important pitch-class relations can be found that are not adequately described above. Again, the sets chosen in Example 4 are sets that are enunciated by the phrasing of the music itself, the simplest rationale for segmentation. The 6z25 set that is heard in the bass in mm. 5–7, for instance, is a set that is marked off by the pauses surrounding the material. It is also true that this set accounts for all the bass's pitch material up to the final phrase. In that

Example 4: "Street Woman"—Coleman's Solo with Bass Part; Sections 1
and 2 and Opening of Section 3 (Transcribed by S. Block)

final phrase, however, while the pitch material for the bass
changes, Coleman takes over the same pitch-classes of the
6z25 set which have been heard in the bass up to that moment
(fourth system, Example 4). Haden's accompaniment, however, is another different 6z25 set, the only other possible set
that can be derived from diatonic A^b major material.

Here is a case where the scale has been clearly segmented
into these two diatonic sets of the exact same intervallic
structure. There are seven possible six-note subsets of the A^b
major scale, so that a clear compositional choice is being made
here. 6z25 is the M-related set to 6z3, the set that had
importance, among other things, as the bass line of the theme

Example 4 (continued)

which immediately precedes this first chorus. One can take the position that this is simply a fortuitous occurrence, but that position would deny the musicianship that enables Coleman and Haden to hear these strong relationships. It is clear that, earlier in the century, Schoenberg did not formulate for many years the structural concepts already present in his music. Thus, if nontonal pitch-class relations were eminently hearable by the master composer Schoenberg, we may assemble that such relations were hearable, also without being formulated, by the master improvisor Coleman.

At the beginning of the second section of Coleman's solo, there is a sense of a chromatic language, as Coleman exploits chromatic upper and lower neighbors to the tonic A^b, which is later transformed back to the diatonic realm. Nevertheless, the counterpoint features a chromatic walking bass, even when the A^b key area is returned to by Ornette in mm. 23–24. After the return to A^b, Ornette moves to a four-note figure which is permuted four times in the chorus and even in the next chorus, further developed and expanded within five-note sets. The motivic nature of the latter part of the solo is clear, but the relation between harmony and counterpoint in this section is more extraordinary. The first four notes of the descent from A^b at the return of the key in m. 24 form a diatonic 4–22 tetrachord which is related to the underlying bass notes (forming a 4–2 tetrachord), spread over the next three measures by the multiplicative operation. Likewise, when Coleman begins the development of a four-note diatonic figure in m. 26, the bass plays a whole-tone figure which is developed further into a chromatic tetrachord, which is itself related by the multiplicative operation to the motive Ornette is enunciating.

The specific operation which maps melody and counterpoint is T_8MI, the same operation for both sets in this passage and the same operation which mapped the final phrase of the theme to the second phrase of the theme earlier (Example 3b). While the performers were probably dealing with the idea of permuting a limited number of note choices, this cannot be construed as accidental. At m. 24–26, for instance, it would be just as logical for the bassist to incorporate G^b into the bass line. At m. 31, F^b would also be logical. Neither choice would disturb the essential nature of the bass line. Yet, neither choice produces the profound network of relationships that were chosen. Thus, we have two performers working two successive four-note permutations in which the specific pitches differ but the relationship between the two parts remains the same.

"LONELY WOMAN"

Coleman's "Lonely Woman," from his 1959 album *The Shape of Jazz to Come,* can be sectioned into the theme, which is only slightly varied when repeated, a bridge eight bars long, which is repeated three times, and the solo sections which encompass Coleman's first solo (22 bars, part 1) until he is joined by Don Cherry for a variation on the bridge (bridge 2) and a second solo (13 measures).[12] As was the case in "Street Woman," this piece can be viewed as tonal, firmly in D-minor (including all forms of the minor), but this knowledge cannot contribute much to an understanding of how Coleman achieves the heights he does in this work, though it does express his relationship to jazz's harmonic past and to jazz's roots in the blues.

Once again, there are a significant number of abstract relationships which can be found between three pairs of tetrachordal sets in the theme, which are all related by the circle-of-fifths mapping common to tonal jazz. What is astonishing, however, is the fact that all three pairs of sets are related by the same process, that is, mapping onto the circle of fifths followed by transposition up a minor third (T3M). Thus, various parts of the phrases in the theme are intimately related to each other, even including such surprises as Coleman's breaking out of the duet structure in m. 15 (Example 5).[13]

Example 6 shows the melodic line of the first bridge and Coleman's solo, part one, with a segmentation by tetrachord. In most circumstances, Coleman's own phrasing has been followed in choosing the segmentation, going beyond phrase boundaries only when a pitch is needed to complete a tetrachord within the previous phrase. Once more, the small number of sets utilized helps project the tautness of the passage.

In Example 7, the same material has been rearranged to show the network of relationships that exist between the sets in this passage. The organization is expressed by operation first, and then the sets which are related by the operation are shown in their musical context. Two sets are omitted, 4–10 and 4–3, because they are not reiterated by Coleman in these two passages.

What emerges from this type of examination is that a small number of operations can explain how pitches are derived and often have great musical import. Taking the first case,

Example 5: "Lonely Woman"—Segmentation of Theme (Parentheses
indicate m-related pairs, asterisks indicate T_3M-related sets)

T_AMI, one sees and hears a very interesting relationship in
the music where two sets, 4–24 and 4–2, are successively
sounded in the passage (and here the sets are separated by
the phrasing); then later, the order of the set succession is
reversed, and their M-related counterparts are sounded
instead. The aural relationship is particularly keen in this
passage both because of the relationships detailed above and
because of the clear whole-tone elements which make up
4–24.

The T_3 relationship comes into play in several places in this
piece as well as operations which may preceed transposition
by a minor third, such as T_3M and T_3MI. One interesting
passage here based upon this relation features the juxtaposition of two 4–12 sets. This can be seen in the third section of

Example 6: "Lonely Woman"—Segmentation of the Melodic Line of
Bridge and Solo (Part 1) (Paretheses indicate m-related sets)

Example 7. In the music itself, the sound is that of a fragment which is announced in the first phrase, followed by the completion of the fragment as it moves to its highest point in the second phrase. One of the reasons the sound of the two phrases seems so right here is that both phrases, as they are being developed within a larger context, are additionally pitch-class transpositions, and therefore directly related on a lower hierarchical level as well.

Two notations in part 4 of Example 7 are given which detail relationships at the moment in the theme when Coleman and Cherry split the line at a cadence (mm. 13–14, Example 5). The transposition up or down a perfect fourth or fifth also is important in this passage, and one striking T_5 relation is formed by the rounding off of the opening of the first bridge and closing of the first part of Coleman's solo by two such T_5-related 4–14 sets.

Lastly, this example shows some of the T_0 relations, i.e., relations where the same pitch-classes are utilized. These are

Example 7: Some Pitch-Class Relations in Bridge and Solo (Part 1)

Example 7 (continued)

not trivial, since they reaffirm the pitch-class content but not the contour of the music. After all, it is a given that much improvisation will naturally feature reinterpretation and variation of the same pitch material on a clear surface level. In "Street Woman," the permutation was on the surface of the piece at the end of the second part and the opening of the third part of Coleman's solo since this involved successive variations based on four primary pitches. In "Lonely Woman," however, the pitch-class permutations are more subtle, since various sets of pitches, as shown in the fifth part of Example 7, are being permuted at nonadjacent sections of the bridge and opening of Coleman's solo. While it is true that these pitch-classes represent different arrangements of what can be construed as scalar material (save for the flat second) related to d-minor, it is still Coleman's genius which groups some of these tetrachordal segments in the manner that produces the rich relationships detailed above. A random breakdown of the d-minor modes into tetrachords will not produce the same tetrachordal sets with the same frequency or intensity of relationship.

It is fruitful to think about larger pitch-class collections that are formed in this work. Example 8 shows a segmentation of the second bridge and second solo melodic line into larger sets, primarily hexachords.[14] Five of the eight melodic segmentations shown form or include one of the two z-related sets, 6z3 and 6z36.[15] *None of these five sets are duplications, a very clear indication that Coleman must be thinking intervallically as he improvises the line.* If one considers only the diatonic scale (7–35) or the natural minor mode, these hexachords are not included. If one considers d-minor with raised sixth and seventh scale degrees (9–7), there are 42 hexachords, other than 6z3 and 6z36, which are included in this larger set. Many of these have greater odds of occurring randomly than 6z3 or 6z36. In fact, for any such given scale, only one possible 6z3 set would be derivable (three possible 6z36 chords). Thus, given all the modes of the d-minor tonality, Coleman has such a wide number of choices to make, if he is utilizing phrases containing six pitch-classes, that the aural relationships presented here in this improvisation must be considered phenomenal.

Example 8: Segmentation of Melodic Line for Bridge 2 and Solo 2
(Slashes [/] indicate z-related sets (sets with the same intervallic structure);
parentheses indicate m-related sets)

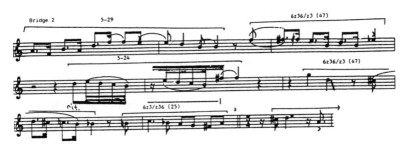

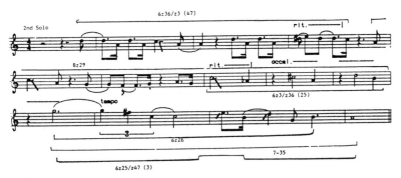

The reason these sets occur here spontaneously is that all three 6z36 sets are related by whole-tone transposition or T_2 (naturally one pair is related by T_4) and the 6z3 pair is also related by T_2. The first 6z3 set which emerges in the fifth segmentation in the third system shown here is related to the 6z25 set shown in the segmentation in the last phrase by T_0M and, in fact, 6z25 can also be considered a superset for the initial five notes. In this section, a pattern of relationships based upon whole-tone transpositions begins to emerge.

The two five-note sets formed here are included in larger sets that have some prominence in the second bridge and second solo material. The first 5–29 set, for instance, is abstractly included in 6z47, a set which is related by the circle of fifths mapping, M, to 6z36. Even more to the point, if F# is added to the 5–29 (it occurs in the next phrase) at the opening of the section, the 6z47 formed would be related to T0MI to the following phrase's 6z36 and T_AMI to the last 6z36 shown in the example. The second pentachord, 5–24, is included in the set 6z26, a set formed by the six notes which precedes the final cadence on A. Specifically, if the pitch-class G is added to the 5–24 shown, and here G is available as the first note of the next phrase, it will form the same pitch-classes sounded at the end of the chorus.

The relationships that are unfolded in this second solo are even more impressive when the harmonic considerations are viewed as has been shown in an earlier article.[16] In the same way that 6z3 and 6z36 sets account for much of the linear structure of Coleman's solo, another pair of related sets, 6z26 and 6z48 (introduced linearly by Coleman at the end of this solo) account for much of the vertical exchange. These relationships are the result of a spontaneous counterpoint where the bass is clearly an independent voice.

SUMMARY

It is important to understand that pitch-class set analysis has been used solely as a tool for understanding some of the relationships that exist in two works by Ornette Coleman, one of which is an acknowledged classic. No assertion has been made that Coleman or any member of his group understood these intervallic relationships in any manner beyond natural and ingenious intuitive construction (although, it is likely that some calculated intellectual understanding existed as well). Set-theoretical analysis has been shown to reveal important new ideas and to model Coleman's compositions in ways which increase our understanding of these works.[17]

In determining that such pitch-class relationships exist in these two compositions of Ornette Coleman's, it has been shown that, while these occur naturally as a result of intervallic transformation, they do not occur by chance. The art of free jazz requires that the improvisors think less in terms of chord changes and more in terms of transforming motives (or chords) which are understood as intervallic events. In Coleman's music, this is harder to grasp because it occurs within a distinctly tonal context. Yet the center of Coleman's genius is not that he simply created a freer rhythmic context for his compositions or sometimes abandoned chord changes in the traditional sense, but that, in eschewing the use of chord changes as a primary basis for improvisation, he applied his considerable improvisational talents to a new manner of variation style based on motivic transformation. This meant that while the listener was hearing such standard chords as a minor seventh, the minor seventh was instead being utilized as an abstract object, not necessarily contextual. The intervallic relationships expressed by such chords as the minor seventh (not its tonal function) became the subject for a Coleman improvisation.[18]

As has also been shown, Coleman went beyond this as well since long-range connections, over the course of a solo or even an entire piece, became an additional concern. Thus, Coleman and other modern giants were hearing pitch-class relationships within the context of their own musical style and history which early 20th century composers, faced with the demise of functional tonality, sought to construct. There is no doubt that Ornette Coleman's entrance into the limelight in 1959 was a singular event in the history of jazz. The deep musical relationships and structures shown here are further testimony to Coleman's highly original and innovative genius.

NOTES

1. Gunther Schuller, *A Collection of the Compositions of Ornette Coleman* (New York: MJQ Music, 1961). Ekkehard Jost, *Free Jazz* (Vienna, Universal, 1974; reprinted by Da Capo.)
2. Ornette Coleman, *Free Jazz* (Atlantic 1364). An alternate take was issued on *Twins.*
3. The term "nontonal" is used here in its strictest sense, referring to common-practice tonality or jazz tonality built on chord changes (though these musics are not equivalent with respect to harmony or voice leading). Thus, the composition "Free Jazz," which is *not* based on chord changes, uses diatonic elements which are developed primarily as motivic

units without harmonic reference and thus would not be considered tonal.

4. The latter process basically defines the term invented by Jost, "motivic chain association," to describe Coleman's music, though Schuller had discussed this earlier.

5. See Schuller's introduction to *A Collection* . . . (cited above), p. 4.

6. Lonely Woman is transcribed from *The Shape of Jazz to Come* (Atlantic 1317), and Street Woman is transcribed from *Science Fiction* (Columbia 31061).

7. The designation "4–1" indicates any transposition of an unordered collection of four pitches, in any octave, with any number of (in this case) successive repetitions which form a chromatic tetrachord. All pitch-class set labeling in this paper utilizes the nomenclature from Robert Morris's *Composition with Pitch Classes: A Theory of Compositional Design* (New Haven: Yale University Press, 1987). Individual pitch classes will be represented by a numeric notation whereby pitch-class "C" = 0, "C#" = 1, "D" = 2. . . ."A" = 9, "A#" = A, and "B" = B. The standard pitch and pitch-class operations of Transposition (T), Inversion (I), Retrogression (R), and Retrogression and Inversion (RI) will be referred to as well as Multiplication (M). Many of the set-theoretic concepts discussed in this paper can be found in Morris's work and in Allen Forte's earlier and seminal work, *The Structure of Atonal Music* (New Haven: Yale University Press, 1973). For a rare use of set-theoretic methodology with jazz, see Jeff Pressing, "Pitch Class Set Structures in Contemporary Jazz" (*Jazzforschung/Jazz Research*, 14, 1983).

8. Robert Morris, review of John Rahn, *Basic Atonal Theory, In Music Theory Spectrum 4* (1982): 152–154. Henry Martin, "Jazz Harmony: A Syntactic Background," *Annual Review of Jazz Studies 4* (1988): 9–30.

9. With the operations performed in this way, MI being equivalent to multiplication by 7, transposition and multiplication can be performed in any order (they are commutative). However, it should be understood that when the operations are separated out, the logical order of operations would be inversion followed by multiplication (by 5) followed by transposition.

10. In dealing with the nomenclature of pitch class sets, the complement of any set (the remaining notes of the twelve-note universe which are not included in the original set), contains the same place in the respective list of sets by that cardinality.

Thus, a seven-note chromatic set, 7–1, would be complemented by the remaining five chromatic notes, which would be named 5–1 since it is a complete five-note chromatic set. Literal complementation exists when the specific remaining notes are present. Thus, a chromatic set, 7–1, whose pitch-classes spanned C-F#, would be a literal complement of the five remaining notes spanning G–B (5–1). An *abstract* complementation would exist, for instance, in a case where a five note-chromatic set (5–1) was included in the original set of seven chromatic notes (7–1). Thus, the notes spanning C–E, C#–F, or D–F# would all represent instances of the set 5–1, an abstract complementation with respect to the 7-note chromatic set spanning all the pitches from C–F#.

11. Regrettably, this paper deals only with pitch relations. However, there are unquestionably important rhythmic-motivic considerations to be examined in this music as well, some of which would likely shed even more light on Coleman's "free" improvisational process. In the author's transcriptions of compositions by Cecil Taylor, for instance, percussion parts are likewise transcribed. For the purposes of this narrow focus, however, the drums have not been included.

12. The form of "Lonely Woman" was enunciated differently in a previous paper (see note 13, below). I am indebted to Lewis Porter, for pointing out a conflict in terms used in that article and thus clarifying the form which is more appropriately explained here.

13. For a further discussion of the theme of "Lonely Woman" and other sections of the composition not included in this paper, see Steven Block, "Pitch-Class Transformation in Free Jazz," *Music Theory Spectrum*, 12/2 (Fall 1990): 181–202. There is wonderful detail present in the theme and elsewhere in the composition.

14. Since the rationale for segmentation has been to stick closely to Coleman's phrasing, in the last two systems of the example, where the phrasing does not break well into hexachordal units, the phrases have been segmented into the sets 8z29, the complement of the very important 4z29 set in this work, and 7–35, which is equivalent to a diatonic scale. Here some of the included hexachords formed by successive pitches are also shown.

15. Z-related sets are pitch-class collections which have the identical interval-class content but which, when reduced to their most compact state within the octave, will not form the same representative pitch classes.

16. See Block, "Pitch-Class Transformation. . . ," p. 200–202.
17. One historical precedent for an analytical tool which does not reflect the composer's manner of composition but is useful in examining vertical sonorities is the use of roman numeral designations, an idea that didn't come to the fore until the "classical" period of music was almost spent. Thus, we can examine a verticality in a composition by Bach as a V6 chord knowing full well that Bach did not think of that sonority as a V6 chord.
18. This, of course, is similar to the manner in which Stravinsky led the neoclassic movement in the earlier part of the century, in which tonality is treated as a static object rather than functional harmonic system.

WORDS AND MUSIC
BY ARTHUR TAYLOR

By Bonnie L. Johnson

On Saturday August 4, 1990 alto saxophonist Jackie McLean
took center stage at Alice Tully Hall in New York City. The
program that evening honored his immense talent as a
composer as well as an intrumentalist and presented his music
in a variety of settings. A quartet with Arthur Taylor on drums
backed a series of guest musicians, including Curtis Fuller,
Benny Golson, Wynton Marsalis, and Wallace Roney. On the
following Tuesday, Peter Watrous's glowing review of the
concert appeared in the New York Times. A portion of it read:

> . . . But as well as the guests played, it was Mr. Taylor
> who defined this section of the concert. Mr. Taylor is
> among jazz's finest drummers, and he made every soloist
> better, making sure they arrived at logical peaks during
> their improvisations, urging them on, dictating the form
> of the pieces, . . . creating a narrative that constantly
> unfolded. It was the sort of virtuosic performance that
> seemed heroic, and the concert achieved an intensity it
> never recaptured and probably couldn't have sustained.

On three separate occasions,[1] I had the opportunity to
conduct interviews with Arthur Taylor in an attempt to glean
insights more personal and substantial and therefore more
meaningful than those found in previous articles about him.
It isn't that abridged versions of biographical information
abound and need fleshing out. Quite the contrary and more
to the point, his achievements have been diminished by
nonrecognition. That he spent 17 years away from the U.S.
may account for some of this neglect. Perhaps being younger
than Max Roach, Art Blakey, and Philly Joe Jones pushed

him out of the limelight. Or maybe the importance of his style in the historical scheme of jazz drumming has yet to be borne out. Whatever the reason, surely any musician whose playing can be heard on nearly three hundred recordings[2]— many of them classics and made in the heyday of the bebop movement and with the leading contributors of the idiom— deserves more.

I consider myself privileged and fortunate to have come to know Arthur Taylor. A lesson I took with him at the suggestion of Jackie McLean three summers ago provided me with a first-hand glimpse of his approach to playing the drums. The telephone conversations we had in preparation for this article were illuminating.

What I have attempted to present here is a two-dimensional view of Arthur Taylor: first, a biographical montage drawn from more than four hours of taped conversation; second, musical examples of two contrasting solos— one a blues at a moderate tempo, the other an extended introduction played considerably faster, both representative of his style when recording with John Coltrane in the late fifties.

THE FORMATIVE YEARS

Arthur Taylor was born on April 6, 1929, in the Sugar Hill section of Harlem, a veritable breeding ground for jazz players. Although he was always an avid music fan, his early life does not reveal those oft-heard stories of the prodigious child who beats on pots and pans in a desperate effort to express himself. Instead, Arthur showed considerable athletic prowess and possessed what he and family members felt were "razor sharp reflexes" on which he had hoped to capitalize.

> I loved track and basketball but what I really loved most was baseball. I had hoped for a career as a professional baseball player but my father said "No, that's no livelihood." Because at that time there were no teams that allowed blacks.

Becoming a jazz musician may not have been the preferred career for Arthur but his father (who is from Belize, then British Honduras) had an interest in music that influenced the young boy.

> My father used to take me to the Apollo Theatre to see people like Billie Holiday, John Kirby, and Duke Ellington. And then I started going downtown to the Paramount to see people like Tommy Dorsey and Charlie Barnet, Sinatra, and groups like that. On Wednesday the show changed at the Paramount and on Friday the show changed at the Apollo. So on Wednesday and Friday I didn't go to school. Nobody would.

Arthur took up playing the drums at the age of 18 or 19, considered late by most standards and admittedly so by Arthur.

> I started very, very late but I always loved music, *always*. I just wanted to learn and I got a practice pad and started going for lessons in the Bronx. I took lessons from a man by the name of Aubrey Brooks, who was really a taskmaster. He couldn't stand me because I wasn't as conscientious as he would like his students to be. He started me out first of all singing. I had to sing notes and so forth. He was getting me into reading, which I really didn't want to be bothered with. I wanted to *play*. Like he was always saying, "You're putting the cart before the horse. You learn this, then you'll be able to do that," which is correct, but when you're young, you cast it aside because you have your own method which you think is right.

Obviously, this teacher/student relationship was not a match made in heaven.

> I didn't study with him long. He got bored with me. He was quite a disciplinarian, which didn't work. Our manners were a little different. It was interesting, though, because later on, when I became professional and started doing gigs and became a little well known, I would meet him and he was amazed that I was able to do it without doing that study.

Taylor was almost 21 years old when he received his first drumset and began performing shortly thereafter.

> My mother bought me a drum set in 1949. That was for Christmas, and in January I started working. We started out in a Catholic church. We used to play on Friday evenings for the kids to dance. That was the St. Charles Church which is in the neighborhood more or less where I live now—140th or 141st near Lenox Ave. We were playing with Sonny [Rollins] and Jackie [McLean], and others would alternate on that job.

It was a stellar beginning for Arthur Taylor, cutting his teeth with neighborhood chums like Jackie McLean, Sonny Rollins and Kenny Drew. As he puts it, "These guys were geniuses. Even when they were young their talents were highly developed."

Arthur cites several drummers as early influences. Some were on the scene at the time, such as Max Roach, Art Blakey, and Philly Joe Jones. Some were from his Apollo Theatre/Paramount days, such as Gene Krupa, Chick Webb, and Buddy Rich. Imbued with a strong sense of "swing" even at this seminal stage of his career, he corroborates the high regard held by all drummers for Buddy Rich.

> The only white bands that could play the Apollo Theatre—because the audiences were really hard—were Buddy Rich and Charlie Barnet, who had a big hit with "Redskin Rhumba" that everyone liked. When I saw Buddy Rich, I can still visualize it in my mind. He had a broken arm, one arm in a cast and a sling, and he played the *whole* show. I mean, you know, with dancers and comedians, and he's got to make these cues and these accents and everything. It was *unbelievable.* He played the whole show and then played a big solo that broke the place down . . . with just his right hand. I said "Yeah, I think I'd like to try that."

But it was J.C. Heard, the drummer for John Kirby, who affected Arthur's playing the most profoundly.

> After seeing Buddy and Krupa, then I heard J.C. Heard. He was really my idol. I fell in love when I saw

him. He was the one who really inspired me, starting out that is. It was the way he played the cymbals. The way he could swing. You know, he could swing so much. He had a really beautiful beat.

CAREER HIGHLIGHTS: 1950–1963

Almost all successful musicians tell of turning points in life which acted as a catalyst in their careers. Often sounding like fairy tales, with immediate and rewarding results, these tales can be misleading. Taylor's episode illustrates this well. In 1950, Oscar Pettiford, arguably the most important and influential bassist after Jimmy Blanton, gave Arthur his first real opportunity by hiring him to be part of his trio along with pianist Wynton Kelly.

> The first break I really got was in 1950 when I went with Oscar Pettiford, the great bassist, to Chicago. It was also with him that I made my first record date. We went into the studio and we made 36 takes of "Love for Sale." If somebody calls "Love For Sale" today, I cringe. There was a part I couldn't get, I just couldn't get it. There was some certain rhythm that was going on that I couldn't grasp at the time. It was tricky and I didn't have enough experience. I was so nervous and getting worse. I was in a state of shock. And every time I played it, it got worse and worse and worse. We made 36 takes and then got in the car and drove to Chicago. So that's about 10 hours in the studio and then off to Chicago. It was traumatic.[3]

It was during this three-week engagement in Chicago that Arthur met for the first time many of the musicians who would later become his colleagues.

> We went to the South Central Hotel [in Chicago] where Dizzy Gillespie's band was staying. Coltrane and Jimmy Heath and Specs Wright and Milt Jackson and all those people were in Dizzy's band and I met them right then and there. I can't remember where Dizzy was playing, but my last set was over before his, so I'd run

and catch about a half hour of his last show. It was very exciting. That's where I met Coltrane.

He also got a glimpse of a remarkable drummer whose name not many people will recognize and I suspect only a few ever heard.

> Sonny Rollins was there at the time too, and that's when I heard the great drummer Ike Day, who was working in the trio with Sonny Rollins and the piano player, Vernon Bivel. Ike Day is the baddest in the history. Art Blakey and Max Roach used to tell me about him. He was the heaviest of any of the drummers. He was a terrible dope fiend and he just died young. Unbelievable! When I heard him, I had to revamp my thinking. I thought about giving up music right then and there. He sounded like Buddy Rich, Tony Williams, Art Blakey, Max Roach, and Kenny Clarke, and all of them rolled into one. I'm telling you, I never heard anything like that in the history of music. In my experience I never heard anyone play that much drums. He could *swing*—he could swing you into bad health and he could solo like Buddy Rich and Tony Williams or Philly Joe and do all kinds of things—unbelievable. It was shocking.

Through most of 1950 and into 1951 Arthur worked with the Pettiford Trio. The young drummer was in awe of Pettiford and attests to his greatness.

> He could play the bass like Charlie Parker could play the saxophone, with that beautiful tone. The first record I ever made was with Oscar Pettiford playing cello. The way he sounded on cello is the way bass players sound today. I swear it's true. You'll hear the record and you'll know what I'm talking about, ting, ting, ting, ting, instead of boom, boom, boom, boom.[4]

After his stint with Pettiford, Taylor performed and recorded with Coleman Hawkins and his quintet which included Harry "Sweets" Edison, Tommy Potter, and Kenny Drew. He stayed with Hawkins through 1951, garnering a lot of road experience touring the Northeast, Midwest, and Canada.

> I was with Coleman Hawkins all of '51—the end of '50 through all of '51. Then Max Roach got me the job with Bud Powell, which is what I always wanted. I replaced Max. He was working a lot with Charlie Parker, and he was ready to form his own group so he recommended me to Bud.

As a youngster, Taylor had tagged along with Jackie McLean. They used to hang out at Bud's house and the pianist "took us under his wing . . . we were his protégés . . . he used to stick up for us if people teased us." Taylor considered Powell his mentor—even more than he did any drummer. The single most important musical event in Arthur Taylor's life was his association with the piano genius.

> The main ambition of my whole life was to play with Bud Powell. I stayed with him for three years straight— longer than I've ever stayed with anybody. Bud was *IT*—drummers and all. I adored him. I admired his music. I use his rhythmic patterns to this day. I base my rhythm off Bud Powell. I don't tell everybody this—but anyway, everybody wouldn't even know how to figure it out, you know. I still will listen to him: I'll put on one of his old records and hear some of those rhythms, and I'll use them just to see how I can duplicate them on the drum. It's very interesting. It's a different type of study.

Taylor spent the remainder of the fifties in a whirlwind of recording activity, playing on over two hundred albums. To say he was in demand is an understatement. By his own accounts, he often felt overworked and expresses incredulity at the thought of ever being able to have accomplished so much: "I may be 62 but I feel like 128. I could *never,* would *never* do that again."

A partial list of the artists that retained his services includes Charlie Parker, Thelonious Monk, Gene Ammons, Jackie McLean, Miles Davis, Sonny Rollins, John Coltrane, Donald Byrd, Red Garland, Gigi Gryce, J.J. Johnson, and

Mal Waldron. Taylor confesses that he was disturbed with
the animosity directed towards him by certain musicians who
complained about his doing "the bulk of the record dates."
He went to Coltrane, who told him plainly, "I use you
because you don't get in the way."

With so many excellent cuts to chose from it is the track "A
Glass Enclosure"[5] made with Bud Powell that is Taylor's
personal favorite ("It's almost more a classical piece than
jazz.")[6] Also making Taylor's top ten list are those dates he
made with Jackie McLean—*456* especially; *Hope Meets
Foster* with Elmo Hope and Frank Foster; and several with
Coltrane, in particular *Soultrane, Traneing-In,* and *Bahia.*
Ironically, *Giant Steps* is one of his least favorites, not so
much because of his playing, but because of the poor sound
quality.

> I can hardly stand to listen to it. The sound is so high
> and tinny. This was at Atlantic and they ruined my
> sound. Not like for Prestige at Rudy Van Gelder's,
> where it was basically a live sound with only one or two
> mikes. I like recording live. *You* have control over your
> sound. With all those mikes, the engineer can fool with
> and mess up your balance.

Two albums with Miles Davis make his list as well: *Milt
and Miles* with vibist Milt Jackson, bassist Percy Heath,
pianist Ray Bryant, and alto saxophonist Jackie McLean,
and the great orchestral album Gil Evans arranged, *Miles
Ahead.* An intimidated Taylor wished he had studied harder
as a youngster.

> When you get into large orchestras it [reading] is
> necessary. But even so, like when I was making that
> record with Miles Davis, *Miles Ahead,* Gil Evans had
> this music that had to have *three* music stands to hold it
> up. I saw that thing when I walked in the studio and I
> said 'Oh my God, how am I going to deal with this?'
> Miles looked at it, walked over and took the music and
> threw it on the floor. He said "I just want you to play
> what you feel." I was relieved. At the time he had all
> those great studio musicians there—people like Bernie

> Glow and Ernie Royal and the heavy guy, Lee
> Konitz—oh so many excellent musicians.

Miles had a special regard for Taylor and on more than one occasion in his recent autobiography he comments on the drummer's sensitivity.[7] Although they had their differences, their relationship was one of great mutual respect and admiration—and protected egos.

This is Taylor's account of the night he walked out on Davis:

> I got angry. We were playing at the Bohemia Club and
> the place was packed—lines around the block and all
> my friends from Uptown were there. And even though
> I played with Bud Powell and Charlie Parker—Miles
> has another kind of charisma you know. He used to
> make me nervous anyway because he would stand there
> and watch me all the time when he finished his solo.
> And I said "Man, why don't you take a walk or
> something, you're making me nervous." He would
> stand there, and he would make comments. He made
> one comment and I said "Yeah." I cursed him out and
> walked off the bandstand, and I say it's the only time I
> saw Red Garland when he couldn't figure out what was
> happening. But the beautiful thing about it—there was
> never anything ever said about it—it never changed
> *anything* about anything. *Miles* never mentioned it
> again; *I* never mentioned it. Other people talk about it.

They certainly do. Drummer Keith Copeland quipped that it was the only time that anybody ever out-Milesed Miles.

The collaboration of percussionists on Art Blakey's *Orgy in Rhythm* albums has a special place in Arthur's heart because of the mutual respect among these drummers.

> It was very exciting doing the *Orgy in Rhythm* albums.
> A series of maybe three albums with Art Blakey where
> he had Philly Joe Jones and old Jo Jones and a host of
> great musicians. We just went into the studio. I had just
> come back from Europe one night before. And the
> phone rings and who is it but Art, and he says "I got a
> record date tonight, get your drums and get down

here." Blue Note records had hired an enormous ballroom on the upper West Side. And I guess Art went to Spanish Harlem and picked guys up off the street; guys were banging on books or bongos, whatever. They had the tympani, and it was a very thrilling setting because Art was in the center of this enormous hall, and they had all of us around him—Philly Joe and Jo Jones and Specs Wright and they had the tympani, the gongs, and the congas. That's one record that I like because it's not dated; it could have been made yesterday, maybe because it's all percussion. They are outstanding records and I enjoyed them. I can put them on and I still enjoy them. That was really a great experience.

So great in fact that it inspired Taylor to organize an annual drumfest.

I used to do Gretsch Night at Birdland. Once every year. And that was with the guys that were using Gretsch: Max Roach, Philly Joe Jones, Charli Persip, Elvin Jones, who else? Well, that's enough right there. But there used to be six of us on the stage. Good God almighty! That was really too much. Can you imagine playing on the same stage with Elvin and Max and Art Blakey and Philly Joe and Charlie Persip? That's too heavy. Just the drums.

EUROPEAN INTERLUDE: 1963–1980

In 1963, Taylor went on a European tour with Johnny Griffin. ("I left for a three-week engagement and ended up staying for 17 years!") As the civil rights movement gained momentum and was giving way to major sociological and cultural changes, an increasing number of African-American artists were making Europe their home.

The same thing exists all over the planet you know. But it's a little more moderate over there. The people are not as—well, they've been through wars and they've suffered quite a bit, so they have a little more compassion, a little human compassion. They told me, especially the older people, what they went through during Hitler's occupation in Paris and so forth. It was really horrible. People here don't know about those things. They'd act in a different manner if they had experienced them.

For ten years he lived in France and for seven years in Belgium. Bop may have had its last hurrah in the U.S. but it was thriving in Paris, and Taylor performed frequently with Dexter Gordon and Johnny Griffin, as well as with touring American musicians.

Europe offered more than just a release from heightened racial tensions and the security of performing for appreciative audiences; it provided a respite from the frenetic pace Taylor kept up in the States. Thus, he had an opportunity to do a few things he probably would not have done had he never left New York. First and foremost, he continued to develop as a drummer.

> J.C. Heard came down to the club one night. And I was so nervous because he was my idol, you know, and naturally I wanted to play my best. He told me that the best thing I ever did was to go to Europe because I came into my own as a drummer there.

> When I look back on it and think about it, when you live in a place like Europe you don't hear anybody, so there's nobody to influence you. Everything you get you're getting from yourself. Like here, I'm in New York, I can go downtown and hear somebody right now if I want to hear somebody play. They may play something I could like and I might try to do it, but in Europe that's out. Well, okay, maybe I could go hear Kenny Clarke or Philly Joe, but I've been hearing them all my life anyway, and it's not on a regular basis either.

Kenny Clarke was one of the first musicians to relocate to Europe; he had been living in Paris since 1956. A very special student-teacher relationship developed between him and Taylor.

> I studied for the first time in my life. Kenny Clarke insisted that I study with him when he opened his

school. He told me that if I didn't study with him I'd
have to fight him, so it was easier to study. I found out
what I was doing all those years, and I was able to
improve on it and do it with more control.

Ironically, as an up-and-coming player, Taylor had neither
been impressed nor influenced by Clarke, who has been
recognized indisputably as the pivotal drummer in the
development of bebop as it evolved from swing.

> I listened to Max of course and Blakey. They used to
> talk about Kenny Clarke; they had such a great respect
> for him. I had listened to him, and I wasn't impressed.
> He was a little different; he wasn't into the same type of
> thing as Art and Max. His cymbal beat was different,
> into another kind of thing. And then I heard him when
> he returned to the U.S., because he had lived in Europe
> even way back then. So naturally he was around all his
> old friends. I heard him, and I still wasn't impressed.
> Then one night, I heard him play. I said, "Oh my
> goodness, this is something *different*. I should check this
> out." It wasn't your regular type of thing. He had
> another kind of timing and everything—little offbeats.
> It wasn't the same basic cymbal beat that he used.
> There were intricate rhythms in his cymbal work.

Another major accomplishment during his stay in Europe
was Taylor's first—and quite successful—attempt at journalism. He collected a remarkable set of interviews that he
conducted with musicians either living in or traveling through
Europe and it resulted in the publication of a critically
acclaimed book entitled *Notes and Tones* (New York:
Putnam, 1977). Subtitled "Musician-to-Musician Interviews," it contains controversial statements concerning the
role of the African-American jazz artist in the mainstream of
American culture. Stitched together by a continuum of
similar questions, the book's value lies in its utter candor and
uniqueness for this genre. A partial list of those interviewed
includes Art Blakey, Miles Davis, Dizzy Gillespie, Sonny
Rollins, Erroll Garner, Carmen McRae, and Freddie Hub-
bard. It is compelling reading.

Family matters, specifically an aging mother, required that

Taylor return to the States and for several years he straddled the two continents. In 1984, he made the U.S. his permanent home again.

BACK IN THE U.S.A.

There are no regrets on Taylor's part about living in the States again. He has maintained a viable performing schedule that takes him to Europe regularly for concerts, festivals, and recordings. Back home, a cultural awakening has finally resulted in a burgeoning recognition of jazz as American art. This, combined with a resurgent interest in bebop specifically, is adding fuel to Taylor's career. He continues to play with his "friends from the neighborhood," Jackie McLean and Sonny Rollins, and others from that era like Jimmy Heath, in addition to artists he had never performed with before the years in Europe, such as the great bassist Ray Brown.

He has resumed performing with his group "Taylor's Wailer's"[8] and now, a full 25 years later, has released his second recording as a leader; it is entitled *Mr. A.T.* (December 9, 1991, Enja Records, R2 79677). He has nearly completed work on an additional volume of *Notes and Tones*[9] and has been approached by a film company in Europe to produce a documentary using videotapes he recorded of Art Blakey, Ron Carter, and Randy Weston.

He is more than a little concerned about the current state of jazz expression, attributing what he feels is a lack of passion to the times in which we live.

> In this life you have to be aware of what happened before you. I guess you have to listen. The times are so different. These people came in different times; when I started out with Jackie and Sonny Rollins, we were twenty years old too, but they were geniuses even then. I was talking to Sonny Rollins about this the other day. We had more opportunities to develop than these people today. They go and develop in the school. We were going into night clubs and beer and gin mills and playing all night long. So you get a chance to really hone

your craft like that. When you're sitting up in some
school you come out sounding like a school. So it's a
different time and different era, which is why these
people sound like that.

He is particularly hard on the current crop of drummers
and, after a lively exchange as we ran through my list, he
considered his responses and requested that I omit specific
names—at least for the time being. ("After I die, you may
print them—I *want* you to print them.")

I don't like any of them. They all play on the same
volume level; they never go up or down. They sound
like they come out of school or something like that. I
was never one to advocate a young person using drugs
or anything, but at least in the Charlie Parker era there
was some excitement. Would he show up? Would he
fall out? Is he drunk or is he doped up or something?
Always an excitement. Today it's just like [makes a
droning sound]; it's just a bore. And I tell them, I tell a
lot of them—I say, "I'm going to get you a box of
Wheaties or something," They're trying but they're not
on the right track. Last one I heard was Tony Williams,
who could really play, I mean really make some
contribution. And they all copy, they all sound alike,
you can't tell one from the other.

HIS MUSIC

If I were given only one word to best describe Arthur
Taylor's playing it would be "swinging." He is blessed with
instincts and good judgment that always keep the music
flowing. And he possesses a powerful right hand that, with all
its energy and drive, creates sheer beauty on the ride cymbal.
That, more than anything else, defines his style of drumming
and is his claim to fame.

Other hallmarks of his style include his rock-solid sense of
the beat which, underlying everything else, is implied by a light
quarter-note pulse on the bass drum that is felt more than
heard, and a strong 2-and-4 on the hi-hat. He has, as well, a

blazing fast right foot that has a mind of its own and can interplay with his left hand at will. In playing fills, he displays technical finesse with tightly controlled double strokes.

Since Taylor is known less for his solos than for his generous comping abilities, his comping will merit future study. After all, that's what a jazz drummer is supposed to do best. Taylor agrees.

> Soloing is not something that ever really interested me. Even when I go on a gig right now . . . when I walk in, everybody's smiling and saying "Oh boy we're gonna have some fun" because I'm going to swing and give everything I have. But with the reputation I have, it is necessary for me to play a solo. It's *necessary*. So I had a devise some things about solos even though I never had a big thing about them. That is not my forte; my forte is swinging. Sometimes I like soloing; sometimes I don't. I really prefer to be playing with the rhythm section. I like the collective thing.

The two solos appended to this article, "Countdown" and "SlowTrane," are representative of Taylor's soloing style during the late fifties. Both were recorded on dates with John Coltrane within two years of each other. The former appeared on *Giant Steps* (Atlantic 1311), recorded in August 1959; the latter can be found on two separate issues, *Lush Life* (Prestige 7581) and *The Last Trane* (Prestige 7378), and was recorded in May 1957.

The "Countdown" solo is an extended introduction. It is 36 bars long, and its form can be viewed as AABA plus a four-bar coda.[10] The coda is Taylor's signature. Snippets of it can be heard on other records, either within the context of a drum solo or as an entire or partial exchange in a "trading-fours" situation. It is a series of rhythmic figures voiced in a manner unique unto Taylor.[11] When he plays the form of the tune up front, please note Taylor's consistency in the final A section. The first measure is exactly that of the first A, and the following three measures are either a clever displacement of the rhythmic figure by one quarter note or a muffed execution of an attempt to reiterate exactly. I suspect the latter because the next four measures comprise the stock "George of the Jungle" riff which provides a graceful recovery. In any event, we can't help but be completely gratified by that wonderful signature coda.

"SlowTrane" is a standard slow blues that was recorded using only bass, drums, and tenor. ("Red [Garland] forgot to show up.") It is another good example of Taylor's sense of the form. After six tenor choruses, bassist Earl May takes two. Midway through May's last chorus, Taylor employs the hi-hat in double time to create a feeling of a faster tempo without speeding up. This enables the drummer to solo in a more comfortable setting. It is very difficult and definitely not preferred by drummers to solo in a slow tempo. Taylor plays four choruses, each of which has its own theme; one can follow the blues changes throughout as he punctuates those measures accordingly. Please notice the relentless hi-hat on beats 2 and 4 that, except for four counts between the fourth and fifth measure of the final chorus, is ever-present.

NOTES

1. The first interview took place in April 1988, the other two in May of 1991, one week apart.
2. Jeff Potter, "Taylor, Art(hur S., Jr.)" in *The New Grove Dictionary of Jazz,* ed. Barry Kernfeld (London: Macmillan, 1988), vol. 2, pp. 520–21.
3. The session was done in New York City on April 28, 1951. Pettiford never used Taylor again on a record date and the track, "Love For Sale," went unissued. Bruyninckx, W., *Sixty Years of Recorded Jazz, 1917–1977* (issued in looseleaf form), "Pettiford," p. P–211.
4. See note 3. Of the four tracks recorded that day, two were issued (Mercer 1966). Taylor is probably not referring to these specifically, but instead to any recording on which Pettiford plays cello.
5. On the album, *The Amazing Bud Powell, Vol. 2* (Blue Note 1504).
6. Leonard Feather's liner notes bear this out. He analyzes the tune as containing four movements.
7. *Miles: The Autobiography,* (with Quincy Troupe) (New York: Simon and Schuster, 1989) pp. 194, 216.

8. "Taylor's Wailers" recorded once. The album *A.T.'s Delight* (Blue Note 4047) was issued in 1957.
9. A German translation of the book is soon to be published.
10. Taylor remembers playing only 32 bars ("I did a chorus.") and was genuinely surprised when I informed him of the additional four measures.
11. The track "Goldsboro Express" on Coltrane's album *Bahia* (Prestige 7353) recorded three months earlier (December 26, 1958), contains several examples of this coda figure, as does Taylor's extended solo on the cut "Sweet Sapphire Blues" on Coltrane's *Black Pearls* (Prestige 7316), also recorded in 1958.

BIBLIOGRAPHY

Bruyninckx, W. *Sixty Years of Recorded Jazz, 1917–1977.* Issued in looseleaf form. Belgium: various dates.

Chambers, Jack. *Milestones I: The Music and Times of Miles Davis to 1960.* Toronto: University of Toronto Press, 1988.

Davis, Miles, with Quincy Troupe. *Miles, The Autobiography.* New York: Simon and Schuster, 1989.

Mintz, Billy. *Different Drummers.* New York: Amsco Music Publishing Co., 1977.

Potter, Jeff. "Taylor, Art(hur S., Jr.)." In Barry Kernfeld, ed., *The New Grove Dictionary of Jazz.* London: Macmillan, 1988.

Taylor, Arthur. *Notes and Tones.* New York: Perigee Books, 1977.

Thomas, J.C. *Coltrane: Chasin' the Trane.* New York: DaCapo Press, 1976.

KEY TO TRANSCRIPTIONS OF DRUM SOLOS

Key:

| hi hat | tom | snare | floor tom | bass | rap stick * | hi hat w/foot | crash cymbal |

*   With the left stick positioned normally on the snare drum, the right stick strikes the left stick's shaft.

MELODIC NOTATION IN JAZZ TRANSCRIPTION

By Mark S. Haywood

Jazz transcriptions often oversimplify or otherwise blur what actually happens in performance, and this can manifest itself in several ways. This paper attempts to define some of the problems which arise and to suggest some solutions. It deals specifically with transcription of melodic line and addresses separately the two issues of pitch and timing.

PITCH

Example A illustrates an inadequate transcription of bent pitches. No standard musical notation exists to express a bend in a note, let alone a particular bend such as an even rise of 1/5 of a tone over the first 1/4 of a note, then a more gradual drop of 1/5 of a tone over the remaining 3/4. Various imprecise attempts have been made to capture effects of this kind on paper, often using arrows

and verbal explanations of the sound by way of footnotes. For many jazz solos, this technique would probably involve writing a book! Such a set of explanations could never convey the sound of the melody as it runs along.

I propose the following solution: a 'pitch chart' can be placed above the melody note in question in order to show how the note varies from normal pitch. Such charts should only be added to notes which do actually vary from what is actually written. The pitch chart is a box in which duration is shown horizontally and pitch vertically. Hence a box for ♩ .

Example A

will be three times wider than one for ♩ ; the height of the
pitch chart can follow a standard whereby a central horizontal line shows the written pitch, the top of the box one
semitone higher, the bottom one semitone lower. Hence we
might have Example B.

Example B

Of course, since the width of the chart is determined by the
note value, the notes themselves must be spaced accordingly
in order that they appear beneath their respective charts. A
key at the top of the transcription should give details, e.g.:

Pitch chart. Vertical range : + /- one semitone.
Horizontal scale : ♪ = 3mm.

The vertical range should be the same for all charts in the
transcription. Once the chart is set up in this way, a line is
drawn within it from left to right, showing as accurately as
possible the pitch envelope of the note as performed. Hence
it is possible to show clearly how a note is affected by pitch
nuance, as in Example C.

Example C

The example now shows how the initial C was bent upwards then downwards, reaching its highest point, almost a semitone above C, about 2/3 of its way through. 2/3 of a whole-note cannot otherwise be easily expressed, nor can the extent of the bend, other than diagrammatically. The A^b is shown to have a downward bend which is at its most pronounced early in the quarter-note. The final G is played as written and therefore requires no pitch chart.

TIMING

Example D

The transcription in Example D illustrates a totally inadequate representation of the timing of a performed melodic phrase. An accurate notation might be represented by Example E.

Example E

This example shows precisely that the notes originally represented as straight quarter- or eighth-notes are in reality delayed or anticipated as follows:

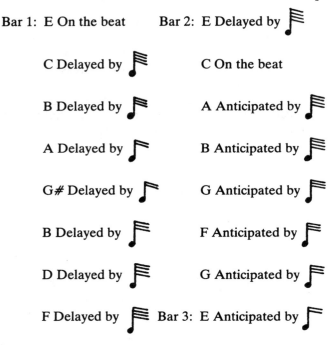

Bar 1: E On the beat   Bar 2: E Delayed by

C Delayed by   C On the beat

B Delayed by   A Anticipated by

A Delayed by   B Anticipated by

G# Delayed by   G Anticipated by

B Delayed by   F Anticipated by

D Delayed by   G Anticipated by

F Delayed by   Bar 3: E Anticipated by

Even this notation cannot be absolutely precise, but it may be as near to the truth as is audibly possible. But is it readable? Does it mean anything? This kind of notation does not clearly show how the various anticipations and delays vary with respect to each other, for example whether a dragging tempo gradually develops but then is swiftly compensated. This notation is no better than the original version using straight quarter- and eighth-notes for someone wishing to see clearly on paper the nuances and nuance relationships in the melody as played.

I propose a solution as follows: slight anticipations or delays to melodic notes can be indicated by adding an arrow beneath the notes in question. To show increased degrees of anticipation or delay the arrow's horizontal stroke can be doubled or trebled. Our passage now appears as in Example F.

Example F

The notation is once again simple and easy to read, as in the original version, but the arrows now show visibly how a dragging tempo gradually develops and is then gradually compensated (bar 1) and how the timing of the notes then increasingly races ahead of the beat (bars 2–3). The arrows should define solely the time relationship between the notes as played and the beat on which they appear in the written transcription. Thus in our example all the notes in the first bar except the initial E are behind the beat and therefore require left-pointing arrows, even though the sixth and seventh eighth-notes actually make up time on their predecessors.

As was the case with the melodic pitch chart, a key should be set up at the beginning of the transcription, showing the full range of arrow symbols to be used (a standard could be those introduced here) plus a note as to how much anticipation or delay is denoted by the most extreme case, for example:

This paper has tried to illustrate some of the difficulties inherent in much jazz transcription today, and to suggest that some standards be set. Two types of musical misrepresentation have been discussed, in order to attempt a broadening of the scope of transcription so as to accommodate the audible language of jazz.

BOOK REVIEWS

Bill Crow, *From Birdland to Broadway: Scenes from a Jazz Life* (New York: Oxford University Press, 1992, 273 pp., $24.00)

Ross Firestone, *Swing, Swing, Swing: The Life and Times of Benny Goodman* (New York: W.W. Norton, 1993, 522 pp., $29.95)

Reviewed by Loren Schoenberg

In his second book, Bill Crow has managed to capture the flavor and vibrancy of one of jazz's golden ages. A skilled observer of his fellow man's attributes and foibles, Crow vividly brings to life many of the fabled, and—perhaps more significantly—under-appreciated, musicians (and selected others) of the last half-century.

This book is an effective antidote to jazz histories peopled with "innovators" only and with musical schools which exist in a vacuum. The author, a skilled (and here thoroughly self-effacing) bassist, has worked over the last 40 years with an astonishing list of musicians from virtually every corner of the large and varied jazz family. Entering the profession at a time when the first generation of jazz musicians were still in their fifties, Crow learned much from hanging around an array of jazz giants, ranging from Sidney Bechet, Hot Lips Page (with whom he met Bunk Johnson!), and Pee Wee Russell to Lennie Tristano, Kenny Clarke, and Duke Ellington. While many musicians of his generation were caught up in immature prejudices against the older players, Crow never let mere chronology stand in the way of a musical experience.

Crow writes in an unassuming, almost journalistic prose. At first, the succession of short sentences is a little jarring, as is the paucity of rhythm within the paragraphs. This is quickly remedied as Crow expands on an early influence and friend, Dave Lambert. The words are driven by Crow's reactions to the person he is writing about; obvious as that sounds, it is not always the case, especially with more "professional" writers. Therefore, he is at his best when recounting special moments. His recollections and anecdotes are always refreshingly to the point. When he stretches out, as he does with a lovely and perceptive reminiscence of the great singer Ivie Anderson, the results are magical.

Friendships and/or encounters with Marian McPartland, Charlie Parker, Gerry Mulligan, Jo Jones, Claude Thornhill (one of the book's greatest joys), Benny Goodman (the 1962 Russian tour), Slim Gaillard, and Mike ("The Music Goes 'Round and 'Round") Riley are recounted with a remarkable clarity and depth of perception. Time and time again, Crow paints a telling portrait with a minimum of keystrokes, in a fashion that would be the envy of many a writer.

At times, Crow's work seems more than tangentially related to that of the great paragon of New York storytelling, Joseph Mitchell. The chapter on Al the Waiter (a fixture at the old Half Note) would have fit right in Mitchell's *McSorley's Wonderful Saloon*. Indeed, the subject of one of Mitchell's greatest essays, Joe Gould (Professor Seagull), shows up in Crow's book.

Crow's warm but unsentimental picture of Birdland and its environs is one of the best portraits of that legendary domain. This in turn magical and seedy area just about a dozen blocks north of Times Square had more great jazz talent per square inch for a while than any other place. Through his depiction of the interiors of these nightclubs and the seemingly unending flow of musicians in their vicinity, Crow gives the reader a real feeling for what it meant to be on the scene at the time. This may be the greatest gift this book can bestow on subsequent generations. It is a written corollary to the famous 1958 Harlem photo that appeared in *Esquire* magazine.

That this jazz world was a living, breathing place where

musicians as diverse as Charles Mingus, Miff Mole, Rex Stewart, Thelonious Monk, Scoville Brown, Art Blakey, and, for that matter, Bill Crow exchanged ideas is well worth keeping in mind these days, when some would have us believe that any time two disparate musicians happened upon the same little phrase it was due to an assiduous copying of a recorded solo. While this undoubtedly did happen occasionally, it was far from the rule. Read Crow's chapters on whom he ran into during his various musical peregrinations, and you'll get a feeling for how the jazz vocabulary evolved. Due to the vagaries of popular taste, the real estate market in New York City, and many other intangibles, those days and the music that came from them are gone forever—except, that is, in these pages.

Himself a gifted raconteur, Crow the author has adhered to the Shakespearian adage "brevity is the soul of wit." Many of the anecdotes get even better on reflection. In a passage about his first New York jam session, we get an indelible portrait of the legendary Brew Moore. Crow encountered him

> lying on the floor with his head propped against the wall. Brew had his tenor sax laying beside him where he could play it without having to hold it up. His florid complexion and the nearly empty half-gallon of wine in the crook of his arm indicated the reason for his supine position. Brew was drunk, but he still sounded good. He hadn't removed the cigarette from the corner of his mouth when he began playing, and as he blew into the mouthpiece, sparks flew from the end of the cigarette. I stood there, saucer-eyed, thinking, "Wow! This is really far out!"

Crow combines a sharp eye with a good ear for dialects, which is used to great advantage in his chapter on Pee Wee Marquette, the major domo at Birdland.

> William Clayton Marquette, three feet nine inches tall, was usually nattily dressed in a brown pin-stripe vested suit and a floral tie, or a dark green velvet suit with a large bow tie. On special occasions he wore tails. His

miniature suits were fairly zoot. His belt line was at his armpits, his trousers were heavily pleated and tightly cuffed, and his box-back jackets featured extra-wide lapels.

Pee-Wee's voice was high-pitched and brassy. Though he did his best to enunciate carefully, he frequently slipped into the dialect of Montgomery, Alabama, his birthplace. He would climb laboriously onto the Birdland bandstand, pull the microphone down to chin and shout officiously:

"AND NOW, LAYDUHS AND GENTLEMEN, BIRDLAND, THE JAZZ CORNAH OF THE WORLD, IS PROUD TO PRESENT, THE ONE AND ONLAH. . . ."

After laboriously naming the bandleader and all the musicians and asking for a "large round of applaw" for the band, he would climb back down to floor level and admonish piercingly "All right, now, fellas, let's get right UP heah! We don't want no LULLS 'roun' heah! no LULLS!"

One of the book's most refreshing aspects is its total lack of pretense. While telling his story with confidence, humor and honesty, Crow goes out of his way to place his own presence in whatever event he is describing in the proper context. He also subtly and sympathetically gauges the differences in temperament from generation to generation. His Henry "Red" Allen story comes to mind on this score. There are also many instances where one can read between the lines—an option seldom granted us in this age of tell-all and ultimately tell-nothing-significant autobiographies.

Crow saves his warmest prose for the lovely and elegant portrait of his long-time friend, John Haley "Zoot" Sims, which closes the book, but Crow manages to convey the essence of Zoot's personality throughout. (I don't want to spoil the reader's opportunity for encountering it for the first time by quoting it here.)

In the course of preparing this review, I began to skim the book; I'd read it completely a few months earlier. As is always the case with the best ones, I wound up reading the whole thing again, and with even more admiration for the many facets of Bill Crow.

Oddly enough, one emerges with a similar feeling of admiration, although of a far more grudging type, for the subject of Ross Firestone's biography of Benny Goodman. While the stories of Goodman's personal eccentricities are legion, Firestone has dug deeply into the personal and social background of this still controversial figure, and has emerged with a balanced and honest portrait.

Never before have Benny's early years been explored in such depth. The lasting effect of a childhood that included occasional days without food, and the sudden and early death of his much-revered father, are here considered seriously for the first time. While misfortunes were by no means unique to Goodman among the early generations of jazzmen, they did have a significant impact on Goodman's almost inhuman quest for instrumental perfection. What makes this book so valuable is Firestone's ability to convey, weigh, and place this material in its proper perspective without becoming an amateur psychoanalyst. His method is clean and transparent when dealing with these matters, and he makes his case convincingly.

Early chapters are rightly devoted at length to a detailed but always interesting study of life in Chicago during Goodman's childhood. After reading about the rise in juvenile lawlessness that overtook the Windy City after World War I, you will appreciate Goodman's comment that if it hadn't been for the clarinet, he might well have wound up as a gangster.

The story moves seamlessly from city to city and decade to decade with a wealth of interesting and, in many cases, new details about Goodman's life. These are all supported, thankfully, in an extensive source list in the back of the book. James T. Maher, whose extensive knowledge of both the music and the music business was an invaluable resource, is prominently credited in the acknowledgements; Firestone has used this living Rosetta stone of American music to its best advantage.

There are many revelations about Goodman's private life, including an early and ill-fated romance with the singer Helen Ward, and his varied medical problems. These are all handled with taste as Firestone respectfully recedes into the distance, letting the participants tell their own stories. This is just one of the many aspects that make this book so far superior to J.L. Collier's myopic and ultimately condescending Goodman book of recent vintage. While Collier went in for misguided musical analysis, Firestone wisely refrains from getting technical. This is not to say that an informed Goodmanophile will agree with all of Firestone's opinions, but they are not tied in some odd way to the author's own musical abilities, or lack thereof (there is no clarinet envy here).

Time after time, eyewitnesses capitivatingly recount their experiences in and around Goodman's world, and, through expert editing of these reminiscences, Firestone has created an engaging tapestry to illustrate Goodman's life and times. Particularly valuable are the quotes from the still unheralded Helen Oakley (not yet Dance) about the winter of 1935–6, when she produced a series of jazz concerts in Chicago that were the first of their kind. Featuring both the Goodman and Fletcher Henderson bands, along with the best Chicago musicians, these events had repercussions for decades. One was the hiring of Teddy Wilson as a permanent part of the Goodman entourage, striking the first of many blows against racial segregation.

Firestone never gets bogged down in speculation about Benny's motives in this or other controversial areas. He gives us first-hand narration whenever possible, sometimes adding a few paragraphs of interpretation, and picks up the story. This is a wonderful way of dealing with a life that spanned more than seven and a half decades, without the telescoping frequently characteristic of Collier's jazz biographies. Firestone deals admirably with the fact that the final decades of Goodman's life were spent far removed from the musical curiosity that he had shown so often before the 1950s. His musical priorities had changed, and this is reflected in the shift to a slight fast-forward that occurs from page 337 on.

Throughout the book, Goodman's occasional episodes of pettiness and financial chicanery are juxtaposed with sincere testimonials to another and better side of this complicated personality. Because he never mentioned it, few knew the degree to which he suffered for decades from chronic back pain, or how he never looked back after a particularly devastating bout with cancer. His friends come off sympathetically as protective of him, and this is another major strength of the book. The reader gleans a feeling for a complete man, not just a clarinet virtuoso, pop idol, or elder statesman. And Goodman's final heroic days are perfectly set down through the recollections of his companion, Carol Phillips.

There is one link, however, between not just Collier and Firestone, but also with the ultimate Goodman chronicler, D. Russ Connor. Each has one major photo misidentification in his book. In Collier, it's Jack Bregman, not Fletcher Henderson; in Connor, it's Harry Sosnick, not George Gershwin; now, in Firestone, it's not Eddie Sauter (perhaps Fud Livingston?). The other photos in *Swing, Swing, Swing,* mostly from the Ken Whitten collection, are fine, and in many instances, relatively rare.

Gene Lees, photographs by John Reeves, *Jazz Lives: 100 Portraits in Jazz* (New York: Firefly Books, 1992, 216 pp., $39.95)

Robert O'Meally, *Lady Day: The Many Faces of Billie Holiday* (New York: Arcade Publishing, 1991, 207 pp., $29.95)

Reviewed by Edward Berger

Jazz Lives is a collaboration between a noted jazz writer, Gene Lees, and an equally distinguished photographer, John Reeves. As its subtitle implies, *Jazz Lives* contains a brief essay and a corresponding full-page black-and-white photo (or in some cases several smaller photos) of some 100 jazz artists, ranging from famous to comparatively unknown. There is no indication of how this selection was made. These verbal and visual portraits appear in order by age of the subjects, an effective departure from the usual alphabetical arrangement. The book begins with the venerable trombonist Spiegle Willcox (b. 1903) and concludes with bass wunderkind Christian McBride (b. 1972). Watching the faces gradually grow younger as one flips the pages does convey a sense of the continuity of the art form. Given the credentials of both writer and photographer, however, the overall results are disappointing, particularly Lees's contribution.

In seeking a new approach to jazz photography, Reeves settled on what he calls the "big face" portrait idea. As he explains, "I thought that straight intimate portraiture might yield viewers useful—and different—information that had not been provided in quite as much quantity as the other photographic approaches to jazz." Thus, Reeves's work for the most part consists of full-page, ultra-close-up, black-and-white head shots which, while often striking and technically impressive, tend to lose their effectiveness due to lack of

variety. Furthermore, many of the portraits are so clinically
stark that they cross the line between insight and invasion of
privacy. Nevertheless, there are some real gems here: Doc
Cheatham with cigar, soulful shots of Benny Carter and
Oscar Peterson, and pensive ones of Clark Terry and Hank
Jones. Some of the best images capture musicians in
somewhat lighter moments, for example Herb Ellis and Ray
Brown together, the Candoli brothers, Kenny Washington,
and Roy Hargrove.

Lees's text gives the impression of having been written in
great haste, with numerous factual errors and occasional
syntactical lapses and misspellings. Among the more glaring
inaccuracies is a reference in the Doc Cheatham entry to the
McKinney's Cotton Pickers. In an aside, Lees asserts that
"there was no one named McKinney" (p. 6). It is well
documented that drummer Bill McKinney organized that
legendary orchestra and remained with it in various capacities for virtually its entire tenure.

Cheatham's colleague and fellow McKinney alumnus
Benny Carter fares particularly badly in *Jazz Lives*. Lee trots
out the old canard about Carter having studied theology at
Wilberforce University, a myth which Carter himself has
dispelled countless times. Lees has Carter in London in the
1930s leading "a BBC staff band of American and British
musicians," which, if only because of British musicians'
union regulations, would have been impossible. (He is
confusing Carter's *arranging* for the BBC Dance Orchestra
with Carter's own international orchestra which played in
Holland in the summer of 1937.) He further claims that, after
penetrating the Hollywood studios, Carter wrote arrangements "usually for black singers such as Lena Horne
appearing in white movies." Such assignments represented a
very small part of Carter's film writing. Finally, we are told
that "in the mid-1940s he [Carter] returned to playing and
travel . . ." This was precisely when Carter disbanded his
orchestra and devoted more and more time to work as a
composer and arranger in Hollywood. All of these blunders
(and a couple of others) occur in the space of four
paragraphs. This treatment is even more disappointing since

Lees lists Carter as "one of my early idols." Indeed, he has written most perceptively and eloquently about Carter in his *Jazzletter*.

Granted that this is one of the worst entries, but such inaccuracies are commonplace. Writing about Marian McPartland, Lees states that the pianist asked him if she and her ex-husband, cornetist Jimmy McPartland (who was gravely ill at the time), should remarry. "Without a second thought I said 'Yes,' " writes Lees, "but there wasn't time." (P. 26) One would think that Lees would have bothered to find out that the McPartlands *were* remarried, particularly since he claims to have been consulted. While this is not a reference book, a writer of Lees's experience and skill should be a bit less cavalier with facts.

As a talented lyricist and respected writer on jazz and popular music, Lees has formed close relationships with many of the figures about whom he writes. His past work has often reflected the deep personal insights such relationships can yield. Here, however, it results in little more than incessant name-dropping and a propensity to inject himself onto almost every page, even when this serves no useful purpose. We are constantly reminded who wrote songs with Lees, who recorded them, who influenced him, and whom he influenced. Even the most inconsequential connections between author and subject are scrupulously pointed out: who once gave him a ride, who called him on the phone, whom he met at Henry Mancini's house, who shares a near-birthday with him, etc.

Occasionally, Lees claims a less modest role: "Kenny [Wheeler] has often said in interviews that he moved to England (in 1952) at my suggestion. . . . Had he (and I) been able to get visas to the United States, we'd have gone there. Thus I, quite inadvertently, influenced jazz in England and on the Continent, because Kenny became one of the major European jazz figures." (P. 102)

On the positive side, it is good to see something written about some deserving but often overlooked artists such as Bill Challis, Jimmy Rowles, Lou Levy, and Bill Kirchner. In addition, there are approximately twenty profiles of musicians under forty, about whom there is relatively little in print. But this is hardly enough to justify this beautifully produced but strangely self-indulgent volume.

Photographs also are a central component of *Lady Day: The Many Faces of Billie Holiday,* but the photos here are historical in nature. Taking advantage of a treasure-trove of photos, interviews and other research assembled by Linda Kuehl, a Holiday devotee who died in 1973 before she could complete her own Holiday study, Robert O'Meally has constructed a fascinating aural and visual picture of the singer. The illustrations include dozens of previously unpublished photos of Holiday—from age two right up until her death in 1959. There are also many wonderful shots of the singer's illustrious musical associates and effective background photographs depicting places where she lived and venues in which she worked. In addition to the photos, there are reproductions of all sorts of memorabilia: newspaper clippings, letters, a baptismal certificate, a passport, even a room service check.

O'Meally modestly calls his accompanying text a biographical essay, not a full biography. Nevertheless, in an entertaining way he sheds new light on Holiday's early years, corrects a number of factual errors, and debunks many oft-repeated myths about the singer and her music. Although he by no means glosses over the seamier aspects of Holiday's personal life, O'Meally admirably focuses on Billie Holiday, the artist:

> We have been so mesmerized by the recital of this singer's private woes that at times we have lost sight of the real reason that history cares about her at all: the lure and spiritedness of her voice, her way of turning bad songs into good or even great songs, and her way of transforming already great songs into music and poetry that will last forever." (P. 10)

O'Meally writes with sympathy and understanding about Holiday's singing style and recordings—the perfect antidote to Michael Brooks's often perverse annotations to the Columbia Jazz Masterpieces *Quintessential Billie Holiday* series. One of the hoary myths tackled by O'Meally is the claim that Holiday had no say in the material foisted upon her by insidious music publishers and crass record company executives—particular bêtes noires of Brooks. Revealing remarks by Teddy Wilson show that she exerted far more control over the selection process than previously assumed: "I would get together with Billie first, and we would take a stack of music, maybe thirty, forty songs, and go through them, and pick out the ones that would appeal to her—the lyric, the melody." (P. 111) O'Meally adds:

> It is important to know that Holiday was not just singing whatever songs she was given, as most accounts report. While it is clear that she sometimes was stuck at the last moment with a song that Columbia insisted she do to honor an obligation to a publisher or song plugger, she usually had some choice in these matters. According to Wilson, the two of them rejected 90 percent of the material they reviewed. (Pp. 111–12)

The Wilson quote is one of dozens of valuable observations by musicians, many published here for the first time. Unfortunately, none of the sources are cited. One presumes that they derive from original interviews conducted by Kuehl or O'Meally, but this fact is not made clear. Similarly, O'Meally includes many insightful but uncited observations by such writers as Gunther Schuller, Stanley Crouch, Leonard Feather, Martin Williams, Albert Murray, and Ralph Ellison. These are presumably from the works by these authors listed in the book's bibliography but, again, even in a nonscholarly work such as this, some more precise method of identifying sources is needed. A more serious citation problem occurs when O'Meally uses a description and attributes it only to "one writer," without even naming the source.

O'Meally's enthusiastic prose sometimes leads to hyperbole: "Between 1935 and 1942 . . . Holiday cut hundreds of titles for Columbia" (p. 114); it was actually around 125. The author cites John Hammond's portentous visit to Monette's in Harlem in 1933, when he first heard Billie Holiday, as "an event for the jazz history book, though so far, aside from [Humphrey] Lyttelton, no jazz historian has noticed it." (P. 55) Virtually every major survey of Holiday's career mentions this event.

Despite these lapses, along with frequent repetition and the absence of an index, the text is a fine complement to the stunning illustrations. Returning to the photos, O'Meally opens Part Three with an astute observation (once again uncredited—it is from Melvin Maddocks's booklet accompanying the Time-Life *Giants of Jazz* series Billie Holiday set), which underscores the book's fitting subtitle, *The Many Faces of Billie Holiday:* " 'No camera,' one writer said, 'could ever contrive to capture once and for all the elusive essence of Billy Holiday . . . [seven] pictures taken in her twenties and thirties are so strikingly dissimilar that they might pass for portraits of seven different women.' " (p. 91)

REVIEW ESSAY

The Hal Leonard Artist Transcription Series

By Lewis Porter

Charlie Christian: The Art of Jazz Guitar
Edited by Dan Fox (Goodman Group, 1964; reprinted and
distributed by Hal Leonard, 1988, 32 pp., $5.95)

The Music of John Coltrane
No editor listed; Alice Coltrane mentioned as a collaborator
(Hal Leonard, 1991, 125 pp., $17.95)

Charles Mingus: More Than a Fake Book
Compiled by Sue Mingus, Andrews Homzy, and Don Sickler
(Jazz Workshop, 1991; distributed by Hal Leonard, joint
publication, 160 pp., $19.95)

Wes Montgomery
Transcribed by Fred Sokolow (Third Earth and Hal Leonard, joint publication, 1988, 96 pp., $14.95)

James Newton: The Improvising Flute
By James Newton (Third Earth and Hal Leonard, joint
publication, 1989, 69 pp., $14.95)

Wayne Shorter
Transcribed by Sanford Marten (Third Earth and Hal
Leonard, joint publication, 1990, 110 pp., $14.95)

Hal Leonard has put together an impressive series of jazz
leadsheets and transcribed solos that musicians and educators will find indispensable. While some collections have

their shortcomings, as noted below, they are all a great place to start, and the collections of Coltrane, Mingus, and Shorter are the first authorized editions for these important artists.

Each book has a unique format. Some offer leadsheets only, some provide transcribed solos, some give both. Most have commentary for each piece, and a few offer technical advice for improvisers. Taking them in the order listed above, the Christian book is the only one that has been issued before. The short biography gives 1919 as Christian's birth year, even though we now know that he was born in 1916, but otherwise this reissue has not become obsolete. The twelve solos are all taken from Christian's studio recordings with Benny Goodman. Most are from originals by Goodman such as "Six Appeal," "Wholly Cats," and "Breakfast Feud," but Christian is represented as coauthor on "Airmail Special," "Solo Flight," "Seven Come Eleven," and "Shivers." The transcriptions are fairly accurate, but ghosted notes are often omitted. Themes and background riffs are usually indicated, although it would have been nice to have shown the guitar part for the theme of "Airmail Special"—he is not playing in unison with the winds, as implied here. The chords provided on "Wholly Cats" are more complicated than the simple blues changes that are actually played. Finally, users should be warned that the versions transcribed of "Breakfast Feud" and "Airmail Special" are the ones once issued on Columbia 652 that spliced together Christian solos from several takes. One will have to compare these aurally when using more recent CD issues. (An article by Clive G. Downs elsewhere in this *Annual Review* details the available Christian transcriptions and their sources.)

Over one hundred compositions are represented in the Coltrane book. Any Coltrane original you are looking for is likely to be there, from "Nita," which was in 1956 among his first originals to be recorded, to the four parts of "A Love Supreme," to the titles on his last album, *Expression.* One can study Coltrane's fascinating and challenging reworkings of "Confirmation" ("26-2," which he begins on tenor and ends on soprano saxophone) and "I Can't Get Started" ("Exotica," also known as "Untitled Original"). Among the few missing items are "Straight Street" from 1957 and "Trane's Blues," also known as "John Paul Jones." The sources are the lead sheets compiled mostly in the 1970s for copyright purposes, and they are for the most part quite accurate. In some cases bass lines and countermelodies are given, and Alice Coltrane has suggested alternate chords for some of the later items. The pieces are in alphabetical order, and a discography at the back gives the album title on which each one may be found. The album numbers are of course mostly out of date, but luckily the titles have mostly remained the same on the CD releases. The dates given in the discography are an odd mix of recording dates (mostly) and release dates.

Many of Coltrane's recordings have no real theme, since he often soloed over the chords or, from 1965 on, worked freely from a set of thematic motives, and here things get interesting. For "Ascension" we get a sketch that amounts to a drastically simplified but useful reduction of the group sound actually heard. For the titles from *Expression* and *Interstellar Space* we essentially get the first page of Coltrane's solo transcribed, although on "Venus" it appears to be the last page. By the way, "Equinox" is given here in the usual key of C-sharp minor, but Coltrane's handwritten version (reproduced on p. 283 of *Coltrane: A Biography,* by C.O. Simpkins, reissued in 1989 by Black Classic Press) shows he wrote it in D-flat minor.

There is quite a bit of confusion here about Coltrane's version of "I Can't Get Started" mentioned above. It was recorded for Roulette on September 8, 1960, as "Exotica," then for Atlantic on October 24, 1960, in a version originally unreleased. In 1970, Atlantic issued its version as "Untitled Original." In this book, for "Exotica" one gets the first A section of Coltrane's solo on the Roulette version and the date is given as 10/24/64 (apparently a typo for 1960, but still incorrect). Under "Untitled Original" one finds the first A section of Coltrane's solo from the Atlantic version, marked with a repeat, than a transcription of Coltrane's solo on the bridge of the last chorus and the last A and coda of the recording. For the date, both 10/24 and 10/26/60 are given.

The Mingus collection is the most authoritative of the batch, due to the active involvement of Mingus's wife Sue, musician Don Sickler, and scholar Andrew Homzy. It includes commentary on each piece by Homzy and is interspersed with photographs and with pages of Mingus's own manuscripts. Two of Mingus's provocative essays are reprinted. For the music, numerous details of the arrangements are provided, including some of the many variations Mingus would throw in at different performances. While these charts may represent what Mingus wrote, one will occasionally spot slight differences in the theme or chords from what was actually recorded. For example, on "Fables of Faubus" the four sixteenths in the second measure should read b-natural, c, b-flat (not b-natural again, as given), a-flat; every occurrence of this pattern—it is found starting on d-flat also—should be corrected accordingly.

There have been previous volumes devoted to Wes Montgomery, compiled by guitarists Steve Khan (Gopam Enterprises, 1978) and Jimmy Stewart (Robbins Music, 1968), and certain favorite tunes show up in this new book by Sokolow that have been available before, among them "Boss City," "Bumpin' On Sunset," "Tear It Down," and "West Coast Blues." Sokolow's transcriptions seem fine—Montgomery's marvelous clarity of phrasing seems to make him an ideal subject—although Stewart's versions also showed the arrangements and bass lines. Sokolow gives an informative introduction that breaks down some of the trademarks of Montgomery's style. All three volumes to date are disappointing in their choice of repertoire. They focus on the Verve and A&M recordings, on which the guitarist sometimes solos entirely in octaves, and sometimes only paraphrases the theme. Out of fifteen solos in Sokolow's book, only one is from the early records with the Mastersounds and only one, the delightful "West Coast Blues," is from the Riverside albums that are generally considered (and I agree) his best jazz work.

James Newton's book will be of great interest because there are few books for jazz flutists and because Newton's own attractive and varied compositions are featured throughout, along with his version of Ellington's "Heaven." The book is for jazz and classical flutists, who already are fairly competent. For each piece, Newton provides guidelines for study. For example, the lead sheet of his tribute to Mingus,

"Forever Charles," is followed by two pages of exercises based on the chords of the piece, then by a transcription of Newton's solo on the piece. Newton provides notes on each piece, in general recommending this procedure of studying the chords first and then mastering one or more solos (transcribed from the recording or written out by the student) on the way to developing one's own improvisations. One piece, "Crystal Texts," is a duet for flute and piano, with the piano part provided. A discography and biography of Newton complete this book.

Because Wayne Shorter is one of the most admired and influential of saxophonists—and composers—the final volume reviewed here has been much awaited. It includes a generous sampling of Shorter's written pieces and saxophone solos, each introduced by an interview with Shorter conducted by Ronny Schiff. The twenty-five pieces include "Lester Left Town," "E.S.P.," "Footprints" (as recorded on Shorter's album *Adam's Apple*), "Ana Maria," "Nefertiti" (only the theme is given for this one because Shorter took no solo on the Miles Davis recording), "Speak No Evil," and other celebrated recordings. The transcriptions are of high quality, with attention to such details as articulation. (One obvious typo will be caught by most musicians: the last two notes at the end of the first line of "Footprints" should of course be e and d, not d and d.)

The Hal Leonard series also includes volumes devoted to Chick Corea's written themes, a David Sanborn book, and a number of guitar books devoted to Al Di Meola, John Scofield, Pat Metheny, and others.

ABOUT THE EDITORS

EDWARD BERGER, assistant director of the Institute of Jazz Studies, is coauthor of the two-volume biodiscography, *Benny Carter: A Life in American Music,* and the autobiography of Teddy Reig, *Reminiscing in Tempo.* His biodiscography of bassist George Duvivier, *Basically Speaking,* will be published by Scarecrow Press this year. He has frequently served as road manager for Benny Carter, has produced and annotated a number of Carter's recent recordings (including the Grammy-winning *Benny Carter: Harlem Renaissance*), and has recently issued, on his own Evening Star label, a CD featuring trumpeter Joe Wilder, *Alone With Just My Dreams.*

DAVID A. CAYER was a founding coeditor of *Journal of Jazz Studies,* the predecessor of *Annual Review of Jazz Studies,* in 1973 and has been affiliated with the Institute of Jazz Studies since 1965. In 1991 he retired from Rutgers University as Associate Vice President for Academic Affairs.

DAN MORGENSTERN, Director of the Institute of Jazz Studies, is a jazz historian and former editor of *Down Beat.* His many publications include *Jazz People,* and he has won five Grammy awards for album notes. He has been a vice president of the National Academy of Recording Arts and Sciences, a jazz panelist for the Music Program of the National Endowment for the Arts, and a teacher of jazz history at Brooklyn College, New York University, the Peabody Institute, and Rutgers.

LEWIS PORTER, associate professor of music at the Newark Campus of Rutgers, is coauthor (with Michael Ullman) of *Jazz: From Its Origins to the Present* (Prentice-

Hall), author of *Lester Young,* and editor of *The Lester Young Reader.* He has been jazz editor and a regular contributor to *Black Perspective in Music.* Other writings have appeared in *The New Grove Dictionary of Music in the United States, The Grove Dictionary of Jazz,* and *Journal of the American Musicological Society.* He performs as pianist, drummer, and vocalist.

ABOUT THE CONTRIBUTORS

WILLIAM BAUER lives in Piermont, New York, with his wife Marjorie and twin sons, Conrad and Isaac. He is currently pursuing a doctorate in composition at the Ph.D. program in music at the Graduate Center of the City University of New York. He teaches choral and elementary music at the Hackley School in Tarrytown and theory at the Hoff-Barthelson Music School in Scarsdale, in addition to conducting workshops nationwide on the Dalcroze approach.

STEVEN BLOCK is assistant professor of composition and theory at the University of New Mexico. His article on free jazz in *Music Theory Spectrum* was the first jazz article ever published in that journal. He has written on contemporary classical music for *Perspectives in New Music, Integrales, High Fidelity/Musical America,* and other publications.

VERNON W. BOGGS, Ph.D., is assistant professor of sociology at the City University of New York and conducts studies of crime and deviance in the U.S. and Scandinavia at CUNY's Center for Social Research. He recently published *Salsiology: Afro-Cuban Music and the Evolution of Salsa in New York City* (New York: Excelsior, 1992). His current musical research is on Cuban influences on doowop and early rhythm and blues.

CLIVE G. DOWNS devotes most of his research to applying Q-analysis (a mathematical methodology) in psychology and is nearing completion of a Ph.D. concerned with applications in representing the structure of knowledge and skills needed in jobs. His musical articles have appeared in *Saxophone Journal* and *Jazz Journal International.* He is currently working also in implementing computer systems in local authorities.

JONATHAN FINKELMAN is a guitarist and is currently pursuing a Ph.D. in composition in the music program at the Graduate Center of the City University of New York. He has freelanced as a jazz and rock musician and conducted research on Frank Zappa and Aaron Copland.

KRIN GABBARD, associate professor of comparative literature at the State University of New York at Stony Brook, is coauthor of *Psychiatry and the Cinema* (Chicago: University of Chicago Press, 1987) and has published widely on film, music, art, and literature. He is currently writing a book, tentatively titled *Jamming at the Margins: Jazz and the American Cinema,* and is editor of two forthcoming anthologies, *Representing Jazz* and *Jazz Among the Discourses.*

MARK S. HAYWOOD works for the British National Health Service and holds a Ph.D. in classics from Liverpool University. A lifelong student of music, he has gained accreditation on several instruments and in music theory from the Associated Board of the Royal Schools of Music.

BONNIE L. JOHNSON is a professional drummer currently performing and teaching in the New York area. She has recorded and toured internationally and has a B.A. in Anthropology from the University of California at Berkeley, a B.M. in Percussion from the Hartt School of Music, and an M.A. in Jazz Performance from Queens College in Flushing, NY. She cites as her mentors Jackie Mclean, Jimmy Heath, Art Taylor, Bernard Purdie, and Sharon Russell.

LOREN SCHOENBERG, a tenor saxophonist and pianist, leads his own big band, and has played and recorded with Benny Carter, Jimmy Heath, and David Murray. He is now associated with the Smithsonian Jazz Masterworks Orchestra (under Gunther Schuller and David Baker) and conducted the American Jazz Orchestra (with John Lewis). He teaches aesthetics at the New School in New York City.

CHARLES H. WATERS, JR., is a practicing lawyer in Houston, Texas. He has a longstanding interest in the life and music of Duke Ellington and is a regular presenter at the annual Ellington Study Group Conferences. An abstract of this essay was presented at the Eighth Annual Ellington Study Group Conference in Ottawa, Ontario, in May 1990.

ABOUT THE INSTITUTE
OF JAZZ STUDIES

The Institute of Jazz Studies of Rutgers, the State University of New Jersey, is a unique research facility and archival collection, the foremost of its kind. IJS was founded in 1952 by Marshall Stearns (1908–1966), a pioneer jazz scholar, professor of medieval English literature at Hunter College, and the author of two essential jazz books: *The Story of Jazz* and *Jazz Dance*. In 1966, Rutgers was chosen as the collection's permanent academic home. IJS is located on the Newark campus of Rutgers and is a branch of the John Cotton Dana Library of the Rutgers University Libraries.

IJS carries on a comprehensive program to preserve and further jazz in all its facets. The archival collection, which has quadrupled its holdings since coming to Rutgers, as of 1991 consists of more than 100,000 sound recordings in all formats, from phonograph cylinders and piano rolls to video cassettes and laser discs; more than 5,000 books on jazz and related subjects, including discographies, bibliographies, and dissertations; and comprehensive holdings in jazz periodicals from throughout the world. In addition, there are extensive vertical files on individuals and selected topics, a large collection of photographs, sheet music, big band arrangements, realia, and memorabilia.

IJS serves a broad range of users, from students to seasoned scholars, authors, and collectors. The facilities are open to the public on weekdays by appointment. In order to allow the widest possible access, there is no charge for routine use of reference materials. Researchers requiring extensive staff assistance, however, are assessed a charge. Due to limited audio facilities, as well as to preserve the record collection, listening and taping are limited to serious research projects.

In addition to students, scholars, and other researchers, IJS routinely assists teachers, musicians, the media, record companies and producers, libraries and archives, arts agencies, and jazz organizations.

For further information on IJS programs and activities, write to:

Institute of Jazz Studies
135 Bradley Hall
Rutgers, The State University
Newark, NJ 07102

A PLUME BOOK

SCATTERSHOT

DAVID LOVELACE is a writer, carpenter, and former owner of The Montague Bookmill, a bookstore near Amherst, Massachusetts. His poetry has been nominated for a Pushcart Prize as well as the *Paterson Literary Review*'s Allen Ginsberg Award. Lovelace lives in western Massachusetts with his wife and children.

"*Scattershot* portrays the reality of this brutal illness with such emotional intensity. Lovelace's journey reminded me so much of my own struggle—except his account is even more devastating because his was a family affair. His chronicle is critical for people to read to understand how mental illness impacts families and gives them hope that recovery is possible."
                    —Andy Behrman, author of *Electroboy: A Memoir of Mania*

"The author describes medications and the process of recovery, but his book's major strength is its language, which beautifully mimics his bipolarity. When Lovelace chronicles a manic episode, the prose comes in breathless, eloquent bursts; when he describes crushing depression, it's as though all the air is being sucked out of the room."
                    —*Kirkus Reviews*

"Memoirs of bipolar disorder are as common as dirt, but Lovelace steers clear of self-pity and self-aggrandizement as he describes, with disarming candor, his childhood with two manic-depressive parents, his time as a drug addict, and his acceptance of his own diagnosis."
                    —*Details* magazine

"Fortunately, *Scattershot* isn't just another memoir of shattered childhood, psychological illness, and drug addiction. It's a consistently engaging, often frightening report from a damaged—but possibly brilliant—mind, and it should resonate with anyone who's dealt with mental disorders or psychological anguish."   —*Charleston City Paper*

SCATTERSHOT

MY BIPOLAR FAMILY

A MEMOIR

DAVID LOVELACE

A PLUME BOOK

PLUME
Published by the Penguin Group
Penguin Group (USA) Inc., 375 Hudson Street, New York, New York 10014, U.S.A. •
Penguin Group (Canada), 90 Eglinton Avenue East, Suite 700, Toronto, Ontario, Canada
M4P 2Y3 (a division of Pearson Penguin Canada Inc.) • Penguin Books Ltd., 80 Strand,
London WC2R 0RL, England • Penguin Ireland, 25 St. Stephen's Green, Dublin 2,
Ireland (a division of Penguin Books Ltd.) • Penguin Group (Australia), 250 Camberwell
Road, Camberwell, Victoria 3124, Australia (a division of Pearson Australia Group Pty.
Ltd.) • Penguin Books India Pvt. Ltd., 11 Community Centre, Panchsheel Park, New
Delhi – 110 017, India • Penguin Group (NZ), 67 Apollo Drive, Rosedale, North Shore
0632, New Zealand (a division of Pearson New Zealand Ltd.) • Penguin Books (South
Africa) (Pty.) Ltd., 24 Sturdee Avenue, Rosebank, Johannesburg 2196, South Africa

Penguin Books Ltd., Registered Offices: 80 Strand, London WC2R 0RL, England

Published by Plume, a member of Penguin Group (USA) Inc. Previously published in
a Dutton edition.

First Plume Printing, December 2009

10   9   8   7   6   5   4   3   2

 REGISTERED TRADEMARK—MARCA REGISTRADA

The Library of Congress has catalogued the Dutton edition as follows:

Lovelace, David.
    Scattershot: my bipolar family / David Lovelace.—1st ed.
        p.   cm.
    ISBN 978-0-525-95078-3 (hc.)
    ISBN 978-0-452-29561-2 (pbk.)
    1. Manic-depressive persons—Family relationships.   2. Manic-depressive illness—
Treatment.   I. Title.
    RC516.L68 2008
    616.89'5—dc22   2008013901

Printed in the United States of America

*Penguin is committed to publishing works of quality and integrity. In that spirit, we are proud to
offer this book to our readers; however, the story, the experiences, and the words are the author's alone.*

C16-895
C898

For Mary and Hunter

SCATTERSHOT

ONE

I opened the door, the kids tackled me, and my wife said, "You need to call your dad. He's been leaving messages for days." I dropped my pack, kissed them all, and sat down. "You need to call him now. I tried to reach you." Hunter pushed onto my lap. "Why? What is it?"

"It's strange. He sounds pretty strange."

I knew what it was already. I should have seen it before I left town. I wanted to come home and tell stories, hear the kids talk, but instead I moved to the bedroom and locked the door. I lay facedown as the kids rattled the doorknob and called from the hall. "What did you bring back, Dad? What did you get us?" They began quarreling. I pulled a stuffed toy, some markers, and a pouch of fool's gold from my carry-on, opened the door, and passed out the gifts. I sat on the bed and tried to think it out slowly but I couldn't. It was pointless. I knew what it was and hit play.

"Hi, David, hello, Roberta. This is Dad Lovelace, Richard Lovelace. Mom is much better now. She's more herself. We've been praying and singing hymns. She enjoys that. Dad Lovelace." Not good. The "Dad Lovelace" thing did not sound good.

"Hello again, David and Roberta. Dad Lovelace again. I just

wanted to mention that there's really no reason for you to come down. Mom is much better, more herself. The family gathering was just a real shock to her system. I think she just needs to rest, so don't come down. It's not a good idea. Thanks, Richard Lovelace." The "Richard" thing was worse.

Before I left for Colorado, I had driven my folks back to Boston's North Shore to see family. I now acted as chauffeur. My mother was eighty-one that year and terrified of driving, has been since 1950. My father was only seventy-four, but suffering from night blindness. When I arrived at their apartment, my mother, Betty Lee, was far from well. She sat on the couch with her forehead clenched and her eyes screwed tight. Her jaw was slack and wet with saliva. I helped her out to their car and felt her thin arm with its hollow bones—just a bird's wing. She curled up in the backseat and fell asleep within minutes.

My father, usually reserved, practically bounced on the seat beside me. He talked nonstop, all the way east. Dad, a theologian, hadn't published in years, but he now carried two manuscripts and spent most of the ride describing them in great detail. It was a long two hours. My parents' car shuddered over sixty. The speedometer had worked loose somewhere in the dash and it fluttered and buzzed. Just past Sturbridge, he pulled out his second work, a memoir, and I winced. He read me his life so fast it was done before we got to our exit.

When we arrived my mother's condition shocked everyone and my father began assuring the family. He said Betty Lee was just adjusting to new medication. I mentioned the onset of Parkinson's but my father broke in. "Now, we're not sure it's Parkinson's. She has some Parkinsonian symptoms—that's all." But

Parkinson's is a progressive disease. It doesn't hit like a stroke. My father said he had all her doctors on the case.

"Including Bryant?" I asked.

"Including the shrink," he said.

The party proceeded while my mother sat on the couch, silent and pinched. Shadows moved through her face as my father squeezed her hand and whispered in her ear, acting as a sort of interpreter for the bright, laughing room. He spoke for her as well, answering questions and almost shielding her from the family's concern. He loves her very much but he was making me nervous. At dinner my father raised his hand in blessing, his ring and pinkie fingers folded down like a saint's. "As an ordained minister of the Presbyterian church, I ask our Lord God's blessing on this gathering. In the grace of Jesus Christ, his only begotten son, amen." My brother, Jonathan, shot me a glance and I shrugged. It was a strange blessing, even for a church historian.

A short time later Jonathan pulled me over by the cheesecake. "Dad's acting weird, Dave. I mean really weird."

"I know."

"He just growled at Jen. He started telling her how to raise our kids and when she started to defend herself he just growled."

"What do you mean, growled?" I asked skeptically. I typically run interference for my dad, and despite the night's odd behavior, I fell into form.

"I mean he growled."

"What? Like, you mean, grrrr?"

"Yeah, like a real dog. And he stared her down. I'm telling you, Dave, it was creepy."

"Okay, that's pretty damn weird," I admitted, and grabbed another beer. "He's weird, all right."

"It's none of his business how we raise our children. If we homeschool them or whatever. It pisses me off." He glared over at Dad. "It's more than weird, it's disrespectful. He doesn't respect Jen. She's almost in tears. It's like he hates her or something."

"No shit." I rarely see my brother angry. He doesn't share my temperament. I got high and cynical in high school; my brother played sports. He believes in fair play and gives everyone the benefit of the doubt. I glanced across the room. Dad was quiet, just whispering to Mom. "He wouldn't shut up the whole way down here, just kept talking. And you know what? He's got a memoir."

"A memoir. Really?" My brother smiled. "Are we in it?"

"No, not really, it's all about his head."

"None of the fishing trips? Nothing?"

"It's all theology—Jonathan Edwards and the Great Awakening. You know. I mean, sure, there's stuff on us, but not much. And now all of a sudden he's giving opinions on all of us." I laughed. "The whole family." My brother and I fell silent and studied our parents there, hunched up on the couch.

"God, it's sad."

"She looks awful," Jon said. "Really bad. She's aged ten years."

"Twenty."

"What do you think?"

"I don't know, Jon. You know how Mom gets," I said, echoing my father. "She's having a spell. As long as Dad lets the doctors figure it out, follows their orders, she'll pull through."

"Dad. Yeah, what about him?"

"I don't know. He closes ranks when Mom gets sick. Gets all

defensive." I pulled at my beer and shrugged. "I'll keep an eye on them," I promised. "Don't worry." Both my siblings consider me the favorite child, my father's golden boy, and it's true he listens best to me. Perhaps it's because I'm the eldest, or the loudest. It's not because I'm the wisest; I'm not. Nevertheless, because I have clout and because I live closest, I work the front lines. When it comes to my parents, I'm the first responder, the medic. I sometimes forget this.

I moved back into the party and tried to reassure the family about my mother, who had sunk into the couch, frightened, her eyes following me. "My mom's all right," I told my cousins. "She gets like this sometimes."

My father cut in. "Betty Lee is just having a little case of the whim-whams."

In our family "whim-wham" is code, a defanged reference to any number of moods and psychological disorders, be they depressive, manic, or schizoaffective. Back in the 1970s and '80s—when they were all straight depression—we called them "dark nights of the soul." St. John of the Cross's phrase ennobled our sickness, spiritualized it. We cut God out of it after the manic breaks started in 1986, the year my dad, brother, and I were all committed. Call it manic depression or by its new, polite name, bipolar disorder. Whichever you wish. We stick to our folklore and call it the whim-whams.

"Her whim-whams happen periodically and she always comes through. We're adjusting her medications. Betty Lee and I pray together every day and that really works wonders. She has wonderful doctors, wonderful—a neurologist for the Parkinsonian symptoms and a general doctor, Dr. Hill, that we just love."

"And Bryant, the shrink?" I asked pointedly. I know my parents' psychiatrist. He's mine as well and he's better than most. In my experience, a psychiatrist's most salient feature is brevity. The therapist's fate—the actual listening to patients—terrifies most psychiatrists. They clock their twelve-minute office visits with ruthless efficiency and write scripts in a flash. It takes longer to flush your radiator than it does to alter your brain chemistry. Before Bryant, I barely knew my psychiatrists; I knew the guys down at Jiffy Lube better.

"Bryant? Oh yes, of course."

"And what does Bryant say?" My father sat surrounded by suspicious relatives.

"I believe it's a combination of factors. The new—"

"What's Bryant believe?"

"Please, let me finish. The new drugs she's taking for the Parkinson's are interacting with the lithium in particular. All the church activities and her artwork. She's just exhausted." My mother wanted to illustrate children's books and she still paints small watercolors, sweet little cards with families like ours, two boys and a girl. She has a fondness for still life and she paints when she's well. As he spoke my father held her hands while she sat mutely beside him. Her expression was clouded, her eyes closed as if she were trying to remember herself. None of us bought my father's explanation. It was clear she hadn't painted in a long time. All of us feared the cycling return of my mom's paranoia, her hallucinatory despair.

"What about church?" my brother asked. "Has she been going? I mean before all of this."

"Yes, of course. She was attending a women's Bible study,

which she really enjoyed. I drive her every week or she gets rides." Rides, most likely. For the large part, my father's avoided church ever since he quit preaching. He says the music's too modern or the preaching's too basic, but it's really the people; there are too many people. Without those rides my mother would never see them, all the people she needs.

"So what does Bryant say?"

"The drugs. We're working together to get the right balance."

He had assured no one. My father is known to maintain a significant back stock of medications, many of them psychotropic. Trays of multicolored pills, generations of them, lay open throughout his apartment; he experiments with an almost alchemical zeal. These pills attest to his faith in technology and the clean workings of mechanized flesh, of the impersonal. For my father, salvation works in two spheres, the spiritual and the chemical. Both realms contain great and authoritative mysteries. The former requires prayer; the latter requires pills and then nothing at all—no family discussions, no fifty-minute sessions, no thought.

Ten years ago at my father's direction I poisoned my mother with lithium. My father's teaching duties had called him away and my mother was staying with me when her paranoia began. She seemed unsteady when Dad dropped her off but he assured me that her medication had been adjusted and would soon set her straight. Her psychiatrist increased her dosage and my father gave me detailed instructions. I did as I was told and she grew worse, much worse. Her psychiatrist would not return my phone calls. My mother lost the power of speech and wandered the house frightened and lost. Food dropped from her mouth. Finally, after days of trying, I spoke with her doctor. "Take her to the hospital" was all he would say. I asked if it was the lithium, if he had prescribed the new dose. "Take her to the hospital." He said that three times and hung up. I never spoke with him again. She spent four days in intensive care. Most of us blame the doctor, some my father. I blame myself—for following orders, for crushing the white pills into her applesauce when she began choking on water.

We left the party early. I held my mother and kept her from falling. She looked cold and frail, like a small animal. I threw my coat over her. I didn't want to talk and turned on the news. But Dad wanted to talk and he turned off the radio. He spoke rapidly on politics and the church, sometimes his boyhood. After an hour I tried the radio again; he switched it off without missing a beat. I was tired and sad and so I stopped listening. Outside Springfield, going seventy on the Mass Pike, a woman ran out in front of the car; she missed our bumper by inches. She disappeared before I hit the brake, out of the black and back into the darkness, just like that. The next day I called my father. He said Mom felt better. I asked to speak with her, but he said she was resting. And the next day I left for Colorado, ignoring the signs.

Now, a week later and back from the mountains, it all crashed into place as I lay on my bed and listened to his rambling messages, the kids laughing in the hall and calling me. Of course. Of course, I knew it. I stopped the messages; they just circled around, making me dizzy. I dialed my parents' apartment. Their phone was disconnected and I got up to go. Driving down to Northampton it all seemed so obvious: my father's new manuscripts—two books in two months, the long dinner when my father spoke openly, his new Web site, the newsletter, and now all of the calls.

Their apartment door was locked. I rapped at it hard with my knuckles. The lights went off. I banged on the door, called out. The lights went back on and my father, through the door, said, "Yes?"

"Dad, it's David."

"David Lovelace?"

"Yeah. David Lovelace. Can I come in?"

"No, I don't think that's a good idea."

"Why? What do you mean, not a good idea? Let me in."

His voice lowered. "No," he said slowly, deliberately, as if he were training a dog. "You will not come in. No, you will not. Your mother is resting." I tried the knob again and stepped back. There wasn't much to see from the window. I knocked again but he had stopped talking. There would be no negotiation. I walked past their building, a long row of modest two-story apartments, pushed through some bushes and onto the rear patios. The weather was wet and cold and I saw no one as I stepped from one small yard to the next. Then I saw my father through his sliding glass door. He sat in front of a dismembered phone, its wires and jacks stripped and spread out. The kitchen waste can overflowed next to him: smoked salmon wrappers, tins of tuna, mayonnaise jars, and newspapers. He saw me and reached for the lock but I beat him and jerked back the door.

He stood, towering over me. "You are not coming in. I forbid it." I pushed past him, into the smell of it, my father's madness: the tang of rotted food and the earthy, nauseating smell of vitamins. He backed off then and shrugged; his anger vanished at once. He smiled and spread out his hands. His shirttails were out and his clothes stained with food. "All right. All right. Maybe you're okay. Maybe it's best. You'll see it's okay, David Lovelace. It's best. Welcome." He sat down smiling and his eyes were sharper than knives and too bright to watch.

I sat down slowly, my back to the wall. "Where's Mom?"

"She's upstairs, resting. She's had a bad shock."

"What do you mean, a shock?"

"The family, Rockport. Seeing the family is always a shock."

"Not for her," I muttered to myself. "Dad, I got your calls. I tried to reach you. What's with the phone?" I asked, pointing at the wires, the gutted phone on the table.

He shook his head. "We're having a terrible time with the phones here, just terrible." He paused, calculated, and struck a casual pose. "So, what brings you down here?"

"I'm concerned about Mom. I'm gonna go up and see her."

My father stood. "Well, okay, if you must. She's really doing much better. She's much more herself. Try not to wake her." I moved through the living room, the scattered plastic pillboxes. My father had found a large book on Goya and had it propped up, open to the crucified Christ, with his holy bleeding head and his hand raised in blessing.

Upstairs, I couldn't wake my mother. She was lying on the floor in her nightgown. Her bed was stripped and someone had pushed foam rubber under her head and back. I thought she was dead. I dropped to my knees. I could hear my father moving slowly up the stairs. The air was fetid and it smelled of urine. I leaned close and heard her breathing, rapid and shallow. Her lower lip trembled; for a brief moment it seemed she would speak. Her thin eyelids fluttered slightly and I could see her eyeballs roll and drop beneath them. Then my father appeared in the doorway, smiling hopefully. "You see, David, much better." I stood and moved back. I was badly frightened by him and felt myself shaking. "Dad, what's this green crap?" It was all over her, some of it wet and bright green, most dry and gray, like clay. Her hair was matted with the stuff. It ran from her mouth across her face and down her neck. The thin blanket she had was covered in it. I checked her breathing again, worried she had choked on it. "What is it?" I asked slowly. I tried not to scream.

"Oh. That's a soy protein product we've been using. Lots of B-twelve. You know that settles her nerves. It's a powder. You mix it with water. I feed it to her."

"I see. Okay. What's she doing on the floor?"

"She fell." My father blocked the door. I couldn't breathe and I felt like retching. I needed help and the phones were all fucked.

"Dad, I gotta go. I'll be back later, but right now I gotta go. I think Mom needs help."

My father smiled; he almost beamed. "Well, David. That makes sense. It's been good to see you. I'll let you know how she's coming along. We pray together every day." My father knew it was a series of tests now and he felt he had passed the first one, held it together. He hadn't raved and I was leaving the apartment. No one would take her away. No one would ask him to leave. They were inseparable.

I didn't have a phone so I drove straight to the cops. I regretted it immediately. The cop behind the Plexiglas made me sit and wait while he talked to his radio. He was younger than I am. This was a waste of time; I should have just called an ambulance. I paced until a shitty little speaker crackled.

"Sir?"

"My mother needs an ambulance. She's unconscious and my father is manic, is having a manic break." Should I say "crazy"? Did he even know what "manic" meant?

"Sir?"

"Crazy." There, I'd done it. Fuck. "My dad's fucking out of it. He's bipolar. My mother needs an ambulance."

"Watch your language, sir. The address?" I gave it to him.

"All right, sir. Just have a seat. I'll send for a patrol car."

"I'll meet them back there."

I paced the parking lot; I should have called an ambulance straightaway. I knew the cops could make it worse, much worse, just by showing up. I remember seeing their lights through the windows when they came for me, and they lit the room red and flashed. I had hit the floor and crawled to the bathroom. I locked the door and looked for razors—just to scare them, I thought. When they came up the steps and rapped on the door, I stripped and ducked into the shower. My friends said, don't worry, Dave, don't worry, and then they let them inside. I could hear them all talking and I clapped my hands on my ears and started to sing. I slid down in the shower and sang.

I waited outside my father's apartment and remembered Woody Woodward, a local man who died up in Brattleboro. He was scared and so he found a church, interrupted the Sunday service, and asked for help. He spoke rapidly and incoherently. Woodward appeared delusional; he claimed the CIA was after him. He had a penknife and when the police came he held it up to his eye and pleaded for help. The cops shot him seven times, including once in the back and once as he lay on the carpet. Then they cuffed him. He died in surgery and both policemen were cleared of wrongdoing.

That's what can happen and that's how we think: seven shots and dying right there at the pulpit. We see how scared all the straights are—how primal that fear is—and we feed off that fear. We know how fast things go bad. One minute you're asking for sanctuary, the next facing guns.

I waited twenty minutes in the parking lot. I knew my father was watching. When the police pulled in I knew he was inside, pacing, making decisions. Fortunately, the police moved calmly. They listened closely and we planned our approach together. I kept saying my father was harmless. "He isn't dangerous," I said, with my mother dying upstairs.

I knocked on the door but my father was spooked and hiding. I led the cops through the bushes and wet patios, the brown oak leaves in drifts. My father sat by the broken phones and when the cop rapped on the glass he turned and smiled. He held his palms out and shrugged.

"Sir, open the door."

"Okay, okay. That would be fine but—"

"Please open the door, sir."

"All right, all right. This is just fine. Just give me a moment." My father stepped into the adjacent bathroom. He came out a few tense minutes later with his hair combed and his shirt tucked in, and he unlocked the door. I could see him throttle down against all the drama, the cops and the lights, against his worst fears: that his mind had burned down, that they'd bury his wife and lock him away. Now here they were, standing in his kitchen with guns and clubs, and somehow he smiled and spoke slowly, a professor again, a calm, reasonable man. One cop stayed with him and one came with me. My mother hadn't moved. The cop cursed slowly, under his breath. He knelt on one knee and felt for her pulse.

"What's all this green crap?" he asked, and I told him. For a moment my mother seemed like some tribal death head, smeared with ritual clay and locked in a trance. The cop gagged. "Open the window," he ordered, then radioed for the ambulance. I went downstairs and found my father explaining his prayers and his potions, the green soy dust all over his table.

"You see that," he said, pointing to an imprinted book bag. "That's the symbol of the Presbyterian church. I am an ordained minister in the Presbyterian church. The mainline Presbyterian church, not one of those split P's." My father leaned and picked up the bag. It was indeed a Presbyterian book bag, clearly emblazoned with a cross and large capital P. My father exhibited the bag's symbol with solemnity. The book bag had become a talisman for him and he rarely let it out of his sight.

I told my dad about the ambulance, that we were taking Betty Lee to the hospital. I knew my father understood the situation deep down, knew he couldn't duck it. Below his smile, his careful manners, beneath his delusions, he knew it was grave. He knew his wife was near death and that he was not right and that he had left her there dying. He knew the soy protein was bullshit, that he sang the hymns all alone. He knew that his chattered prayers were all bent and broken and still he prayed to God they would work. And they did, too, because I came to triage his mind and pick up my mother, because I knew what to do; I'd been on both sides. My father watched from his full-blown mania, from his paranoid seat at the right hand of God, as the disgusted EMTs stared at his smile and lifted my mother onto the gurney.

I love my father. I knew what he was attempting because I've done it at times, passed myself off as sane by sheer force of will. Like my father, I've seen the beautiful cartwheel of thoughts pitch past and crash and I've learned not to speak of them, to let them all go. I can stand inside a desperate circus and force my mind to slow, if only for a few moments. It is the hardest work I've ever known. And now I watched my father attempt it, try to gather a mind much deeper than mine, try to hold back a green interior ocean full of monsters and wonders. I watched as he reeled in each rocking moment, as he stood in her bedroom and loved her and smiled.

I left him alone in his apartment and drove up to the hospital. They taped oxygen tubes under my mother's nose, pushed a needle in her arm, and taped it for the glucose drip. They said she was severely dehydrated, that her blood was like sludge. They pulled some of it for a lithium level. I explained the green soy drink again. We talked about strokes. I mentioned her state at my cousin's in Rockport and I mentioned her lithium poisoning. Still, she was unconscious and a stroke seemed most likely. I walked with my mom and a nurse up to intensive care. There'd be an MRI in the morning. I sat a long time by her bed and it felt like a grave, but her eyelids still fluttered. I left her, called Roberta from the lobby and ran out of change. I went back to my dad. It was long past midnight and he was awake. His bed was stripped, too. I suspect it hadn't been slept in for weeks. I told him that Mom was all right now and resting, that we would go over in the morning. I was exhausted. I asked for his car keys. He stood then, his smile tightened, and he spat out his words. "Absolutely not. I'm legally entitled to drive. We've been all through that."

"Dad, I can't let you drive."

"Oh, you can't, can you?" He rose up and snarled. "That's enough. That's more than enough. Get out now, David Lovelace." I threw up my hand and left without another word. Hell, he could light out for anywhere.

I slept hard and woke early at home. I called my brother to let him know it had busted wide open. He said he'd come on the weekend. I waited an hour, called my sister Peggy, and said Mom might be dying.

"She's still not conscious?"

"No. I mean I haven't been there today but it looks pretty bad."

"So, Dad just left her like that? On the floor?"

"Peg, he's out of his mind. You can't blame him. I mean maybe you can but that's not important right now. I've got to get him somewhere, into a hospital."

"Right," she said, and slipped into gear. She doesn't have it but she knows all about our disease. She knows the drill; she's a professional, a therapist with a practice out west. I needed her badly.

"Get him to the psychiatrist—what's his name?"

"Bryant."

"Get him over to Bryant right away, like this morning. It's an emergency and he'll make room in his schedule. We need to get Dad safe and back on his meds today. He's a loose cannon right now. Bryant should give you the paperwork to commit Dad if he won't sign voluntarily."

"He probably won't, not after yesterday."

"Right. Make sure you get the form. Each state's different. I don't know what it's called out there, but Bryant will know. Okay? I'll book a flight but it might be a few days. I'll see. Now, call Bryant immediately and then keep me posted. Use my cell."

I booked an appointment and drove back to my father's. This time he let me in before I could knock. He was waiting for me, playing *Don Giovanni* loudly and pacing. His clothes were the same. Books and papers littered the floor. He held out his strangely limp, sweaty hand and I shook it. "Thanks, David, for coming. I'm so glad you did what you did. You know best." He smiled. "Everything's just marvelous here."

"Good."

"Listen, David, I did just as you suggested. I dumped Bank of America."

"You did what?"

"I went in a few days ago and closed my account. I got everything out of safe-deposit." He thought I'd be pleased. He'd heard my complaints about the mega-bank, how they turned me down for a loan. I realized he had taken my financial rant seriously.

"Where is it?"

"What?"

"I don't know, the stuff you had in your safe-deposit box. What was in the box?"

"Oh, our will, a few of Grandmère's rings, I think our life insurance policy. And the gold, of course."

"Gold?"

"British gold sovereigns."

"Sovereigns. How much?"

"Well, the markets fluctuate, of course. You know, Peter Grady got us to cash out all our stocks and buy gold. Remember Peter Grady? From church? A marvelous idea, just wonderful. Y2K?" He shrugged. "No problem at all. There's always gold, no matter what—"

"Dad, that was five years ago. Besides, it didn't even happen."

"What didn't happen?"

"Y2K."

"Yes, it did. Clearly it did. Just look at the date."

"Okay, okay. How much?"

"Sixty, seventy thousand if you want just a rough figure. If you'd like, we can look it up. I have today's paper." He had the whole month's papers in a pile by the welcome mat.

"Where?"

"It's in the basement."

"In the laundry room? The building's laundry room?"

"No, no," he reassured me, "next to it. It's in a yellow tackle box."

"Do you mind if I go get it?"

"Not at all, not at all."

The yellow tackle box was there all right, on the concrete floor next to my father's snow tires. I hauled it upstairs. I suggested we walk downtown to my bank. I assured my father it was local and benevolent, a good place for a safe deposit box. He shrugged and put on his coat. An aria finished as we stepped out the door. "Wonderful piece that," my father said. "Wonderful."

Sixty grand worth of gold is heavy. I worried the tackle box might snap open, its tiny hinges give out, so I held it under my arm, hoping my dad wouldn't change his mind, hoping I wouldn't end up chasing him around town with a plastic box full of gold.

The bank's atmosphere quieted my father somewhat. I sat with the tackle box on my lap and tried to offer as little information as possible. "You know," my father said, "gold is a much sounder investment these days than paper—bonds and such."

The manager fiddled with some keys on her desk. She wore one of those unfortunate business suits and her nails had been done up with tiny stars. "Oh, that may be so, sir. I get a number of questions about it."

"British sovereigns. That's the way to go. Here, I'll write that down for you."

"Dad, she doesn't need you to write it down."

My father's voice slowed, became emphatic. "I am writing it down." He finished and handed his note to the banker with a flourish. He smiled. "When the meltdown comes, your best bet is gold." You couldn't argue with that. I smiled at the manager. She moved through the forms, my father filled his box up with gold, and we escaped without incident.

Now, with the gold safely squirreled away, I considered my father and how best to help him. I got the car and we drove to the hospital. To visit Mom, I told him, and then go from there. My mother seemed unchanged—cleaned up, but no better. No one at the desk knew anything. My father leaned over her bed and whispered encouragement. He pulled her beat-up old Bible from his Presbyterian bag and read a psalm quietly, his face close to hers. He prayed for her. He loves her so much.

Next, I brought Dad to our psychiatrist. Bryant was efficient. He asked one simple question and let my father do the rest. "So, Richard, how are you doing?" At that my father rambled for five minutes, discussing medicine, interdenominational feuds, God, opera, his mother and mine. He modeled his Presbyterian book bag, holding the great P to his chest—a sort of crazed denominational superhero. Bryant finally cut in. "So, Richard, you would say you are—"

"Wonderful."

"Well. Quite frankly, Richard, you shouldn't be. Your wife's in the ICU; she may have had a stroke. You shouldn't be wonderful."

My father dropped his smile and took another tack. "Yes, yes, of course. I am quite concerned. I think it was the medicine you were giving her, frankly. But she's in good hands now. David Lovelace is here and things are moving along well."

"I'm afraid you're acting inappropriately. I understand religion is important to you, but you're using grandiose religious terms—"

"You're Irish Catholic," my father injected dismissively. "You're antireligious."

"Richard, you're delusional. You've given me every indication of a manic break." He pulled out the green pad. "I'm giving you a prescription for Seroquel. That should help you sleep. I've got some samples here somewhere." He rummaged in his file cabinet. Psychiatrists' cabinets may or may not contain files, but are regularly filled with brightly boxed samples: psychotropic candies, Wellbutrin pens, and Zoloft staplers.

Bryant found what he was looking for and gave me two boxes. He asked my father to wait outside. "I agree with you. Your father's full-blown. I suspected as much and he's just confirmed it. He left three increasingly incoherent messages on our machine last night."

"He loves answering machines."

"Yes, well. Are you all right?" he asked me. I nodded. "Your meds good? You'll need to keep it together. Stay in touch. Now, we should get him in right away. We'll try Northampton first. Can you get him to go with you, sign himself in?"

"I don't know."

"I'll call Cooley Dick and recommend hospitalization."

I told my father we'd head back to the hospital around dinnertime to check on Mom. No change. I took my dad to the snack bar and told him what I thought, what Bryant thought. I could see his thoughts race now, looking for an out. "Look. It's up to you, but the psych ward isn't bad here. You should consider spending a few days, just to get your meds straightened out, get some regular sleep." The last thing he wanted was sleep—he had too much to do—and there was no chance in hell he'd take Seroquel without supervision. Your average mood stabilizers—lithium, Depakote—are aspirin compared to antipsychotics like Seroquel. Seroquel is better than most, but any antipsychotic hits like a club to the head. They knock manic patients out of the trees. Twenty years ago doctors had given me the granddaddy of them all, Thorazine, and it hammered me. My muscles went rigid and my mind stopped dead and I lurched through the ward like Frankenstein's monster. I want to say I'd take it again if I needed it, but I fear that I wouldn't. I'd run.

I know my father considered it and he might have done it but for my mom. "Mom will be right downstairs," I said. "You'll be on the fifth floor and Mom on the third. You could visit." I knew there would be no visits. The fifth floor was a lockdown. This was the first of my lies. "Look, Dad, you're a little out of whack. That's all. You'll be out in a few days." Another lie. "You heard what Bryant said, you just need to slow down a bit so you can take care of Mom. She needs you." That much was true.

"Bryant is antireligion. He doesn't believe in the efficacy of prayer. He's friendly enough, sure"—my father's face twisted— "but he's not a Presbyterian. He's not even Protestant."

"Okay. Forget Bryant. He's a papist. I'm sorry I brought him up." It was strange. I was reasoning with Oliver Cromwell: milord, the blood-letter is not a heretic. "Listen," I said, "let's get you away from Bryant, get you hooked up with folks who understand." And so, Bryant's judgments were rendered null, just like that. He was my father's enemy now, perhaps all Christendom's, and I wouldn't mention him again. Dad would never take his drugs now.

"You know the drill, Dad. If you sign yourself in here, you can leave whenever you wish. But if you decide not to sign yourself in, well, then I'll have to do it. Then a whole bunch of bureaucracy gums up the works. Just sign in. For Mom's sake." I looked at him straight. I could smell his mind working fast, sparking. His eyes spun just like slots and I waited for the payoff.

"All right, David. If you think it best. Personally I think it's overkill. I'm perfectly fine."

"But you'll do it?"

"I guess."

I moved quickly now. We exited the hospital's main doors and walked around to the emergency entrance. A bit dramatic, I thought—provocative—but psychiatric admissions pass through those gates. Walking past the stacked ambulances, I prayed he wouldn't stop, wouldn't turn and ask questions. The ER was bright, a scratchy electric yellow that hurt my eyes. It was a limbo and I've waited here, too, waited for the wheelchair upstairs, the next ferry over the Styx. Over there, on the ward, they knock you down dead and hope you rise again sane on the third day or month. My father was jittery, mercurial; the triage nurse was harried and dismissive. She pushed us back on the list. In the ER a cut finger—a handful of stitches—takes precedence over our often fatal disease, despite the bad odds. One out of every four untreated bipolar individuals dies by suicide. Not there on the ER floor, mind you, but later, after they give up and leave. Suicide is simply the finishing touch, an end to slow death by depression. You can't blame them.

But my father stayed because I did, because I asked him not to leave. I did everything short of card tricks to keep him occupied, keep his paranoia at bay. A social worker finally took us in hand. She did not work for the hospital; she was not a psychiatric nurse. She worked for Safety Net, an independent, state-funded advocacy group. I had to get past her first, prove to her I was a good son, that my father was indeed mad. It was unfortunate that at this moment he looked remarkably sane, relaxed even, charming.

He was good, all right; he managed the act better than I ever did. But after a forty-five-minute chat with my father, the social worker took me aside. "I agree with you and Dr. Bryant. Your father could benefit from hospitalization. He's agreed to sign himself in, and that makes it so much easier. Unfortunately, there are no available beds on ward tonight. Could you come back tomorrow?"

I looked at her incredulously.

"You think I can get him back to commit himself again tomorrow? After two and half hours in the ER?"

"I don't know." Why did they wait to tell me? Were they just practicing? My father would have to wait a day for the next ferry.

When I got home Roberta pulled out her calendar and we scheduled the crisis. She told me not to worry about the children; she could make it home for Mary's bus and we'd get extra days at Hunter's preschool. "Get someone to cover the bookstore. Just concentrate on your parents and I'll do the rest."

Mary overheard us and came into the kitchen. "What about my play?" She was ten years old and had the lead. "Dress rehearsal's tomorrow."

"I've got to teach tomorrow afternoon," Roberta said. "I can't get out of that. You'll have to take her." Mary had her costume on, just a big sweater. She was Charlie Brown and had a date with a pumpkin.

"I'll take you, Mary. We'll just have to go a little early and pick up Papa. All right?"

"I guess so. Is he coming to rehearsal?"

"No, he has an appointment."

"Good," she said. "I need to practice first. Papa might get bored."

"Don't worry about that, darling." I glanced at Roberta. "That's the least of our worries. He's not coming. We just need to drop him off at the hospital. It won't take long." It seemed like a reasonable plan, not ideal, of course, but reasonable. It wouldn't take long—the paperwork was done. My father wasn't dangerous and if I worked it right he wouldn't be scary. It was okay for Mary to see this, to begin understanding this part of the family. How bad could it be?

Bad. It was another day, and so another round of forms was required, another psychiatric evaluation by a non-psychiatrist, another long wait. I had promised that today would be quick and told Mary that we could have ice cream afterward, but we'd already spent forty minutes in the waiting area. Now, waiting again in the small, bright examination room, my father and I tried out some small talk as Mary sat in the corner and whispered her lines. We pretended nothing was out of the ordinary, just another errand: pick up milk, drop off kids, commit Dad to asylum.

Finally, the door opened and a slight man in a white coat and holding a clipboard slipped inside. "Hi, I'm Mark," he said. That's it, just Mark. Not Dr. Mark, not even Mr. Mark. He was balding but had managed to coax a wispy gray ponytail back from his temples. He was Safety Net and he was letting his freak flag fly. He was on our side, defending us from doctors and other medical professionals. After another forty-five-minute interview, wherein my father lost his much-abused patience, brandished his Presbyterian book bag over his head, insisted Bryant was a heathen

Irishman, and repeatedly referred to me by my full, somewhat unfortunate given name—David Brainerd Lovelace—the interview concluded. I realized Mary had wandered off. My father now refused to enter voluntarily, to commit himself. It was hard to blame him; I wanted out, too. Both the breadth of my father's knowledge and the force of his controlled mania seemed to diminish our friend Mark. He warbled like Joan Baez while my father belted Rossini. Mark seemed unsure as we stepped into the hallway. Where the hell did Mary go? I'd been too busy bottling my rage to notice. Mark put his hand on my shoulder, an attempt at compassion. "Well, I have good news. Your father seems okay. He's presently not a danger to himself or others. I cannot recommend that your father be involuntarily committed at this time."

I pushed back from him, stunned. "Okay? You think he's okay? My mother's upstairs in a coma. He left her on the floor for days. Tried to force-feed her some green, soylent product. He's off his meds. He's noncompliant. He's driving around. Last night he saw some infomercial and bought a three-thousand-dollar mattress."

"The incident with your mother was a few days ago now. He seems better."

"What the fuck?" I was close to losing it. "How the fuck do you know?" Nurses watched from their stations, agog. When she heard my voice from down the hall Mary returned, her hands and pockets full of candy corn raided from somewhere out back. I stepped into Mark's face and he backed away, held his clipboard out, and ducked slightly.

"How do you know he's off his meds?" he asked defensively. "Has he had a blood level?"

"A blood level? No, I've been too busy visiting my mother in the ICU and talking with not-even-doctors to arrange a fucking blood level." I'd lost it and Mark moved closer to the nurses. Mary stood riveted, popping her candy. "What? Are you trying to protect my father? Do you think I want to do this? Do you think this is fun? Do you think he's a victim, that I'm victimizing him?" I was loud now. I wanted to hit him.

"Mr. Lovelace, I understand you're upset, that this is upsetting." Mark looked sympathetic and nervous. His eyes grew large and moist. He was breathing rapidly. "We all want what's best for your father." I snorted. "We all want what's best for him." Mark gestured to the caring ER staff—three openmouthed nurses and two newly arrived and very large orderlies. "You have to understand. Your father needs an advocate. I'm his advocate. You know, they used to warehouse patients—"

"This isn't a fucking warehouse, it's a hospital and I want a doctor. His psychiatrist called and said to admit him."

"Yesterday, he called yesterday," Mark clarified.

I leaned in to the well-meaning Mark and grabbed his nametag. "You're a chickenshit, Mark. Do your fucking job. I'm not leaving until my father's locked up." I stepped back, disgusted. "I don't want to talk to Safety fucking Net anymore. I want a doctor." An orderly closed in behind me and I saw security approach fast down the hall. I stopped and smiled grimly.

Mary stood beside me. It was time for her play. "C'mon, Charlie Brown," I said softly, and pulled her close. I held her tight and turned toward the orderlies. They stared me down and I said under my breath, "You're not locking me up. You can't lock anyone up." I looked around at them all and back toward my father. He sat quietly in the bright examination room and smiled at my scene. "Goddammit," I said, and grabbed my daughter's hand, pulled her away from all this and marched toward the door. "C'mon, Dad!" I yelled over my shoulder, and I kicked their swinging door as hard as I could. It hit the wall loud, like a rifle crack.

I unlocked the truck and Mary climbed up quietly. She wouldn't look at me. Great, I thought, now my daughter needs therapy—already. Good grief. I saw my father moving slowly across the lot. "Sorry, darling," I said. "Sorry about all this." She just nodded and picked at her sweater. I held the door for my father and he stayed quiet as well. "I'm driving you home, Dad. I need to get Mary to rehearsal."

"Of course, of course," he said, and fell silent for most of the drive. I thought he was gloating until we got to his door. "What about Betty Lee? We didn't see Mom."

"I know, Dad, I—"

"She's all right, isn't she? She'll be all right?"

"Sure. Sure, Dad. Try to get some sleep and I'll see you tomorrow."

Back in the truck I apologized again. "Sorry, Mary. I had no idea it would be like that, take so long. Lousy way to spend the afternoon, huh?"

"Yeah, I guess." She pulled on Charlie Brown's sweater and smiled. "It was kind of funny, Dad."

"Funny." Nothing was funny. My father was out; he had won the first battle. I had no way to slow him or keep him safe.

"The way you yelled at that guy in there and when you

slammed the door. I've never seen you get mad like that. I thought it was funny."

"What about Papa? How did he seem?"

"Crazy, I guess. But okay. I mean he wasn't scary or anything." Then Mary opened her script and began practicing her role. She seemed fine; she was learning. My mother stayed with us once and fell sick. Mary was just a toddler, and she watched Grammy move through the house all heartsick and broken and unable to speak. She's seen my medicines. Five years ago I was manic and sat on our porch with her and her brother. Mary was seven and Hunter just three; I was forty-two and full-blown. She had some clay and we sat and made figures while my mind rushed away and I tried not to follow; I tried to stay home. My wife, Roberta, came home and rescued me just like the first time, twenty-two years ago. Roberta is quiet, strong. She knows the school calendar and remembers the mortgage. She leaves me notes in the morning. She says the kids will be fine, that they take after her side on this, my family's disease. They'll have, she said, the best of both worlds, and I want to believe her.

But I want to be ready. I've seen both my parents drown in the sickness. I've seen my brother sink down. I've denied my own madness and I've loved it almost to death. All my life I've heard my family blame each other, some devil, some church, genetics, and shrinks. We're ashamed and afraid of our minds. I want to believe my wife and not worry. I want to get strong and show my kids how. I want my family fearless and proud.

TWO

My parents met in 1954 at the Peniel Bible Conference, a small church camp in upstate New York. This camp shaped my parents' courtship, their marriage, and the rest of their lives—all of our lives, really. It's the closest my brother, sister, and I ever got to a hometown. Peniel sat at the base of Mount Cobble, best described as an oversized hill with a good view. The camp took its old-time religion straight from the tent revivals of the Great Depression and it looked it. Unaffiliated with any specific denomination, any real source of funds, the camp was built from the basics: sweat, rough lumber, God, and the Devil.

The dining hall was sheathed in wooden slats pulled from World War II ammunition crates. It was a long, utilitarian building with a massive stone fireplace set at one end and it smelled of wood smoke and oatmeal. The pine woods were full of cabins built from damp, greenish pine and dotted by red and white lichen. Each section, the boys' and the girls', had two outhouses. Our assembly field was the packed earth between the dining hall and the chapel, and it doubled as the playing field. Peniel had an underused baseball diamond in a place we called the Dustbowl.

The Channel, our swimming hole, was a cleared stretch of marsh full of soft mud and sharp grasses. There were redwing blackbirds and painted turtles, too, and there was no swimming on Sundays. The chapel was a simple pine building with a great bronze bell on its porch. This bell woke us, sent us to calisthenics, meetings (Bible study), meals, more meetings (prayer), and bed. Peniel washed my whole family in the blood of the Lamb—regularly—and that's something each of us carries in various ways. It's hard to forget.

My mother was born in 1925, the youngest of three children. Her father was a banker and the family lost almost everything in the Crash of 1929. He lost the rest five years later when his wife died. My grandfather continued; he kept his suits pressed and found work, but his sorrow went bitter and poisoned him. He began attending the fire-and-brimstone crusades and was saved by the infamous Billy Sunday, the preacher who rallied for Prohibition. "There isn't a man who votes for the saloon who doesn't deserve to have his boy die a drunkard," Sunday thundered. "He deserves to have his girl live out her life with a drunken husband." This made good, stern sense to my grandfather. He renounced the Devil and set about raising his children, my mother, Betty Lee, her sister, Rose, and her brother, Frank, in a dark world full of sinners. My grandfather ruled his house absolutely, with righteousness and a hard hand, and my mother, the youngest, served him from breakfast to bedtime. He remarried but his new wife resented the children. Their stepmother berated them all for years and then she just left.

My mom was the youngest and seemed to suffer in her childhood the most. She was nine when her mother died. At sixteen, her brother, Frank, took charge of the family's happiness. He staged my mother's dearest memories with magic, vaudeville acts, and art. He called her "Midget" and she was his magician's assistant. He scoured the city for costumes and wigs and had his younger sisters up on his backyard stage every day after school. Rose dressed my mother; she turned her baby sister into princesses and cowgirls and fairies. The three of them pretended together; they acted out other people's stories, happy ones. Frank and Rose are the heroes of her happiest memories. Mom is the one who still carries her father's heartbreak. She was his favorite, and all of her love is stitched down by worry.

My dad was born in Hollywood, where his father fixed scripts for Twentieth Century Fox and drank. When he smashed my grandmother's Rolls Royce she initiated divorce proceedings immediately. As soon as the court allowed she moved my six-year-old father to Albuquerque, New Mexico, where she burned every letter, photograph, and press clipping concerned with the man. If my grandmother could have extracted her ex-husband's DNA from her son, she would have done so immediately. She never spoke of Hunter Lovelace again, not even with my father. She told him Japanese submarines were the reason they left California. An attack, she said, was imminent.

My father grew up a virtual orphan on the high New Mexican desert. By the time he turned nine he discovered books could rescue him and let him leave his autocratic mother far behind.

The farther the better, and for my father that meant spaceships. Back then, before the Bomb, science still conjured a utopian future. The classic science fiction of the era took this on faith, built its castles in the air and sometimes destroyed them. My father never quite outgrew these stories. He let go of the hardware, sure, but he never let go of the vision, his hope for a shining city on a hill.

Gus Armstrong, my father's only high school friend, dragged him out of the books and into the desert. They caught Gila monsters and hunted, jumping ducks from irrigation ditches along the Rio Grande. They found a case of dynamite down in an old mineshaft and they spent weeks blowing boulders from cliffs. They spied on a Hopi snake dance and afterward caught two of the rattlesnakes and brought them back to town. The rattlers' fangs had been ripped out for the dance. My grandmother tolerated them until new fangs appeared.

In the summer of 1948, just before my father went east, Gus Armstrong decided to round out my father's preparatory education with a trip to a brothel he knew in Juarez. Driving south, the boys entertained themselves with a twenty-two-caliber pistol, shooting road signs and groundhogs from the car window. A groundhog ducked; my father pulled back the pistol and slipped the gun's hammer. Bang. Silence ensued and then Gus asked calmly, "Richard. Did you just shoot a hole in my Buick?"

"No, Gus," my father answered, just as slow and deliberate. "I did not. I shot a hole in my leg." Gus pulled over, fashioned a sort of tourniquet, and they turned back home.

"I guess that trip just wasn't God's will," my father remarked to me years later. The doctors left the slug in my father, just above his right knee, and when I was a boy I'd ask to see the bullet all the time. The bullet is still lodged right there in his muscle, like a piece of God's will, coppery green and buried in flesh. Shortly after the aborted trip to Juarez, my father limped into Yale on crutches, a gun-shot atheist.

In 1943 Frank encouraged my mother to enroll at the Pratt Institute in New York City. He had become a successful photographer and supported his worried kid sister with money and love. My mother hoped to illustrate children's books and she worked extremely hard, repaying Frank with her happy watercolors: the girls all in pigtails, their brothers with slingshots, calico aprons for Mom, and for Dad a pipe and the paper. But her normal undergraduate concerns began building and mutating. She stopped worrying about grades but feared for her soul. She worked harder and harder to stay with her painting, to keep her paranoia contained.

She finally broke at the end of her senior year, just prior to project deadlines and exams. She had been studying and painting for days. She was jacked up on coffee and had stopped sleeping, just pushing herself. And then late one night she looked up from her paintings, the blue skies and children, and she saw a wicked figure, a demon hunched in the corner of her room, watching. She snapped and heard voices; the creature just stayed in the corner, waiting. Her close friend and roommate, Margaret, sought help. By the next day she was labeled schizophrenic and put away. Her diagnosis didn't change for forty years.

It was 1949 and psychiatrists diagnosed almost all delusional

illness as schizophrenia—"shattered mind." Nervous break-
downs were one thing, but with hallucinations it was pretty
damn hopeless. They didn't have antipsychotic drugs. They didn't
have Thorazine, Stelazine, Trilafon, Zyprexa, and the rest. All
they had was electroshock. They'd been using it for eight or nine
years when my mother got sick. The treatment wasn't yet perfected, but it was a fairly simple procedure. Electrodes are placed
on either side of the patient's head. An electric stimulus is applied, causing seizure and convulsions lasting fifteen seconds or
so. Patients may experience short-term memory loss but no evidence of brain damage has been linked to proper dosages. They
had established the proper doses by the time my mother got sick.
Now it's called ECT and technicians use muscle relaxants to
inhibit the full-scale convulsions. This removes physical dangers such as the breaking or dislocation of bones. Sedatives are
administered to quell panic. ECT is often effective, especially
with chronic, drug-resistant depression. It seems to work for
some people—no one knows why exactly.

It seemed to work for my mom. She was there for quite a time
but her delusions did pass and before long she returned to her
painting. It remained unclear when my mother would be released but in those days, before all the medicines, a diagnosis of
schizophrenia usually meant long-term hospitalization and even
lifelong institutionalization. Eventually, one of the nurses noticed her artwork, the healing it had brought, and she began
advocating for her release. My mother's college roommate, Margaret, enlisted help from her church camp and Peniel brought
in its big guns. Miss Beers was the central leader and spiritual
guide of the camp. She was formidable, a veteran of the prewar

mission fields of Japan. Grover Wilcox was a fundamentalist preacher from Newark, a firebrand who turned his house into a church and combed the ghetto streets for souls to save. His sense of righteousness made him fearless and he hit like a freight train. Beers and Wilcox descended on the hospital like twin holy terrors and demanded my mother's release.

Wilcox brought my mother home to his house church, where his family gave her a room and a place at their table. My mother stayed afraid but Wilcox had built a mighty fortress and he kept her safe for a time. He kept my mother from slipping out of the world, even as he renounced it. He didn't approve of art, but he helped my mother graduate, finally, from Pratt. She took a job teaching art in Newark's elementary schools. Every morning my mother stood in front of kids from the projects, handed out scissors and glue, and tried to organize art. Art teachers are just a step removed from substitutes. Their motives are pure and their discipline vague. They make excellent time-honored targets and provide ammunition in the form of art supplies. And my mother, she was a hopeless disciplinarian. She raised me. Mom says teaching art in the Newark public schools was the most terrifying experience of her life. The next summer, when the pastor offered her a ride to Peniel she jumped at it. He packed up his family, thirty-odd church kids, a few lost souls, and my mother and headed upstate.

As for my father, he soon outgrew science fiction, pistols, and groundhogs. He majored in philosophy and music composition. He studied existentialism seriously enough to be terrified and found Schoenberg's twelve-tone scale appalling. He packed up his life and moved everything into his head. He often closed his eyes in concentration, as if hearing some silent, slow music. This slow music made driving dangerous and dating awkward; by his senior year my father had dug himself into a social and ideological hole. It wasn't long before an odd student named John Guray stepped into it.

Guray was prematurely bald, walked with a limp and a cane, and wrote light verse. He wore berets and had discovered psychoanalysis. Guray was made for psychoanalysis and began practicing his art on my father incessantly. He kept notes and made charts. He pondered my father's dreams. It was Guray who convinced my dad to travel west and find his father. In fact Guray went along for the ride, guiding my father and his subconscious across the country.

My dad had not seen or heard from his father until the day he and Guray tracked him down. They found him in Hollywood, working on a studio lot. "He was nice enough. Somewhat reserved," my father said to me recently. "He introduced us to some blond starlet. I think he wanted to make sure we weren't gay, that we showed some interest."

His father then introduced them to Cecil B. DeMille, and when my father asked, "How did you part the Red Sea, Mr. DeMille?" DeMille replied, "I didn't, son. God did." And that was it. That's all my father told me. That's all he knew of his father. A blond bombshell and Cecil B. DeMille stole the show.

Upon their return to New Haven, a crestfallen John Guray claimed the analysis and their relationship could go no further, that my father had experienced a great breakthrough. He then produced a bill for four thousand dollars. All my father got from plumbing his subconscious was a road trip and a ridiculous invoice. My father felt he really owed Guray—that's how lost he was. He looked for guidance in his books and found it in Thomas Merton's autobiography, *The Seven Storey Mountain*. Merton's story brought him to God. Yale's so-called New Critics, Cleanth Brooks among them, had given my father a well-lit, archetypically ordered universe, and now Merton's God would give it meaning. My father even considered monastic life in Merton's order.

About this time John Guray began sending my father handwritten bills that he marked "Overdue." My father avoided him and began attending church. Guray began attending church and suggested my father meet a minister acquaintance, Don Mostrom. Before long my father was attending a weekly Bible study run by Mostrom and some other theologically astute, serious men. A number of them spoke highly of the Peniel Bible Conference; a few were in leadership roles as members of Peniel's Prayer Council. They tore up John Guray's bills and began mentoring my father.

My dad had recently been fired from Berman Salvage & Scrap, where he had earned his way by scraping gold tracings from discarded spark plugs. He had few prospects. But he had a Yale philosophy degree, so he found a job teaching seventh graders at the Riverdale Country School. Like my mother, he found the experience unrewarding. He's referred to his pupils as "snarling, derisive children of affluence." He fled in a hail of spitwads and headed straight for Peniel—again, just like my mother. His career had stalled, perhaps, but he was now clear about what he wanted to do. He wanted to help build the Kingdom of God—that "shining city upon a hill" proclaimed by the Puritan leader John Winthrop. He went to Peniel because it was a big job and he was unsure where to begin. That was 1954, the summer he met my mother.

It's a wonder Peniel Bible Conference ever brought my parents together, a tribute to the biological imperative. Love is a great mystery, and nowhere more mysterious than at Bible camp. In my experience the place routinely smothered romance with spiritual angst and Bible study. We were taught that no matter how attractive we found fellow campers, we were all clothed in the Old Man or the Flesh, camp-speak for our corrupt, fallen natures. My father, of course, has a different view. I know my father believes they were set up. Why else, he argues, would they have made him assist in my mother's arts and crafts class? But in the end, it wasn't church history or Peniel's machinations that drew them together, it was my mother when she's well—her empathy, her ease and laughter with friends, and what my father calls her "cheery, elfin smile."

They were married in 1958, just after my father graduated from Westminster Seminary. My parents honeymooned in Lenox, Massachusetts, where Dad commenced Mom's education at the Tanglewood Music Festival. When they returned from Lenox, Grover Wilcox ordained my father as his assistant pastor. He moved in, and so my parents began their life together on the top floor of a house church in Newark, New Jersey. Wilcox was known for his legalism, a worldview held by the hardest of the hard core, the separatists of fundamentalism. Wilcox labeled anything secular—art, sports, politics right or left, beer—"of the World," a distraction from God. He disapproved of my father reading the *New York Times*. He threw out the arts section. His church piano was for hymns only—certain ones—and my father remembers playing a Beethoven sonata when Wilcox barged in. "What is that, Richard?" he yelled. "Scales?" Wilcox and other Peniel leaders took pride in their cultural isolation, in the blessed assurance of songs known by heart. My father was suspect; he worked on a whole different scale.

But the following summer Dad connected with Julian Alexander, a like-minded minister from Scotch Plains, New Jersey. They were washing dishes together in the camp kitchen when my father began complaining about Wilcox and legalism. "The elders at Mostrom's church drink beer all the time. And John Murray, at Westminster, the theologian, he drinks sherry." He threw a pot down in the sink. "Did you know, Julian, that Calvin's salary included forty gallons of wine annually? Or that Luther recommended drinking a beer before confronting the Devil?"

Alexander was himself an intellectual and allergic to legalism. He enjoyed my dad's mind and loved his idiosyncrasies. I believe he hired my father on as youth pastor just so he had someone with whom to discuss Luther, Calvin, and Kierkegaard. His church provided my parents a house, furniture, and a generous stipend. Freed from the Wilcox house church, my mother could wear her lipstick again and my father could listen to anything.

They were finally making their life together and things proceeded smoothly until I was born in 1960. It took my mother six months to recover. Her postpartum depression soon deepened into paranoia and delusion. It had been ten years since her last breakdown. She lay on the couch and suffered Old Testament fears and delusions—she was damned or maybe a prophet, Elijah perhaps—and all the while church ladies came with their casseroles and left with their gossip, their prayer concerns. That summer, as my mother recovered, Dad carried me around camp in an unzipped plaid suitcase. I was swaddled in blankets, a sort of precious luggage. It was as if I'd been found in the rushes down by the channel, or perhaps baggage claim. If I returned to Peniel tomorrow—and it's still there—I'm sure some ancient camper would chuckle and say, "I remember that suitcase. Your father was a riot." My father has long been the camp's celebrated eccentric, a subject of lore and apocrypha.

My mother recovered over that summer and when we returned my parents discussed having another child. They consulted a psychiatrist, who advised against it in no uncertain terms. It could "aggravate my mother's schizophrenia and pass it on," he said. They ignored him and my mother gave birth to the sanest Lovelace in the bunch, my sister, Peggy. Again, my mother slipped into the black. I was just two years old but I remember her black eyes. I remember how frightened I was growing up, scared my mother would leave and never come back. Peggy says at age three she began worrying for our mother, afraid she would make Mom cry.

I didn't share that worry until later. By age three I had thrown church picnic chicken and coleslaw at deacons. Desperate, God-fearing adults had tethered me to trees. Bucktoothed, thin, and agitated, I resembled the young Jerry Lewis to my sister's

Judy Garland. She was a beautiful kid, crowned with brown curls. She possessed a quiet, reflective spirit and a holy terror for a brother. By all accounts, but especially by the accounts my sister still continues to share every Christmas, our sibling rivalry was intense and one-sided. I did get the most attention. Any kid who deploys airborne sprocket weapons built from smashed clocks, spikes breakfast cereals with stockpiled Tabasco sauce, and generally lays in wait for his saintly sister will get the most attention. My sister retreated to her room and read for the greater part of her childhood. She resents it to this day. Still, she was better off on the moors with Heathcliff than in the backyard with me.

My mother was happiest at Peniel, where she spent her summers painting still lifes and camp signs, and always painting Bible verses on banners. I remember helping my mother decorate the chapel with the armor of God. Together we cut the cardboard shapes: the helmet of salvation, the breastplate of righteousness, the sword and the shield of faith. Mom painted them silver and black and we hung them from the rafters. Peniel made clear to the children that we were at war. In the camp nursery—the Olive Yard—all of us sang, "We may never march in the infantry, ride in the cavalry, shoot the artillery, but we're in the Lord's army." As soldiers of Christ ours was a battle "not against flesh and blood, but against principalities, against the darkness of this world." I loved it. A holy war is the best kind of war a boy can have, full of demons and superheroes. Vietnam wasn't important when the Prince of Darkness himself hid under our bunks and threw darts from our woods.

Peniel was more think tank than camp. Its program was a veritable wailing wall of religious training and I spent each July and August ducking out from the tent. It didn't matter. By the time I was ten Grover Wilcox had my loud mouth testifying on the streets of Lake George, confessing sins before I had committed them and diagramming the Four Spiritual Laws on signboards with marker. Peniel's religion was hard to dodge, even twenty miles away. I suspect Peniel's founders, Miss Beers and Mrs. Mac, viewed recreation as a gateway to sin—exercise heats up the flesh and leads to temptation. They made no excuse for the camp's asceticism, its unrelenting schedule of chapel meetings. It was our evangelical heritage, stiffened through Prohibition and run straight through the Depression.

I remember my cabin challenging another set of boys to an eating contest in the dining hall. Before it was over the camp's cofounder and disciplinarian, Mr. Mac, hauled us up in front of the camp. We stood shamefaced as he glowered. And then, after a long silence, he began.

"Gluttony, campers, is one of the deadly sins. Gluttony makes a mockery of the gifts God brings us. Gluttony is wasteful. It is selfish. Now, these boys are no more sinful than the rest of us. They want to be good, mindful of God's blessings. But gluttony is an abomination to the Lord..." He continued straight through dessert.

Today's Republican megachurches have no problem with gluttony. Evangelical churches lure children to camp with imitation rock bands, Jet Skis, and parasailing. Peniel, with its outhouses, its stick-framed chapel and broken-spined hymnals, seems a poor country cousin, its children just a motley crew of preachers' kids and other unfortunates. It was hardscrabble but we made our own fun or we stole it. There were plenty of rules and we broke them. We swam on Sundays, stole canoes, and kissed girls. We ran away but never long enough, really, to leave.

It was fine, a boyhood surrounded by austere mystery, by dusty prayers, with the small mountain behind us and all the white pines, a place threshed and winnowed by prayer. We sang the old, muscular hymns I still love—"Lead on, O King Eternal"; "A Mighty Fortress"; "Power in the Blood"—and Sunday suppers were brimstone and honey, and it all made you hungry. There was no entertainment, no frippery. The camp got its name from an Old Testament story in which Jacob demands his god's blessing. He wrestles the angel all night for it, and at dawn the creature relents; it twists Jacob's hip, blesses him, and leaves. He called the place Peniel and that's what we learned there. We were crippled and blessed and taught to be thankful.

Every August, after leaving Peniel and before heading back to Scotch Plains, we visited my dad's mother in Woodstock. We never called her Grandma; we weren't allowed. As a young woman my grandmother had taken her inheritance to Europe, where she came of age and commenced a lifetime of seasonal grand tours. Although her means came from unwashed cowboys once removed, my grandmother adopted old money and the old world as her own. Shortly following my birth she actually willed herself French and insisted the family call her "Grandmère." She got her table manners from Marie Antoinette and enforced them with a cold imperial stare. She was a lifelong member of the John

Birch Society and supported Woodstock's Christian Science Reading Room. She had sent her food back to kitchens and dressed down their chefs all across the Western world. My mother, of course, was terrified by the time we hit Albany. By the Catskills the grooming had begun in earnest. She picked at our clothes and plastered our hair with her spit. "Now, David," she'd say, "remember to stay at the table until she lets you go. She will excuse you." My sister and I sat in the backseat holding our infant brother and happily fending off our mother's fluttering hands. We were off to see the matriarch, her meadow and the trout stream, but my mother continued to fret. Our station wagon filled with hairspray and fear. "Richard," my mother would say, "you should polish your shoes. I didn't have a chance to wash the children's outfits. Please don't bring up money with your mother."

My father, oblivious to my mother's growing panic, usually responded by turning up the radio and commenting, "Now, listen to this. This is a beautiful movement; listen to how the horn comes in." He would look up in the rearview mirror and say, "David, do you know what horn that is?"

"French," I'd answer. They were always French and he'd nod approvingly. He never asked our mother or Peggy what horn it was, he always asked me.

It was 1967 and we'd pass through Woodstock and ogle the hippies, turn left at the Bear restaurant and then down her long drive, past the ruined well, the leaning stone post with its BEWARE OF DOG sign. Grandmère was terrified of hippies. When we arrived, just after she assessed and welcomed us, she asked, "How was it in town? Were they out on the green?"

"Yeah. Tons of 'em!" I answered enthusiastically.

"Yes. Well." She turned from us and to her son. "The town, Richard, is in a state of siege, nothing less."

"It's lively, all right," he agreed.

"Well, the place looks beautiful," my mother said hopefully. "Your lilacs are lovely."

"Yes, aren't they?" Grandmère allowed, and looked back to my father. "It's nice to see all of you."

"So, Mother," my father asked. "How's the mildew this year?" Grandmère was obsessed with the hippies, my father with the mold. And with good reason; Grandmère's house was famous for its virulent strains. A river ran through it—literally. Groundwater sluiced down the shale mountain behind her and it flowed straight through her stone crypt of a basement. All the water smelled of sulfur; her rooms smelled of rotten eggs and Chanel No. 5. Mold attacked the house from below but Grandmère had a solution of sorts. She painted the interiors teal green, a color we called "Catskill Mold." She painted everything that color, the oak beams arching above our heads, the fieldstone fireplace, the furniture. She imported the massive teal-green curtains to hold back the north light. She installed green carpets. Her living room was a perfumed grotto, a wet place at the bottom of the sea.

But water saved Grandmère's house as well. The house overlooked a gently sloping meadow with apple trees and a trout stream flowing along its far side against birches. Years ago, someone had built a large stone pool in its path and the brook flowed through its wooden slat gates. It had begun to collapse before I was born, and over the years it gradually filled with silt until the stream broke down its bank and swept around the old ruin. The pool drowned in mud and wildflowers and tadpoles. My sister and I would greet Grandmère, cut loose, and run down to the water. Dad waved and said, "David, hey, David. Try to spot some trout."

Then my father always brought in the bags and stood in the kitchen with my mother and Grandmère, where he'd announce: "I need to run downtown. I can see the allergy situation is bad this year." He'd leave Mom and my infant brother alone in the house with Grandmère and dash back to the car. After two or three hours my father always returned with two dozen night crawler worms, a stack of lurid science fiction paperbacks, and a stockpile of allergy medications. He doped himself up on anti-histamines and disappeared into his books and his space travel, alone again in the New Mexican desert.

"In our family," Norman Maclean famously wrote, "there was no clear line between religion and fly fishing." Norman's father, also a Presbyterian minister, taught him the counts of a fly cast. "He certainly believed," Maclean wrote, "that God could count and that only by picking up his rhythms were we able to regain power and beauty." It was different for my family. In Woodstock, just after dinner my father and I would take our Styrofoam cup of worms and our rods and walk down through the meadow. When we were close Dad would crouch down and we'd whisper and thread the thick night crawlers onto the hooks. We'd crawl closer and flip the baits over the grassy bank and my father would count to twenty. If nothing happened we'd leave the worms drowning and go watch television. In the morning I'd run down and pull out a trout, dead and all twisted up with the line. In fact, it wasn't really fishing, it was trapping, and an ignoble introduction to something I love. Discipline and patience are hard-won in my family. Years later, after Grandmère was gone, I lived in her house until I learned fly casting, how to fish all her streams. I came home to teach my father and brother and together we fished through the Catskills' own legends: the Esopus and Willowemock and Beaverkill.

When I was nine, Peggy and I brought a cassette tape we had made especially for Grandmère on Dad's new machine. After dinner we begged Grandmère to turn down William F. Buckley—the man somehow dominated her television—and listen to us, to the new tape we had made. "Well," Grandmère said. "If we must. We shall wait until the next commercial." Peggy and I squirmed while Bill Buckley listed our gains in Southeast Asia. It was a long list but finally Grandmère turned the sound off and my father popped the cassette into his portable recorder.

"HI, GRANDMÈRE. THIS IS DAVID," it said. "I'M GO-ING TO READ YOU SOME RECORDS. WORLD RECORDS FROM THE GUINNESS BOOK."

"Hi, Grandmère, this is Peggy. I want to say a poem that—"

"THE WORLD'S FATTEST MAN WEIGHS FIVE HUN-DRED SIXTY-TWO POUNDS TEN OUNCES STRIPPED NAKED. A MONSTER PIG WAS KILLED BY AN ELEVEN-YEAR-OLD PHILL-I-PINO BOY IN 1962 AND IS CONSID-ERED THE WORLD'S LARGEST SWINE. THE WORLD'S MOST—hey, cut it out, Peg, I'm reading. THE WORLD'S MOST PRO-LIF-FIC MOTHER WAS RUSSIAN. NADIA BUKansky or something GAVE BIRTH—stop it, c'mon, stop it—TO SIXTY-NINE CHILDREN FROM 1725 TO 1765. THE MOST HOT DOGS CONSUMED IN..."

Grandmère's smile, normally frozen, had calcified. She was clutching the arms of an antique chair, her eyes fixed on my mortified mother. Just under my tinny voice you could hear my sister crying. Dad and I thought it was great. Everyone just loved it.

Grandmère said a quick thank-you and lapsed into silence, watching William F. Buckley talk on the screen. My father picked up his science fiction and my mother picked up Jonathan. Grandmère finally broke her silence. "It was quiet here," she said. "Just the real artists before that communist boy moved in up the road." It all went to hell, my grandmother maintained, when Bob Dylan came in 1965. "You know his manager, that Jewish man, what's his name? Grossman. He owns property in Bearsville. Just over the stream."

"Oh, really," my father said. He held his book on his lap and kept reading.

"Richard, I was speaking to Henry Maust yesterday." The Mausts were Grandmère's only Woodstock friends. "Henry came home yesterday and found a number of naked hippies just lying on the lower field. Just lying there. Imagine, Richard." The red menace and flower children kept Grandmère on her toes. When she drove us to town in her Cadillac, she had us lock all the doors. "Put your hands in. I'm rolling up the windows." We were pushing twenty miles an hour. "Hilda Maust said a hippie on a bicycle actually reached into her car. Imagine," I couldn't imagine. I couldn't believe a hippie tried to grope Hilda Maust. There were far more interesting things to do in Woodstock than grope Hilda Maust. The town was full of psychedelia and head shops. Even the hardware store was a head shop. I loved it.

Our last mornings in Woodstock had ritual. My father and I would clean the last brace of brown trout. My mother had finished packing by eight a.m. and lay on the green couch in a state of nervous collapse while Grandmère fried the trout in bacon fat, filling her kitchen with sweet smoke. After the trout and English muffins Grandmère would give us all stiff little hugs and we left. Grandmère would soon leave herself, decamp to her winter lodging at the Women's Republican Club in New York City.

My father always slowed at the base of Grandmère's long gravel drive; he'd honk and we'd shout, "Good-bye, Grandmère," and then, finally, relax. Mom and Dad would start laughing again; Peggy and I could get back to our quarrels and jokes. Despite all the forced manners, the endless wait to be excused from her table, I never wanted to leave my grandmother's. I loved its ruined slate pool, the meadow, the trout with their red spots circled by orange, their brown sides sliding into buttery yellows. The Catskills are old mountains, worn down and haunted; Woodstock was an old artists' colony shot through with new colors. Scotch Plains, New Jersey, stood in stark contrast to all this, a flat patch of white suburbia, my father's church full of middle-management parents and bored kids.

I know my father struggled as much as I did. It was hard to just blend into the normalcy of a suburban pastorate, especially at the helm of a youth group. His occasional sermons often confused the congregation with concerns they viewed as tangential to the gospel, things like poetry, music, and film. My father was aloof and cerebral and lacked many of the basic ministerial tools, social skills like facial recognition. Dad was terrible with names. He once buried a body without knowing its gender, fudging the pronouns. When he looked out over the faithful, I'm convinced Dad simply had no idea who most of these people were or what they were doing in his church.

Nevertheless, he grew close with Willow Grove's pastor, Julian Alexander, and before long they were staging all manner of unlikely cultural events. The church youth group performed my father's adaptation of *Waiting for Godot.* Julian and my father presented a series of dramatic readings, including *No Exit* and *Franny and Zooey.* My dad's flock of teenagers grew both in numbers and enthusiasm. My father and his group began dismantling preconceptions, the distinctions between high culture and low. "They got me into the Beatles," my father told me, "and I got them into Schumann." Eventually, my father embraced the artistic bloom of the '60s and in doing so inflamed Willow Grove's cultural anxieties. He quoted Bob Dylan in sermons. The church mothers didn't know what to do.

Christ taught his followers to be "in the world but not of it." My father emphasized the former and, moreover, he argued for total immersion, and it wasn't all Bach. He took me to see *A Clockwork Orange* and *Deliverance* when I was twelve. The good Presbyterians of Willow Grove still remember when their church sign announced:

Sunday Services 9 & 11 am
This Sunday: God's Eternal Grace
Next Sunday: Rosemary's Baby

The deacons protested and Julian asked us over to dinner. After grace and the passing of pot roast, Reverend Alexander allowed that the sign had spiked interest. "We've been getting calls, Richard. Are you aware that the film is a horror film? An R-rated horror film?"

"Yes. Have you seen it?"

"Certainly not. I understand it involves Satan."

"Absolutely. It is Satanic," my father enthusiastically concurred. He helped himself to seconds. "It emphasizes how counterfeit spiritualities promise heaven without a real Christ."

"Look, Richard. I'm not sure I can help you if you go through with this. I'm not convinced a sermon on *Rosemary's Baby* is a good idea." Julian chuckled in spite of himself. "You know, they might riot."

"Julian, I would not recommend this film without a good reason, without a real message."

Julian remained skeptical. "That's all well and good, Richard. But I don't think it—" A thought struck him. He put down his water glass. "Richard, you don't plan to show the film, do you? I cannot allow it. We don't have a projector." He winced. "Do we?"

"No, no. Of course not." My father laughed. "It's a good movie—I loved it—but I'm not going to show it. It's just a sermon illustration, that's all it is."

Julian smiled in spite of himself. "A pornographic sermon illustration?"

"The film is about modern witchcraft. There's some sexual magic, I suppose—offscreen. It's not pornographic. I wouldn't recommend it if it didn't have redeeming social values."

"Such as?"

"Such as witchcraft is bad news."

Julian relented and the Rosemary sermon was a huge success. People poured in that Sunday to see what rough beast was lurching toward them. It was standing-room-only and my father made them stand in a church a little bit larger, a little more open to the world. Excepting the witches, of course; they had to stand outside.

Meanwhile I ranged with a band of neighborhood boys through frog ponds and vacant lots. We were all seven, eight, or nine, busy testing the boundaries of backyards and parents and school. I was the minister's kid; I pushed harder than the rest because I had much more to push—all the weight of my sin, my father's congregation, and all the heavenly host. I couldn't listen anymore. My kindergarten teacher dragged me by my ear to the office. By second grade I was sneaking out after dark to soap cars and egg houses. I stole copies of *Mad* magazine. When we went to the circus I convinced my parents to buy me a real leather whip. I terrorized church picnics and flunked out of Sunday school. I was not a bad child, simply my father's. It's kid stuff, but ministers' children must run amok. They maintain the cosmic balance.

One Saturday morning, the neighborhood bully, a large dim-witted boy named Eric, began taunting my band of friends. My whip had been confiscated by then but I still had my slingshot. Eric said I was a lousy shot, that I couldn't hit a barn, and then the rock hit his forehead. He stood there, stunned, until blood covered his face. Everyone scattered. I ran home, hid in my closet, and cried for twenty minutes until I heard Eric's mother arrive. I crept into the hall and listened.

"Your son," began Eric's mother, "is out of control. My boy could have very easily lost his eye."

"I'm terribly sorry. I'm sure David didn't mean to hit him."

"He didn't, did he? Where did he get that slingshot, that weapon?"

"I'm afraid I bought it for him. After he lost his whip." Mom suspects she's guilty of everything and confesses at every opportunity.

"Does his father know this? Does the church know about your son?"

"Yes, I'm afraid so."

"You will punish him. He can't just roam the streets with weapons." I heard a chair scrape and ran for my room. "I'll be leaving now, Mrs. Lovelace—"

"Please, Betty Lee."

"I hope your son understands what he's done."

She left and I crept down to the kitchen. My mother sat very still and I thought she would cry. I crawled up into her lap and she kissed my streaked face, pushed back my hair, and just held me.

By now my father was attending Princeton, working toward his doctorate in church history. Julian and he had long since agreed that my father's strengths lay with academia. He couldn't run a church. He was, as my dad puts it, "administratively incompetent." In 1968 he published his thesis as *The American Pietism of Cotton Mather.* I remember his doctoral thesis in piles— three-by-four note cards stacked on the cold linoleum of his church basement office. And I remember standing with my father in the church office, helping as he mimeographed and collated late into the night, meeting his doctoral deadline by the hour.

It was clear to the deacons that my father possessed negligible management skills and found discipline tedious. But it was his eccentricities, the ones Willow Grove's teenagers found so cool, that alarmed the church as a whole. It was widely rumored my father closed his eyes in prayer while driving the church kids to camp. He let the teenagers listen to "Sympathy for the Devil." He rode around on a Japanese motorcycle far too small for his frame and, worse, he regularly perched me on the bike's gas tank, stuck a peewee football helmet on my head, and cruised the streets. By the end of summer the church officially forbade dangerous spectacles involving six-year-olds. They put my dad on a short leash.

It wasn't simple culture shock. Beyond the ridiculously small motorcycle, the rock and roll, the salacious sermons, and Mahler blasting from his church office, my father had one other consuming interest, one that clinched his suspect identity at the church: snakes. Mostly snakes, and also some lizards. He had never kicked the reptile-hunting habits of his desert boyhood. Claiming he was allergic to any common, domesticated pet, he spent large sums on reptiles. He began haunting exotic pet stores in the city, rank basements lit only by heat lamps and run by unshaven snake enthusiasts with names like Sal or Jerry.

If my father had left his pets to their reptilian stupors, safe in their terrarium homes, his collection would have remained no more than an eccentric's hobby, harmless. Instead, he insisted on taking one or two of the animals to his church office daily, barricading the door with his thesis draft, jacking the thermostat up to eighty, and blasting his music. He flaunted the snakes. The habits of the hognose, in particular, provided my father with colorful sermon illustrations and he spent an inordinate amount of pulpit time exculpating common, garden-variety snakes from the sins of Eden's symbolic dark serpent.

As my father completed his doctorate, a general and inevitable consensus formed. My father was, in a word, ill-suited for the ministry. My mother was unstable, a poor choice. A growing chorus of alarmed parishioners brought a wide range of Lovelace anecdotes to the church deacons. Their youth pastor had allied with the scourge, the unwashed, the counterculture. Church members wanted my father dismissed. At the deacons' meeting, a phalanx of balding, relatively unimaginative midlevel managers found my father deeply strange but all agreed he was doctrinally sound and appreciated his affinity with the church teenagers. My father's eccentricities were duly noted and discussions ensued, but no disciplinary action was taken.

Their mood darkened considerably, however, when Willow Grove's cleaning woman quit abruptly after encountering a small alligator snapping at her from the church organ's keyboard. An emergency meeting was called; my father reclaimed the vicious little reptile from the deacons and promised to leave him at home with the rest. He listened to their dire warnings with equanimity as his loathsome pet scratched and hissed from the cardboard box on his lap. By now my father had perfected his classic deacon meeting defense. He simply wandered off in his head, rhapsodic, detached from any parish concerns.

He wasn't worried. Princeton would award his doctorate in

church history that spring. He would send out his impressive credentials and just wait for the right teaching position to open. He was a ministerial lame duck; he was on his way out. Now he could devote his time to Brahms and his reptiles, take more father-son trips to the Jersey shore to catch sea robins and blowfish. It was a great relief to all involved.

Meanwhile my mother had her trials, shy and thrust into the role of a minister's wife, God's hostess. She bravely bought Tupperware, chatted awkwardly through Jell-O mold suppers, and kept me in Band-Aids. My sister retreated and my father was busy. I needed an accomplice and so I spent my entire seventh year praying nightly for a brother. When Jonathan finally showed I took all the credit. It was the power of prayer. I just kept at it till God relented.

I forgot what my prayers would cost. Mom lay on our couch in New Jersey, holding my infant brother, unable to speak, afraid for her mind and her soul. My mother soon drifted into paranoia and then deeper into delusion. She was damned and everyone damned her. When the churchwomen began arriving with food, began holding her baby, my mother's fear grew worse. They had plotted to take her family, to poison her, to carry out Satan's terrible will. I watched her each morning as she lay on that brown couch. She haunted the room. And then my mother was gone and we couldn't go see her. My father smiled and said Mom was just resting but I knew better. I knew she was crazy. Mom's mind, my father said, had begun skipping and just needed a knock, a bounce back into its groove. But I knew things. I had heard things. I knew what had happened before I was born. They took her away. They locked her up. She lost the power of speech and she growled like a dog. When I was seven a nightmare lodged in my chest and never left. Alone late at night I saw my mother snarling and snapping. On some level, I think, my siblings and I felt responsible for the sickness that followed our births. My mother's postpartum delusions threw shadows over my family's world. She broke into black rooms we never could enter. My father began to shield my mother from the outside, from trouble and finances, from parties and friends—even from us. I spent my childhood afraid for my mother, afraid I would lose her to hospitals, to all the whispered secrets. It became my lifelong fear—our family madness, my mother barking, my mother convulsed.

THREE

In 1968 my father was named professor of church history at Conwell Seminary, a small evangelical school outside Philadelphia. Conwell soon merged with another conservative school and we all moved to Hamilton, Massachusetts. We didn't really belong in Hamilton. In fact, my father's employer didn't belong in Hamilton. Theologians do not mix well at the hunt club. On Boston's North Shore matters of religion were settled properly ages ago. God chose sides and the hunt club won. Sunday mornings are set aside for polo games and horse trials, not church. The Catholics had already fled the place, leaving a large, empty campus above town, and, in a sort of religious lateral pass, they sold it to us.

Dad went on ahead to Hamilton and Mom stayed behind with us and packed. She seemed fine then, fully recovered from Jonathan's birth. He was almost two, my sister seven, and I was nine years old. Dad brought his mother house shopping and Grandmère put a down payment on a low-slung, damp house surrounded by oaks and scrub saplings. He found it in Hamilton's scruffy outback, where ranch homes with mulch-pile lawns were hidden away in the woods like the servants' quarters. Dad wired the house for sound, set up his snake room full of heat lamps, unpacked his typewriter, and sent for us. Grandmère loved Hamilton. She believed there was hope for us yet. In any third grade the new kid always gets it in the neck. And in New England, the new kid is new until two or three generations stack up in the town graveyard. I was pilloried at the bus stop and shunned at school. The heir to a major banking concern beat the tar out of me by the lockers. The children of law firms gathered to taunt me. My fistfights all degenerated into inconclusive heaps; they won me no allies. I hated school and every afternoon I ran home, dumped my books by the door, and headed for the woods. Just across our street was a series of bridle paths that went for miles, through marshes, thickets, and streams, until reaching the rolling estates closer to town.

Before long I tired of aimless walks and begged for a BB gun. I snuck along the bridle paths and took ambivalent shots at squirrels and songbirds. I fancied myself a poacher of the king's deer when I carried that gun, and incredibly, the cream of Hamilton society played along with me. On one gray November afternoon, miles from home, I heard what sounded like a pack of wild dogs barking and baying. There must have been dozens. I held my popgun tightly as the noise got closer, and then it arrived. The hounds tore around the corner and came straight at me. They were mad, the whole slobbering, yelping lot of them were mad and charging full tilt. I slipped behind an oak tree and looked for a limb. The dogs didn't slow, their tongues lashing and eyes rolling as they passed, chasing something, not me.

I heard a horn and then it made sense—at least in a limited, theatrical way. It was the aptly named Myopia Hunt Club, my new neighbors. I dropped the gun and kicked leaves over it just as the first horse and rider came into view. Another dozen or so rounded the bend, resplendent and ridiculous in brass buttons, red swallowtail jackets, and boots. The man in the top hat blew his horn again and the entire spectacle rode past swiftly and awkwardly.

None of the riders acknowledged or even made eye contact with me, a scruffy, modern American boy who had wandered into their game. Myopia has guarded their club's mix of nearsighted tradition and horses since 1882. Nevertheless, by the time I arrived lax zoning and thoughtless development had degraded both fox and Brahmin habitats. The club had stooped to dragging fox scent through the lower class of Hamilton neighborhoods. It was embarrassing for all of us, my poaching deer that didn't exist and the whole gang of them, costumed by P. G. Wodehouse and chasing a nonexistent fox.

I was overjoyed. I had found people—grown-ups—who were stranger than us, stranger than my family. Next time maybe I'd get caught and they could place me in their imaginary stocks down in front of their English-like club. I was heartened and redoubled my hunting efforts.

My father flourished at Gordon-Conwell and hit his stride as a church historian. His doctoral thesis, *The American Pietism of Cotton Mather*, was now in print and well regarded. Academia, even evangelical academia, gave my father's eccentricities license and he was respected by the school's faculty. The social graces required of ministers are not expected of professors. The students loved his lecturing style and his classes filled immediately. He was forgetful and distracted and they loved him for it. He couldn't remember their names but he knew his stuff cold. My father argued that Cotton Mather, of Salem witch trial fame, had laid the foundations for modern evangelicalism. Dad asked his readers to look past the trial, but I put it front and center. Mather played a pivotal role, arguing for the court's admission of "spectral evidence": dreams, visions, and nightmares. Years later he defended the trials in his work *Wonders of the Invisible World*. In short, Mather legitimized hallucination in the New World; he brought hysteria into the courtroom. I'm no church historian but I am a Lovelace. I've heard my mother speak of demons and my father of angels. I've watched my family's religion conspire with our brain disease to conjure spectral evidence and trumpet it.

Mather's world proved too dark for my father, and he soon jumped a generation and focused on Jonathan Edwards and the Great Awakening. Edwards's sermons sparked a wildfire revival that spread through the colonies and across the Atlantic. He had it all: rock and roll fame, brimstone, and poetry. Edwards was a theologian's action hero, America's answer to Luther, and he became my father's intellectual touchstone. My brother was named for Edwards, and I was named for his missionary friend, David Brainerd. These two preachers stand at the opposite poles of my family's religion and give witness to its ongoing cycle of redemptive ecstasy and damning guilt.

Edwards claimed that true grace was evidenced by a supernatural illumination of the soul. Further, he argued that as "visible saints" his congregation should expect the bodily effects and feverish symptoms of salvation. Before long he had his congregants swooning in the aisles, crying and convulsing. Neighboring preachers denounced the church as hysterical, even possessed. Ultimately, Edwards conceded that some of these signs were suspect, but not before he had raised the psychological bar: the evangelical rush, the high as conversion's sure sign. I tried to catch this ecstatic proof all through my youth. All of us did.

I've never received this blessed assurance, but I've found its complement. I found what David Brainerd suffered at the faith's other pole: the sickness of the soul, the self-loathing that marks a true pilgrim's progress. Brainerd renounced the colonial world and lived in self-imposed exile. He lived, he said, in a "hideous and howling wilderness." Brainerd complained ceaselessly of "vapoury disorders," of distraction and despair. At the end of his life, he retreated to Edwards's spare room, finished up his sad notes, and died. He said he was unworthy of love, foul and sinful. His heart, he wrote, was a cage of unclean birds. My sister, Margaret Lee, has never seen this place. She's the only one of us who isn't bipolar, the only one of us named for a loved one rather than a Puritan.

When he wasn't lecturing, my father preferred to write at home in the living room. He would hole up with symphonies blasting and a constrictor draped around his shoulders. The three of us children were altogether too young for my father's distracted, intellectual disciplines. Even my mother lacked the critical tools necessary to share in my father's cerebral world. I'd lose myself in the woods, and my sister lost herself in books. My mother put flowers and vases on her kitchen table and worked on her paintings while Dad hunkered down in a low upholstered chair, hunched over his typewriter and insulated from the family by a wall of classical music. There was always music in the living room. Finally he ran speaker wires out to the kitchen and our dinners were swamped in Brahms and Bartók. My father would sit at the head of the table and hum, his eyes closed as his right hand hovered with the strings. He ate between movements.

"Who can tell me the composer of this piece?" he'd ask, and my sister and I vied for his approval. My mother never guessed. Once she had me pull the wires out of the speakers.

"Now listen to this. This passage gives it away. Who wrote it?"

"Mozart." My guess was always Mozart with a Beethoven fallback. The occasional choral work had to be Bach.

"No, no. Here's a hint. *Afternoon of a Faun.*"

"What's a fawn?" my sister asked.

"Bambi's a fawn," I said. "Duh."

"Okay then, it's Beethoven," my sister said confidently. "It has to be Beethoven."

"What's Beethoven have to do with fawns?" I challenged.

My sister faltered. "Okay," she said. "Okay, Bach."

My father smiled broadly. "Wrong. You're both wrong. It's Debussy!"

Of course, Debussy.

But my father had other records, records the Willow Grove kids had given him. He didn't have much rock and roll but he had Dylan's *Highway 61 Revisited.* I listened to it over and over and memorized its lines, especially: "God said to Abraham kill me a son / Abe said man you must be putting me on / God said no Abe said what / God said you can do what you want Abe but / The next time you see me coming you better run." Dad had his Debussy and I had my "Desolation Row."

Some nights, when he was sick of Puritans, my father bundled me up and we went fishing. It was always just my Dad and I. Jonathan was too young and my father rarely invited my mother or Peggy. My father cited their complete and utter lack of interest and I think deep down he welcomed it. After all, they were girls. But Dad and I, we always fished.

We returned again and again to Salem Willows, a broken-down amusement park beside smokestacks and the harbor. It smelled of fried food, cigarettes, and drunks. At night—it was always at night—we would walk out on the long, dark pier, twenty feet above the water. Thirty-five years ago, before all the draggers clear-cut the ocean, my father and I could regularly catch twelve-pound cod on cut clams and jigs just out from shore. When the fish hit I lowered our rusted Coleman lantern just about down to the water and lashed the line. The cod flashed white in the bright green water and I'd hold the rod while my father dropped a nasty fist of grappling hooks. I'd horse the fish toward Dad and he would wait for the moment, yank and haul the fish up hand over hand. When we stood on that pier, I couldn't have cared less for the sad merry-go-round behind us, its seasick music and moldering horses. I didn't need cotton candy, spinning lights, and rides. And I don't think Dad needed Debussy. We were happy just standing in the dark with some hooks and a box of slippery, translucent clams for bait, waiting for fish.

Waiting for ducks was an entirely different matter. I remember sitting in duck blinds all through dark November afternoons, scanning the horizon for anything other than seagulls. "Seagulls are protected," my father explained, to my great disappointment. "We can't shoot seagulls." We used a small skiff to navigate through the salt marshes and, if necessary, retrieve ducks. I wanted a dog, of course, a retriever, but my father pleaded allergies and said the snakes were enough. We didn't really need the dog; we rarely hit ducks. Instead, we sat and watched our rather sad group of plastic decoys bob out in front of our hovel while I listened to my father talk about jumping ducks along the Rio Grande of his youth: whole rafts of them, he'd say. I don't remember bringing home edible ducks, but the family feasted on sea duck occasionally, a kind of feathered herring. I was too young for a gun and just played with the duck call. My father had a twelve-gauge monster of a Browning, a goose gun if there ever was one. It was an automatic and it jammed every time.

Although our duck hunts never lived up to their promise, I loved the idea of hunting. Anything. I spent more and more time on the bridle paths killing small innocent things with my BB gun: chickadees, nuthatches, large beetles. I knew it was wrong but I kept score. I played for keeps. I longed to poach larger game from Myopia's forest but stags were scarce, as were pheasants and partridge. This left squirrel. It was clear I needed more gun.

"Dad," I said, "it's perfectly fine to shoot squirrels. There's a season and everything."

"I don't know, David. It just seems cruel."

"People eat them all the time, Dad. Really."

"I've never seen anyone eat a squirrel. Maybe in Appalachia."

"Dad, there's tons and tons of squirrels out there. A few less wouldn't matter." My father resisted the idea, but I kept at it. I found recipes.

The Browning was useless on ducks but we knocked down a half dozen gray squirrels in no time. Hitting squirrels with a twelve-gauge shotgun is as easy as it is pointless, and although the gun's kickback knocked me into the leaves repeatedly, I quickly mastered the skill. I could squirrel hunt and trout trap like a professional. My father and I had left legal concerns such as trespass, gun law, and license vague, so when we heard the shouting my first instinct was to run but my father stood his ground. It was Mr. Mosley, our neighbor. His son, Dick, beat me regularly down at the bus stop.

"What the hell do you think you're doing?" Mosley asked.

I dropped the squirrels and my father said, "Oh. Hello, Mr., Mr.—"

"Mosley."

"Right, Mosley. Mr. Mosley. I'm Richard Lovelace and this is—"

"I know who you are. I want to know why you're out here killing squirrels with a damn shotgun." My father stared at him blankly. What could he say? That we needed the food? That squirrels were overrunning our lawn? Killing our livestock?

"Listen, Lovelace. This is no way to teach a boy. Take him to the dump and shoot rats if you have to. Go ahead. But if you kill another goddamn squirrel with a shotgun around my house I'll have you arrested. Understand?" My father nodded silently and Mosley stalked off, back through the woods. I picked up the dead squirrels by their tails and ran for home; Dad caught up with me on the back porch. He gave me some pointers on gutting and skinning the poor things, put his gun away, and went back to his typing. I threw the innards, the heads, and the feet into the woods.

My mother had not been apprised of the hunt but was unconcerned when I came into the kitchen and slung a sack full of dressed squirrel into her sink. She was standing over the kitchen table, fretting over her calligraphy. "Hi, dear," she said, and looked over. "Oh, David. That's a good pillowcase, dear. I could have given you an old one. What's in there?"

"Mom, I'm making up a surprise for dinner," I told her. "I need onions and carrots." I pulled the recipe from my back pocket. "Let's see. I need chicken stock. Do we have any chicken stock? I'm making a stew."

"All right, dear, use bouillion—those cubes up in the cabinet. Just look at that pillowcase." It was filthy and spots of blood had soaked through the flowered cotton fabric.

"I'll wash it. I promise." I peeked in at the sadly diminished squirrels. Bits of thread and fuzz stuck to their shiny, sinewy bodies. "Never mind, Mom. Just don't worry about dinner." I pushed her out of the kitchen.

By this time my mother had seen just about everything. She wasn't worried about my surprise; she'd find out soon enough. Mom had enough concerns. She dressed us, got us on the bus, cooked our meals, and washed our clothes. She periodically

wrested the checkbook from my father and pleaded for bud-
getary management. She kept our family presentable, even with
snakes in her spare room and dead squirrels on her stove. And
yet, banished from her kitchen, she just stood in the hall at a loss.
There was nowhere for her to go. The front of the house with its
sonic-boom speakers and Dad was off-limits, their bedroom was
dark and small, and the family room smelled of snakes.

Dinner was horrible, of course, a shocking, watery mess with
the rodents floating up out of the boil. My sister began crying
immediately. I myself was racked by guilt and nausea but recognized I must eat squirrel or admit to wanton slaughter. My
mother made toast. Only my father tucked in with gusto. "Not
bad," he said. "Not bad. Better than eating frogs."

Mom cleared the table and made me promise to throw the left-
overs, my entire stew, into the woods after family devotions. Every
evening, my father shut down his music, read a passage from the
New Testament or Psalms, and asked our opinions. I always had
opinions and Dad always followed them with his own, longer and
more coherent, commentary. After that came the prayer.

"Does anyone have something they would like to thank God
for? Any prayer requests?"

My mother spoke up. "We need to rake the leaves, Richard.
I'm worried about the leaves. It will snow before we know it." No
one wanted to pray about the leaves, not again. God couldn't do
anything about the leaves; our house was in the middle of the
woods—what lawn we had was moss. Raking was a Sisyphean
task my mother asked us to perform every autumn, an offering
to the neighbors.

"Betty Lee, we are aware of the leaf situation and have been for some time. We will put that before the Lord. Are there any other requests?"

"Peggy won't let me watch *The Three Stooges*. She says it's stupid."

"She's correct." My sister beamed. "Watch the Marx Brothers. Does anyone have concerns other than the leaves and *The Three Stooges*? Does anyone have anything to be thankful for?"

"Squirrels," my sister said softly. "I want to pray for the squirrels."

Then we held hands, my father prayed for spiritual awakening to sweep the globe, and we were dismissed. Generally, I'd go back to the television, my sister to her novel, and Mom to the sink. On Friday or Saturday nights we'd go down to the basement and play poker. My father liked what he called "classical poker," five-card stud, and he would roll his eyes when I called one-eyed jacks or suicide kings wild. We all enjoyed playing, even my mother, who had been raised to believe cards were sinful. We had done our best to make the basement into a family room. We glued colorful carpet remnants to the linoleum floor and the walls, a patchwork of shag rectangles and tightly woven squares. But the basement would flood every spring and the scraps would lift up, and the snake cages always needed cleaning.

The squirrels exacted their revenge the next spring. My sister and I convinced my parents to take the requisite trip to Disney World. My father bought a pop-up camper and loaded it with fishing gear. We hooked it to the back of our station wagon and together with the rest of the East Coast we headed south to

Orlando. We forgot Jonathan at a gas station in South Carolina. It took us some time to reach an exit and effect a U-turn. When we returned, horror-stricken, Jonathan was just sitting on the curb with his special blanket, calmly sucking his thumb. He wasn't worried; he'd made the necessary Lovelace adjustments already. When we got to Florida my sister contracted sun poisoning, I was bitten by a barracuda, and my screaming brother was forcibly removed from Captain Nemo's submarine. Back home, my father parked the camper in the backyard and we all did our best to forget. The squirrels shredded the pop-up, just totaled it. My father paid cash to a passing backhoe operator and he dug an enormous hole in our backyard and buried it. That was our last family vacation. We never went farther than Peniel again.

Dad's snake habit was becoming a problem, undeniably. Upon moving to Hamilton, no longer regulated by life in a parsonage, my father's affair with reptiles reached crisis proportions. An entire room of our small ranch house was dedicated to terrariums, heat lamps, rodent foodstuffs, and the like. It was a humid cave of a room, reeking of mouse fear and snake droppings. It smelled fermented and nutty, like burned cheese and acorns. The snakes drove my mother to despair. My father simply refused to consider their removal. He seemed incapable of even smelling them.

We owned a reticulated python of considerable size named Ringo; a boa named Boris; an anaconda; any number of indigenous snakes; two alligator-like caimans, Wally and Jinx; and Igor, who hung baleful and motionless on our living room curtain. It was Igor, not Camus, who taught me life could very well prove meaningless. Lettuce was his only comfort. Generally, Igor was removed from the curtain and sequestered with the other reptiles only when company was expected. He was forgotten on occasion. Once, to my mother's horror, he joined the faculty wives' prayer group.

If Igor hinted at the immutable, absurd nature of the universe, the caimans argued for its undying malevolence. It was Jinx who commandeered Willow Grove's organ and threatened my father's ministry. Now the beasts glared up at us from my old bassinet. They never slept. We force-fed them using bits of raw meat pushed down their beastly throats with pencil erasers. At every opportunity they sank their needle teeth into our hands and held on until we swung them over our heads and tore them free. The relationship proved so bloody awful that their eventual death and dismemberment by Woodstock raccoons was viewed as a blessing, the best for all concerned. I should emphasize, there is no reason to entrap, purchase, or possess a pair of caimans. They don't keep each other company, they don't wait for you to get off the bus, and they don't play fetch.

As for the snakes, I was my father's willing accomplice. I gave up hunting the king's squirrels and joined my father, who spent his leisure hours stalking the local snake population. We drove slowly through the surrounding neighborhoods in the early evenings, watching for garter, corn, and hognose snakes sunning themselves on the blacktop, pulling the last heat of the day from the road. Down by the bridle paths, we found an old white door lying in weeds, peeling and pulling apart with the rain. It was the perfect snake trap, providing a dark lair of soft earth covered by a warm solar collecting roof. We visited the door regularly and I snatched any number of garter snakes from under it, including a pregnant one that bore twenty-one squiggling babies back in my room. Once I lifted the door and found a young milk snake; its orange, brown, and white patterns made it a jewel, as beautiful as a brook trout.

The summer I turned twelve my dad dragged home a sorry-looking fiberglass hull. Ipswich Marine said it sank out behind Crane's beach when the bilge pump crapped out. Second time. They pulled the boat out of the channel. "She just filled up with rainwater," they assured my father. "Twice. It's nothing structural. No holes. It's just the bilge pump. We'll put in a new one." They said all the owner wanted was salvage costs. The Coast Guard had called the boat a "navigational hazard." My father called it a stripped-down, no-nonsense fishing machine. It was a 1965 Cathedral Trihull.

The boat, my father, and I spent considerable time at Ipswich Marine. The mechanics liked my father; they called him the Professor. "It's like this, Professor. All you've got is a hull. That's it. Just a hull. But it's bulletproof. When she has an engine she'll plow through anything, four-foot seas, rips, sandbars. She's a fishing machine, Professor, you're right. She sure is." They sold us an ancient and rectangular outboard, spray-painted and mounted it. The boat got new steering and wiring harnesses. We named her *Strider* and commenced plowing through four-foot seas, rips, and sandbars.

We fished weekends and after school, day or night, early spring through the first snow, most often with weather permitting but most notably not. We fished the mouth of the Merrimack River primarily. The Merrimack powered New England's shift from the small farms to massive brick workhouses and it pushes past the great textile mills of Lawrence and Lowell, past miles of brick, stone, and broken glass, all of it shuttered now, bricked-up and silent. The river drains all this. It floods the mud flats just past Newburyport and then roars out to the Atlantic through a pair of massive granite jetties, a great engineered channel. The ocean's ingoing tide pushes up huge standing waves at the mouth and its outgoing pulls wicked rips. We plied it at night in a two-time loser of a bulletproof hull with a tired, spray-painted engine. Confused seas and questionable piloting plagued the *Strider,* but we came back because along with everything else, the river dumps out an enormous amount of bait—herring, alewives, crabs, worms, silversides, and sand eels. Mackerel moved through; striped bass, bluefish and sharks, even five-hundred-pound tuna patrol here. And back then there were cod, actual codfish.

Launching and loading the *Strider* was not the most danger-ous phase of operations but it was the most humiliating. Misfor-tune at sea, for that matter stupidity at sea, is a private matter. At sea no one is watching when you, say, let the anchor line's bitter end slide overboard (we did that), run aground (we always did that), run out of gas (yes), or fall overboard (see below). Death at sea is considered heroic—even ennobling—quite unlike, say, forgetting to set the station wagon's parking brake on a ramp while it's attached to a three-thousand-pound boat, or drilling a hole in the hull while mounting a deck chair, or forgetting the boat's drain plug prior to launching.

We pushed our luck and the nearby Coast Guard station's

patience, and one night the worst almost happened. It was in the fall and my father was alone at the mouth hoping for cod-fish. He set anchor in a hard running tide and the *Strider* swung round fast. The engine's prop caught the anchor line and held its stern down into the current. The river poured past the engine and swamped the boat almost immediately. Dad grabbed a knife and leaned over the transom; he fell into the water and cut the boat free. He pulled himself up onto the half-sunken boat and it spun past the jetties. The engine was underwater, its batteries dead. He said he prayed for all of us, that we'd be all right. Out past the jetties the boat slowly drifted out of the current. The tide turned. My father found an oar we had stashed, stood in the water, and paddled for Salisbury Beach. Hours later he walked up and banged on a door. They gave him rum, scavenged an anchor, and made our boat fast against the incoming tide.

Twenty years later I sold the boat to an old friend for pocket change and didn't see it for years until I stumbled across it in Rockport. It was up on stanchions behind some tourist shops on Bearskin Neck. Five or six kids were scraping away at its hull and I asked them how they ended up with it. "Me and my brother found it out past Salvages," one said. "Just floating, banging against the rocks. No one claimed it. The number's expired." His story seemed unlikely but maybe it was true. I couldn't ask my friend; he was gone. Long ago I decided to believe it, that the *Strider* kept floating without us.

Back home in Hamilton, undrowned and admired by his colleagues, my father began a new book that became the central work of his life. Using Edwards's writings as a template, my father hoped to shape the next Great Awakening. It had already begun, Dad believed, within the counterculture. By 1968 the media brought wild tales of Jesus Freaks and their movement to my father back east. Gone were the blue-eyed, pastel images of Christ from Sunday school; his profile began resembling Che Guevara's. It was a strange, paradoxical movement—the marriage of hippie rebellion and fundamentalist religion—and for a season the press could not get enough, nor could my father.

My father believed Peniel should get into this act and so he arranged a field trip. Twelve skeptical church folk boarded a van bound for Love In, a Jesus commune in Freeville, New York. It was a massive barnlike structure, embellished by the requisite stained glass, hippie towers, and flags. Dad had made arrangements with the so-called freaks for lunch but we stood tightly grouped in their driveway like frightened birds. A few tense moments passed, and then a bell like Peniel's rang and the fabled Jesus People emerged from the pines. My father's great hope for the church approached in overalls, bandanas, and hair. A tall, smiling man said, "Brothers, sisters, welcome," and my father allowed himself to be hugged. "Are you from, from…"

"Peniel Bible Conference."

"Yes. Peniel." All of us stood quite still. "Welcome."

My father stepped forward. "All of us are very excited about what you are doing here. Living together."

"Thank you." The man threw an arm over Dad's shoulder. He had straw or something in his beard. "My name is Ed. Please, everyone, come and eat with us."

He led us into a large dining area outfitted with picnic tables and packed with believers. "Everyone, everyone," Ed in-
toned, "we have visitors here for lunch. These brothers and
sisters are from Peniel Bible Conference." Ed ushered us to
the front of a buffet line and we helped ourselves to lentils.
We returned and sat in uncomfortable silence until a group
prayer welled up around us, a marathon grace involving hand
waving, swaying, and shouts. There were murmurs in an unknown language comprised of the letters L, M, and N. It was
tongues! They were speaking in tongues, the language of angels! I was thrilled. And also the angelic young women weren't
wearing bras! I was thirteen years old and surrounded by
women without bras waving their arms around. Their eyes were
blissfully clamped shut. They were oblivious to my wide-eyed
prayers. God, I was thankful. I saw my dad smile as well.
He had his first chapter: "Jonathan Edwards and the Jesus
Movement."

My father believed in an artistic and spiritual renaissance
that would flush all the mediocrity out of his church: the shallow
self-help books, its awful attempts at musical relevance, its path-
ological fear of art and outsiders. He welcomed the curiosity and
rebellion he found in the youth movements and wanted to chart
a way out of what he called "dead orthodoxy." He wanted to find
the sublime. Instead, the Jesus People became the worst kind of
latter-day Puritans, isolated and judgmental. Dad's new culturally hip church filled with believers in book-burning apocalypse,
in rapture and flight from the world. They stopped listening
and, sadly, my father stopped speaking. Eventually, my father,
whose mind had welcomed so many artists and thinkers,

locked out his tone-deaf peers. Dad learned to love his music in silence.

He was most present, at least for me, on the ocean and duck marsh. My father wouldn't give me a shotgun; I was too young. He wouldn't allow a pet retriever and so when we shot ducks we lost them. But we rarely hit ducks. In short, waterfowl hunting was cold, boring, and pointless. But when my father asked me to go, I jumped. I loved to be with him. We hunted on the salt marshes behind Plum Island. The Merrimack River lies to the island's north, the Ipswich River to its south, and it's cut from the mainland by the Parker River and acres of salt marsh. The island is protected as a bird sanctuary, an essential stopover of the Atlantic Flyway. The salt marshes are essential as well but they're not protected, a gauntlet. My father and I figured we could bag our limit of ducks there easily. Bang, bang, bang. Dad had an aluminum skiff and we loaded it with decoys and ammunition. We put in a few miles inland on the Parker River. It was November and cold and the sky was a white blank. Aluminum skiffs are loud: they clang and ring at every wave and footfall. Ours was dented and old; it popped rivets and sprung leaks every time. It wasn't worth much but the engine was good.

The marsh looked all the same to me but Dad marked a point where the grass and black mud jutted into the river and turned. There was an empty duck blind; my father nosed toward it and I plopped the decoys down in a nice-looking, sociable group. We drifted down with the river for a few minutes and then Dad gunned the engine quickly and cut it. He tilted it up and we slid onto the bank. We never got ducks but this time we would; I knew it. This was the Parker River National Wildlife Refuge, a sure bet for dead ducks. It was low tide. Dad and I dragged the skiff up through the crushed mussel shells and soft muck until it got hard. Dad picked up his shotgun and we climbed up over the bank. It was a good walk to the blind but the silver boat was best stashed at a distance. The damp ground sucked at our boots and the hollow spartina grass popped.

We saw two ducks and they saw us as well. I hadn't complained but I was cold and I wanted to go home. By dusk we both wanted to go home but the boat had already left. It was almost high tide and the river was slapping against the spot where we had left it. I hadn't thrown the anchor, nor had my father.

"Well," my father said with remarkable equanimity, "it can't have gone far. It would have hung up on something." He didn't even curse. And so we started downstream, hopping ditches and slogging through mud—keeping busy. I knew my feet were wet but I couldn't feel them. There was no point in crying. Just before dark my father said, "All right, David. I think we should forget about the boat and get to the highest hump we can find. The tide's still coming." I knew I would cry and he looked at me and smiled. "It's not coming that far up, don't worry. We'll see someone. I've got three shells here and I'll use them to signal."

When it was pitch dark and all I could hear was the salt water moving on the marsh, my father said, "I think we should pray. Let's pray for your mother to call the Coast Guard."

It worked—not right away, but it worked. She grew concerned and reported us missing around ten p.m. By then I was hypothermic. My father had me stand and walk in circles, stomping my feet. He sang the old hymns from Peniel and had me sing along. He knew all the verses, each more somber than the last. I was delirious and the songs turned from triumphant assurance. I heard lost graveyard sounds. At eleven p.m. the Coast Guard found our skiff capsized off Crane's Beach, the engine dangling by its fuel line. After that they called out a helicopter. We could see its searchlight sweep back and forth over the river moving up from the sea. When it got close Dad lifted his shotgun and blasted three times. A boat was radioed. I was hustled aboard and wrapped in blankets. They wanted to take me to a hospital but Dad and I refused. It made the local papers: HAMILTON MAN MAROONED WITH SON. "'We sang hymns and prayed to keep warm,' Lovelace said."

The next day my sixth grade gym teacher lined us all up and then he said, "Hey, Lovelace. I heard you got stuck on a marsh." I nodded and looked at the floor. "Heard you sang hymns." He smiled and chewed at his gum. "How'd that work, huh?" The kids all stared and some of them laughed. I didn't speak. I wanted to know why I had to pray all the time, why I had to sing. I wanted to know why the world kept floating off, whose mistake that was, and why my family felt so alone. I began to realize that our beautiful ocean could drown us. That we shot animals dead or put them in cages. That my mother could drift and that my father lost boats. That my father's God said to Abraham, kill me a son.

FOUR

In 1974 Dad transferred the reptiles, my mother sprayed dis-infectant, and my grandfather moved into the snake room. Mom's father had spent the last decade working the family cir-cuit. He'd spend six months with my aunt Rose, long enough to confirm all his long-standing paternal judgments and begin shouting. Rose would get on the phone and plead with her brother, Frank, who would host Grandpa until his anger refocused, gath-ered momentum, and turned on his family. Then Frank called Mom and it was our turn. It was emotional tag team, except Mom never called on her siblings. She never shook off Grandpa's dis-dain but assumed he had cause and that cause was her fault. She saw herself through his eyes: her shortcomings as a daughter, a wife, and a mother, the disappointing family she'd made.

There was no grace period with Grandpa, no honeymoon month spoiling his youngest grandchild, telling us stories, or feigning interest in snakes. Instead, he immediately began rak-ing leaves—obsessively raking leaves—and shooting dark glances at the men of the household. Whenever I looked out a window Grandpa was there, muttering angrily and wrestling a tarp filled with wet leaves, seasons upon seasons of them. I was fourteen that fall and I was awkward and sullen. Above all I was lazy. I spent my afternoons watching reruns and expended what energy I possessed in odd, useless projects. I drank Moxie and collected the cans. I lined the walls of my room with my empty orange cans. I caught pregnant snakes and named all their babies. I didn't do homework and I never ever raked.

"Richard," my mother said one night as we gathered for dinner, "look at Grandpa out there. I'm worried for him."

"Who?"

"Grandpa. Right there under the window. In the shrubs. He's been raking for weeks."

"He has?"

"Yes. And none of us are helping." My mother gave Grandpa a little wave from the kitchen window and mouthed the word "dinner." "Look, he's not coming in. He's shaking his head." It was true. Grandpa had redoubled his efforts. He had a stiff mustache and a gray crew cut and jabbed his work gloves at the tarp like a boxer. He waved Mom off and started dragging his tarp toward the woods.

"He's going to kill himself," I said. "He shouldn't be doing that."

"Who asked him to?" my father asked. "We live in the woods. We don't need the leaves raked." My mother sat slowly. She stopped arguing and twisted her hands until they dropped in a hard little ball. Grandpa wouldn't stop, the ugly brown leaves wouldn't stop, and Dad wouldn't start. I wouldn't start either, no way. Grandpa was none of my concern.

Mom stopped talking. She stared at her empty plate and forgot about food. She moved into her worry, stepped further and further from our bright kitchen. My mother saw darkness so often in daylight that we stopped paying her heed. My father counted on Peggy to hold Mom's hand, to keep her from falling while he typed. I watched television with my seven-year-old brother. I wore headphones. She'd have been on her own in the dark if it hadn't been for Peggy.

"You know," I said, "Grandpa said I was planning to kill him. He said I was trying to poison him."

"Let's have dinner!" Jonathan shouted. My mother rose.

Dad smiled. "Oh, you're kidding, right? He said you were going to kill him?"

"Yup. That's what he said. I came in from school yesterday and he started shouting at me. He said, 'Don't think you're getting away with it, Buster. I'm watching you.' Stuff like that."

"Poison!" my brother screamed gleefully. "What poison?" Peggy sat quietly and my mother busied herself at the stove.

My father was fascinated. "He really said that?" I nodded. "Wow. What did you say?"

"I said I wasn't planning to kill him. What do you think? He's crazy, that's all. I just pushed past him and went upstairs." I looked past my father to the window and watched Grandpa scrape at the yard.

Dad chuckled and shook his head. My mother quietly set a platter of chicken on the table. She set the cauliflower and cheese sauce down. "I'll just make him up a plate," she said in a whisper, gathered the food, and wrapped it in foil. Then Mom sat and waited for grace.

Grandpa had transformed the snake room into a comfortable den and hid there when he wasn't outside raking leaves into guilt.

He still ate our suspect food, but he ate most of it alone in his den. It wasn't difficult to avoid Grandpa, but one afternoon he ambushed me. He hopped out of the kitchen and stood at the top of the stairs. "I know what you're up to, boy. You can't fool me." He held a can of Moxie in one hand and a broom in the other.

"What, Grandpa?" I stopped on the stairs, well out of his reach, and smiled mockingly. "What have you got on me?"

"You're on drugs, boy. I know it. I can prove it." He held up the orange can and shook it at me. "Right here."

"What do you mean, Grandpa? What do you mean, 'right here'?"

"It says it right here, on the can. You're on acid. I knew it."

"Acid."

"That's right." He smiled triumphantly. "Carbonic acid. This Moxie's full of it."

"That's what makes soda fizz," I said dismissively, and climbed toward him. "It's just soda, Grandpa. Christ."

"Watch your mouth, David." He took up the doorway and refused to move. "Don't you take the Lord's name in vain." I kept moving up and tried to duck past him but Grandpa jabbed his broom into my neck. I stumbled back, fell, and slid down the stairs. "Jesus," I cursed at the floor. I got up and shook out my arms as he glowered above me. "I mean, goddammit, Grandpa." I turned before he could shout, walked through the garage and back into the woods. Dad sent Grandpa back to Rose.

The first year I got hit with depression it seemed warranted, reasonable. My depression wasn't clinical; it wasn't grave; it was just natural. I had hormones. I'd read *The Catcher in the Rye*. Besides, it was 1975 and the music was terrible, just entirely wrong. My classmates and I inherited very little from our older brothers and sisters: no sense of purpose, no hippie dream, just dirt weed and old records. There were no antiwar marches—there was hardly even a war—no Woodstock, no tragic overdoses, nothing. There sure as hell wasn't any free love. We were ten years late. We'd been swindled and my classmates were oblivious. I shunned them, and so I spent most of my time sewing patches on blue jeans and listening to Neil Young records. I had round glasses and brown hair down to my shoulders, where it curled up with an unfortunate sort of bounce. I was voted "Most Earthy" in my class and dragged to *Saturday Night Fever* in overalls. I wanted a cultural watershed, and when President Carter reinstated draft registration I ran down to the post office looking for something to burn.

I had three friends in Hamilton and all of us were cultural misfits. Our fathers taught at Gordon Conwell, an isolated hothouse of midwestern evangelicalism. My friends and I were regarded as a sort of invasive species at school. All of us had washed out socially early in the first grueling rounds of puberty, and so there was a certain Darwinian inevitability to our friendship. We had been raised by theologians and thrown to the wolves, to the beautiful daughters of bankers and their lacrosse captain boyfriends. William Beck was the only one of us without evangelical ties, but after he stood in front of our class and announced his papal ambitions he too was shunned. "I intend to be Pope," read the opening of his career essay, "I will live in the Vatican." After that we took him in; he was one of us. We sat in our parents' basements with black lights and posters. We talked about Jesus, the moral problem of breasts, and what went wrong with Paul McCartney and Wings.

Hamilton's parties, football, and polo games couldn't hold us; they wouldn't have us. Local church youth groups were an obvious choice, the last social outpost. They had to take us in, but they didn't. Finally, we found a church out of town where no one knew us. West Peabody Congregational welcomed us with open arms. That church was filled with lapsed Peabody girls and religious fervor. Our retreats featured nonstop French kisses and prayer requests. I got baptized (again) in a cold Maine lake just to impress the girls. I was shameless. I mimicked the kid beside me when he spoke in tongues. I belonged.

I didn't belong in school. My chemistry teacher returned my midyear exam and shook his head. "I don't know how you did this, David. But you have flunked flunking." My wood shop teacher placed my project, a deformed little pencil box, on the center of a bench and smashed it with a three-pound sledge. I was in my third year of algebra. I skipped out of gym and had numerous fistfights with a pair of ill-tempered brothers, identical twins. It was all terribly confusing. Only my English teacher and her *Scarlet Letter* made sense. She had long dark hair, was partial to miniskirts, and possessed a tremendous set of black leather boots. She gave me a copy of Keith Jarrett's *Köln Concert* and I was sure that I loved her. I spent passionate moments alone with the record and afterward lay spent and weak with shame. I am worse than Arthur Dimmesdale, I thought. I should be made to wear a great scarlet M for my sins.

Meanwhile, my father's book, *The Dynamics of Spiritual Life*, had been published to good—if largely evangelical—reviews. It had made quite a splash, in fact, and my father's calendar filled with speaking dates and side projects. He spoke against the church's isolation from the greater world, and especially the world of art. He promoted cultural awareness, an appreciation of anything fine— high, low, sacred, and secular. He put "Howl" on his required reading lists. "Quite simply, this poem is about loss—loss of purpose, loss of mind, loss of God." Students complained it was obscene and my father glowered. "Of course it's obscene."

He began dragging our stereo up to the seminary once or twice a semester. His music lectures were soon packed; they drew crowds of earnest seminarians, skeptical colleagues, and random onlookers. I went. He started lectures with Bach and then broke the cultural ice with some Simon and Garfunkel:

> And the people bowed and prayed / To the neon god they made / And the sign flashed out its warning / In the words that it was forming / And the sign said the words of the prophets / Are written on the subway walls / And tenement halls / And whispered in the sounds of silence.

My dad hit stop and looked up from the tape deck. "Okay. How about that? The neon God." He stopped and scanned his puzzled audience. "Don't you see what's going on here? Culturally? This isn't just pop. 'Hello, Darkness my old friend.' That's not Frank

Sinatra. You wouldn't hear Frank Sinatra singing about false prophets, people writing songs that voices never share." My father was big on the Beatles. He liked Joni Mitchell, Leonard Cohen, and Dylan but avoided the Stones and was downright scared of the Doors. And then he discovered a strange new hybrid, Christian rock. He stacked our living room with vinyl, some of it good, most of it poorly produced and mediocre. He championed the decent musicians and befriended a number of them. He even produced a record or two. My friends and I took up the cause. We believed one musician in particular, Larry Norman, was the ultimate outsider. He was our model rebel: too Christian for rock and roll, too rock and roll for the church. He met with my father once in the living room and my brother and I spied through the door. He was due to perform and dressed at our house. After he left we looked in the shower. I found a few wisps of his long blond hair and we saved them. We were, undoubtedly, in an alternate universe.

My mother blamed coffee and Satan for her anxieties. She always had a jar of instant decaf and drank cup after thin cup of the stuff. She took her vitamin B pills and sat with her brushes and paints, and every three or four years her worries curdled into paranoia. She was sure the neighbors were reading our mail. The mail carrier let them. They knew we hadn't paid the phone bill. The bank knew and Dad was hiding the checkbook. Or Grandmère would call. All Grandmère had to do was call and leave a message for Richard. That was enough. The seminary trustees planned to fire Dad because of the snakes, because of the records.

My father reassured my mother every morning and he prayed with her dutifully. But when we arrived home from school he often called Peggy into the living room. "See what you can do for Mom. All right? She needs you; she's getting the whim-whams."

"But, Dad, I don't know what I can do for her. Why don't you take her out? Or call some of her friends and invite them to dinner. How about David? Why doesn't he do something?"

"That might be too much of a shock. No. You just go talk with her."

My sister always did. She dragged all her childhood guilt into the kitchen and sat holding Mom's hand. She did this for years until her guilt turned to anger. Why didn't Dad do something? It was Dad's fault and he did nothing but control Mom and keep her from friends. As for me, I stayed downstairs by the snakes, watching television with my kid brother.

My first depression found me watching television. I got farther and farther away and lost with Gilligan until one day I stopped understanding. I couldn't follow situation comedy, its plots, mishaps, or jokes. I found *The Brady Bunch* incomprehensible. Its laugh track made me weep. When I spoke I heard my words unravel into just sounds. Nothing was in sequence and my thoughts blinked off one by one. I could see them. I was scared that my little brother could see. I was like Mom. Jonathan avoided me now, I could tell. I could see him in sepia, those brown heartbroken shades where dead people pose. I saw us all now in sepia. I stopped washing my hair and brushing my teeth. It was pointless. If I did it I'd have to do it again. I saw my mom. I knew the way she stuttered in the kitchen, the way she turned from us and dropped into some hell. The muscles in my face let go. Alone in the bathroom I made a smile in the mirror and it strangled my eyes. I saw my mom. I found tears on my face. I shuttered my room, refused meals, and gave in to my stupor. I now know the symptoms of clinical depression well: changes in brain chemistry, a quantifiable loss in electrical brain activity, speech and thought slowed to a crawl, delusions, in short a complete exhaustion of the mind. All I knew then was the mark. I was marked for it, for madness, just like my mother. I waited for the hallucinations, watched for them. I lay in bed and stared into nothing at all. My heart was a nest of unclean birds—just like my namesake's. I stopped attending school. I couldn't dress myself. The hours lasted days and every hour I sat and considered my suicide. I wanted to drown. I wanted to take the boat out past Dry Salvages, five, maybe six miles past, and then gun it, hit the throttle and jump. But I knew I'd never do it and that knowledge disgusted me. I was just a kid and lacked the courage. I was a fucking coward. Suicide was a big decision and I couldn't even choose my socks. I despised my socks; their smell made me sick.

I couldn't even stand up and no one could help me. In fact, there wasn't much anyone could do for me back then—just take away the razors and watch me. There weren't many drugs. Today they feed suicides antidepressants, stoke the poor suffering kids with chemical courage. They help most of the time but sometimes, rarely, the medicines hasten tragedy. Sometimes they work just halfway, just enough to get them to jump.

I couldn't sleep and day was identical to night, just shadows sliding across blue bedroom walls. My friends visited once, spoke at me, and left. I told my mother to turn them away after that. I didn't speak the same language as they did. I couldn't even feel the same emotions. Mom brought me food and took it back to the kitchen. She opened the curtains and made me sit up. I could hear her talking to Dad in the kitchen and I knew she blamed herself for my sickness. My father knocked.

"David. Hey, David, are you awake in there? Can I come in?" I was awake. I was always awake. You never sleep; you just lie down and beg to.

"David?" He came in and sat at the foot of my bed. He asked how I was feeling.

"Tired. I'm just tired. I'm trying to sleep."

"I just came in to try and cheer you up." I stared at him. He smiled and tapped at my knee. "You know, Mom and I were just saying how nice it's been to have you around. I mean you're hardly ever here anymore, out running around with your friends doing... well, who knows what you're doing."

"Yeah."

"Look, what I'm trying to say is that we like you this way. I mean you're more thoughtful, more sensitive. You're not blaring bad music through the house." It was a calculated jab and he hoped for a response, but I couldn't respond. I just stared at my blankets and my father continued reluctantly. "Don't get me wrong, David. I don't mean to belittle what you're going through. I think it's extremely difficult. St. John of the Cross called it a 'dark night of the soul.' This is normal. This is Satan testing you. He's tempting you just like he tempted Jesus in the desert. You're in the Slough of Despond. Once you pass through this, you'll be a stronger Christian."

"Slough?"

"Bunyan. *Pilgrim's Progress.*" He stood and moved to the door.

"I'm proud of you."

When I felt stronger I made myself leave the house. Later that winter, I was hiding in the seminary library, curled into a carrel with my head in my hands. Someone said, "Excuse me." I knew no one at the seminary; that's why I was there. They couldn't be speaking to me. "Um. Excuse me," a man said again. "Are you David Lovelace?"

I turned my head and squinted up at him. "Yeah. So?" Two well-scrubbed seminarians beamed down at me.

"Are you, um… are you having a dark night of the soul? I mean, excuse me, but your father, Dr. Lovelace, says you're having a dark night of the soul."

"He does."

"Yes. You know, St. John of the Cross."

"I know St. John of the Cross. I know the dark night of the soul. Yes."

"What's it like?"

"Oh, come on," I said. "Fuck off. Please? Just fuck off." I got up and stumbled past them. Evidently my father had been bragging about my depression, about his son, St. John of the Cross.

By early spring I began improving. The Sanka and vitamin B my mother pushed started kicking in, I guess. I went back to school and let everyone whisper, and I whispered, too. My voice frightened me; it sounded like cancer. I avoided my friends and I sat at our family dinner table under duress.

One night my father had big news. "Guess who's coming to dinner next week? Chuck Colson!"

"Chuck Colson." I looked down at my plate. "Wow."

It seems Chuck Colson, Nixon's own hatchet man, had experienced a jailhouse conversion, read my father's book, and started up his own Bible study with some of the old gang. My father had been flying down to DC regularly and mentoring a select group of Watergate conspirators. Revival makes for strange bedfellows, and Chuck Colson and my father had become fast friends. Wow. I couldn't wait.

When Colson arrived I wore my patched jeans and I pulled out my ponytail and dragged hair across my face. Dad introduced us and I shook his hand silently. At the table Dad chatted with Colson while my mother flitted nervously and served up the steaks. My father kept trying to pull me into the conversation.

"Well, you know, David and I are great fishermen. We love the ocean." Colson thought that was grand. I just stared at him.

"David's been considering Wheaton College. The one in Illinois. Evangelical." A fine choice, said Colson. I didn't eat anything. The smell of food still made me nauseous; I hadn't eaten in days. I just moved my silverware while the hatchet man sawed at his meat. Dad leaned closer to the big man. "Confidentially," he said, "David's been having a bit of the dark night of the soul." I excused myself from the table.

Apparently my family and friends could not understand me and it was quite clear I would never appreciate St. John. I just got angrier and angrier until I punched at the walls and got up and left. I ran through the woods. I quit church. I looked at my mother, saw her eyes all clouded with cataract fear, and I knew that my death would return. We'd been dealt a raw deal, Mom and I. She was stuck with her hand but I figured on folding.

I went back to church one last time, back to West Peabody. I wasn't sure but I was sick of the praying and all the old answers. My godly parents had been fruitful; they had multiplied and had commenced my religious training at once. It's like this: when you're a preacher's kid, eternal life is a done deal by the time you are baptized—all you have left is mortified flesh. It seemed such a cheat and so I raised hell. It was a matter, I think, of cosmic balance. So, of course, I came back to church to raise hell, to blow my goddamn dark night all to pieces.

I skipped out of youth group and wandered the church halls. I pushed into the pastor's office. He was upstairs in the sanctuary, meeting with the deacons, or elders, or some bullshit mission committee. There was nothing of interest on his desk; the office was neat. I didn't know what I wanted but I soon found it: a fire extinguisher, chemical, type II. I pulled the pin and squeezed the trigger just a bit. A tiny, noxious dust cloud appeared. I squeezed again and once more, ringing the preacher's desk with small, perfect clouds of sulfurous yellow. A light, postapocalyptic dust was falling. It was lovely, I thought, and then the cylinder kicked back into my chest and opened up like a flamethrower. I ran for the door holding the thing while its hose thrashed at my arm. "Fuck!" I screamed down the hall, "Fuck!" and ran through the church hollering with the thing and with the smoke alarms screaming. I got to a side door and pitched the extinguisher out on the pavement, where it spun like a huge broken bottle rocket. The deacons were standing out front because inside was hell. I told the firemen I didn't know why it happened. The thing just went off. Boom.

Anger pushed me back into the world but it was the fishing that freed me—Ipswich Bay. By now I had floated over most of it and run aground on the rest. It was something about drifting, just standing alone on the currents, that made me grateful again. The flat line of horizon stayed quiet and the fishing pulled me close. It was a different, more serious prayer and it saved me. It was the spring run of mackerel—shoals of small tinker mackerel moving beneath me, quickly, just under the surface. I jigged up five at a time on a long line of small, silvery hooks. I live-lined the smallest, pushing a large hook through its lips and flipping it back, watching it flash down. I wanted the big fish, the first migrating stripers or bluefish. Deep down I wanted what the old man caught and lost to the sea. I love waiting for the hit, the living, thrashing hit from the blank green. I love what pushes silversides up in a spray, what swings the gulls down and leaves the boat bloody and feeds us.

I recovered, but my room was stale with my sickness. I had maybe sixty-five dollars. I was a broke preacher's kid with wanderlust and so I turned to the mission field. It offered the best opportunity for a boy with my talents and connections, and before long I was mass-mailing frightening little cards asking for tithes. My awkward yearbook photo gawked above the bold caption: "Please Help Me Witness for CHRIST with Teen Missions!" A small write-up followed, describing the mission project, the construction of a Christian orphanage outside Manaus, Brazil. Finally, in bold letters below my pitch, Teen Missions' trademarked call to action ordered, "Go Lay a Brick for God!" I could lay bricks; how hard could it be? I had been called to Manaus and I shamelessly hit up every relative and every Peniel preacher I could find.

In truth, all I'd been called to was a chance to get out of the country, all expenses paid. As for the gospel, that was a bit more complicated. I had lost it somewhere in that dark night but I knew it cold. I could deliver the Good News at a moment's notice. If asked by a Brazilian with average English skills, I could explain the basics. If necessary I even could discuss the mysteries of the triune God or the problem of evil. Lack of belief could not dissuade me from the mission field. Besides, I still liked Jesus. I now practiced a sort of benign pothead agnosticism counterbalanced with sporadic contempt. In short, I was seventeen. I was bipolar, seventeen, and ready to cycle. I no longer wanted to save the world. I wanted to see the world, sure, but mostly I wanted to meet exotic girls and convince them I'd seen it. I cut my hair, signed the Teen Missions doctrinal statement, and caught a bus for the Lord's Boot Camp in Merritt Island, Florida.

Prior to shipping out, teenagers from all over the country received training at the Lord's Boot Camp. We lodged in mildewed tents where nocturnal armadillos crawled under the canvas and our backs, seeking body heat. Reveille came through a loudspeaker system just before dawn; we got some grub at the mess hall and then commenced the laying on of brick. Lecture subjects alternated between Jesus's infinite love and my unacceptable behavior. It was a nightmare. What the hell had I been thinking? I must have been sick.

One morning at break I was playing my harmonica when a Lord's Boot Camp staffer walked up. He squinted at me. He had a crew cut. "What's the name of that song, son?"

I shrugged. "I don't know. It's not really a song."

"Yes it is, son. It's a song. Is that a Christian song?" Non-Christian songs were forbidden at the Lord's Boot Camp.

I rolled my eyes. "Right, right," I said. "It's called 'Jesus Loves Me Blues.'" I was given work detail and lost my harmonica. I lost my copy of *Walden*—No Secular Humanism. I lost the girlfriend I'd met on the bus down—No Pairing Off. I even lost my shorts—No Immodest Dress. And so, stripped of my sins, I flew to Manaus with twenty other brainwashed workers. At seventeen I found myself one thousand miles up the Amazon, stacking misshapen bricks and sleeping in a hammock alongside fundamentalists. I should have joined the fucking army.

The first week we ate canned chicken and gravy over reconstituted potatoes. By the second week we settled for gravy with reconstituted potatoes. Soon after the gravy changed from a meaty brown to tan to a sort of milky gray color and resembled soupy reconstituted potatoes. We had lots of green Jell-O. We ate green Jell-O until the bitter end. We lived in a compound hacked from the forest—a baked dirt exercise yard beside a rudimentary kitchen and a thatched area with benches and tables. There were tin cups and Kool-Aid. I now understand how Jim Jones did it, how he achieved his dark ends.

By the third week I and two other missionary youths began sneaking down to the river at night to fish. We built small fires and ate small fish that had fangs. We smoked cigarettes bummed from workers we met in the forest clearcuts, broken-looking men with machetes who stood beside billowing brushfires. We bought a turkey from a man who lived in a stick hut a mile or so downstream. It had one eye and was sickly. We fed it our baked oatmeal and fully intended to kill it and eat it when the time came. The mortar and bricks ate into my infected hands. I knew I could get sick there, that I couldn't hide there, that I had run straight into my darkness. I stayed up and waited for Colonel Kurtz.

Six days a week we ate salt tablets and malaria pills and slaved relentlessly in the clearing. It felt more like a swamp in the heat. We carried bricks, mixed mortar, cleared brush, and cut the tin roofing. I dug an outhouse pit through ten inches of rainforest loam and six feet of sand. Nevertheless we kept up appearances; the missionaries taught us how. Every day after lunch we spent one blessed hour in the shade and we learned. The men's course was entitled God's Gentleman. I learned how to shave—never against the grain; this causes pimples—and how to part my hair. In *The God's Gentleman Workbook* I found line drawings of various head and face shapes, with suggested hair parts. I have a thin face, and the authors suggested I should part my hair in the middle. The workbook was filled with cautions. There was a picture of a long-haired man with a black X across his face.

Beards were advised only when confronted with weak chins or other, more serious disfigurements. The girls' workbook, *From Grubby to Grace*, was kept away from the boys but my fellow gentlemen and I surmised that it dealt with more intimate matters. I still possess my *God's Gentleman Workbook*. I brought it back from Brazil and placed it in a box in my mother's attic, along with a blow dart and a lacquered candy dish carved from a root. But I'm a backslider, I confess. I shave against the grain and I renounced combs years ago.

On Sundays we would eat a special baked reconstituted oatmeal with raisin sauce and then board the missionary's van and head toward the city to evangelize. It was shameful. I talked about a savior I didn't know to destitute strangers without English. I had lost twenty pounds. I'd broken my front tooth. Someone had stepped on my eyeglasses and one lens was Scotch tape. I needed phrase books for town; I needed phrase books for camp. In Manaus, only the fleeting glimpse of the ubiquitous, thin-tied Mormon missionaries could cheer me. Evidently, a circle lower than Teen Missions existed, haunted by pairs of dark-suited young men from Utah, cruising the cities of the world like Buddy Holly's sanctified ghosts.

Toward the end, when our building was close to completion, we were driven to a leper colony about twenty kilometers outside Manaus, a desolate outpost of concrete and tin buildings built on a series of dusty, deforested hills. Everything had been burned long ago. We met the sorriest-looking people I had ever seen, their faces bandaged, fingers and ears eaten away, some with open sores. I remember how they stood off from us and pointed, laughing. A tired uniformed woman coerced them into the damp chapel, where we commenced singing songs in English. But we had practiced singing "Jesus Loves Me" in Portuguese for the occasion. It was a big hit. In fact, the lepers laughed and clapped and joked with one another throughout that suffering afternoon. The sun outside stayed hard and bright as we stood in the small, dark room with our eyes cast to the floor. I had nothing for these people. I heard ghosts again and I thought I'd be lucky just to get home. My friends and I never ate the turkey but returned it to the man in the forest. He thanked us and then he got out a machete and killed it right there while we stood beside his smoky hut, queasy and mute witnesses for Christ.

We had flown into Manaus from the city of Belem, on the delta coast. For our return, Teen Missions had booked a twelve-day, one-thousand-mile boat trip down the Amazon. We were all tremendously excited until we saw the riverboat, a rusty steel barge with its upper deck half-fitted with sloppy welds. It could have been the boat Werner Herzog pushed over a mountain while shooting *Fitzcarraldo*, his film based on the rubber barons and their fabled Manaus opera house. It certainly looked like it had been pushed over a mountain by Werner Herzog.

The Brazilian crew and passengers kept to the lower deck. Some slept in cabins, some in hammocks hung from the rails. Our group had the upper deck, where we stood watching brown water slide past the dull green mangroves and vines. The Amazonian rain forest isn't all toucans and shamans. It's more than that. For me it was the drone and skip of an old diesel engine, an endless swamped tangle that pushed back toward low clouds and rain and then white towers and sun. Sometimes the river seemed as wide and slow as a lake and we steamed down it day and night.

The third day out, the captain blasted a whistle and our boat sidled up to a clearing, where there was a small thatched building and a pier made of sticks. A handful of Indians appeared, ragged and shoeless, some with straw hats. The crew threw over the lines and within minutes the clearing teemed with people laughing and shouting, Indians selling baskets of dried fish, passengers embarking with filthy woven bags or disembarking with planking or chickens or children. A battered red pickup careened out from the trees and swung toward the pier. Half a cow hung from the tailgate. The deck hands grabbed the cow by its two legs and dragged it down the stick pier. They hoisted the meat aboard with some difficulty and winched it up over center deck, second class, where it hung for days while the flies and the galley cook worked like piranhas. Up in first class we ate it for a solid week, in stews.

I slept under the sky in my hammock. It was August, and the Perseid meteor showers rained down into the forest as the stars climbed up from the trees. It was all god, I was sure of it: the Southern Cross above us, the butchered cow below. It was god haunting the sad dust of equatorial opera houses, god in the malarial rivers and leper colonies, in all of this terrible beauty. All the old words like "savior" and "faith" seemed broken now. All of it was broken and I most of all. I didn't have long. I figured it was a matter of months.

FIVE

The morning after I returned from Brazil my mother began force-feeding me. She was painting again and watercolors lay on the kitchen table every morning with fresh flowers, calligraphy, and scripture. She'd clear them away every evening and apologize. She hadn't believed in her art since college. Peggy was still reading; I spent days with my brother and the television. The house was either silent or filled with Dad's music. Not much had changed.

I was twenty pounds underweight and had a broken tooth, a serious intestinal complaint, and no plan. College loomed. I had some options, some acceptances, but I could not decide. I was sliding back toward despair and my mind was slowing down. I couldn't even plan the afternoon. The first week of August my father interrupted one of my stuttering reveries and called me into the living room. "Listen," he said. "Let's clear this up. It's not necessary to have career goals. You'll figure that out once you get to college. Remember, David, careers aren't important. What's important is your calling, your vocation—how you will help build the Kingdom of God."

"Well, that's good," I mumbled. "I'm glad I don't have to

worry about getting a job." I was getting uncomfortable even before Dad mentioned St. John, but when he brought in the Devil I rushed from the room.

I tried to take the long view, I really did. I knew Dad's spiritual approach was traditional and time-tested. Humans have spent thousands of years studying the soul and less than thirty studying neuroscience. Until quite recently, the world blamed mental illness on devils—black bile and devils. In my family it was never the bile. All questions remained religious questions, questions that my father channeled through seventeenth-century Puritan divines. According to Dad, God and Satan are having a long, drawn-out game of capture the soul and we are all up for grabs. I seemed to be the only one losing.

I shook off Dad's Puritans. It wasn't too hard; England did it in 1620. A year after they left for their new world, a depressed mathematician named Robert Burton published the world's largest compendium of depression. He called the Puritans a "mad, giddy company of Precisians" and explained that they doubted of "their Election, how they shall know it, by what signs ... [and] with such nice points, torture themselves, that they are almost mad." Burton stressed bile over demons, "obsession over possession." His tome became wildly popular and created a royal court glutted with moody, world-weary posers. Burton wrote it, he said, to keep busy and called it *The Anatomy of Melancholy, What it is, With all the Kinds, Causes, Symptomes, Prognostickes, and Several Cures of it. In Three Maine Partitions with their several Sections, Members, and Subsections Philosophically, Medicinally, Historically, opened & cut up.* For starters he named the Head Melancholy, the Body Melancholy, and the Bowel Melancholy or "windie melancholy." The

subclassifications followed: Jealous Melancholy, Hypochondri-
acal Melancholy, Solitary, Romantic, Religious, and so on. Burton might have saved his ink. In my family it was always Religious
Melancholy, twenty-four-seven. There weren't any others. The
spirit ruled the mind and the mind ruled the brain.

Everyone knows the only cure for Religious Melancholy is more
religious training—prayer, certainly, but mostly more religious
training. I was in a tough spot. For months my father had been
praying and pushing me toward a midwestern, evangelical school:
Wheaton College. I no longer had the strength to push back. I
couldn't confront my family about our God. I couldn't announce
my desertion. That would mean leaving the evangelical trenches,
a rush into no-man's-land, straight toward the guns and barbed
wire. Instead I crawled out of the faith in secret and soon I was
tangled. I knew if I struggled I'd reveal my godless position and
so I came home from Brazil and played dead and hung on the
wires. I hoped that when night fell my family would crawl through
my blackness, cut me down, and carry me home.

My father flew me out to Wheaton College. He bought a
leather-bound Bible, inscribed it to me, and left. Wheaton was
awful. I soon discovered that I much preferred wasting away in
an equatorial white-slave work camp run by religious fanatics
over wasting away in a well-stocked cafeteria as classmates
argued for the Pope's eternal damnation. Every class session
opened with devotional prayers. I remember bowing solemnly
over my pickled, partially dissected fetal pig. We had all signed
a pledge not to curse, drink, gamble, have sex—especially

homosexual sex—or dance. We could not listen to jazz. It was eerie, as if some sort of cultural virus had swept through the place, had left us all standing and smiling and hollowed out from the world. Theologians will discuss the problem of evil forever but I'm more interested in the problem of goodness, why piety so often breeds zombies.

I guess I was called to tour the new building on campus, the Billy Graham Center. It was there I realized that the jig was up and I could no longer pass as evangelical. Upon entering I was ushered through the Rotunda of Witnesses and then on to a sort of wax museum history of evangelicalism. The tour ended in a small, well-lighted place, a room made of mirrors, blue sky, and clouds. From a walkway arched over mirrors I witnessed myself hovering in midair. Bach chorales rose from cheap, hidden speakers—the very sound of rapture, full of wow and flutter. At eighteen I found myself trapped in a phony Heaven, staring at myself. Nothing had prepared me for this, not church, not drugs, nothing. It focuses the mind, floating in Heaven, staring at oneself. I bolted and never returned.

If God couldn't cure my religious melancholy I figured it must not be religious. And it wasn't black bile, I knew that. The stuff doesn't exist—God maybe, but not black bile. As for doctors, I sure as hell wasn't schizophrenic, and if I was headed there, I didn't want to know. No way was I going to a doctor. I just had bad moods. All I needed was some fun, a lot of fun, and that meant Colorado and skis.

My Volkswagen blew its seals at twelve thousand feet,

somewhere inside the Eisenhower Tunnel, the very top of a pass blasted through a mountain peak. I didn't care. I just coasted six miles down and into my promised land. I pushed my car into a gas station lot, scavenged what I needed, and starting walking. It was three in the morning and the snow shone blue and lunar and the air tasted like steel. I walked through the night toward Breckinridge, toward the mountains, my cure.

The cure didn't take. I was determined, I did everything right, but it just didn't take. I landed a job at a local lodge, a modest, ramshackle place that gave me a room. I worked at a shop called Spurs and sold cowboy hats and phony snakeskin boots to tourists. I quit when the mountain opened and got a job teaching four-year-olds how to ski. Mostly they stood in the snow and cried, but I had my season pass. That was fun. I fell for a blond, blue-eyed girl with a turned-up nose and a closet full of tight sweaters. She was Lana Turner on skis. Her bedroom was like some delirious untethered satellite and I'd leave in the morning sleepless and dazed. That was really fun. I had what amounted to it all in a ski town: a beautiful girlfriend and a ski pass. But it wasn't enough. It would never be enough. I didn't need fun. I just needed a doctor.

At age twenty, I had only experienced half the disease— depression—and an accurate diagnosis was unlikely. Instead I spent years believing that my agitation and unhappiness were my fault, and my periodic depressions simply confirmed my self-loathing. Increasingly, fear and anxiety made my decisions. I found stopgap solutions and sad little hideouts. It would have

taken a full-blown crisis to pull me out my trenches. I didn't
want this disease. I had no intention of stepping out to meet it.
Denial wasn't difficult, not yet. No one in my family had experienced mania. My father and brother weren't sick at all. My
mother suffered from depression, she could get delusional, but
her quiet paranoia always passed. On average bipolar disease—
aka manic depression—hits patients in their late teens and
twenties. My father held out into his fifties. Classically, the disease hits in adolescence, as it did with me, and it most often descends like black death. My father, brother, and I had six years
before the shit hit the fan.

Simply put, bipolar disease results from the inability of the brain
to regulate emotion. Manic-depressives are mercurial and experience their highs and lows intensely. The illness is often called
a mood disease but this term obscures its deadly nature. Bipolar
disorder is a brain disease. No doubt it can be exacerbated by
lousy childhoods, whiskey, and stupidity, but it is biological in
origin. Psychoanalysis, abstinence, and education can't hurt, but
they cannot cure this sickness. Many sufferers do not experience
the disorder's more extreme, psychotic symptoms, but the disease is chronic and life-threatening, the most lethal form of mental illness. Left untreated, one out of every five manic-depressives
commits suicide. Considering the average onset age for bipolar
disease, it's no accident that suicide is the second leading cause
of death among college students.

Depression is a painfully slow, crushing death. Mania is the
other extreme, a wild roller coaster run off its tracks, an eight

ball of coke cut with speed. It's fun and it's frightening as hell. Some patients—bipolar type I—experience both extremes; others—bipolar type II—suffer depression almost exclusively. But the "mixed state," the mercurial churning of both high and low, is the most dangerous, the most deadly. Suicide too often results from the impulsive nature and physical speed of psychotic mania coupled with depression's paranoid self-loathing.

Patients who move between the two poles many times within the course of a year are called "rapid cyclers." A milder form of the disease, in which mood fluctuates but pulls back from extremes, is called cyclothymic disorder—bipolar lite. Properly understood and managed this form of the illness can prove extremely creative and productive. I've nibbled at the edges of hypomania all my life and I know I've benefited from it. It's hypomania, that precious, semilucid phase before mania, that is so seductive. It's brilliant—a quicksilver state charged with poetry, charisma, and sex. I believe it is possible to touch it and love it and leave. I believe it's a gift. But then I imagine cocaine addicts feel much the same way.

I'm more suited to counting angels dancing on a pinhead than to amateur discussions of neuroscience, and so I'll be brief. The brain communicates with electric signals. Neurons package chemical information into neurotransmitters and then fire them off to other neurons across spaces called synaptic clefts. If all goes well, the intended neuron—the receptor—catches the message, processes it, and then gets rid of it, gets ready for another. Most often the cell that sent the message gets it back to repackage; this is called reuptake. All this hums right along, with various neurons turning off or on, slowing and speeding, as needed. There are a great many chemical circuits in the brain, but two neurotransmitters are of special interest to the bipolar: serotonin and dopamine. These produce pleasure—they're lovely. But if the brain can't regulate their movement, if they pool up or drain down, there's trouble.

There are two categories of drugs presently used to treat manic-depressives: mood stabilizers such as lithium, and antidepressants. Mood stabilizers do just that: they build an emotional ceiling and floor, keep patients from going off the deep end. Lithium is used both to regain equilibrium and to prevent future episodes. It works at both ends but is best as a ceiling against mania. Scientists now think it affects enzymes involved in the processing of information within the neurons. I don't know how it works and I suspect no one really does.

The new generation of antidepressants, including Prozac, Zoloft, and others, is called SSRIs—selective serotonin reuptake inhibitors. They help you feel better by keeping your serotonin out there. I don't know how they work but I do know they can work too well; they can push a depressed bipolar patient right through the roof. They are a dangerous godsend.

I couldn't stay in Breckinridge; melancholy doesn't mix with hot tubs and ski slopes. I cashed out my fun when the mountain closed, broke it off with my girlfriend, and drifted back east. I moved in with my family one last time and found carpentry work, framing houses on the North Shore. I hung rafters in the bright sunlight, stood in pine sawdust, and measured and cut. For a while the work fixed me. I banked my money and applied to Colorado College.

In all likelihood, it was the last summer my family would live together, and no one acknowledged it. My father was alone and hard at it, stripped down to his boxers and undershirt and hunched at his typewriter. His outlook began darkening. The great cultural shifts of the '60s ground out and evangelical culture was never redeemed. His colleagues had circled the wagons. Jonathan and my mother were quiet that summer; Jonathan turned thirteen and found basketball, and my mother seemed well. She was painting. Peggy planned on attending Wheaton in the fall. Her news filled me with quiet rage. It was as if some insidious blue-eyed caste system preordained my family to evangelicalism. It seemed none of us could escape, but I bought a motorcycle and tried.

I rode west on the small roads past the upstate vineyards, the Finger Lakes, and on through Pennsylvania. I skirted the rust belt and left the East all behind. I traveled the small roads across Nebraska, Route 20 and Route 2, through tiny one-blink towns like Broken Bow and Valentine. The wind spilled the light yellow and the Sand Hills went rolling just like Ipswich Bay. If I couldn't be happy, stay simple and fun, if some soul sickness had me, I'd gamble for beauty like this. When I bought that motorcycle I bought the romance of sadness; I wanted to stay lost on the moors. Technically I was just headed to college, but still, I pushed it. I ran out of gas and money on Colorado's desolate eastern plains, about one hundred miles from school. I hitched to a truck stop and sold my new plaid shirt for three bucks' worth of gas. I got to Colorado College after midnight, unrolled my sleeping bag on the football field, and fell asleep, a melancholy poet, a broke, tired, and extremely happy melancholy poet. I could finally study what I loved and not have to pray about it.

I was twenty-two when I slept on that football field. I'd never heard the term "bipolar." Manic depression was a Jimi Hendrix song. Mom was just slightly schizophrenic; that's what I heard. That's what the hospital called her in 1949. But she wasn't; she was manic depressive. They could have done better. After all, the German psychiatrist Emil Kraepelin had written the book on manic depression fifty years earlier. His seminal textbook revolutionized the understanding of mental illnesses. Kraepelin posited the "manic-depressive synthesis": the two extremes were components of the same disease. He described it as a circular, periodic disease and differentiated it from schizophrenia, a far worse, degenerative condition. Kraepelin's detailed description took over two hundred pages but his suggested treatments only took five: bed rest, restraints, cold baths, and morphine.

Fifty years later the American psychiatrists labeled nearly all severe cases schizophrenic, including my mother. In a sense they had given up. Medicine had been dissecting the brains of schizophrenics and manic-depressives for decades and had found nothing abnormal, no cause. Slide after slide of "diseased" brain tissue showed no difference from healthy brains. Nothing seemed broken. Science had isolated the microorganisms that caused syphilitic madness; Alzheimer had found his tangles of cellular brain debris; and psychiatrists knew about hormones and thyroid dysfunction. But they could find no biological basis for manic depression or schizophrenia, and the radical advances of neuroscience were decades away. Psychiatry took another path and followed Freud. Schizophrenia and manic depression were diseases of the mind, they said, not of the brain. Psychoanalysis was all the rage in 1949. German psychiatry had been disgraced by Nazism for its complicity in Hitler's savage eugenics. Postwar psychiatrists dismissed Kraepelin's earlier work, considered his categories too obsessive, too German. Unfortunately schizophrenics did not respond to the new talk therapy; neither did the manic-depressives. Nothing could be done so psychiatrists lumped them together and shipped them off to state hospitals and custodial care: bed rest, restraints, cold baths, morphine, and electroshock.

Lithium could have helped. It was out there. The ancient Greeks wrote of its healing powers. It had been used as a sedative as far back as the 1870s, but the salt proved difficult to patent and thereby profit from, and its use died out. But lithium still claimed some vague therapeutic value in the public's mind. Back when Coke had cocaine, 7Up was called "Lithiated Lemon-Lime Soda," but it took an Australian researcher named John Cade to rediscover the efficacy of lithium therapy. He proved it in 1949, the year my mother was committed. He didn't buy the psychoanalytic thesis and felt sure that the causes of manic depression could be found not in biography but in biology. He began studying the urine samples of manic-depressives, looking for a toxin common to all. He isolated their uric acid and tried injecting it into guinea pigs. Why not? It was awkward, for one thing; uric acid is not terribly soluble in water and the doses were lumpy. He added some lithium to increase solubility and began shooting the guinea pigs full of lithium urate. He switched to lithium carbonate and the poor little pigs calmed down, way down. They even sat still for their daily urine shots. Cade speculated that lithium might work on raving lunatics and he found a few desperate cases. After two weeks on lithium, a man who had raved for five years quieted. He stayed at the hospital but soon returned to his old job. Similar results were observed with other manic patients and a large test group proved its effect. Cade published his findings: "Lithium Salts in the Treatment of Psychotic Excitement." He didn't know how it worked; he just knew that it did. Scientists still aren't sure how it works. But lithium proved a magic bullet against mood disorders. Psychiatry was off to the races.

Though not quite. Psychoanalysts still called the shots in America and they remained skeptical of drug therapies. And then came the table salt fiasco. While Cade was shooting up guinea pigs, lithium was introduced as a salt substitute and American cardiac patients filled their shakers with the stuff. Some dropped dead, and this is how doctors first learned of lithium's low-dose toxicity. After that it took psychiatry twenty years to convince the Food and Drug Administration of the drug's value. It was finally approved for use in 1970, and it saved my family sixteen years later.

When I got to Colorado College I knew nothing about psychiatric medicines, had no inkling I could benefit from them. I studied street drugs in college, not legal medicines. Colorado College is a small, very private liberal arts school, idyllic, really, and the perfect place for learning. The college organized class schedules under the "block plan," wherein students took one intensive course at a time. One month it was Joyce, the next Nabokov. The system was perfectly calibrated to the attention spans of manic-depressive poets and drug-addled youths. And Grandmère paid tuition, room, and board. I was suddenly, even understandably happy—nothing manic about it. I was the happiest I'd ever been. The English department loved me and I loved them dearly. I edited the school's literary magazine, brilliantly, for two dazzling weeks. I should have been content and hardworking; I should have edited the lit magazine for more than two weeks, but I was nervous and flighty, afraid of my mind. And the school housed me with all the other transfers, all the other brilliant washouts. We had all the best drugs and I used them like medicine but considered them fun, recreational. It worked great for a while, the best medicine I could buy without seeing a shrink, without confronting my sickness. Pot was a party mask I pulled over my symptoms. Besides, all the good antidepressants hadn't been invented yet.

Colorado College opened its welcoming, laissez-faire arms and I found that my drug of choice was acceptable, not a problem. As soon as class ended I made the campus rounds, smoking strong, sticky weed with various friends. My afternoons were slow, lovely. I unraveled quietly and it was the quiet I craved. I lay on the grass and read chapters of *Ulysses* and they made sense for ten to twelve minutes. I couldn't sit still without pot. It was a mild hallucinogen back then—before hydroponics and super strains—and it brought me the dreamy, sedative calm that I needed. It slowed my skittery mind.

Nevertheless I was a self-medicating fuckup. I just smoked, drank, and snorted whatever turned up. I was young, smart, and squandering my grandmother's money. Some kids get drunk and smash up Dad's car; I did drugs and smashed up my mind. I fucked up my own self-medication. I took whatever turned up. Maybe I was getting sicker, maybe my steering was shot, but it was my decision. I held the wheel and floored it. I hit the ditch and flew through the trees.

I wasn't alone; manic-depressives like their drugs. Street drugs are not chosen randomly; addictions don't just happen. For many of us, drugs provided a coping method of sorts. Some never get over their first loves. Studies show that 40 percent of the bipolar population is alcoholic. Only 7 percent of the general population needs that drink. Alcohol blunts agitation. It makes depression more interesting. Cocaine is very popular with manic-depressives; I loved it. A few lines can tap into that fast mind, that euphoric bravado that marks the first, beautiful stage of a manic break, hypomania. Manic-depressives use coke to augment or jumpstart their highs. The cocaine deals high and fast with dopamine and mimics mania quite well; its crash is a mini depression. Cocaine is bipolar disease in powder form, convenient and fast. Crack's even faster. Ecstasy dumps massive amounts of serotonin and dopamine straight into the system and damages the cells where it's stored in swaths. Permanently. It destroys future happiness. And the psychedelics—LSD, peyote, mushrooms—they can trigger manic breaks, blow a latent disease sky-high.

My friend Thomas was brilliant, a psych major with swagger and an elegant death wish. He would vanish for weeks at a time and then reappear mysteriously bearing cocaine and cognac. Our conversations ranged widely and rapidly—from poetry and religion straight through to psychology and getting more drugs. I had my requisite and seminal psychedelic experience with Thomas, when we ate mushrooms one morning in New Mexico. We had driven down to Bandelier National Monument, a canyon full of Anasazi petroglyphs and cliff dwellings, a sort of psychedelic field trip. No one knows much about the people the Navajo called Anasazi, "the ancient ones." They were gone before the Navajo arrived. The trip site was genius, all Thomas. I lost Thomas early on, ran past him as he fell for a cactus. I lost my shoes and my shirt as well. It was hot and I was running up and down the canyon floor. A tour group arrived and stared at me. The canyon was getting busy so I walked a mile or so and found a series of sketchy ladders climbing up to a dwelling. I spent the afternoon sitting on what I hoped was a stone altar, quietly watching over the desert. I could see miles. I watched a hawk wheeling and assumed he was looking for me. Call it delusional, synthetic, or decadent, whatever, that shining sky was heartbroke and beautiful. I'd see it again if I could. But I can't. Besides, I know now that psychedelics are just shortcuts. They're not as good as the real thing, as madness. They're not even close.

I signed up for Melville, for a four-week seminar on *Moby-Dick*. Our class would meet in Chicago, at the Newberry Library, and study its impressive collection of Melville manuscripts and trinkets. There were twelve of us. The college had arranged our housing in a kind of academic flophouse with rooms by the week. I first read *Moby-Dick* in high school and I believed every word. I still do. The evangelicals call this inerrancy; I call it art.

Everyone else flew; I took a Greyhound. It started snowing pretty hard somewhere in Nebraska and the bus slowed to a crawl. I had nothing to read. So I ate just a bit, just a small cap of a mushroom. Just to take the edge off the trip. A short time later the bus turned sideways and the driver yelled to get down and I looked out the window and down to a ditch. There was screaming. The driver steered into the slide and recovered while I just sat thinking. A woman was weeping but I knew dying in Nebraska on a bus in a ditch would not happen. It was a hallucination, and you just ride out hallucinations. Still, with time moving so slow it took forever for the driver and God to work that out.

My next near-death wasn't as random; I felt I deserved it. I even approved its aesthetic. It was a slow descent down into the bowels of the Newberry, into the vault of the Melville Room. Down there, under all that great library's books, I knew it was true what he wrote: "To grope down into the bottom of the sea after them: to have one's hands among the unspeakable foundations, ribs, and very pelvis of the world; this is a fearful thing." I felt flushed, claustrophobic in that close little room squeezed between metal shelves. I got dizzy, speedy, and scared. It seemed crazy. I was just a kid and the book was just a novel. Relax.

Of course I loved the class, meeting for hours every morning to discuss the cosmos—the beautiful, appalling whiteness of the Whale. My classmates were sharp and beautiful, and Dan Tynan, our professor turned friend, revered the work. I cannot imagine a better adventure. I tried to stay happy and smart but I had struck a match on that bus while I pushed through the white Nebraskan prairie. In eating just that small bit of a fungus I started a fire that would burn down my mind. The experts call what happened to me "kindling"—a perfect, poetic term. It's the brain's "escalating response to a repetitive stimulus," as Drs. Jameson and Goodwin explained in their seminal text *Manic-Depressive Illness*. This escalation reaches a point at which the mind continues to flare long after the match burns out.

For me, the disturbance continued for months. Just a bit of that mushroom, a crumb, dropped the floor out from under me. I barely got high but I plunged into Melville's bottomless sea by way of Alice's rabbit hole. I went down fast, way down below the Melville Room. I was among bones, the ribs and pelvis of the world. My thoughts broke and tumbled in my head, the same dead pieces falling over and over again in the spin. I was drowning, quite literally, in my own mind and I went quietly and excruciatingly mad. My consciousness clouded into a feverish, sleepless dreamscape; I held on to what I had and by dumb luck I had Melville. He gave me what language I had and was right when he wrote, "The whale-fishery furnishes an asylum of many romantic, melancholy, and absent-minded young men, disgusted with the carking cares of earth." While I could still read I wandered that asylum. I still have that copy of *Moby-Dick*, its pages bent and stained, scribbled with illegible notes. I've waved it through hospitals like a talisman. My wife looks concerned every time I pick it up.

Before Chicago and Melville I believed in beneficence, in the unwavering beauty of the world. I was broke but undoubtedly coddled, unworried about home or love, and I was young, unacquainted with death. I believed in a sort of Deadhead transcendence, a pantheistic mellow, and I ate mushrooms to find it. In Melville's parlance, I clung to the masthead, one hundred fifty feet in the air. I can't say he didn't warn me. "Close your eyes in this mystic reverie," he wrote, "and you'll fall with a half-throttled shriek and drown in a summer sea."

Melville lets his orphan, Ishmael, swing open "the great floodgates of the wonder-world," where he sees the god-horror whale, the "grand hooded phantom," Moby Dick. "It was the whiteness of the whale," says Ishmael, "that above all things appalled me." It was the white of holiness and death shrouds and angels, the white of the shark, of corpse lips and absence and God. I drowned with all my stoned head transcendence and everyone, everything bled to this white, this monstrous ghost-bodied blank.

By the second week of class I stopped coming and hid in my flophouse room. My sleeping bag lay on an old blue-ticked mattress with a gray pillow, no case. I had a lamp, a hot plate on a battered white stove, and a small empty fridge. I pulled the shades and locked the door. I stopped bathing. My body disgusted me. I stopped eating and felt my thoughts slow, lurching to what felt like a halt in a matter of days. My thoughts were broken, actually broken. Neurologists demonstrate this, the crash in brain activity, loss of memory, inability to speak. If I dreamed I woke with a start, my heart banging, and so I stopped sleeping. My tongue was slow, uncoordinated. I bit it when I spoke. My new friends were all concerned. They visited me often and their visits were horrible. I sat up for them and was nauseated. I just wanted them to go away. I could not speak their language. Worse, I could not feel or understand their emotions. I was dead.

For one week in Chicago I had been the life of the tea party, everybody's friend, and then I was gone, a ghost with a withered smile. I only spoke with suicide. Suicide understood me, never would judge. I considered all the options. The little oven I had—its size just perfect for my head—was electric but I knew I had knives. I knew I could jump out the window, eleven floors, the simplest solution. I wanted the oven, though, no mess, no scene. The electric oven became my excuse because I was weak. I knew I couldn't do it. I knew I'd fuck it up. I couldn't even sit up. Who was I kidding? I didn't have the courage. I had to do it, it wasn't my choice. Suicide never is; it's just not volitional. It's just a tool and sometimes we are forced to use it.

Someone knocked at the door, kept knocking and knocking. Finally I dressed and opened the door and the light pushed me back. It was Dan, my professor, and I didn't let him in, just kept my hand to the doorknob and squinted.

"David, how are you?" I shook my head and stared at his shoes. "The class, all of us have missed you. It hasn't been the same." I didn't move, didn't look up. "We're having a big dinner tonight, the last day of the class, and you have to come. All of us want you to come." I couldn't let him in and I hated myself for it. I hated myself for fucking up. For worrying my friends. For becoming a ghoul and wrecking their party. Why should they have to deal with me? They were dead wrong. I wasn't worth their pity.

Dan stood at the door, perplexed. He didn't want to cause pain. "Look, David, look. Don't worry. You don't have to come down. But I'm going to send some food up. I want you to eat." This time I nodded. "And you know, David. You have an extension now. Don't worry about Melville right now. I'll get your paper sometime later. It's not important. All right?" I said okay and turned back toward my bed. My tongue tasted like sand. I didn't want fucking food.

The afternoon moved past. The brown light pooled behind the shades and leaked away slowly. Sylvia Plath. How long does it take to die with an oven? How long with your thighs pushed against the door? Or do you close up the door, crane your neck? I should do it, get out of the way. If I jumped would it be graceful? How would I fall? How long? Could it feel good, like sleeping? And then another knock on the door. A woman's voice. Oh, how would it look if she came and found me? A scream and blue lights. Cops. My family, my mother.

"What?" I called from the bed, lying on my side toward the stained plaster wall. "What?" I was hoarse.

"David, let me in. It's Sarah. I have food."

"Leave it." I was so stupid and mean, such a mess she couldn't see me.

"David," she teased, "now don't make me break in here."

I saw her standing there, perfect, blond, sorority sister. Cute as hell and utterly different from me, from this. I'd flirted with her through the first week, through "Loomings" and Queequeg. I can't see her, I thought, not like this, all wound in my sheets. "Hi, Sarah. I'm sorry, just leave it, I'm sorry."

"I won't just leave it."

So I stood slowly, naked and sick. I pulled up the sheet and covered my sickness and stood by the door. "All right, Sarah. All right." I cracked open the door and she was shining. I took the tin-foiled plate and she stopped the door with her foot.

"I'll see you later, David. I'm coming to check."

"No. Please." My old mind knew I should love this, anticipate this, her coming to me. But that was gone, I knew it, and this cold, sharp piece of knowledge cut at my chest. I took Sarah's food and leaned over the stove. I ate chicken. I ate at a thigh till I saw the bone, the small veins, and I spat at the sink. I ate rice. My jaw felt like a cramp in the chewing. I bit the side of my cheek again and again, shredded it. There was cake. I couldn't even look at the cake.

I sat on the bed. I wanted to call Sarah and tell her not to come, but I couldn't. I couldn't even do that, let alone stick my head in the oven. Sarah was wrong. She could get hurt, I could hurt her. She wouldn't come, she was just being nice. She won't. It's just pity, like you pity small animals that twitch on the road. I don't need a fucking night nurse. I need this to stop. This horseshit body all pasty and white, my filthy cock and idiot stare. It was wrong of me to eat their food, to mumble, to go to their party. They shouldn't have asked me. They shouldn't have had to. I'm a sinner. Okay? Okay, so I said it. Sinner. Flesh. I'm garbage, and Christ, if he ever existed, would spit in my face and I'd fucking clock him. No no no not that I'm sorry forgive me all that. Go ahead. Cast out my demons, go ahead try. I'm Legion. The door has a lock. It locks. I should be dead—dead dead. Nothing after, no stupid Heaven. If there is a fucking God and he cares he will leave us all dead. He'll slit open my belly and suck out my soul. Leave it dead on his cloud or some shit.

I moved across the room like an arthritic and checked the locks on the door. I knew I could keep her out, that I would, but I moved toward the bathroom, toward the shower. I scrubbed my white stomach raw and scraped at my groin. I smelled of soap and rot and went back to the mattress to wait. Sarah came and I just let her. I was wrapped in my sheet and she moved to the window and let up the blind. She was beautiful by that window, painted with light like a Vermeer. She turned and looked at me and I had to watch her face. I could not look away but I thought that I should. She undressed and all the time she looked in my bee-stung eyes.

I laid my mind in her breasts and she smelled of sunlight. I curled up against her belly, my leg caught over her soft, perfect hip. Her breath was the only air in that undersea room and she saved me from drowning. She whispered but all I heard was her breathing, and her hair fell down across my eyes and I slept. The following day the Melville seminar ended. I returned to Colorado and Sarah went elsewhere. I never saw her again.

I limped back to campus and barricaded my door. Thomas came by to cheer me up, carrying his cocaine and Remy. I asked him to leave. I didn't want his medicine. It got so bad I knew I would die, I was dying. I hadn't slept or eaten in weeks.

I called the school's health center and made an appointment, knowing the therapist would hate me, think me spoiled or faking or screwed up on drugs. I worried. I chose my appointment clothes days ahead of time, swapped out my shirts, counted the hours, and knew I couldn't go.

I arrived at the student health center and stood quietly at the reception desk. A woman stepped out of a room, glanced at the schedule, and asked, "And are you David?" I nodded. "Well, David, I'm terribly sorry. I need to go to my office downtown. Something's come up suddenly. I'm afraid you'll have to reschedule."

And that's how it happened, the rest of my life. A scheduling flap, an apology, and a linchpin pulls out. I could have gotten some medicine, some idea that this wasn't my fault. Maybe my father's God could have stepped aside long enough for me to discover my illness and steady my hand. No chance. The therapist hated me, that's all. I was just a spoiled kid who fell down with his drugs and scraped his knee. She was right, I decided. She was right not to waste her time on me. I couldn't even pick myself up off the ground. I could never go back to that office. I went back to my room and sweated it out like some junkie. Spring came and I crawled home.

I was almost better. My brain or my soul had purged its bad chemistry and righted itself. I went back to the North Shore for some carpentry work, for my mom and Ipswich Bay, but the other ocean hit when I got home—the same sour air, the corpse light, the dark crush when I walked in the door. I found my father in bed. I almost smelled lilies in the brown light. It was two in the afternoon.

"He's all right, darling," my mother said. "He'll get up later. He's just resting." He wasn't. It's nothing like rest. I wouldn't see him that day. I knew where he was, and he wasn't with us. Days later I caught him at the bathroom door, hunched in his boxer shorts, his eyes like smoke. I waved as he opened the door. I wanted to stop him, grab at his arm, and see if together the two of us could stop ourselves from drowning.

SIX

My father and I were like drunken sailors. I staggered the decks while my dad lay passed out in his bunk. Before long I took to my room and began sliding down. I hid for over a week until my brother barged in and shook me. "Dave, you got to get up. You got to do something. Don't just lie around. Please." He looked like he might cry. I sat up. "Dad's been lying in his bed for a year. He's been lying there since I was a sophomore. He doesn't even try." He walked to my window and snapped up the shade.

I squinted and said, "I know, Jon. I know all about it. It's awful."

"You don't know. You haven't been here. Mom can't handle it. Get up, Dave. Please."

"All right," I said. "All right, I will, but I can't talk right now. I just can't." I turned to the wall and pulled my knees up. I closed my eyes. Jon pulled the door shut. I was a fuckup and my brother was an orphan. Jon was adrift and I couldn't help him. Peggy lived in Chicago and Mom did everything now. She woke Jon for school; she fed him breakfast. She picked him up from his games and from practice and fed him again. Mom managed because there was no one else left, just this frail little bird with her two hollow shells.

Dad had taken a paid leave of absence from the seminary and they were kind enough to call it a sabbatical. Mom fielded all the calls from his students. She went to Dad's office and found their old, ungraded term papers. She explained to his colleagues and to the trustees that he was sick. "We don't really know. He's just exhausted," she said, but she knew. She knew how it was. My father was fading. He had joined in her sickness and so he was lost to her now, lost to all of us. Mom took a job as a home health aide, her first job in thirty years. She spent her days bathing the old, sick, and dying, then she came home and cooked dinners her husband refused. She went to bed alone with him, wrapped herself in his stale sheets, and prayed.

My father stopped listening to music: all he needed was the machine hum of his dehumidifier—white noise in a black room. He couldn't bear to hear us move through the house. He used an old coffee pot for his bedpan now and never came out until the house had gone dark. He thawed frozen shrimp in our sink and ate them with crackers. He watched television, drank wine, and hid his empty bottles in the garage. He abandoned our mother, that's how we saw it, and my siblings and I wanted to scream. I wanted to stand up, kick Dad out of bed, and show him how it was done. My rage pushed me out of my room. I didn't know shrinks or medicines or therapists. I just got angry and walked for hours through the woods.

I sat down and wrote my Melville paper and I took Ishmael's advice: "Whenever I find myself growing grim about the mouth ... whenever my hypos get such an upper hand of me, that it requires a strong moral principle to prevent me from deliberately stepping into the street, and methodically knocking people's hats off—then, I account it high time to get to sea as soon as I can." I went back to Colorado and left them all there.

I finished school but my confidence was shot. My depression hadn't been conquered or even considered. It had just ebbed away, leaked out from my body. I was terrified, really frightened that it would come back and never leave, like my father's. I stopped making plans for the future, stopped considering grad school and academia. I couldn't teach. I couldn't stand in front of others; I'd break down and lose it. I relied on my cynicism to keep myself white and the rest of it black because it was the gray that really scared me, the twilight. I didn't want to see where I was going. I didn't want to look down and see where I was, and cocaine helped me with that. For a quarter gram I edited and typed my friends' papers. For a half I composed them. I had settled for some brittle glaze of happiness, just a little boy clutching his candy.

I graduated and drifted back to the North Shore. I had no plans; I just wanted to live in Gloucester, fish, and stay close to the bay. I found my mother just where I'd left her, alone in her kitchen. The table was blank, no color, no brushes, nothing. She was happy to see me but her eyes soon fell to the floor. I sat down at her table—tired from the motorcycle, sunburned, and utterly stoned. The living room was shut and Dad's papers were covered with dust. For two years my father had hidden in his bedroom and his shade now frightened the family. My brother's boyhood was damaged and now he was sick. His disease came on just like mine, with suicide thoughts in the spring. He was sixteen, same as I had been, just like clockwork. My mother ran out of words. Down the hall to the left lay her husband's shadow, to the right was

her son's. I was scared, more frightened than angry. My father
was dead and he spooked me. His depression had killed him, was
killing my brother, and I thought I might catch it. I could smell
the infection in Hamilton, in the stale, yellow air of the bathroom, the kitchen, and the hallways.

I knocked on my father's door. I opened it and stepped into
the dark. "Dad. Dad, it's David," I whispered. "I'm home."

He rolled toward me, cleared his throat, and said, "Dave. It's
you, you're back. Good. It's good to have you back. If you'll wait
just a minute I'll—"

"It's okay, Dad. Don't get up. You don't have to get up now. I'll
see you later." I backed up and closed his door softly.

My mother made pork chops. I pulled my brother from his
room and sat him down at the table. I knew he was glad I'd come
home, believed that somehow I'd help. He pushed at his food silently. My mother and I spoke about Peggy—out in grad school,
Chicago, for social work. She was okay; she was fine; that's nice,
I should call her. When it was over my brother exhaled and stood
up. He stood still when I hugged him. He was sweaty and rank. I
kissed my mother good night. Everyone was in bed by nine
o'clock and I couldn't sleep. This disease was contagious. My
brother had proved it.

I needed a place to live and I knew who to ask: William, my high
school friend with the papal fixation. He had remade himself
into a sort of fast-talking Brahmin and his real estate machinations were becoming legendary. Starting in college, he had
maneuvered his way into a string of magnificent North Shore

homes: beach houses, old captain's houses, mansions built upon seawalls. I'd return each Christmas and attend William's parties, lavish events thrown on bad credit in the elegant homes of strangers. All of them were winter rentals, each one as lovely and transient as his stories. He read Latin on occasion, knew the rules of polo, pretended to enjoy lacrosse, and bored his dates bragging of nonexistent stock portfolios. He'd given up on the Vatican; he wanted Gatsby's place now. He looked me in the eye and claimed he had gone to Phillips Andover, not our public high school. Our conversations grew increasingly short and confusing and our friendship waned. But William remained a genial, somewhat surreal host and he continued to find beautiful, inexpensive rentals.

I called him at his mother's. "David. How nice to hear from you," he said officiously. "Goodness. It's been some time. What can I do for you?"

"Do for me?"

"Yes."

"William, how are you?"

"I'm well, thank you. And you?"

"Good. I'm good." Bad grammar appalled him. "I'm back on the North Shore for the winter and I need a place to live. Do you have anything?"

"I see. Well, David, it's fortunate you've called. I'm negotiating an agreement right now for a house up in Gloucester. Turn of the century, stone construction, granite. It has a tennis court and a number of outbuildings: a barn, an old forge. There's a stone tower."

"A stone tower. You're kidding me, right?"

"I can assure you," he huffed, "that I am not. I will need some housemates and you're welcome to apply. Rent should be reasonable. As I say, I'm presently negotiating."

"I'm in."

"David, I—"

"I'm in, William. Cut the shtick, okay?" I knew I was inconvenient for William, a witness to his plebian past, but I charged past his defenses.

There was a pause and then William's clipped response: "Fine. Very well. I'll arrange a tour and ring back. Now, I'm quite busy at the moment, so if you don't mind."

"Sure, William. Whatever. I'll talk to you later." I hung up and smiled. I couldn't trust him, of course, I knew that, but William made me feel honest, upright, and sane.

Any misgivings vanished when I saw the house. It was set on a hill above the Annisquam River and the forest behind stretched across the heart of Cape Ann from Gloucester to Rockport. I found the stone tower back in the woods beside a small pond. It was maybe fourteen feet across and two stories high. Two goats grazed beside it. The tower was overgrown with thick vines and served no apparent purpose. It was a poet's tower. Perfect.

I walked back to the main house and found William and the landlord speaking on the front lawn. "David. Let me introduce Mrs. Morrison. She's the owner."

She thrust her hand at me. It was covered with dirt. "I've been gardening," she explained. "Call me Pat." I liked her immediately.

"David's a developer and he—"

"No, I'm not, William. I'm just a carpenter. I'm working in

Charlestown right now." I heard a loud, piercing squawk and another, and I started. We all looked up at an enormous green and red macaw perched twenty feet above us.

"Aw, goddammit," Pat said, and called her husband. "Norris! Hey, Norris. Get the ladder. The goddamn parrot's stuck in the tree again. Norris!"

"Help. Help me. Help," the parrot screeched.

"My son Tiger taught him to say that. That's Sebastian. He's a royal pain in the ass and he's filthy. My husband smuggled him back from somewhere. He was a pilot." William and I met more of Pat's family, various adult children. Pat pointed out a llama stabled under the tower. "His name's Butch. Don't get too close," she laughed. "Damn thing spat in Norris's eye once. We had to take him to the hospital."

Pat saw through William immediately and just rolled her eyes. Looking back, I know Pat saw William just as I did. He was a character, a self-deluded character, perhaps, but amusing. "Well, boys, the house is yours. I like you well enough. No big parties. Norris has all the paperwork and he'll take your money. You can move in after Labor Day. Something like that." Pat welcomed me into her house and before long I loved her and wanted her to adopt me. Her family was like mine, I thought, without the religion, the depression, and the ranch house.

I called Nathan Sargent in Breckenridge, told him about the place, and convinced him to move east. He was my closest and most levelheaded friend and I needed to shift the household's balance toward sanity. Besides, Nathan was a carpenter, a good one, and I had work for him. Frankly, I begged Nathan to come. I needed his help. I had landed a contracting job and was in over my head. A college friend named Dalton had moved east for law school, bought a property, and tracked me down. Boston's condo market was booming and properties were flipping right and left. Carpenters were scarce and unemployed English majors with tools could name their own price. I named mine and it was way too low. "It will be fun, Dave. Relaxed," Dalton said. "I'm living on the second floor. We'll convert the third floor first. I'll help."

The building was an asphalt-shingled three-decker in Charlestown, Massachusetts. It looked sallow from the street and out back it had more of an air shaft than a yard. Its linoleum was curled and its roof was shot. All of its lead-painted surfaces were begrimed with exhaust and neglect. Nevertheless my law student friend had high hopes. He saw exposed brick and period trim with a deck off the back and lots of houseplants. He wanted gas lamps and Back Bay Henry James, and he planned to make a killing. He outlined his vision over bong hits upstairs.

We wandered the building while I made up numbers and then Dalton summoned resolve. "Come on, Dave, let me introduce you to Mrs. Rourke. She lives on the first." He turned at the landing. "Listen, don't worry about her. We'll try to keep her happy until she leaves." Dalton knocked at her door and she invited us in. She was pleasant, in her late sixties and a widow. Her apartment was filled with religious icons and cats. She offered us tea.

The following week Mrs. Rourke met me on the front stoop. "Here, let me get the door for you, dear," she said as I struggled inside with a table saw. "What a big tool. I hope that won't be too loud." She couldn't stay, that much was clear. I hadn't even set up my workbench and there it was, all laid out. It was going to get loud and very apparent that I had come to evict her.

Nathan and I took sledges and crowbars and gutted the upstairs apartment. We cut through the plaster; insulation poured out like cancer, bits of brown shredded newspaper and dust clouds. We filled garbage bags with the stuff and left them in corners for weeks until they punctured and spilled out again. We pitched the trashed lumber out the back windows. We hacked at the walls until coffee break, when we sat on the stairs, our faces like chalk with our mouths little pink rings left by the dust masks. About the third week I asked Nathan how to read blueprints, what the smaller lines and some of the symbols meant. I bluffed with electricians and lost sleep over plumbers. I was failing badly and I knew it. I had never worked as a lead carpenter, let alone contracted a job. My original cost estimates were laughable, fictions written by a lapsed English major. I kept the crumpled lumberyard receipts in a battered red Sawzall box and became increasingly reluctant to add them together.

Dust and noise rained down upon Mrs. Rourke and by Christmas she no longer called me "dear." We were making that woman's life a living hell. We heard curses and mutterings when we passed by her door. She had sharp fingernails and an odor of cats followed her. Mrs. Rourke frightened us. She caught me once and asked me in for coffee. I sat nervously on her fur-covered couch and she brought me a cup. "I wish you could meet my son, Danny. He's a cop over in Chelsea." She smiled. "He should come by soon. He should see all of this. All the work you have done." She narrowed her eyes. "My other son's dead. A good boy, too. Went to mass. Died of lung cancer." She coughed. "He got it from plaster dust. You know that stuff's full of asbestos? Full of it. It killed my son."

I stared into my coffee and said softly, "No, it's not."

"What's that?"

"It's not asbestos, Mrs. Rourke. It's horsehair plaster."

She ignored me. "You know, I'm afraid to breathe down here. A lot of days I tie a wet towel around my mouth." Drywall scraps dropped past the windows behind her. Mrs. Rourke was a victim of progress; it wasn't even my progress and I had to push her. She had maybe six weeks before I moved downstairs. It made me heartsick.

I drove over to Hamilton and I always found my mother in the kitchen, worrying over her paintings. She was always so happy to see me. I sat and watched the anxiety ebb from her body. I always asked, "Where's Dad? Is he up?" And she always shook her head. "He's just lying in there?"

"I'm afraid so. David, I think we should just let him rest."

"Oh, c'mon, Mom. He's been resting for two years."

"Not quite." I made her nervous.

"How's Jonathan? Is he here?"

"No, dear, he's at practice. He should be home soon. Do you want something to eat? A grilled cheese sandwich or something?"

"Sure, Mom, I'll eat. So he's doing better? Jonathan's doing better? He's not depressed, is he?"

"I don't think so. He's playing basketball again." My mother got out the bread and cheese and I went down to inventory the garage. Our old fishing coolers were stacked against the back wall and filled with empty wine bottles. I was furious. My mother was alone and she was suffering and Dad hid away like a coward. I'd been drained of empathy, all pity. I was sick of blaming some mystery, some spirit or ghost. Just like Grandpa, all I had now was rage. I went back upstairs, walked passed my mother, and knocked on Dad's door.

"Dad. It's David. I'm coming in." I charged to his bedside, glared down, and ordered him up. I told him Mom needed him. "Dad, it's beautiful outside—pretty warm, a nice sunny day. It's daytime, Dad. Did you know that, Dad?" My father didn't move; he didn't speak; he just stared at the opposite wall. He played dead and I stood there and watched. I knew how it was; I knew all about this despair. I knew my words worked like knives and I opened his veins. I knew I could kill him. I heard my mother call from the hallway: "Your sandwich is ready, come on, dear, Dad's resting." Peggy and I agreed that our mother's deathwatch had gone on too long. Her sorrow had broken our hearts. We blamed Dad for all Mom's unhappiness, for Jonathan's ghost of a childhood. We blamed Dad for sadness. I blamed him for me.

Dalton introduced me to Daphne at one of his law school parties and we hit it off immediately. I convinced her to visit Gloucester and picked her up the next morning. On the ride I pitched her the story of Dogtown, the site of Gloucester's first settlement. I'd been hunting for the place for weeks—just a string of small cellar holes somewhere in the woods. The village was largely abandoned after the Revolutionary War and left to its widows, stray dogs, and the indigent. People in town called them all witches and named the place Dogtown. It was the stuff of romance—at least my kind of romance—and Daphne and I spent the day rambling on the trails behind my house, getting lost and discovering flooded quarries, fields grown over with brambles. After that we were inseparable.

She was beautiful and serious, with long black hair and dark eyes. Her father had emigrated from Greece and struggled to send his only daughter to college. She was grateful and driven, and had captured a full scholarship to law school. After Daphne began spending her weekends in Gloucester she asked me my plans.

"My plans," I said flatly.

"Yes, your plans. You can't stay here. Remember? The lease ends in June."

"Well, I have to finish Dalton's job. That should take forever."

"That's because you shouldn't be doing it. You should be applying to graduate school."

"Why? Just because I don't know what I'm doing? I like it here." I waved my arm over the coffee table. "This is fun." Nathan was in the kitchen sharpening his chisels and avoiding Daphne. William was upstairs barricaded in the master bedroom ironing his vast collection of faded secondhand ties. Our third roommate was upstairs in bed, chain-smoking and reading Kafka. He'd been there for weeks but when he first arrived he was cheerfully delivering pizzas and waving *Cannery Row*. He insisted we call him Doc and aspired to a life of bohemian ease. His outlook had darkened.

"Fun," she repeated, and shook her head. I couldn't afford to lose Daphne; I couldn't afford to scuttle her faith in me. And so a few weeks later I applied for a graduate publishing seminar. It was only twelve weeks; I figured I could hold it together for twelve weeks.

Nathan and I hired Doc to help out in Charlestown and each morning we stuffed ourselves and our tools into my Volkswagen Rabbit. Its starter was dead, so I parked on a slope and we rolled, and I popped the clutch and we smoked until we hit Boston. The lumberyard had put my account on hold; materials were scarce so Nathan and I were making bricks out of straw. Doc was the only one still enjoying the job. He was philosophical and spent weeks stripping paint from the original woodwork with a brass-bristle brush. He wore a series of disintegrating yellow rubber gloves and wrapped himself in Zip Strip fumes and cigarette smoke. By January I no longer cared about doing the work right; I just wanted it done, slapped up. Nathan took issue with this and held on to his pride. Doc and I just left him alone and repaired to the second floor, to Dalton's apartment. We raided his stash and smoked bong hit after acrylic bong hit until all the anxious drama boiled out of the place.

Mrs. Rourke's complaints became a daily occurrence. We locked ourselves away upstairs. The beautiful apartment we had set out to make filled with end cuts and ill will. Dalton hid his bong and his dope and began tallying the numbers daily. Each week I'd present a punch list of tasks to Dalton. Each week he would check our slow progress against my good intentions. It had become pretty obvious to all what was going down by the time we sat in Rosie's Diner on Main Street and watched the space shuttle *Challenger* launch on the twelve-inch television behind the counter. It showed the doomed teacher and astronauts, and then the shuttle would launch again and explode again all through our lunch.

The budget was dead and gone, but every afternoon I'd report downstairs to Dalton's apartment. He'd offer me a beer and I'd sit covered in dust with one or two knuckles bleeding. I'd make my excuses while my friend listened patiently with his necktie and checkbook and notes. "Look, Dave," he kept saying, "it's not your fault. This is a big job, bigger than either of us imagined." I smiled at the floor ruefully. "The third floor's almost finished and buyers are interested. I'll pay down the lumberyard and we'll get the third done. After that you can start with Mrs. Rourke's. We'll adjust your old numbers and blow out the walls."

"Okay," I said, unconvinced. I wished he would just fire me.

"Jennifer and I are going down to the city in a few weeks. A friend of mine's throwing a party. You should come down."

"Maybe," I said. Dalton valued my friendship more than the numbers and that made me feel awkward. I questioned his judgment.

Radcliffe called to schedule an interview but I was stoned and scribbled the time and address on the back of an envelope. I lost it and a week later I arrived just past three. "Sorry I'm late," I said. "The parking was tricky."

The director looked up from his desk. "Late? Your appointment was for one p.m. You're two hours and ten minutes late." I stared, thunderstruck. "I have others scheduled, I'm afraid, but thank you for coming." I suggested rescheduling and he thanked me again. I drove over to Daphne's apartment and she sat me down. She said I wasn't ready to grow up and that she had big plans. She wanted a law firm and a forty-foot sailboat. She quit me; it hardly mattered. I agreed with her, told her it was a smart move. I decided to go down to New York with Dalton, drink heavily, and quit.

I got to Gloucester late Sunday night. I wanted to sleep and then I wanted to drive into Charlestown, collect my tools, and then sleep for a week. I got to the door and Nathan pulled it open, grabbed my arm. "Where have you been?"

"I went to New York with Dalton, you know that. I think we worked out a—"

"Never mind about that. Look, your dad's not right."

"What? What are you talking about? What do you mean 'not right'?"

"He means whacked," Doc clarified from the kitchen. "Crazy." Nathan nodded. I narrowed my eyes and looked at him. He was grinding his teeth. "We've been, um, doing a few lines," he said sheepishly. I threw my bag down, walked toward the kitchen, and found Doc sitting in front of a mirror.

"It's all gone," he said. "Just as well."

"What the hell do you guys mean, my father went crazy?"

"Dave," Nathan said calmly, "your grandmother called us."

"Grandmère? She called you?"

"Yeah, Grandmère. The Matriarch. She was trying to reach you, obviously. She needed you to go over to Hamilton and see what was going on. Your father called her in Woodstock and freaked her out. We told her you were in New York and then Doc decided we should go over and see."

Doc nodded proudly. "You need to call the Matriarch."

"And tell her what?"

"That your father is 'crazy.'"

"It's after midnight."

"Doesn't matter."

"What the fuck do you mean 'crazy'?"

"Okay, okay, calm down," Nathan said. "I'll tell you."

"I need a drink." Doc found some whiskey while Nathan continued.

"Everything's all right, now. Don't worry. Your mother's fine."

"Christ, could you just tell me what happened?"

"No one answered at your parents'. I don't know where your brother was. Anyway, after your grandmother called, Doc and I jumped in the car. It was, I don't know, about three this afternoon."

"We were kind of high," Doc allowed.

I had told them all the great family stories, the same Professor Lovelace lore that circulated through Peniel and the seminary. They knew my parents and now they had spoken with Grandmère. They were high, excited for some wacky Lovelace adventure. My family was a bit odd, that's all, not a problem. Cars were blown up, snakes lost in libraries, boats sunk, iguanas left on curtains and children at gas stations. So what? We were eccentric and fun. We were madcap. My friends thought it sounded fun and mostly it was, until our disease made it serious.

Whole seasons had been lost to despair, and spring most of all, curled to a desiccate brown outside our bedrooms. When one of us was well we set food out for the others. We left them in silence and waited our turn for the sadness. It was all so horribly polite. We didn't want a fuss. We weren't crazy. It was spiritual, we said, and we almost believed it. It wasn't that hard to believe. Until this point my family had suffered only from night sickness. None of us had stared at bright blindness, not one of us had struck toward the sun. My dad was the first.

"Wait, wait. What exactly did Grandmère say?"

"She said, 'Richard sounds terribly excited.'"

"'Terribly excited.' All she said was 'terribly excited'?"

"Pretty much." Nathan shrugged. "But she sounded pretty scared."

My grandmother rarely called us, but Dad called her dutifully. The most unsettling thing the two had ever discussed was Grandmère's Christian Science church. None of us discussed our feelings with Grandmère, our sorrows and fears, our joys. Quite frankly, my grandmother was more interested in the proper placement of flatware. And now after thirty-odd years came this phone call. God knows what my father told his mother, what terrible floodgate had opened.

"Really," I said, considering. "So you went there?"

"Sure. We figured we could help."

Apparently Dad had been watching for cars because he met my friends at the garage. He cracked open the door and demanded, "Who is it?" He seemed all right. My friends were disappointed; they'd been hoping for drama.

Nathan smiled and said, "Hi, Doctor Lovelace. It's me, Nathan Sargent, David's friend. And this is Doc."

"Peter," Doc whispered.

"I mean Peter. Doc's his nickname."

"It's about *Cannery Row*," Doc interjected.

"He's not a real doctor," Nathan clarified. "Anyway, we're David's housemates over in Gloucester."

My father relaxed and swung the door open. "Oh, yes, yes. Of course. Come in, come in. Friends of David Lovelace. Welcome." My father smiled broadly. "Welcome. Please call me Richard." Something was off. My reclusive father had thrown his arms open wide. My friends smiled furtively at each other. The synthetically high had met the real thing. "Please, please, come up the stairs."

My mother stood in the kitchen. She immediately moved toward my friends. "Richard's feeling a bit frisky tonight," she said with a crooked smile. She was afraid they might leave her. "It's nothing, really. Where's David?"

"He's down in New York. It's just us," Nathan said. "What's going on?"

"He's been singing hymns," she whispered. "Since this morning." Dad glared down at my small, helpless mother.

"Okay," Nathan said. "That's okay. I'm sure we can—"

"We need to sing!" my father thundered, and he grabbed Nathan's hand. He grabbed Doc's. "Do you boys know 'Michael, Row Your Boat Ashore'?" They stared at him. "Come on, you must know it." They stood in an awkward circle beside the refrigerator, embarrassed. Nathan and Doc avoided looking at each other; they tried not to smile.

"I don't know it," said Doc. "I don't think we should sing it."

"You're going to sing it." My father raised his voice. "Now, please take Betty Lee's hands and we'll begin." Doc stopped smirking and Nathan sobered up. My mother held up her hands to my friends and Dad started in his strong baritone. "Michael, row your boat ashore, alleluia, Michael row..."

Nathan leaned toward my mother. "Where's Jonathan?"

"He left this morning. He's over at the—"

"Keep singing. You're not singing."

My mother wouldn't sing. She stared at the floor. "High school. He's at the high school."

"Sister helps to trim the sails, alleluia, sister...Come on, now. Sing." Nathan and Doc mumbled the chorus. It was all chorus. My father ran out of verses and Michael kept rowing back and back. It wasn't funny anymore. It was never funny and the song made my friends queasy. Finally my father stopped and everyone dropped their hands, relieved. Suddenly it was quiet and scary and no one knew what to do. My father went to the window and checked the driveway.

"How did you boys know to come?" my mother asked quietly.

"Grandmère called us. She was worried. I guess he called her."

"I heard that." My father swung around. "I heard that! Grand-mère called you. Get out. Both of you. Get out now! You are agents of my mother. You came to spy for her." Doc and Nathan watched dumbstruck as my father's face darkened. He squared his shoulders and moved toward them. "Get out! You are agents of Grandmère." "Honest, Dr. Lovelace," Nathan said. "She just asked us to check on things. David's away and—"

My father pushed past Mom, opened a drawer, and pulled out a large flathead screwdriver. He waved it in the air and then pointed it at Nathan and Doc, his face splotched and red. "You boys are agents of Grandmère. I knew it." He stepped toward them. They bolted and Dad chased them outside. He stopped by the garage and shook his weapon as they scrambled into their car. My father stepped into the driveway and scowled as they sped past. My mother was alone.

I woke her at one a.m. She said it was quiet. My brother was home and my father had been taken by ambulance somewhere. A psychiatric hospital. "Okay, Mom, okay," I said. "It's all right. I'll be over in the morning. Go back to sleep."

The days followed in whispers. We knew very little. "Dad woke me up," my brother said. "He was in the hall around five a.m., just pacing up and down and singing creepy hymns. I mean the scary ones, Dave. You know—minor key, blood of the Lamb stuff. Medieval. He wouldn't stop."

"What did you do?"

"I got out of there. I had stuff to do. I was freaked."

"You just left Mom? You left her alone?"

"She said it was fine. That Dad was okay. So I left." I might have left, too. None of us had seen a full-blown manic break; we didn't know what it was. There had been no discernible warning, no hypomania leading up to Dad's hymns. He spent more than a year twisted in sheets and silent, and then, *bang*, he launched into space. Our family's disease had a second act, a real show stopper. It had us coming and going now, up and then down. The great fear, the madness that had stalked my mother every day of her adult life, that had whispered up crazy from under my childhood bed, the fear that had driven my sister to Loyola and a degree in psychology, had come for us now. It starts with depression, I surmised. So that's how it starts.

The ambulance had taken my father to a nearby psychiatric hospital named Baldpate. I drove over with my brother the next morning. "Baldpate," I said. "They called the fucking place Baldpate? What is this, the twelfth century?" Jon and I laughed nervously. "Sounds like skulls; the Place of Skulls. Nice." We spent the rest of the ride worrying in silence. I was disappointed by Baldpate. I had hoped, perversely, that Baldpate could live up to its name, but it proved a series of low-slung, nondescript buildings filled with addicts and drunks. We passed through security and sat in the visiting area, waiting for Dad. He came through the door slow and stiff. He looked confused and pushed out his words with some effort.

I told him he'd be all right. That he'd be out soon. "Of course, of course," he said, "I'm fine. How's Mom?"

"Good, Dad. She's fine."

We sat there and stared at the floor in silence, and finally we left.

Two or three days later my father called my mother from the ward's pay phone. He asked her to come at six sharp. When she pulled up to his building, my father jumped out of the bushes and into the passenger seat. He looked at my startled mother. "Everything's fine, Betty Lee, wonderful. Now, just drive. Drive." We never went back for his clothes.

Dad didn't go back. He refused. My mother filled the prescriptions called in by Baldpate—an antipsychotic and lithium— and Dad complied. He went back to his bedroom, knocked out and counting his pills in a cotton-mouthed hush. My mother bought him plastic pillboxes with snaps and small trays and he slid his slack-jaw meds like rosary beads. She found a psychiatrist, a Christian involved with the seminary. No one said much.

Dad slept through the days, his eyes half-open in a room filled with undersea noise. My mother's watercolor still hung on the wall—daffodils and calligraphy that read "Rejoice in the Lord always and again I say rejoice." There was no music in the house. My mother answered phones and whispered like a ghost to doctors and friends. It's all right now. We're praying. Yes, thank you. I'd visit and Mom would say, it's all right now. He's all right now, just sleeping.

Back in Gloucester my friends Nathan and Doc worked up their story—a Dr. Lovelace story so strange, so gothic, that it beat all the others. They called each other Agent One and Agent Two. I'd sit by the woodstove and stare and hear the Agents of Grandmère as they laughed in the kitchen. Daphne had left,

Charlestown was in shambles, and Dalton wouldn't let me quit. I owed it to him, he said, to stay and to finish. I took his check for eight hundred dollars. I cashed it and called him and said I'd be back in two weeks. I drove to Hamilton and told my mother I was leaving on a short vacation, that I'd be home soon. I told myself the same thing and knew I was lying.

SEVEN

My father's break confirmed my worst fears. His mania introduced my own demon. There was something more frightening than despair, something uglier and more humiliating, and it stalked me. My medicine, my pot smoke, proved useless against this cold fear. I got high and then I was wing shot and flapping and dread ran me down. I needed to run. I loved my family, they needed me, but I needed to run. I feared my father's sickness was inexorable, pulling me closer toward madness, and so I cut him loose and never looked back. I couldn't hide anymore in Gloucester; I couldn't float on Ipswich Bay. I needed a far ocean. I wanted to sink, disappear from New England, from my family and our devils.

I chose the Blue Hole, a massive dark circle punched through a turquoise reef off the coast of Belize. It drops straight past the bottom of the sea and into a vast subterranean cave system. I packed all my dive gear—my mask, fins, buoyancy vest, and regulator. I packed my tank and a sixty-pound weight belt. Writing would be my excuse, my work. I packed a primitive twenty-pound laptop in one briefcase and a dot matrix printer in another. All this ridiculous weight—these props—announced my intentions and proved my resolve. I bought a cheap flight and paid extra for baggage.

At Belize City the bus driver heaved out my bags. My tank hit the concrete and rang through the station like a great empty bell. I dragged all my stuff into bright sun and the city, a decayed shantytown built by pirates, all its wooden buildings leaning on stilts and splashed with faded turquoise and pink. A clutch of children watched me stagger down the street under my luggage and laughed, jumping over the orange septic gutters and pointing. I crossed an iron swing bridge and found a cheap room overlooking the brown stinking river. Toward dusk I ate fried pork and bought dope at a Chinese restaurant. It was everything I had hoped and I was happy.

The next morning I caught a speedboat out to a small fishing village called San Pedro on Ambergris Cay, an island just behind the barrier reef. Its main street was short and made of sand, a few cheap hotels and shops with two modest gated resorts at either end. Past those there were just tangled mangroves. I unpacked at the cheapest hotel and went to bed with the best of intentions. In the morning I'd hire a dive boat. But I got stoned after breakfast, too stoned for diving, and wandered beyond town on a foot trail that snaked along the island's edge. I didn't find beaches; the surf crashed on reef a mile out from shore, just a line of white laid before the horizon, a dull distant roar. I found a camp near the end of the island—an empty cluster of tarps and plywood, a tree house that flew Rasta colors. The air smelled foul and clung to the tangled undergrowth. I turned and at the island's north end the reef came close. I floated and kicked above its bright colors and fish.

The second night I found the Tackle Box Bar at the end of a wood pier, just a shack with Guinness and rum. Out front a deck encircled the pier's old turtle pen, a wooden cage about twelve feet across where a morose sea turtle swam circles all day and nosed at the bars. The Tackle Box kept the turtle for tourists but the bartender, Clive, ran the place like his private club. We hit it off and before long my routine centered on the place. By my second week I had scheduled and cancelled trips with every dive boat on the island. I made excuses each morning and had coffee and joints with Clive until lunch. I drank up my dive money fast and I gradually gave up on the idea. I was too stoned to count my breaths coming up, to avoid the bends and drowning.

Clive believed that maintaining a dissolute expatriate writer on premises provided ambience. His bar already had a depressed, endlessly circling sea turtle and now it had me. I became the bar's second mascot—typing ostentatiously at a novel through the afternoons and shooting darts for drinks late into the nights. Every day after lunch Clive ran an extension cord out from the bar and I plugged in and typed. He let me keep my briefcases behind the bar so I could play writer. It was perfect, really. I had rum, a laptop, and fishing boats out the window. I was Hemingway in Cuba without the right words.

"Brother David," Clive asked every day, "how is the book?"

"Oh, great, great. I mean good." I could tell Clive anything. He didn't read and didn't much care. "I mean it's coming along." The novel wasn't coming along, of course. It was floating facedown and unconscious. Every afternoon I flipped it over and poked at it for an hour or two. I had spent weeks sitting in a bar two thousand miles from my sick family and the novel was my excuse, my justification. As long as it didn't die I could stay here at the Tackle Box, a shack at the end of a pier on an island off the Mosquito Coast. But the book was a goner, an absolute dirge. On the bus down I had convinced myself that Ed, a troubled adolescent tollbooth operator from Chagrin, Indiana, would rivet the reader, that Ed could give alienation a fresh face. But by the second chapter Ed just sat in his cold metal box and grumbled. And I sat on an island staring into a blinking, sun-bleached screen, empty and high.

San Pedro is a small village and locals started to talk. The dive shop had given up on me weeks earlier. I stuck to snorkeling on the north end of the island and hadn't used my tank and regulator once. One morning an American dive instructor stopped me as I walked on the beach. "You know," he said, "it's not like people don't notice."

I smiled. "Notice what?"

"How you are. How you wander around this place, up and down. Who your friends are."

"What about my friends? You mean the Tackle Box?" He smiled slightly, looked out at the white line of reef, and walked away. I cursed at him under my breath but I knew he was right. I watched everyone now and I knew how they saw me. I wasn't a diver or a writer, I wasn't even a tourist, just a kid staying stupid with hardly a dime. By now, the thought of diving the Blue Hole terrified me, the idea of dropping down along its outer wall, down past all the colors with the black cutouts of sharks hanging above.

I was a coward; I knew it. I had left my family in crisis, my mother in shock and my father gone blank. I left my brother with hardly a word and I blunted my guilt with island rum and smoke and bright water. My novel spiraled into incoherence but I told no one and typed pointlessly, tangentially, for appearance's sake. Clive knew I was broke but he didn't mind; he knew I was wasted but then so was he. I stuck to the bar and when money got tight Clive let me string a hammock after closing and sleep there. My dart game got sharp and I won all my drinks from the tourists.

One evening I noticed a pretty girl from the States. We danced to Clive's endless reggae outside on the pier, spinning and flirting beside the Tackle Box and its poor, hopeless turtle. That was all it took. I fell into some sort of desperate amphetamine love right there in the dark. I blew up against the girl and held on for dear life. June was flattered at first and we kissed. The next day we hiked to the north of the island. I gave her my mask and showed her all of the beautiful fish. We were drunk on rum by dinner when June's friend entered the bar. She gave me a cold stare, moved close, and they whispered together. They stepped outside. Clive leered after them and turned to me laughing.

"I guess I'm screwing up her vacation." I shrugged.

"I'd like to screw up her vacation," Clive said. "Just fine."

June came back, sat down, and looked serious. "This isn't real."

"What do you mean, this isn't real? It's real." I knocked on the mahogany bar. "We're sitting right here. In Belize. In Clive's bar."

"Home is real. I go home in a week. I have a boyfriend at home and he's real."

"Okay, okay." I backtracked. "This isn't entirely real, but so what? You're not home. You're on vacation." She looked skeptical—drunkenly skeptical, but a tough sell nonetheless. "It's not supposed to be real."

"Exactly."

"What's home, anyway? Is that all you want? Wisconsin?"

"Illinois."

"Whatever, the Midwest." I waved an inebriated hand. "Look around. Look at this place. Look at me." She smiled but I knew my logic was failing. I knew it wasn't even logic. I was bluffing and ordered more rum.

"When are you going home, David?"

I shrugged. "Who knows?" I laughed and picked up my drink. I tried to act insouciant but June shook her head sadly. Her pity scared me serious and I looked down at the bar. "After I finish the book, I suppose."

We danced again and drank. I told her I loved her and thought that I did. I was hypomanic by then, clever and charming. I could seduce anyone and wanted to try. I was madly in love with a girl I'd known for a day and I wanted to prove it. I asked June down to the beach and tried to undress her. I couldn't convince her; I couldn't seduce her; "It's not real," she kept saying.

"All right then," I said. "I know what to do. Let's make it real and get some tattoos, matching tattoos." She smiled and thought I was joking, and I was when I said it. No one had tattoos back then, just bikers and sailors. "Yeah," I said. "Let's go. I dare you. So when you get home you can prove this was real. You pick the design." She started to laugh. "It can be small."

She pushed back at my chest and considered my smile. She

stumbled and kissed me. "All right, okay. I'll do it. Let's do it." I was charming, all right.

I knew there was a barbershop and tattoo parlor straight up from the pier, and I knew it stayed open late, a place where fishermen played cards and drank quietly. No one smiled when we walked in. No one spoke; a radio somewhere played static and salsa. The men stared at June. They looked her up and down without expression, grave. The owner moved behind his desk and asked, "What you want?"

"We want tattoos, both of us." Someone whistled low. The card players frowned and shifted in their seats.

"No, you don't want any tattoos." He looked at me skeptically. "Where you been? The Tackle Box?"

"Been on the beach," I said. "What's it matter? We want tattoos. Can you do it?"

"Yeah, man. I can do it. But you don't want it. Your lady there, she doesn't want it. What you want to mark her up for?" I looked back at June where she stood in the doorway. "Sure she wants a tattoo," I said, and showed him my money. "The lady chooses the design. Go get your book."

"Okay, okay. Yes, sir," the barber said. He was done reasoning with drunks. I intended to brand a young woman and the men against the wall stared contemptuously.

In retrospect, the love of my life chose poorly: a complicated little seascape featuring two seagulls, a palm tree, and a trite sunset that took a half hour to carve into my ankle. When it was finished, I stepped out from behind the curtain and June was gone. The men chuckled and shook their heads. I saw her once more on a sandy backstreet. She looked up, panicked, and ducked into a tourist trap. I knew not to follow her. She was frightened and her fear knocked me out. I'd been dizzy for weeks like a punch-drunk fighter and finally fell down.

I was scared, too. The locals just stared at me. I was sure they were talking about me, joking. I hauled my dive gear down to the Tackle Box. I laid out my new, shiny-chromed regulator, my mask, my fins, and my buoyancy vest on the bar, stood my tank in the corner. I was broke and I needed to leave. My ankle hurt and I felt humiliated. Nothing was real. The diving was a lie, the novel was a lie, and true love was just an angry red blotch above my left foot. Clive put the word out; some local divers ran over and the bidding lasted fifteen minutes. I gave away unnecessary clothes, sold my backpack, and cut my luggage down to a rucksack. Clive let me leave the laptop behind the bar. I said I'd be back in a few weeks, when my money ran out.

Years later, when I returned to the Tackle Box, Clive yelled, "Brother David! We have your machines! We have your machines." The cases were stashed in the rafters and dusty. I traded Clive my sunglasses for them. The turtle was gone. "The tourists complained it was dying," Clive told me. "It was bad for business."

"I suppose you're right." I smiled. "Greenback turtles are an endangered species, you know."

"Yeah, yeah, I know. So what?"

I boarded a boat for the city at dawn and caught a bus for the Guatemalan border. I crossed in the morning, moved through by young soldiers with rifles. My scuba gear netted good money and Guatemala's poverty doubled it. The checkpoints and soldiers continued all day through the jungle and right into Tikal, nothing but local color to me. I felt just fine away from the ocean, free of my book and blue holes. I met some American kids on the bus and none of us were tourists. We claimed to be travelers deep in the northern jungles of Guatemala and headed for Mayan ruins.

Tikal's ancient temples rise from a vast tract of jungle filled with partially excavated and buried palaces, temples, and tombs. There are parrots and toucans and the roar of howler monkeys at dawn. The place was transcendent and crawling with soldiers. Guatemala had been at war with itself for thirty years. Four rebel armies hid in the mountains. The soldiers fanned out from a barracks just past the ruins, patrolled the whole region, and blocked every road.

My friends and I decided to sleep in a temple. We hid in the jungle while guards and soldiers cleared the park. At dusk we climbed a half-buried temple, using roots and undergrowth for hand- and footholds. We saw the last of the sunset from a small room at the top and watched the jungle fade into gloom. All of us made wild conjectures concerning Mayan spirituality. One of my friends expounded upon Quetzalcoatl and the ancient Mayan calendar. It promised, she said, the apocalypse in 2012.

Apocalypse. I wasn't quite right, and like many before me I found the word itself intoxicating. I loved the very sound of it. "Look around," I said. "Look at this place. Apocalypse happened a long time ago. Look at the soldiers. Apocalypse is happening right now." The howler monkeys had started up, a low wall of sound from the jungle. We watched flashlights move up and down the main temples. My friends unrolled their sleeping bags and slept. But I couldn't; my mind was too fast. I thought about the Mayans, about human sacrifice, the Last Supper, and cannibals. I sat until morning, wide awake with the jittery ghosts of disease and religion. I figured I didn't need some fool sacrifice; I had road dust to cover my sins.

I got to Antigua and found Doña Luisa's restaurant. It wasn't hard—gringo hippies buzzed around its entrance like bees. Doña's interior courtyard functions as the central switching station on the gringo trail and its corkboard is plastered with notes: "Darien Gap—Safe?"; "Elvis from Puerto Barrios is a COP!"; "Need starter for VW bus"; "Sally from Denver: I was sick. I'm sorry. Headed to Copan. Meet in two weeks?" I scanned Doña's board for something, some reason to stand there short on cash, miles from home and pushing for farther. There were relief work and Spanish lessons and yoga.

I stood in the white stucco entrance with my pack slung down sideways and I fell for it all, for the never going back, just the endless south, its jungles and deserts and ruins. I saw the women around me all lovely and tattered, the ones who rode high on the roofs of ancient Bluebird school buses lumbering down through the hills. I fell for the happenstance jigsaw of traveling broke, the beautiful puzzle before lostness got found by e-mail and cell phone, before the global got positioned by satellite. I loved it more than the ocean.

My crumpled tollbooth novel still lined the bottom of my pack and I settled on its old, time-tested excuse. I ordered coffee and eggs and wrote my own note: "Typewriter needed to rent or borrow." I would find an old black Royal and type it all over again in this ancient colonial city. I'd learn Spanish. I would live with the people. But first, I needed a typewriter. I was quite clear on that. A writer needs his typewriter and my quest for the perfect black Royal bought me a month of leisurely, unwriterly days. Every morning I would check in with my note and spend the remainder of the morning drinking coffee, meeting Americans, and plotting far-flung itineraries.

I moved into a hostel and secured a fine room surrounded by English-speaking stoners for three bucks a night. I fell in with a tight group of travelers—a Norwegian photographer named Per, my American friends from Tikal, and a traveling love triangle involving three Germans. We spent our afternoons in the ruined cloisters of a colonial monastery, playing guitars, scribbling poetry, and studying Spanish. I climbed through the ruins ecstatic; my thoughts frayed and snapped in the wind like blown sails. I smoked my pot to let go of the wind, to spill the sails and just drift. I was in love with the sky now, a small band of friends, and every woman who smiled.

I sought out my highs. I slept with the German women, took full advantage of their stalled love triangle, but I soon fell for Elizabeth, a quiet student from California. She studied Spanish through the afternoons, her picnic blanket laid out on the cloister's grass courtyard, her long, elegant legs delicately tucked beneath lovely cotton skirts. I spent my days gazing down from the arched ruins above her, utterly smitten. It was quiet most days and peaceful, but once a large group of tourists descended. Their leader moved toward Elizabeth and I jumped down from the stones like Errol Flynn. I could move from dewy-eyed love to swashbuckler rage that fast.

"Yes. Yes," the woman kept saying to Elizabeth. The word gave her speech a rhythm, a sort of clockwork, reflexive peace. "Yes. We're gathering to invoke the spiritual essence of this place. Yes." Elizabeth smiled politely. I looked around at the convent, screwed up my face, and asked, "The essence of what? Catholicism?"

The woman stepped back and stiffened. "No, no, oh God, no." Her face, twitched. "Yes. No, it's not that at all. It's more, you know, the life force, its energy." I looked around at the broken stones and pocked walls that had seemed so beautiful, so ruined, before this woman appeared.

"What," I continued, "sort of a nun energy?"

"Well, yes. Yes and no. This place was a sacred Mayan site long before the Spanish arrived, long before Catholics."

"Really?" Elizabeth asked wryly.

"A Mayan site?" I offered. "You mean a temple? Human sacrifice? That sort of thing?"

"Hey, listen, pal." A swarthy man garbed in batik, heavy wooden necklaces, and chest hair stepped into my face. "The Mayans never fucking sacrificed humans."

"Well, actually I—"

"Now, the Catholics. Don't get me started on the Catholics."

"Bill, please." The woman stepped in front of the strongman. "Look. Why don't you just join us? There is room for all faiths, all spirits here. Yes." Evidently, Elizabeth and I were now considered crackpots, some sort of retro-religious Catholic throwbacks, and this by a group cozying up to Quetzalcoatl. They murmured and pitied us. "Yes, come. We are going down into the holy catacomb of this place to chant." Elizabeth smiled.

"All right, all right," I said, laughing. "Lead on." Their holy catacomb was an old cistern, damp and smelling of toads. I grabbed Elizabeth's hand as we descended the broken stairs into pitch darkness. Someone sparked a lighter, then a few more like a rock show, and we saw the room—circular, with its roof curving in from stone walls. It resembled a hollowed-out subterranean gourd, one infested with hippielike moles. Our leader spoke. "Please, quiet please. Is everyone down? Could we please douse the light?" We stood now, silent, expectant, and deeply claustrophobic. "Could we please everyone hold hands? Good." I was already holding hands with Elizabeth and had no desire to hold hands with anyone else, ever. I pulled her back, out of the dark circle. The group started humming; everyone in the hole started humming ferociously and then they just stopped. Everyone waited and I could hear the walls drip. I couldn't see a damn thing. People kept waiting. Silence. A few stragglers across the cistern started up humming again, unsure and nervous, and then suddenly all hell broke loose with the hums. I kissed Elizabeth quietly, her shoulders pushed against the wet holy stones.

My money was running out fast. I ate bread, avocados, and onions every day, bought harsh Guatemalan cigarettes in pairs, and nursed beer at the bar. I'd been in Antigua three months, I'd overstayed my visa by two, and my friends were drifting away. Elizabeth flew home to California, Per back to Norway, and the

Germans went south. I still had a ticket, a flight out of Mexico that I'd pushed back indefinitely. I figured to get to Mexico I needed two hundred bucks if the ticket still worked. I didn't want it to work but I still needed money. I hadn't called home in four months. If my father had recovered I knew he'd order me home, and if he hadn't I didn't want to know. I still had some time, I thought; I planned to enjoy it and figured I was.

I sat in the plaza across from Doña Luisa's and watched the new kids arrive. I'd have to start all over again, learn their names, where they were from and where they were going. They'd find the cloisters soon enough. The great cathedral towered behind me; pilgrims and wafts of incense pushed through the park. I loved the smell of that pinion smoke. I loved Antigua but I couldn't stay. I walked across the plaza toward the bank, past all the soldiers, and pushed into Guatel, the national phone bank.

Wooden booths lined the walls. Benches were packed with strung-out travelers, Mayan mothers, old men, and children. Every few minutes a name and booth number were called from the desk but I had heard it took hours. I waited in line, took a ticket, wrote down my name and my family's number, and sat down to wait. Then I was too nervous to sit and stood by the door smoking. I could still leave. I lit another cigarette and tried not to think of Mom alone in her kitchen with the house gone quiet, or worse, my father still broken and singing. I thought of my brother, orphaned and left all alone. I couldn't go back; I'd get sick. I'd get stuck.

I stubbed my cigarette on the wall and put it behind my ear. I cut in at the desk and spoke fast, ragged Spanish: *"Disculpe, disculpe.* I'm sorry. *Mi numero es mal. Otro numero."* I felt panicked, grabbed a pen and waved it. The woman found my card. I scratched out my parents' number and jotted down Nathan's. Forty minutes later they called my name and I jumped.

"Hello. Hello."

"Bueno, señor. Adelante."

"Hello?"

"Yeah, hi. Is Nathan there?"

"Dave? Is that you?"

"Who's this?"

"Shit, it is you. This is Chris."

"Chris. You're living there now?" Chris was a friend of Doc's.

"I took your room. Listen, have you called home? Your parents have been calling everybody—me, Nathan, that guy in Charlestown. You need to call home."

"Yeah, I know. They want me to come home. I know I haven't—"

"Man, listen to me. They *need* you to come home." Chris paused. "You don't know, do you?"

"Know what?"

"It's your brother, man. He's in the hospital." Chris waited for me to respond. I didn't. I didn't breathe. "Dave, you still there?"

"Yeah."

"He's okay, he's okay. I don't know much but he went off like your father did. He punched your father out, broke into someone's house."

"Punched him out?"

"Your dad."

"He went crazy?"

"I guess. I mean I don't know." Chris was embarrassed.

"When?"

"Maybe three or four weeks ago. Someone called the cops. He's at some hospital in Boston, I think. Lookit, you've got to call your parents. You need to get home. They need you." There was no air in the booth. It was hot and collapsing. "Dave, you there?"

"But he's okay, everyone's okay?"

"I guess. You need to call."

"I will, I will. Listen, I was looking for Nathan. I'm broke. I need like two hundred dollars."

"Your folks will give you that. It's not a prob—"

"I can't ask them for it. It's complicated and I can't explain it right now. How about one hundred? Can you wire me a hundred? I'll pay you back when I get home. I need it to get to the airport."

"Look, man, I—"

"Shut up, Chris! I can't talk anymore. Goddammit. These calls aren't cheap. I'll give you the bank information. All right?" I read off the routing numbers. My notebook was shaking. "Get it from Nathan if you have to. Scrape up two hundred or two hundred and fifty if you can."

"Okay, okay," Chris said. "Just come back, all right?"

"All right, man. I will. Thanks. I gotta go."

I hung up and pushed back against the dark booth. I slid my foot against the door and felt myself buried. I heard dirt hit the coffin. It was my kid brother gone now. They had locked up my kid brother, the sweetest guy in the world. He didn't even do drugs. I was smothered already and knew I was next. We were God's twisted joke, some kind of wrecked trinity: the Father, the Son, and me in this holy ghost town. I wanted more distance.

Our father's manic break drew my brother and I together. It rattled the knob and opened the door we both feared. Like my own sickness, Jon's hypomania built through the weeks after Dad's hospitalization. His mild temperament gave way to anger. His basketball game grew increasingly rough. He cursed referees and friends and fouled out in minutes. The long-standing tension between Jon and the neighbors' boy escalated into a feud with lockers trashed and lies spread. My brother stomped around the house for weeks. He stopped sleeping and then he blew up.

He started yelling about the neighbors. He yelled at Mom—she wasn't listening. He was going to settle things once and for all with that kid up the hill. "I'll kick the shit out of him," he said, "and then I'll forgive him." He went to his room and made some sort of cape and tied it over his shoulders. He stomped back to the kitchen. Dad appeared. "I'm just going up to forgive him," Jon said. "That's all. I'm going up to forgive my neighbors." Jon headed for the door and made it to the driveway before Dad caught him by the shoulder.

Dad tightened his grip and Jon spun and coldcocked him, pushed Dad's glasses into his eyes, cut him up, and he fell to the ground moaning. The neighbors' kitchen door was locked so Jon punched his fist through the glass and fumbled for the lock. The neighbors leapt up from their dinner screaming.

"I'm forgiving you," Jonathan announced. "I'm forgiving you with my blood." They ran for the back of the house. "I'm not going to hurt you," Jon called. "Don't run away. Look, I'm forgiving you." Blood dripped down onto their carpet and Jon smeared gory lyrics on their walls. He was singing them when the cops arrived: "The public gets what the public wants but I don't get what society wants / I'm going underground, I'm going underground." He bolted out and down through the woods and the cops were out of breath when they cuffed him. Jon was sent to the Human Research Institute in Boston, where they strapped him down and dosed him with antipsychotics.

But I didn't want to hear my brother's story, not in Guatemala. And I didn't want to hear it later. I didn't ask him about it for years. Someone banged on the phone booth. I dug my way out and went to my room. I knew what was happening back home was bad and believed it could kill me. If I tried to rescue my brother he'd pull me under for sure; if I returned now I'd never come back. I packed my filthy clothes, counted my money, and walked to the plaza. The cathedral was behind me, Doña Luisa's beside me, and Guatel straight ahead. After twenty minutes I walked toward the phones and straight past to the bus station. I caught a bus toward Panahachel. I'd wait for my money there.

Panahachel is made for prodigal sons, a sad little Riviera beside a deep mountain lake. The mountains look quiet and peaceful and the lake is braided with blue and green currents. Nightclubs play the latest American hits and the video bars show all the latest American films. The only violence in Pana is entertainment on small screens in English. Every morning Mayan widows come from across the lake and sell woven bracelets and embroidered clothes. There are hummingbirds in the gardens and retired US career soldiers, too; the air tastes like spring and blood carries oxygen and alcohol and we share copies of *USA Today* where they worry about crime in Miami. And we worry, too: about the long ride to Tikal or the phone lines and exchange rates, and always the water. What about ice cubes? Can we use ice cubes? In Pana the currents tangle across to the murderous mountains and if we get sick the *farmacía* sells antibiotics that poison the small things inside.

I belonged there and I hated the place. I ate organic yogurt and granola each morning just like the rest. I drank at the Circus Bar and waited for money, for my next round of friends. I carried my bible, *The South American Handbook*, everywhere and plotted my itinerary south. One night an American commandeered the bar. He was over six feet, covered in wiry red hair, and barraging the bartender with terrible Spanish.

"*Zapato*," he said loudly. "*Mi nombre es Zapato.*" He pulled off his sandal and held it next to his face. The bartender found this hilarious; we all did. He told me his last name was Schuster—or Shoe—hence the nickname.

"It's Zapata," I said, "with an A."

"It's Shoe, my nickname is Shoe. It's masculine."

"Not the revolutionary?"

"Not the revolutionary."

I smiled. "Too bad." He moved back to his table and rejoined a tough-looking blond kid. Zapato was loud and kept gesturing. He was selling something the kid didn't want.

"What do you mean, dangerous?" Zapato blustered. "The whole damn country's dangerous. If you don't want dangerous, you shouldn't have come here. Right?" The kid didn't answer. "Look, what I'm saying is we could have an adventure, see the place." Zapato swung his arm up toward the lake. "Look at those mountains. Look at all that. Do you want to just sit here and listen to fucking Michael Jackson in some gringo bar, or do you want to explore?" I liked this Zapato.

"Listen, my truck is full of shit and the roads are bad," the blond kid said. "I've had three flats since Mexico." I decided I liked the kid too; he had a truck.

I turned and said, "The roads aren't that bad, not if you go slow."

"That's all right," Zapato concurred. "You got to go slow, Jim. Hell, I'll buy you a spare if that's all you're worried about."

"And the gas," I interjected from the bar.

Zapato glanced up. "Yeah, and the gas. We'll pitch in for gas."

Jim stared at me. "Who the hell is this guy?" Zapato shrugged and Jim continued. "Look, it's not the gas, y'all. There's a fucking war up there."

Zapato dropped his hands to the table, exasperated. "Nah, not really a *war*, Jim. Just some guerrillas. Way out. There's roadblocks up there but there's fucking roadblocks all over."

I pulled out the guidebook, joined their table, and flipped to the index. "Now," I asked, "where are we talking?"

"Nebaj, Cotzul, you know." Zapato gestured dismissively. "Beautiful weavings, real Indians, quetzales."

"Quetzales? You mean the bird?" Now I was skeptical. The

animal boasts a close relationship with most Mayan gods, and is extremely rare. It's almost mythical. Male quetzales sport a crest and a long, iridescent tail that streams out behind them. They resemble a sort of holy Dr. Seuss bird. "We're not going to see any quetzales."

"We might, you know."

"Jesus Christ, y'all," Jim blurted. "I don't give a damn about birds. What about the soldiers?"

"It says here the security situation is improving," I said helpfully.

Jim turned to me. "Oh, really. Are they still mowing down Indians, or what?"

"They don't seem to be . . . ," I said inconclusively. I scanned the book. " 'For lodging Nebaj has Las Tres Hermanas—delightful. Alternatively you can get a room in a private house for slightly less. There is also an army camp.' "

"Exactly," said Jim.

I ignored him. " 'There are magnificent walks from Nebaj along the river or in the surrounding hills, but north of the town is still not safe.' Well, there you go," I said, "we just won't go north. 'All houses have been burnt between Nebaj, Chajul, and Cotzal; no one lives in this area and most traffic is accompanied by military personnel. Views of the Cuchumatanes Mountains are spectacular.' " The book wasn't helping. I pushed it across the table, away from Jim.

Zapato kept buying rounds until Jim agreed. We'd go for a ride up into the mountains, spend a few days away from it all. The next morning all three of us crammed into Jim's truck and drove slowly and rather stupidly toward the Ixil Triangle and its three Mayan towns: Cotzul, Nebaj, and Chajul. There wasn't much to see: the land and its people were in shock, featureless, almost blank. At points along the road the dust were nearly black from ash. We encountered few people and all we had were each other and Jim's tiny pickup—a white Ford Ranger with Texas plates, a silver camper cap with a blue surfboard proudly lashed to its top. By noon we were dehydrated, stoned, and relatively optimistic. By the noon the next day we were dehydrated, stoned, and sick of each other. The truck's fan belt started squealing and Jim's mood worsened.

He slapped at his dash. "Why the fuck am I driving around in these mountains?" he asked. "I could be surfing, goddammit." Jim had a couple of grand and told us he was headed to El Salvador for the surfing.

Zapato had maybe five hundred bucks, a fortune, and just wanted to "get laid," which meant any number of things in his cosmology: go on a bender, climb a volcano, screw a German tourist. I had twelve bucks US, enough, I hoped, for the bus back to Antigua after throwing in for the trip. It was tight and I tried to pawn Jim my Nikon. He had a camera—"a perfectly good fucking camera, thank you very much"—and wasn't interested. I wasn't too worried—Zapato lent me cash against my money wire. I wasn't worried about anything as long as we didn't drive home.

We were off to see Indians but there weren't many around. After the military coup in 1982, the civil war had escalated into full-scale genocide and thousands were butchered. Four hundred forty Mayan villages were razed in the four years preceding our tour. Cotzul was a ghost town: less than one hundred Mayans were left from a city of twenty thousand; the rest were dead or in hiding. Death squads used late-model trucks much like Jim's. We were scary and most survivors just ran from us. We pulled into a small village and a young boy began screaming while his mother stood slowly and gathered him up. Jim tried to illustrate our irrelevance by gesturing to his surfboard but it merely furthered the confusion. Soldiers stared at our chests but never our eyes. Inevitably, Zapato would try to lighten the mood, but all he had left was sarcasm. "Well, this is a friendly town. Nice place for dinner."

Jim kicked at the stones. "Fuck this, y'all. This fucking trip of yours sucks. Look, it's my truck, and if I say, we just turn right around." Zapato and I groaned and turned away. We'd heard this before. "Listen, I'm the fucking captain of this ship."

We bickered by the town well and smoked cigarettes till the children came out from hiding. Zapato juggled something and I gave away Chiclet gum. Their mothers, and some men now, called from dark windows and the children ran off again laughing. It was clear no one would die. We strolled down a few blocks and turned back toward the store. The Mayans quietly gathered our items and spoke softly to one another worriedly in Ixil. We bought stale bread and tinned sardines, cigarettes and warm beer—a few dollars—and then we left quietly with our heads down, ashamed and strangely triumphant. We had seen Indians and they had seen us.

Those mountains are more haunted than my family ever was, more haunted than a thousand asylums, and I hid there. The Ixil Triangle dwarfed all the guilt that I bore for my family, all my impotent, cowardly love. I couldn't return to my parents and kiss

SCATTERSHOT   171

them and pick up my brother. I couldn't think of them for the
fear but I could drive through a genocide. I could rage against
strangers; I could mourn for their untold victims, but I couldn't
face home.

On the third day we drove past Acul—just a grid of concrete
huts, high on a hill and surrounded by soldiers. This was the first
of Guatemala's new "model villages" and was made for the widows and orphans of Nebaj. The televangelist Pat Robertson built
it with Guatemala's first evangelical president, General Rios
Montt. Robertson paid for Acul's construction with a fund-raiser
he called the International Love Lift. None of us commented as
we passed the dreadful place. We were exhausted by then; even
the truck felt worn out and sad. Three kilometers later we hit a
checkpoint.

"Where's the pot?" Jim asked, and threw his beer under
the seat.

"Under the seat," Zapato answered. "Fuck. Under the fucking
seat, fucking brilliant." Zapato whistled softly.

I lit a cigarette and a soldier leaned into Jim's window.
"Buenas tardes." He smiled, sizing us up. He put his right hand
on his holster; his left he placed on the surfboard. He gestured
at it with his chin, still smiling. His teeth were rotten, brown
and wet.

Jim sat stone-faced. "El surfboard," he said slowly, staring at
the uniformed boy, daring him to laugh. Zapato and I groaned,
started whispering something about money, bribes, *mordida*. There
were four or five soldiers total, ranging in age between about
sixteen and nineteen, bored and dressed in fatigues. They had
been sitting at a plank table under a makeshift thatched

sunscreen by a blank dirt road in the dry hills. They were bored and encircled our truck. A transistor radio played tinny salsa. The others were up and circling the truck. It was over eighty degrees outside and way hotter in the cab. The one in charge stepped away and Jim began slapping his palms against the wheel.

Zapato pulled at his red beard. "Put out that cigarette, Dave, will ya? Christ." The soldiers were now standing in a tight circle in front of the truck, alternately smiling then stopping as the oldest spoke and gestured—bad gestures, short chopping motions, fists into palms. We couldn't hear a goddamn thing. Fifteen minutes passed. One leaned against the quarter panel; one had a boot up on the bumper. It became apparent they were laughing at the surfboard, pointing at it. One held out his arms, moved his hips in a slow circle. Soon two others jumped in, adding surf moves—hilarious. They watched us, laughing and jerking in the road. Jim watched and shook his head slowly. "Fuck this, y'all," he said. "This sucks, this really sucks."

A brown dog moved up to the leader nervously, sniffed at his boot, and jumped back. It was the kind of dog you see anywhere poor—useless and starving. It was covered with mange and dust. The dog began moving in a strange ocean current himself, slipping sideways between the surfing boys, moving forward and back, whimpering. Then the soldier kicked it sideways, his boot catching the dog's exposed rib cage and landing the sad thing beside the others. And immediately, like they'd done this before, like this was their job—and perhaps it was—all the soldiers lifted their rifle butts and brought them down on the dog and kicked it and crushed it.

Zapato was out of the truck before it had finished. "*Muy mal, señors!"* he screamed, *"muy mal!"* I followed Zapato out and dragged him back into the broiling truck. The dog was dead now and twitching. It hadn't made a sound. "Shut the fuck up, Zapato." I said. "Please just shut the fuck up." The boys with their guns were laughing louder now, pointing at Zapato, pointing at us. After a time, the soldiers moved back under their thatch and sat down. Two Mayan women appeared from nowhere and dragged the broken dog down off the road and away. Ten minutes passed and the serious soldier stood. He waved our truck through, smiling. They were all laughing now beside a bloody smear in the dust. I waved and said, *"Gracias,"* and meant it, as Zapato beat the dash with his fingers and Jim cursed into the wheel. He said he was sick of this stupid shit, that he was going surfing.

We drove straight through to Antigua and the retreat made us fast friends, *compañeros.* We talked about summer work in Alaska and made future plans to meet in Seattle. I got my two hundred bucks and Jim left a day later for La Libertad, El Salvador. I saw him a week or two later in Livingston, Guatemala. La Libertad was a ghost town, he said, just soldiers and dogs. Jim said there were two Aussie surfers left. He said they ate nothing but Frosted Flakes and seemed damaged. He stayed with them for two days then headed back north. Zapato headed south for Costa Rica, a country without a standing army, without soldiers.

I cashed out my wire, booked another room, and returned to Doña Luisa's. Funds were short but I figured I had three or four weeks left to find the next windfall. I met some more travelers and played the life of the party even while I cut my budget down to the bone. An American couple, a woman named Katherine and her friend Jeff, moved into the room next door and we struck up a fast friendship. We cooked dinners in the hostel's kitchen and drank coffee together each morning. They were unhappy. I showed them the cloisters and hikes and places to swim while they argued quietly. They suffered their friendship in the hostel, on the buses, over coffee and beer. Katherine knocked on my door early one morning and climbed into bed. This trip was all her old boyfriend's idea, she said, a way to woo her back. She wanted to leave, she wanted to go home to Washington State, and she asked me to come. I said sure, why not, that makes sense. I knew I had to get back to the States. I needed money. I'd go to Alaska if I could swing it. I'd stay out west if I couldn't and find a quick carpentry gig. I'd find the farthest point from my family where I could work and save money, and then I'd head south, really south.

Katherine and I took buses as far as we could till we ran short on money. Buying bus tickets farther, to Tijuana, would break us and we'd have to cross the Sonora hungry. We sat mute and exhausted in a dusty town square across from a bus station. Together we had done it: two middle-class American kids had managed to find themselves out of money, sick, and staring at the desert, almost and finally lost.

We were fine, I assured Katherine, just fine. I was high as a kite, hypomanic, and I joked about stopping in Mexico City. "We could paint murals," I said. "Or I could. I know. I'll be Diego and you could paint those painful self-portraits, like Frida."

Katherine ignored me. "If we could just buy some plane tickets, get up to San Francisco. I have friends there."

"We could try," I said, and pulled out my last card, a blown Visa.

It was good for an imprint; beyond that my Visa was worse than useless—it was larcenous, thousands over its limit. For months, I had strategically deployed my bad credit throughout Central America at places too isolated for card authorizations. I spotted a promising travel agency just across the *zócalo*. It looked defunct with its blind drawn, with its sun-faded posters of Machu Picchu, the St. Louis arch, white women on white beaches.

Katherine and I took our best shot. We sat across from a travel agent and exuded all the American confidence we had left. I booked two flights to San Francisco and handed my Visa to the polite man with excellent English. My stomach was shot already but it gurgled in earnest when he reached for the phone. I kicked Katherine's foot and shot a glance at the door but it was too late. The agent set down his phone and he smiled. For the first time he really smiled, looked straight into my gringo eyes, and said, "I'm sorry, señor, but they have instructed me to destroy your card." He drew the scissors from his desk with a flourish, like a matador, and he cut my card in two, slid the pieces across his desk, and sniffed. There wasn't much to say. Katherine stood and left. I asked for the bathroom.

We bought avocados, bread, and bottled water and then took the next bus bound for Tijuana. The bus was packed with peasants, all of them grim-faced but friendly, all of us headed to the north. Things changed. The desert began to undulate beside the bus and I loved it. I loved the bus driver's salsa music coming over cheap speakers. I decided I loved Katherine. I loved the upholstery.

The bus idled at a truck stop and Katherine slept as I watched a man perform at the curbside. His hands moved fast in the hard desert light as he worked his shell game. I knew I was the mark; he had come for me. I rose and stepped into the sun. I knew I could win because of the sway and the change—the hallucinatory wave of heat off concrete, my wasted body, my mind all quick like a blink—and I followed the rhythm and put money down and lost and knew I could stay and beat this and win. A Mayan woman grabbed my sleeve and said, "*Cuidado, señor.*" I shook her off irritably and put more money down. The men were laughing. Women on the bus woke Katherine and pointed at me, shouting. The shell man stood from his squat and gestured angrily. We got back to the game. Then Katherine appeared over me with her brown hair like a snarled halo and she grabbed my wrist and our money and pulled me back on the bus.

Tijuana was a mess, and I don't remember how we made it north to Olympia because my mind moved faster than we ever could. And I don't remember Katherine as well as I should; she saved my life.

EIGHT

Olympia, Washington, was dense and green with summer, a rain forest after the desert. My brain flooded with dopamine and I was walking on water. I was walking through Eden on soft carpets of moss. We stayed with her friends in a huge converted barn. Katherine busied herself with chores while I wandered. Everything—the houses and barns, the roads, the telephone poles—was painted in myth. I stood in a story I began telling myself and I shook symbols out from my pockets. I kept them all hidden from Katherine at first and she thought I was happy. My mind swooped in sudden, exhilarating gusts. I knew I had changed and I liked it, almost. I could have gotten better; I could have found help.

Summer solstice hit on a full moon that year. I soon gathered that as astrological omens go, this was a biggie. Preparations began for a traditional Olympian blowout, complete with innumerable bonfires spread out through the woods, Kesey-like supplies of hallucinogens, a fourteen-foot stack of tripped-up TVs, and just a remarkable number of women in sundresses. It was like Altamont had never happened.

When we arrived Katherine found friends and I wandered

into somebody's kitchen and a four-gallon pot of simmering mushroom tea. It looked bad and smelled worse—a vat of boiled liver bits, bats' wings, what have you. I tried just a sip and it wasn't half-bad. Those resourceful Olympians, with their vast stores of fennel and years of alchemical experience, made the stuff almost tasty. Right then I knew I was standing at my brink, resolving to pull some subconscious pin and blow things to hell. I stood alone by the untended pot and drank the stuff like beer. Dosing myself with hallucinogens was not heroic, despite what I thought. I was not embracing my destiny. I wasn't even embracing my stupidity. I lacked the judgment necessary for stupidity, let alone courage, but in my mind I was brave Orpheus plunging into the underworld to rescue my family. I was delusional and valiant and drank two more cups.

I weathered the night in a broken-down hippie bus in a bad-smelling sleeping bag without Katherine. I stayed awake all that night and through all the nights after. Every day I ran through primeval forests and epic adventures. After a week I knew it wasn't the mushrooms anymore. I had stood on druggy cliffs before but this time was different, very different. I was way, way higher and I'd jumped past the ledge. I was falling and I just couldn't hit. I couldn't wake up and I wasn't asleep. I gave up sleep. I gave up food. I didn't have the time.

Thought rose out of its banks and it spilled through sex, God, and dreams, mysterious places the mind should not trespass. Mania flooded my tidy little village of memory and constructs, the sunny little place where I play, where I keep my desires amused. All lines fell and connections sparked and went black and hissed through the water.

What I knew of the world mutated continually, all a huge metaphor now—broken and heavy and rolling straight toward me. When I pulled on a thought it unraveled to trees, asphalt, spilled horizons, and suns. I needed to look away and I knew it was already too late; I was blind and just babbling. This is it, I thought, this is madness and my family was chosen. I wanted my father, my brother, and I knew I could talk with them now, that I could meet them out on electric fields. I knew why my father held hands and tried to share these visions. And I knew why my brother punched him out trying to save them.

My thoughts moved so fast they began to hum, and that humming was music, absolutely sublime movements strafed with dissonance and twelve-tone. My father sang all his hymns because everything did. Twenty years later, I know that music well. It's symphonic and fast and above all it is inclusive and sung by everything—every tree, rock, and smokestack. These song cycles draw a skein up under experience, increasing its tempos, tightening the harmonies, connecting it all. There's a transcendental romance to mania, to this drawing together. And I believed, still believe, that this music is true, that the scattershot visions of madness are holy. They are also fucking crazy and hopeless and sad. At its core the transcendental manic experience remains one of great loneliness. It transcends, but it rarely translates. True visions find their grounding and validity in the universal, the spiritual, but these visions are poured into each cooking skull, one at a time. You'll burn down before you can share them. The face of God blinds and it burns, make no mistake. Approach these breaks in a sentimental fashion and you'll find yourself seduced by nervous, chattering ghosts, maybe lost there for good. Worse, put your vision in a pulpit, wrap it up in some patchwork doctrinal robe, and you're absolutely finished, done.

In Olympia that summer I fell into a bottomless, unpeopled hell—the absolute cold knowledge that I'd gone quite mad, that no one could ever hold me again. Still, I thought maybe I could work out the sense. I needed to remember it, write it, and speak it. I needed to organize and so fell to my knees, gathering rocks and muttering. So what if I was mad? Of course I was mad. Everyone should be mad.

To hell with all the people who stared. I had done it, broken through Ahab's pasteboard mask and harpooned my whale. I would justify my mania, all this quicksilver. I would speak it and write it before it all burnt, before it was smote down to ash and forgotten. The others would see, the ones who stared at the floor to avoid my fucked eyes, who whispered while leaving and never came back. I wrote broken poetry; I spun and I shouted past all the sweet music.

I was a god and I was scared shitless.

But Olympia was beautiful and Katherine loved me. She held my hands and led me down through the woods to the water. She told me to eat; she told me to sleep. She surrounded my bath with incense and candles. She gave me tinctures and teas while I shuddered and twitched. Every evening Katherine laid out the tarot, insisting it would prove therapeutic. She was wrong, of course. Dealing tarot cards to a psychotic is like pouring shots for a drunk. Katherine continually turned over the death card. "That's good," she would say. "It means change. Really."

When she was asleep I'd steal out of the barn and walk through the woods, collecting portents—bits of twigs, stones. Often I'd walk through to the college, look for someone awake, anyone, an audience. The lush smell of the forest, the rhythmic buzz of the insects, and the yellow streetlamps reminded me of Vietnam. A student walked by and I said, "Excuse me, excuse me. Doesn't this seem like Vietnam?"

He stopped and looked me over. I was shirtless and bathed in sweat from running through the woods. "Huh?"

"Vietnam. I think there should be helicopters. Don't you think?" His face screwed up with suspicion and he backed away. "Hey," I called after him. "I asked you a fucking question." I was gravely disappointed in him. People are so unimaginative. Fucking MBA pre-law frat dick. Hate those guys. He'd probably call security.

I walked into a dorm and wandered its halls looking for like-minded enthusiasts. I found them drinking beer in a cinder block dorm room and invited myself in. I was great and they loved me. We were all messed up and figuring it out. I taped some typing paper together, took a marker, and diagrammed our collective purpose.

I placed Man and the Word in the center with scribbles radiating out. I underlined the word "sphere" repeatedly. One of the kids downed his can and stood up. "Yeah, yeah. That's it. Sure, that's fucking it." He took my work and held it up. He taped it on their wall. Everyone approved absolutely. I was their fool and my cosmic schema a souvenir. They loved me. Of course, who could blame them? We drank a lot more beer and when security arrived I did not panic. Evergreen College security would understand me; I could teach them. They weren't interested. I was disappointed again. Nevertheless, I convinced them not to call the actual police and they dropped me off campus.

I found a pay phone and called my cousin back east, a psychiatric nurse. It was the first time I had spoken to anyone in my family in months. I told her I was fine but thought I'd check in. I hung up. I called my friend Paul in San Francisco and told him to get the fuck up to Olympia. I told him it was like Vietnam and William Blake and thought he understood. I might have told him I was William Blake. I told him Katherine was a witch and had spells. I asked him to help me and he came the next day.

If Katherine seemed conflicted upon my departure, her friends seemed delirious. I was too busy talking to kiss Katherine good-bye but as Paul grabbed my arm and pushed me into his rental car, I swore I'd return. I rolled down the window and spoke of Alaska, how we had to keep moving. All the way down the dirt driveway I stuck my head out the window like a kid and kept talking. Paul never told me to shut up, not once.

Katherine and I had seen Paul weeks earlier in San Francisco, after the desert. I had been at sea. I sat on his couch waist-deep in the saltwater flats of Sonora. I talked at Paul late into the evening, incessantly, symptomatically, all the while watching the horizon just across the room, how it curved with the earth's surface. I was preparing to drown.

None of this troubled Paul too terribly. Paul had one passion, Russian literature, and short of Blakean visions, nothing prepares one for madness quite like a passion for Russian literature. Paul himself had never gone mad but he openly admired, even envied, those who had. He aspired to a sort of controlled, manic transcendence and described it with longing and reverence. He spoke admiringly of a brilliant friend, a doctoral student who became "unhinged and enlightened." In that particular case Paul blamed Hegel, straight up. "Have you read Hegel?" he'd ask.

I would lie and say, "Some." I knew the word "dialectic."

"If you read Hegel, I mean really read Hegel, you will go insane." He loved this.

"Really. Insane."

"Absolutely. He encompasses so much, everything. And it's all paradoxical."

"Dialectical."

"That's right, exactly," Paul would say excitedly, and then, before you knew it, you would be in Montreal or Prague or somewhere.

So when Paul flew to Olympia and rented the rescue car, I believe he anticipated real metaphysical drama—a cogent struggle with existential dread, a chance to referee my wrestling match with God. He was sorely disappointed. All he got for his ticket were sleepless nights and a perfectly excruciating flight back to San Francisco on his dime.

At the gate, waiting to board, waiting for the VIPs to settle first class, one inevitably spots the problematic—individuals of large girth; harried mothers with colicky babies; loud men strutting with cell phones; certified lunatics. I was the latter, the person with and to whom Paul had to sit and listen. Listen while I studied the cloud columns beyond my small plastic window, comparing them to Michelangelo's "phony clouds," noting any number of likenesses, wondering aloud if clouds could be read for portents, like tea leaves or entrails; listen while I asked the concerned stewardess for two cups of tea; watch while I ripped open the tea bags and sprinkled the tea into my peanuts.

I asked Paul if he'd ever met an oracle. I asked him to drop the oxygen mask and then I bid him farewell. I space-walked to the bathroom, shut myself in that plastic closet, all lit up and flying. I stood there a long time, wanting to get off, frightened by the whoosh of blue flushes, worried for the pilots. When Paul finally retrieved me and escorted me past the small, irritated crowd assembled by the bathroom, I forgot all about crashing, all about the wreckage of living. I asked the stewardess for a cigarette.

Paul's wife, Jehanne, picked us up at the airport. Jehanne spoke Russian and was busily earning a Stanford doctorate in Slavic literature. Anytime Paul suspected a botched translation she quietly clarified matters. She clarified me right out of the gate. As soon as she heard my broken syntax and jagged statements, she knew what to do. The drive home from the airport to East Palo Alto mirrored the flight. I continued my commentary from thirty thousand feet up while Paul and Jehanne exchanged worried glances.

Most sane people possess an irrational fear of mental illness, see it as a contagion. Frankly, you're more likely to catch a broken arm in a ski lodge than brain disease in a psych ward; nevertheless few civilians dare contact with the crazies. Perhaps it's superstition, a primal fear of possession. Perhaps the demons that Jesus cast out are still in the neighborhood.

Paul had no such fear; he was positively nineteenth century in his romantic vision of madness. Sentence by run-on sentence, I took apart that wistful romanticism. Free association is not always a poetic tool; sometimes it's just a shovel in a dead field full of holes. Paul, my dear and brilliant friend, was exhausted—even disillusioned—by the time we got home.

As for me, I found my return to San Francisco tremendously

invigorating. I was so excited by the time we arrived at the apartment that Paul and Jehanne immediately announced they were off to the movies. They made me promise several times to stay put, pointed out the fridge and television clicker, and then fled my company.

Okay, I thought, okay. I'll just settle in. I'll get out some stuff so I can show them where I've been, figure out where I'm headed. I dumped out my pack by the door and kicked away all my thin, sour-smelling clothes. From a gray plastic bag I drew out a *huipil*, an embroidered Mayan blouse, an heirloom that granddaughters sell for nothing to tourists. This particular one was a real bargain. I worked the woman down just at nightfall, just as her bus was preparing to leave. It was yellow, my mother's favorite color. I laid out small weavings, bracelets, gifts and mementos from travelers and lovers scattered over the continent.

I found books on Paul's shelves, marked the right passages with pencils, pens, and paper clips. I laid them down in a circle. I got some food, some fruit and cheese. I opened a trunk, found blankets, and searched for old letters. A photo would strike me and of course it had to go next to that bit by Melville, or under that window. Everything, every beautiful fucking thing in that apartment, in my pack, in my head was connected, and I circled it round through the rooms, retracing and refining and scribbling footnotes.

Before I broke through, all of this stuff was just junk, just cardboard props standing in for the real. But now it was all heavy as hell, shining and sucking everything toward it. Here I was, little old me, tidying up the event horizon, aligning the chunks of a collapsed star.

Four hours later and it was nearly done. It was just about making sense when Paul and Jehanne swung open their door. Shoved it open, actually, pushing some framed prints out of the way. "Careful of those," I cautioned. Their faces dropped and I smiled reassuringly. "Don't worry. I can explain this. I can explain myself. It's all here."

Jehanne went directly to their bedroom but Paul listened politely, picked up some items, and carefully placed them back on the floor. He moved slowly and with great feigned interest down through the installation and toward their bedroom. "I haven't got to the bedroom yet," I said apologetically as he closed the door.

The cops arrived twenty minutes later. Paul and Jehanne were sitting on their couch, quite close together and not saying much. I was sitting on the floor talking, surrounded by a trainload of meaning all hitched onto items—some of them mine, most theirs. When I saw the flashing lights out their front window, I stood and acted decisively. "Right," I said. "Time for a shower."

I went into the bathroom, shut the door, locked it twice, and stripped. I'd just adjusted the water temperature when the knocking commenced. "Yes, just a minute," I said hospitably.

"Sir, could you please step out?"

"I'm in here. Who is it?"

"The police, sir. What are you doing in there?"

"What do you think I'm doing? I'm taking a shower." I shook my head. "Obviously."

"Open the door, sir."

"Just a moment. It will be just a moment. I've got shampoo all over the place."

"Where?"

"Specifically? On my head, in my hair. Christ." I could hear the cops—there were at least two—talking to each other and then to Paul. I couldn't hear much but I knew what they wanted. Was I dangerous? Suicidal? "I'm not dangerous," I called helpfully from the shower. "I'm not suicidal."

That's when they started banging at the cheap hollow door and shaking its knob. "Open the door or we'll be forced to open it for you. You don't want me to kick your friend's door in, do you?" I pictured Paul and Jehanne, seated on their couch and shaking their heads.

"All right, all right," I said, feigning exasperation, smacking the chrome mixing valve down. "Hold your horses."

"Open it."

"Just a sec. Drying off." And then I looked in the mirror and grinned. I couldn't resist. "Do I have time for a shave?"

"That's it. We're coming in." I opened the door on cue, dripping, a towel wrapped around my waist, the perfect, imperturbable host.

Both cops were huge, one of them black, one white. They stayed serious as I genially fended off questions. I consciously slowed myself way, way down, editing my words for the first time since Olympia. "But of course, of course, I can see how it might seem that way, officers. If you would just allow me a moment to dress, I'm sure we can sort all this out. Actually"—I gestured to the cluttered floor and laughed nonchalantly—"I've been sorting things out all night." I shrugged. "You know how it is—traveling." I got up to get dressed; they sat me right down. Still so serious.

At the time, East Palo Alto had one of the highest murder rates in California. They didn't have time to waste on fucked-up white kids. I rated a clear waste of time. They led me to the bathroom, watched as I pulled on my jeans. An ambulance arrived. I got pissed and I spit out a question. "So, you gonna cuff me or what?"

The white cop shook his head. "No, we're not going to cuff you. You're just going to walk out to the ambulance with us."

Shit. I wanted them to cuff me, I wanted the drama. "Fuck you," I said. "Fuck all of you. Fuck this," I said, and I kicked all the shit out of my way as they led me outside. Paul stood by me, close to weeping. Before I climbed into the ambulance, he embraced me and said he was sorry. I quoted our beloved Dylan and said, "Jesus was betrayed by a kiss." He smiled grimly—"I knew you would say that," he replied—and I climbed into the ambulance, messianic, radiant, and sadly mistaken.

I remember commenting on the ambulance driver's boots, combat boots—heavy-soled with tight-laced canvas uppers. The kind of boot you'd wear to kick picket fences or teeth back into their roots. "Nice boots," I said, making conversation, sarcastic and strapped to a seat in the back while the two-way radio popped with squelch. She glanced around toward where I sat grinning and cuffed, and she sneered as she spoke to her radio. Coordinates. The streetlights like helicopters.

"Where's your shirt?" they asked at the hospital and I had to explain that the cops dragged me out without a shirt. "Where are your shoes?" I explained how they dragged me out without shoes.

"I know how this looks," I said. "I was taking a shower." They wheeled a guy past in a straitjacket and tied to a gurney who kept shouting, "I'm gonna fuck you up! I'm gonna fuck you up!" He said that all down the hall.

"Don't worry about him," they said. "Are you on drugs?"

"Not particularly."

"Where's your family?"

"On the East Coast."

"What's their phone number?"

"I don't recall."

I Love Lucy was on the television mounted to the ceiling of the waiting room beyond the desk. The guy on the gurney kept frothing "fuck" over and over and that corny Desilu Productions heart was on the television screen above the triage doctor, who said, "Give him a piss test." I focused on the TV. Lucy was in trouble and Desi seemed exasperated—a Batista lost in Fred and Ethel's apartment building. I mentioned it but the nurses tended to ignore conversation. Just: "Are you allergic to any drugs? Is your family on the East Coast?"

I pissed in a cup in a washroom with stainless steel mirrors and stuck the soap in for laughs.

"Test this," I told them with all the cracked bravery of a lost kid who'd walked past the strapped-down convulsions rolled into the corner, the concrete underworld-lit Lincoln Tunnel, past the doors that stop screams, toward the desk where I placed the hot piss and the soap on the admittance forms, refusing to sign, watching a commercial for *PM* magazine in the room beyond. "Test this."

They were disappointed. One nurse told me she had had a long night and really wished I could give them another sample, so I complied and they led me into the waiting room, where I sat with a black guy dressed as an orderly on break who said he wasn't allowed to give me a smoke. We watched Mary Tyler Moore and I decided he was watching me, not Mary, and this was no break.

I took some notes with a borrowed pen on the back of a magazine. I made connections between situation comedy and the poor bastard raving in the hall. I quoted Melville to the guard and included Hendrix, and he chain-smoked and wanted none of it. After a while a nurse came in and said, "The doctor wants you to drink this." She held out a plastic cup with the words LILLY CORP stamped on its side. It held thick orange syrup. I asked what it was. "It'll help you relax," she said.

"Well, hold on, I'm just finishing this project," I said, and pointed at the magazine, where models smiled up under my scribbles. It was a standoff, I guess, but the orderly just watched the tip of his smoke. So I listened and I gave in and I downed the syrup okay. I walked past the front desk out of the magazine room to a room with just me and they slid the bolt shut but the TV kept going. I listened all night and it took forever to end.

There were no windows and I slept through that day and well into the next. I woke underwater and slow, and the nurses swam by, gurgled, and left. I lay unrestrained on a gurney in the center of a white, featureless room. I knew where I was and why, and my tongue felt swollen and dead, stuck to my teeth and palate. I tasted of sickness and I spat a thick white paste into the sheets. I sat up and waited out the dizziness for—what? Five minutes, an hour? Finally, I swung my feet from the gurney. I stood up and stumbled forward. I caught the bed and pushed at my legs till the knees locked. I saw I was scared and knew I had nothing. I'd lost my body and they'd repossessed my mind. I understood, then, that my brave spiritual quest was just a cartoon, and I just stood by the bed, rubbery. I felt like Gumby, after the humans got him, after they had put down Pokey.

A cute nurse entered as I slowly took stock. I steadied myself beside the gurney and made a sort of smile. I wore a blue hospital shift and I wondered if it covered my ass. The nurse stood across from my thin, tangled blanket. "How are we today?" We? I thought. We? She was one of them. She wasn't so cute. I worked my mouth and asked for coffee. "I'll bring you some juice," she promised, and left. I twisted around to check my ass but couldn't. I could not turn my head. I reached up and the muscles in my neck were taut and hard, like vulcanized rubber. I got back into bed.

It didn't matter. I wasn't bored. I wasn't going anywhere. There was nowhere to go and I had no one to go with, not even myself. The nurse returned, cranked up my bed, and gave me the juice. Some spilled over my chin and she caught it in her cupped hand. She gave me another plastic cup, more bittersweet syrup. I shot it back into my throat without questions. I would go back to sleep.

Near-death survivors speak of white light and often describe floating serenely above their dying body, the nurses and surgeons and loved ones. After the drugs I lay on my back covered in sheets and departed. I saw fluorescent light tubes. I saw my body lying there perfectly well, rosy-cheeked and ready to walk but for me, the dead mind in the corner, the ghost watching his body and longing for life. I called for the nurse. I gave her the number in Hamilton and then I slid under.

The nurse reached my house and Mom woke my father. "Richard, it's David. It's a hospital calling." My father pulled at his sheets, swung his legs over the side, and climbed out from his haunt. He was dizzy and frightened and picked up the phone. The nurse told my father what he already knew: another child had his sickness, another son had been damaged. She said I was resting and that I'd be fine. She described my symptoms and assured my father that mania was not permanent, that they had medicines now, and my father asked her to stop. He didn't need a tutorial, he knew it all cold. He knew what it was, now, and it wasn't St. John's dark night, or Satan's temptation, or even the whim-whams. He knew what it was: just genetics, our birthright, our brain disease. The nurse explained California's laws on involuntary commitment. If he did not sign and accompany me out of the hospital soon, I was in for weeks of observation, no exceptions.

Dad told my mother just what the nurse said: that I was all right, that we had medicines now, and that nothing was permanent. But it was and he knew it and we all know it now: that our sickness is chronic and there isn't a cure. My sister is well. She isn't bipolar. But the rest of our family—my parents, myself, and my brother—must take medicines for the rest of our lives. We've learned that our happiness will always be suspect and simple sadness must taste of despair.

My father went back to his room and flipped the light switch and packed a small bag. He called his travel agent and booked a red-eye round-trip. He shaved in front of a painful mirror and then knotted his tie. Dad arrived in the morning. Paul met him at the airport. They drove straight to the hospital, where Dad

met with a doctor while the nurses pumped me with antipsychotics. I was virtually paralyzed when I met my father and Paul
by the front desk. They double-dosed me for the plane, I'm sure.
"I'm sorry, Dad," I said. "Sorry that you had to come here." I was
wearing my jeans, the blue hospital gown, and some slippers.

Paul said, "I've got your pack in the car, Dave. Let me go get
a shirt and your shoes."

"Sorry," I said, and stared after him.

My father squinted in the bright hospital light. He had been
pulled from his shell and forced to seem confident, well. I knew
then that he loved me and that he was brave, and I wanted to tell
him how much I had missed him. "Dad," I said, and made a rubbery smile.

"David, we've all missed you. I'm glad you're coming home."

"Sorry, Dad," I said, and went back to numb.

"Don't worry, David. Don't worry. I'll get you home and then
we can talk."

Paul drove us to the airport. My father realized he hadn't
bought me a ticket. When his credit card bounced just like mine,
Paul paid for my flight. I couldn't even thank him. I avoided
Paul's eyes; he left us long before our departure. I hadn't seen my
father in months. I'd traveled thousands of miles to join his secret
bipolar circle and now we were mute, with our roles reversed. I
wanted to ask my father, ask him what would come next, but my
tongue felt lifeless and sticky. Dad steered me onto the airplane
and got me to my seat. He bought earphones, tore open the plastic bag, and listened to Mozart. The hours moved as I stared
straight ahead, drooling—just the back of a beige headrest, the
engines, and black windows.

NINE

It was late when we arrived home. My father went straight to bed. I found a small watercolor on the kitchen table—a note from my mother. "Welcome Home, David!" it said. "We love you." And it showed a boy with a thatch of black hair standing outside a happy storybook house. I pushed into my old room, climbed over some boxes, and slept in my clothes.

My mother had been up for hours when I finally got up. "Good morning, dear," she chirped. "I'm so glad you're home, David. It's an answer to prayer." She kissed my cheek. "We've been worried sick."

"I know, I know, Mom. I'm sorry," I said. I lifted my arms like dead weights and hugged her. "I'm sorry."

"No need to be sorry." She stepped back and looked for her son. The kitchen was bright and loud but I didn't talk. It felt wrong, not talking; I retreated into the bathroom. It was a slow and reasonable decision, I thought, quite sane. I am sane, I told myself. I closed my eyes in the dim light and sat on the toilet. I spat at the floor and wiped gray slime from my thick, clumsy lips. I needed water and stood and reached for the faucet and steadied myself. There wasn't a cup. I leaned slowly down into the sink. I turned my head to drink and my shoulder came with it; water spilled over my cheek and into my ear. I looked at the mirror and my face hung from its cheekbones. I came out, worked my jaw, and smiled.

"Do you want breakfast, dear?" I stared and my mother decided. "I'll make you some eggs." I sat down and the table was set: a glass of orange juice, silverware, a plate, and three pills.

I drank the orange juice and pushed my tongue forward and back. "Mom," I asked, "what are these pills?"

"Those pills? I'm not really sure, dear." She paused and worried. "I think one of them is lithium." Pills have always confounded my mother—such powerful mysteries in such small secular pieces. She's afraid of making mistakes, afraid of her confusion. Since January her family had collapsed all around her, suffocated with medicines and silence. I was dazed with antipsychotics and my dear mother was heartsick and shell-shocked. "Richard told me their names," she said. "Was it Thoritane, Thorzone?"

"Thorazine. What's this pink one?"

"I just don't know, dear."

"Can I have some coffee, is that all right?"

"Yes, yes, of course." My mother moved hurriedly with the coffeepot. I watched her hand shake as she poured it. "Your father gave them to me this morning, I—"

"Never mind, Mom," I said. "It's all right." We stopped talking. Mom stood watching my eggs fry. The coffee had cooled and I slugged the pills down in one gulp. "Where's Dad? Where's Jonathan?"

"They're both in bed. I imagine Jon will be up soon. He's excited to see you."

"Yeah. When's Dad getting up? I want to know where he got those pills."

My mother sat down beside me and crumpled a napkin. "He's not. He's not getting up." She was grieving alone and she watched my blank face. "He's not getting up. He's on leave from the seminary." Her voice got quiet. "He's drinking, David. I found wine bottles in the garage."

Wine was the least of her worries. Wine was nothing. The room looked small, the pine cabinets tired and shot full of dark knots. My forearms rested on the sticky table as I waited for the drugs to hit. How could I help her? I stood slowly. I wanted to leave but there was nowhere to go, so I just stood.

My brother came into the kitchen. He looked gaunt. "Hey, Dave. Welcome home. How you doing?"

"I'm home at least. And you? You graduated?"

His face fell and he glanced toward Mom. "Yeah, yeah, I did, Dave. Barely. It was hard, really hard going back." He looked up and smiled. "I'm going to Gordon in the fall."

"Good. You're on campus, right?" He nodded. "Good. You need to get out of here."

"Dad's not doing so well, Dave."

"I know. Mom said. What do they have you on?"

"Who?"

"You know. For pills. What are you on?"

"Lithium, mostly."

"Did you ever have pink pills? Do you know what's pink?"

He shook his head. "Never had pink."

"Maybe it's lithium."

"I don't think so, Dave. My lithium's white."

"Well, I've got pink, whatever it is," I said. "And I'm on Thorazine. I know that."

"That sucks. You got to get them to take you off that stuff. It's hard-core."

"I know, believe me," I said as I sat in our old kitchen, waiting for it with the back of my neck, for the paralysis. I shouldn't have taken those fucking pills.

"Mom," I asked, "where did the pills come from?"

"California," my mother said softly. "They gave them to Dad in California."

"My shrink's in Hamilton," my brother informed me. "He's not bad. He's Dad's shrink."

"You mean that Christian place?"

"Yeah, Haven Associates. It's not that Christian, Dave." I stared at him. "I mean they're real shrinks. They don't just pray over you."

"Screw that," I said, and finished my coffee. My mouth leaked and coffee dripped from my chin. "I'm not going there."

"Betty Lee," my father called from his bedroom. "Betty Lee, please come here." He'd been listening.

When Mom left, Jonathan rolled his eyes and whispered. "It's bad, Dave. He doesn't even get up to pee anymore. He's got a jar under the bed."

I couldn't turn my head toward him. I heaved my legs and spun my whole body to face him. Was it good to be home? Was it good to see my brother? Like this? "It's fucked. Jon, this whole place is fucked. Get out. Help me get out." He just stared at me and then Mom was back.

"Richard says you have an appointment today, David. This

afternoon. Jojo set it up. You know she works over in Gloucester at the hospital. In the psychology ward or something." Everyone knew I trusted my cousin Jo, that she was the only one I called from Olympia. Mom handed me a note. "Here. Richard wrote down the address and the doctor's name. Jon can drive you." She took my plate. "Do you want any more coffee?"

"No, Mom. No. I'm just going to lay down for a bit." My brother moved from the doorway. "See you, Jon." He nodded gravely and my mother turned to the sink.

"Yes, dear. You must be tired."

We were all so very tired.

My mother woke me up for my appointment. I was already dressed so I went outside and waited for Jonathan. I picked up Jon's basketball and tried to dribble but it bounced all wrong—too crooked and fast. It scared me how bad I'd become, and I let the ball roll away. I had no idea what Jon was on, but I was on all of it. Shut down. Our ride to the hospital was quiet. Jonathan wouldn't go in with me. He hated the place.

The psychiatrist was quick; my cousin had briefed him. Manic or possibly mixed state. Bipolar type I—both manic and depressive history. Strong family history of the disease. Father, brother. Mother? He wrote two prescriptions: lithium and Thorazine. On a separate sheet he wrote out careful dosage instructions and the names of two local therapists, and shuffled me out.

I was old-school now, a classically doped mental patient on time-tested pills. In 1986, psychiatry was on the cusp of major breakthroughs, but in Gloucester, at least, the docs stuck to the old guns. I was taking drugs from the 1950s, the old standbys. I have no quarrel with lithium. Lithium was proven effective against mania in 1949 and remains among the best mood-stabilizing drugs known. Lithium made me sane and it continues to make my life livable. Drugs such as lithium and Depakote regulate levels of dopamine, a neurotransmitter associated with pleasure. My basic—and primitive—understanding is that too much dopamine and thoughts can speed out of control; too little and depression often results. Some enthusiastic neuroscientists even claim that profound religious experiences, visions both ecstatic and hellish, are essentially dopaminergic—just dopamine and nerve endings—the result of too many or too few neurotransmitters. It appears reductionism is a professional hazard among brain chemists.

Thorazine is another thing entirely. It is not a mood stabilizer; it's a mood strangler, a blunt instrument. Thorazine arrived in 1954 and is the founding member of a group known as the "major antipsychotics." They are neuroleptics, literally "nerve-seizing" medicines. They don't regulate dopamine as lithium does; they shut it down. They are faster, stronger, and more dangerous than the mood stabilizers and they feel scary as hell. If lithium is a glass of merlot with your dinner, Thorazine is a quart of scotch with your breakfast. Long-term use of neuroleptics is primarily limited to chronic schizophrenics, but in the short-term these drugs remain the front-line weapons against mania. They stop patients cold and keep them quiet for a week or so until the long-term mood stabilizers like lithium kick in.

Thorazine was the first of these blunt instruments to be

approved and was used extensively through the 1950s and '60s. It is a quick-acting sedative and proved especially useful through the psychedelic years, when it became known as the "LSD antidote." It remains one of the fastest, if not one of the safest, drugs to treat delusions, hallucinations, and manias. Administered as a syrup it can drop a maniac in minutes, although I'm proud to say it took a double dose to knock me out in San Francisco. Possible side effects include withdrawal, autism, and tremors. A severe movement disorder called tardive dyskinesia can be triggered by long-term use of the drug. Tardive dyskinesia doesn't stop once it starts, and there's no known cure for its muscle spasms and tics, tongue protrusion and finger twitching. It is constant and lifelong.

I don't claim to comprehend neuroscience. I understand the role of transubstantiation in Holy Communion more than the dopaminergic causation of visions. I've been accustomed to mysteries, holy and otherwise, since I was a child. Some of us care for orphans, amass fortunes, raise protests or Nielsen ratings; some of us take communion or whiskey or poison. Some of us take lithium and antidepressants, and most everyone believes these pills are fundamentally wrong, a crutch, a sign of moral weakness, the surrender of art and individuality. Bullshit. Such thinking guarantees tragedy for the bipolar. Without medicine, 20 percent of us, one in five, will commit suicide. Six-gun Russian roulette gives better odds. Denouncing these medicines makes as much sense as denouncing the immorality of motor oil. Without them, sooner or later the bipolar brain will go bang. I know plenty of potheads who sermonize against the pharmaceutical companies; I know plenty of born-again yoga instructors, plenty of missionaries who tell me I'm wrong about lithium. They don't have a clue.

Back then, though, just knocked down from my high, I despised the pills and considered them all the same—the balance of lithium and the death haze of Thorazine. I hated the fact that I needed them. I had been pulled from the road back to Hamilton and my friends had all scattered. I felt stranded. The Morrison place was just a winter rental; Doc was in Baltimore and Nathan out west. My mother had saved a card that arrived for me from New Mexico: "Dave, Get down here. We've got a house surrounded by mesas and cacti. Tam and Tony are here. Bob's here. Need spiritual guidance. There might be work. Nathan."

I would have gone in a shot. I wanted to go. I wanted to stop eating their fucking pills and head back west. I couldn't help my family, not like this. My brother was on his own. He just needed to leave. It was too late for my father. He had chosen his life—curled up in a dark bedroom at noon. My father's drugs made living death possible, a blank still life with pills. I hated the smarmy psychiatrist's cure that hollowed me out and stuffed me with cotton and headaches and fear. But I hated my damaged mind even more. I knew I'd been crazy; on that I was clear. I knew I was still crazy and thought if I missed a dose I'd be gone. So I kept taking the stuff. I was scared of myself.

I convinced my mom to give me the keys. I told her I had a doctor's appointment and insisted upon driving. There was no stopping me. I had my old car and drove back to the winter rental, back to the Morrisons'. I knew they were back for the summer and that the main house was full. I knew the Morrisons had enough grown children to pack the place, but I also knew that Pat, their mother, loved me, and that she gathered strays up, made them breakfast, and put them to work.

Pat's son Tiger had his eyes on the stone water tower out back. He planned to break into the cistern itself, which comprised the tower's first sixteen feet, and create an apartment. But he was fishing on a trawler off Maine, so Pat let me move in for the summer. Butch and the goats lived downstairs, stabled next to the cistern, and I had the top floor, a round room of stone circled by small arched windows and topped with a cone-shaped roof.

Byron and Shelley are completely correct. There is no better place to go crazy than a stone tower in the forest. Romanticism fed and enabled my madness. My aesthetic was made for madness and madness made it. I would not give up and rot away in Hamilton. I would find as romantic a tomb as possible. I would light a pyre in my head, stand by the sea, and throw sparks. I now had my tower. I had the haunted wood. I had my goats with satanic eyes. I even had a llama whose significance I had yet to plumb. I had it all. I had everything a young, romantic poet could need, excepting opium and the ability to walk, speak, or think well.

I tried to get better. I kept taking the drugs. In fact, I took a lot of the drugs. I avoided doubling up on the lithium but I began loving the Thorazine...I seemed to remember the shrink telling me it was fine. "Take two if you are still feeling racy." I'm sure he said that. Apparently, Thorazine was having a paradoxical effect on me. I believe it sped me up, way up, back up to where I wanted to be. And as soon as it did I downed another and took to the woods or the ocean. It's a difficult feat—almost impossible—but I developed a pronounced taste for recreational antipsychotics. I wandered Cape Ann happily stoned.

I found my old boat, *Strider*, half-swamped in its berth at Gloucester Marine. It was a wreck but I cleaned it, pulled its battery, and swapped in my car's. I flooded the engine and waited impatiently, chain-smoking beside the tank. I pretended I was headed to England. It wasn't hard. I could play make-believe at will. The more outlandish a notion, the quicker I claimed it. I wasn't completely insane: part of me recognized the impossibility of a transatlantic voyage but I suppressed the killjoy in me. I loved playacting, took the absurd seriously, and loved to tell others about it. It was, after all, remarkable.

I fueled the boat downriver at Lobster Cove, bought some beer and ice. I pounded out the mouth of the Annisquam and into Ipswich Bay. The bay opened to the northeast, toward Maine. I planned to pass Lane's Cove and Folly, round Halibut Point, cut across Sandy Bay past Pigeon Cove and the Dogbar, then shoot behind Straightsmouth and out to Thatcher's Woe. I knew that Thatcher's Woe is the island where Salem's minister had wrecked en route from Ipswich, all hands and his family lost, all but him. I knew this and I had the chart in my head; I had its poetry. I knew where the names came from and I thought this made me heroic, unsinkable. After Thatcher's were Milk Island,

Pebble Beach, Good Harbor, and Gloucester. I'd dart through the cut and gas up again, just to be sure. Then it was "straight on until morning," for "they that go down in ships": George's Bank, the open Atlantic, England—at least through the first tank.

I got lucky and found glory much sooner, in the monstrous, injection-molded shape of a cabin cruiser, drifting out near Salvages. An overweight man in a tangerine sweater and shorts waved from its flying bridge, his arms making the international symbol for distress and a clear call to destiny. I cut back the engine, threw out some fenders, and pulled alongside. A bikini-clad woman moved in the galley.

I tried to sound competent. "Trouble?"

"Yes," he called down. "Do you have a radio?"

"What? You don't?"

"I dunno. It's not working or something."

"Flares?"

"What?"

"Flares. Do you have flares?" I love flares.

"What the hell are you talking about, flares?"

"Flares. Morse code. All that stuff." He stared at me blankly. "Listen, do you want help or what?" The man looked disgusted and started down the ladder.

We would have a gam. According to Melville, a gam occurs when two boats, preferably whale boats, meet at sea and exchange news. I was insane—nautically proficient and insane, a time-honored tradition. The guy made it down and commenced to sweat. "Listen," I said. "How 'bout I give you a tow into Rockport? Where you out of?"

"Newburyport."

"Yeah, well." His boat was two and a half stories of solid plastic, a thirty-eight-foot slab loaded with every inoperable navigational and nautical convenience known. It weighed more than most marinas. I wasn't towing him to Newburyport.

"Okay, Skip. Tell you what. Throw me the bowline and I'll tow you into Rockport." This was better than imaginary transatlantic crossings. This was real. I could really rescue this guy. I could pretend he was sinking, even.

He stared down at my presunk craft and her ancient Evinrude. "I don't know," he said, and scanned the empty horizon.

"Just throw me the line. C'mon, Skip. I don't have all day." I caught his line. Fed through a chock on his bow, the line dropped at a sixty-degree angle down to my stern. The *Strider* was nearly under his boat. I could have added line but hadn't the time—he was sinking. I cranked the engine and we were off, marking maybe two knots. My engine coughed and the bow pitched strangely. I lost steerage intermittently.

Twenty minutes into the operation I glanced over my shoulder and I saw Skip yelling at me. He started waving his arms again. The international sign of distress. Of course, he was sinking. I waved him off. We waved at each other for another five minutes until my boat jumped forward and the towline shot over my head. He cut it, cut his own line. Nice one too, one-inch braided. I looked back. The guy was screaming and I just gunned it.

You try to help people out and they just cut you off. You try to teach people a thing or two and they run. After my thwarted ocean rescue, I retreated to my tower, to solitude. No one understood a goddamn thing. I wrote run-on poems. I tried to reread *Moby-Dick* and turned its margins black with my scrawls. My situation was seriously dangerous, and this welcome realization filled my days with adventure. But the nights, the nights were horrible. The tower had no electricity; all I had were candles and a gas camp stove. I spent the hours pacing and muttering, full of fear and paranoia, waiting for the bats to flit down from the ceiling. I thought of my father and how if I did what everyone wanted—if I got sane—I'd end up like him, half-dead and laid out. I slept less and less.

When the Thorazine ran out I grabbed the empty bottle, walked through Dogtown and down into Gloucester. The drugstore refused to refill it and said I should call the doctor. No chance. I walked down to the Main Street Café, sat down, and pulled out my notebook. It was a mess, fat with notes and scraps, filled with exclamations and cosmic errand reminders. I pulled out a Guatemalan road map, consulted, and set to work on my epic poem, *Extranjeros.* I still have that notebook. The poem features dead, bloody tongues, clubbed bluefish, and churches. It was art. The best thing I had ever written, I was sure, but it wasn't quite done. It needed more. Everything needed more.

So I got back to it, scraping away at that notebook in the empty midafternoon café. I thought I cut a dashing and unusual figure for Gloucester, carrying notebooks like it was Cambridge, ostentatiously flipping the ruined pages of my talismanic *Moby-Dick.* When the young waitress walked over I redoubled my effort. I held my finger up and asked her patience as I scribbled.

I looked up. She was beautiful. "Do you know, by chance," I asked, "how to conjugate the verb 'murder' in Spanish?"

She didn't skip a beat. "Past, present, or imperfect? What do you want?"

"Um, coffee, I mean past." I was impressed. "You know Spanish?"

"Sure." She smiled at the papers I had spread over the table, turned, and walked off for the coffee.

"What's your name?"

"Roberta."

"I'm David."

"I didn't ask."

"You from Gloucester?" I asked. "You don't seem like you're from Gloucester."

"Sure I am. Lanesville." She looked me over. "You're not."

"Well, no. Not exactly. I've been in Guatemala. Mostly. Colorado."

"I went to school in Colorado."

"Huh," I said. What I wanted to say was, *Jesus, you went to school in Colorado? So did I! When? Exactly! This is no coincidence. It's fate, pure and simple. Quit this place and let's go back. I have friends outside Taos!* But fortunately all I could manage was, "Huh." It's incredibly difficult, nearly impossible, for a maniac to effectively chat up a girl, but I soldiered on.

Roberta smiled. "You've been traveling. Me too. I just got back from Greece and Africa. Now I'm figuring out what to do."

"Wow," I said, completely agog. "Greece. How long?"

"Six months or so."

"Where'd you stay?"

"Under a sort of bush."

"A bush. You lived under a bush?"

"It was a large bush. It was down by a beach. A number of us lived there. We picked olives." Roberta had lived under a Greek bush by the ocean. I was in love.

"What about Africa?"

"I might tell you later. I don't know." She glanced over at her boss. "Listen, I've got to get to work."

Roberta, Africa, Greece—I was clobbered with romance. I was in love again and planned to sweep her off her feet. I began writing love letters immediately: tearing sheets from my notebook, jumping from prose to verse, sketching far-flung dreams for our future. I drew a treasure map of Gloucester with an X marking my tower. I had pages and pages and I left them on the table with a five-dollar tip. She shrugged it all off and figured she'd never see me again.

I left the café, walked down Main, and entered a hair salon. I don't have the faintest idea why. The last thing I wanted was a haircut. Romantic poets do not get haircuts. Before long I was explaining the subconscious to an amused hairstylist named Diane. I had *Moby-Dick* out and open to the masthead chapter. I must have seemed harmless, because before long we were comparing pharmaceuticals. I'd found a fellow enthusiast. I littered the front counter with various pills and my scribbled descriptions and dosage instructions. I shamelessly traded three Thorazines for two Percocets. I made Diane promise to read *Moby-Dick* and I tried to give her my copy. And then Roberta walked in.

I looked up and we startled each other. Diane jumped up and smiled mischievously. "Hey, Bert. Let me introduce you to Dave."

"We've met." Roberta rolled her eyes. "He was just in the café."

Diane laughed. "Really. Did he make you read *Moby-Dick*?"

"I did nothing of the sort," I interjected while collecting my pills from the counter. "I just suggested she should read a few chapters. Do you know the masthead chapter?"

Diane smiled. "No, I can't say I've read the masthead chapter."

Roberta and Diane smiled at each other.

"Well," I explained, "the masthead chapter just hammers transcendentalism—all that fuzzyheadedness."

They laughed out loud and then Roberta said, "Listen, David, we have to pick up Di's brother at the airport. It was nice to see you again."

"Oh, sure, sure," I said, and hurried outside, feeling suddenly foolish. I spent the rest of the afternoon wandering the town: Pavilion Beach, Halfmoon, Rosie's Wharf, the galleries over on Rocky Neck. I made people nervous and knew it, and so I kept moving. By nine o'clock I was in Blackburn's Tavern, drinking beer and sharing random thoughts with the bar's disc jockey as he set up. I was tangential. I was global.

"Have you ever considered classical?" I asked.

"Classical," he scoffed. "No. Why would I play that?"

"Just for a break, a sort of breather between, I dunno, Bob Seger and Aerosmith."

He smiled. I was amusing in short doses, good for cameo appearances. He kept fiddling with knobs, pulling cables from milk crates.

"How about African drumming?" I asked. He looked past me and I heard Roberta's voice.

"What are you, everywhere?" I turned and there were Roberta and Diane, Bert and Di, back from the airport and laughing.

"Ubiquitous," I said. "Like the whale."

"Hey, this is my cousin," the DJ said. "The one I was talking about. She's the one whose boyfriend does all the work in, what, Nicaragua?" We both looked at Roberta. Her eyes fell and she nodded, then she and Diane wandered off.

I looked for them later but they were gone. No matter. I learned from my new friend, DJ Mark, that Roberta was staying with him up in Lanesville, a small village to the north. I thought I knew Lanesville. At least I knew how to walk there through Dogtown. I knew its granite cove and the quarries scattered through its woods. I didn't know Roberta's family owned two of those quarries, or that her family spread through the woods and down to the bay. I didn't yet know that dating Roberta meant courting all of Lanesville.

Mark said his house was on Emerald Street. I was in luck. There was only one house on Emerald. I sat on its front steps and waited for Roberta to come home. Mark pulled into the drive around 1 a.m. I ran out from the dark and said, "Hey, Mark. How'd everything go?"

"Jesus!" He jumped. "What are you doing here?"

"Waiting for Roberta, I guess. Do you need any help unloading stuff?"

"Roberta? She's not here?" I shook my head. "Shit. Wait here for a minute. I'll see..." He stopped at the door. "Oh, just come in already. Just for a second."

I was in the living room flipping through his records when Mark tracked Roberta down at Diane's. "Bert," he said in a stage whisper. "Listen, that guy's here... The guy from the Black-burn... I know, I know... Yeah, I figured. He was sitting here waiting for you. Huh? Well, what am I supposed to do with him? Shit. All right, all right. I'll take care of it. Christ." Mark stepped into the living room. I smiled and he threw me out fast, like a bouncer.

Most women would have gotten a restraining order, but not Roberta, not after living under a bush and hitchhiking through Zimbabwe.

The next day I was still out of Thorazine. The situation was desperate. I couldn't go to the doctor, out of the question. But my cousin Joanna, down at the hospital, she could get me some. I showed up at Addison Gilbert just flying. Joanna looked concerned. "This doesn't seem to be working out, David."

"What do you mean?" I blustered. What had tipped her off?

"Your situation. Where are you staying?"

"In a water tower. Out in the woods."

"Right."

"By Dogtown. Do you know the history of Dogtown? It's fascinating—"

"Right. Forget Dogtown. Have you been taking your meds?"

"Yeah. Sure. I took all of them. I need more. Especially the Thorazine. I've run dangerously low on Thorazine."

"I see. Why don't you give me the name of your doctor?"

"Short guy," I said. "Mustache and glasses. Works next door in the other wing."

"Right."

By dinnertime I was locked in the psych ward over at Beverly Hospital. My father had driven me over. "Just for an idea you might want to consider, an option," he said. I found the nurses quite charming. We chatted forever and then they invited me on a tour, which sounded lovely. They had me sign some papers—just a formality, they said—in order for me to view the entire facility. And so I committed myself. It wasn't voluntary, more of a bait and switch. They explained I was stuck there for at least four days, and then they gave me the complimentary syrup.

The next morning I sat down to a fine breakfast of oatmeal and drugs. Afterward the nurses sent me down to the psychiatrist's office. He was reviewing some papers when I entered.

"Hmm." He set down his glasses and looked me over. "Have you ever been on Trilafon?"

"What the hell is that?"

"An antipsychotic. It seemed to be effective on your brother."

"Another one. How much of that crap is out there?" I asked.

"Quite a bit."

I was in a fog and sat for a moment. Trilafon. It looked like I'd never see Thorazine again. I blew that. The doctors had me where they wanted me. They were going to run down the list of chemical options until they hit pay dirt. "Okay," I said. "Bring it on; bring on the Trilafon."

Trilafon was a disappointment but the hospital itself was a pleasant surprise. The psychiatric ward at Beverly dispelled the standard images of bedlam I carried. When I was a kid in neighboring Hamilton, we didn't call each other nuts or mental, we just said, "You're Danvers." Danvers's State Lunatic Hospital had warehoused the region's chronic, violent, and hopeless since 1878. It was an astoundingly gothic structure set high on a hill. It was so astoundingly gothic, in fact, that it inspired H. P. Lovecraft's Arkham Sanitarium, the one featured in *Batman*. Its spires and turrets are visible for miles and dark legends about it are numerous. The hospital had seventy-seven acres that once belonged to John Hathorne, a judge in Salem's infamous witch trials. People spent their whole lives behind those walls. Its graveyard doesn't have stones, just small metal markers with numbers, no names. Before lithium, before its approval in 1970, I would have gone there and I might have stayed there, institutionalized.

Instead I played *One Flew Over the Cuckoo's Nest* in a sunny common area with compassionate nurses. Granted, I was manic, but I loved the place. My fellow patients took me seriously and I befriended two in particular, a kid my age who was in for attempted suicide and a young schizophrenic woman. I fancied myself Randall Patrick Murphy, gambling for cigarettes and telling tall tales.

And then suddenly, I was sane—not completely well, but fundamentally sane. The Trilafon stuff worked, just as it had for my brother. The hospital wasn't an adventure anymore; it wasn't a novel or movie, it was just dull. I was actually bored. The depressed guy was depressing, the nurses humorless. Only the schizophrenic could get me to laugh. She was brilliant. By the second week I reached an understanding with the nurses. I would take my medicine if they would let me out after the morning's group therapy. I promised to return for dinner and meds. I had more leverage than I realized. Technically, I had voluntarily committed myself; I was free to go whenever I wished.

As soon as they sprung me I headed back over to Lane's Cove. I spied Roberta sunbathing on the bow of a lobster boat and the sight filled me with courage. I hoped I could explain—or at least distance myself from—most of my madness. I approached Roberta because I believed she could understand me, that she wanted to understand me. But first, I had to get past the phalanx of lobstermen on the boat's deck. New England's lobstermen are an insular bunch, suspicious of all outsiders. Any out-of-town mental patient who expresses interest in their young female relatives can expect formidable opposition. I knew that. But hell, I was a New Englander. I was a New Englander on medication and I was up to the challenge. I walked down the ramp to the float and the lobstermen stared. "Hey, guys," I said. "Nice day."

"What? Are you that guy from Danvers?" They chuckled. Evidently, I needed no introduction. My questioner drained his beer, threw his can toward a white five-gallon bucket, and missed. All of them looked a bit sunstruck and beery.

"Not exactly," I said. "I'm living up in Dogtown."

This was greeted with general hilarity. "Dogtown? You live up in Dogtown? No one lives up in Dogtown."

"Well, I mean I—"

"You're that crazy guy that knows Bert and Di."

"No, ha ha. I wouldn't say that, ha ha. I'm not really crazy. Ha. Just a misunderstanding." They leaned on the rails and waited for my story. This was becoming difficult. My newfound sanity had eroded my ability to chat up anyone—cops, waitresses, stonewalls, or lobstermen. Where was Roberta? Hadn't she seen me?

"Yeah, well, listen, guys. All right if I go forward and say hi to Roberta?"

Mercifully, one of them stepped forward. "Yeah, fine, fine. Knock yourself out. You want a beer?" I took it gratefully and pushed around the wheelhouse.

Roberta immediately jumped overboard. She was treading water under the bow and I could hear the lobstermen laughing. "Roberta. Roberta, come on. Look, I'm better now. Honest. I'm straight. I want to apologize." No answer. I knew her options were limited. She could swim for it—melodramatic and awkward—or she could climb back aboard—just awkward. A few tense minutes passed on deck, just me and the guys. No one said much. Then Roberta swam down the length of the boat, climbed over the transom, and smiled.

My chances with Roberta had improved substantially along with my mental state. I told her about Olympia, about my break and the hospital. I even attempted to listen, a difficult feat for any man but especially taxing for the manic gentleman caller. The afternoon moved slowly, so slowly it was tonic. I came back to the cove the next day, and Main Street Café the next, and I still made it back for lockdown and meds. I asked Roberta to lunch and took her to the Willow Rest, a gas station lunch counter. I bought her a Superburger for two bucks and told her I couldn't stay long; I had to get back to the ward. Last Christmas she gave me a Willow Rest mug.

TEN

I wanted out. I promised the nurses anything they wanted. They arranged for a therapist and I promised to see her. They found a psychiatrist and I promised to take all his pills. I promised to avoid "excitement" and "overstimulation." I vowed to eat vegetables, drink plenty of fluids, and swear off hallucinogens. I meant it, too, every last word. I didn't need Yeats to tell me the center could not hold. My gift for metaphor, my free associations, had reached past poetry and into illness. A phrase or image spilled into my mind and flew back in splatters, a kind of dreadful spin art. I wanted sleep and I wanted more sleep; I wanted to wake under a medicine spell and drift into whiteness.

I went back to the tower and considered all the tiny altars I'd built throughout the room, little piles of meaningful bits: a broken blue bottle, scrawled notes, a key, a ball of wax. I swept them up with my boot and pushed them from windows. I had nothing left beside the pills and my family and still I wouldn't go home. I feared the sadness; I feared I'd stay sick with it, never leave my father's dark room.

Instead, I pushed back at sadness with long hikes and carpentry's hard, physical work. I was lucky and strong enough to dodge mania's blowback depression. I renounced mania and faced down its subsequent humiliations. And yet, I still loved my poles. I always will. After Beverly Hospital I walked a fine, dangerous line between romanticizing the aesthetic of madness and courting disease. I wanted quiet but not some hospital hush. I needed a beautiful calm, a capital-R Romantic calm. My recovery required the proper setting and architecture. I didn't want a room; I wanted a landscape, a painting, and I found it in Rockport. A friend introduced me to the owner of the oldest house in Pigeon Cove. Nadia lived elsewhere in Rockport and the house needed a caretaker. I was to sleep in the house, call the plumbers or the fire department if necessary, and pay fifty dollars a month.

Nadia's place was off the Byronic charts; it out-Shelleyed even the stone tower. And it had heat; it had glass in the windows. It was hidden from the road by massive oak trees but everyone knew the place and called it the Old Witch House. According to local lore, two Salem brothers had fled to Pigeon Cove with their mother, an accused witch. They built the house in 1692 and hid themselves away in the woods. It certainly looked like a witch house: a dark brown garrison with swirled glass in diamond-pane windows, low ceilings, and high fireplaces. Hallways went back and back through centuries of cobbled additions. I remember opening a closet to find another nest of rooms, and another and another until I was lost.

The rooms were all very beautiful, but it was the barn that I loved. It had sheltered the boyhood of Nadia's son, who had committed suicide. Model train tracks ran through the rafters and the bookcases bulged with Jules Verne. There were notebooks and drawings and old wooden toys. And then he grew up, moved to the city, and returned; he stepped off the Stone Pier and swam out to sea. He met death just as I once hoped to meet it, by drowning. I never touched his things, never moved them, but watched the room, all quiet and ghostly. It was the antipsychotics that kept me so still. I could sit for hours, watching daylight crumble, watching the shadowy brooms sweep it away. The barn frightened me with all its heartbreaking little pieces that Nadia never boxed or hid away. And yet I was drawn there by its melancholy undertow. I found it fascinating and lovely and all this was dangerous.

My psychiatrist said I "wasn't out of the woods" and I would need to be on a low dose of antipsychotics for some time to come. He said I could expect, eventually, to maintain proper equilibrium with lithium alone. I could look forward to that, he said. I stayed alone at the Witch House and took the doctor's drugs two, three times a day. I took care with the doses and times. I bought a watch.

I avoided friends. I saw their sadness as I tottered around and answered their questions with rubbery, stupid words. Dalton came up from Charlestown once. My housemate Doc was gone and William was just too crazy to visit. Nathan came back from New Mexico and tracked me down at the Witch House. "Hey, man. It's good to see you," he said. I marked his dismay. "We got your cassettes down in Taos. We loved them." I didn't remember making tapes. I didn't remember sending anything to New Mexico. "We listened to them every night like they were some kind of surreal *Prairie Home Companion*." I winced. "They were a frickin' riot."

I spent my mornings dividing up doses, my afternoons tromping through Dogtown, and my evenings convincing Roberta to see me. She was calm, quieting, and she never gave up on my mind. She stayed over on occasion and we slept together and I had hopes for the future. But I was fresh out of a psych ward, unemployed, and blunted by drugs, by the Trilafon. I remained physically awkward and my tongue was bloated and dry. Roberta was understandably noncommittal but I pressed on with a sort of primitive, Frankenstein-by-the-well charm. It was all I had left, and it worked.

One morning I sat down with my coffee and shook out my daily dose on the scarred kitchen table. Roberta walked in and said, "That stuff's going to kill you."

"What, the coffee?"

She smiled. "No, those pills. What is that stuff anyway?"

We'd been through this before. "This capsule's lithium and this here's Trilafon."

She sat close and touched my arm. "You seem a lot better, David. You're not crazy at all. That stuff scares me. It's industrial."

"Would you say it's a chemical straitjacket?" I smiled. I just loved that phrase. "A way for the doctors to keep me down?"

"Seriously, do you really think this shit makes you better? Cures you or something? It just shuts you down."

"Okay, I'll grant you the Trilafon. It's not exactly fun, but it did get me down in a hurry. They've got me on a low dose now." I held the gray pill up between my thumb and forefinger, considered, and popped it back like a chocolate.

"It's a sedative."

"Actually, I think it might be a horse tranquilizer. Really. I'm serious." She didn't laugh. "Look, I don't want to go nuts again, just go off. Ever. I'm taking this stuff until they tell me to stop. I don't think the lithium is all that bad, at least that's what they tell me. It's not as bad as the Trilafon. It's not an antipsychotic."

"What is it then?" She turned to the stove. "Do you want some eggs?"

I nodded. This was exhausting, the longest conversation I'd had in weeks. "Lithium? Lithium's a salt, that's all."

"A salt?"

"Yeah, it occurs naturally. In groundwater. It's good for you. I think they drink it at spas."

"They make batteries out of it."

"True," I said. She had me there.

I enjoyed my assigned therapist. She was pleasant and caring. She was brilliant and addressed the practical and philosophical ramifications of psychopharmacology while I stared and drooled on her couch. I voiced Roberta's concerns. I complained about my slow, rubbery body and the sludge in my head. I asked about lithium batteries. She did her best to downplay the side effects and stress the therapeutic necessity of the medicines. She knew I couldn't afford a frank discussion of tremors and tics, kidney and thyroid functions. I didn't need excuses. She said I'd be off the Trilafon very soon, that my dose had been lowered. She said lithium's side effects were far less pronounced than the antipsychotic's. But it was very likely, she said, that I'd need lithium the rest of my life.

I didn't believe her. I couldn't separate the antipsychotic's gruesome effects from the lithium's workings. I took them together and I lumped them together: the zombie pill Trilafon and the mood-stabilizing lithium. It was all or nothing in my mind. If I dumped the Trilafon the lithium went as well. I wanted my body back. I wanted my soul. I craved just a touch of dopamine grace. Compared to bipolar's magic, reality seems a raw deal. It's not just the boredom that makes recovery so difficult, it's the slow dawning pain that comes with sanity—the realization of illness, the humiliating scenes, the blown money and friendships and confidence. Depression seems almost inevitable. The pendulum swings back from transcendence in shards, a bloody, dangerous mess. Crazy high is better than crazy low. So we gamble, dump the pills, and stick it to the control freaks and doctors. They don't understand, we say. They just don't get it. They'll never be artists.

I needed Roberta but I knew she wouldn't coddle a head case forever. She wouldn't shack up with Frankenstein. She had been threatening to leave for New York City. A few of her lefty college friends were squatting in a building on the Lower East Side. They promised her plenty of room. New York was clearly the next adventure and I wanted her to go, even without me. She couldn't stay in Gloucester any more than I could live in Hamilton. I told her I'd join her as soon as I could, as soon as I was all better.

I still thought that way, that I could get better—all better. That I could recover, dump the drugs, and move on. I wasn't about to surrender and sit quietly in a pale-colored room with a pill tray and Muzak. It took me years to understand that the only way to recover from the disease is to greet it each morning and raise a lithium toast every night. I didn't want that. I wouldn't listen. I wanted to pitch the pills and go off with Roberta. But deep down, I knew I needed the quiet of Dogtown and the Witch House and time. I still needed my medicines.

By the early 1980s Manhattan's Lower East Side was a mess of empty, burned-out buildings, rubble, and crack houses. Tompkins Square Park resembled a refugee camp, a tent city full of the homeless. Real estate speculators had abandoned their properties and so the city condemned the empty tenements and took possession. It wasn't worth investing in these buildings at the height of the AIDS and crack epidemics. They weren't saleable. They weren't worth fixing. The city was stuck and it blocked up the tenement doorways and windows; it deterred squatters and drug dealers by demolishing stairs and trashing the roofs.

It didn't work. There was a critical lack of housing in New York and, what's more, a critical lack of frontier left in America. Squatters had a reason, a grand cause, to further their adventure. Advance troops crawled through back windows until the squats established themselves, had a critical mass of occupants. Then the sledgehammers came out, the agitprop posters and spray cans. The squat symbol—a circle bisected by a zigzag arrow— announced the new neighbors; a poster told the city YOUR HOUSE IS MINE. The neighborhood had dozens of squats by the time we arrived.

It was late September when I drove Roberta and her belongings down. Her college friends, John and Pete, lived in a fledgling squat on Thirteenth Street, between Avenues A and B. It was hard to miss. The old tenement's brick front was covered with wheat-pasted agitprop posters, defiant slogans, and great swoops of punk graffiti. Its first-floor windows were barricaded with cinder blocks and its metal front door was battered and streaked with rust. To the building's left was Life Squat, to its right Camouflage building, then Squat Theater, and then Sucker's Hole, all of them fortified bunkers filled with politicos, artists, and punks.

A handful of grubby people were smoking next door on the stoop when we arrived. The only clean person on the stoop, the only one without a dust mask dangling from his neck, stood as we approached. He wore camo and combat boots and his hair was hacked into a blunt pageboy.

"Who are you?" he said. "Are you here to see someone?"

"We're here to see Pete and John in 537. We're friends," Roberta said. "Who are you?"

"He's John the Commie," someone said, and then laughed. "Don't mind him. He gives speeches while we do the work."

"Fuck off," John the Commie said. "I work same as you." He turned to us. "Yeah, okay. I think they're inside." He went out to the street and hollered up at the broken windows. "John, Pete, are you up there?" There was a shout and we waited for revolutionaries to pull back the barricades. But there weren't any liberated masses, just another guy covered in plaster, with a big grin and heavy black glasses all white with the dust.

"Berta, hey, Berta. Come in, come in." He slapped me on the back. "I'm John." We walked toward the back and on up a dark stairwell. It was cold inside and dank like a tomb. It was a five-story cave. We got to the fourth floor and John proudly welcomed us into his space. It was windowless and illuminated with Catholic saint candles. A radio played opera and a large tub of wet plaster covered the table. "I put some red into the mix," he said. "It makes for a nice salmon color, don't you think?" It was beautiful and John was beaming. We all were.

"Alex lives upstairs on the fifth," John said. "Come on, I'll introduce you. He was the first guy in here. He's been here all summer." We climbed up. John put his shoulder to the door and it opened out into the back half of the building. Most of the walls were gone, including, I noticed, the main weight-bearing wall. Rubble was everywhere—piles of lathe, tile, and horsehair plaster. Most exterior walls were stripped to gray mortar and red brick. The roof was bad and much of the room was wet. There was pigeon shit in the far corners and glass crunched underfoot, but the room's center was swept and Alex had pitched his blue dome tent in the clearing.

"Alex. Hey, Alex," John called. "Are you in there?" The tent rustled. "Alex, I want you to meet a friend from Boulder. She's going to stay here for a while."

The tent moved again; a flap unzipped and Alex crawled out with a groan. "Alex is an anthropologist. From Princeton," John whispered. He looked the part. Alex wore a graying beard, round wire glasses, and a pained expression. We sat on folding metal chairs arranged around a milk crate and plywood table, a stack of books, two cook pots, and a gas camp stove.

"So, you opened this building up?" I asked.

"Yes."

"Wow," I said. "That's something." He nodded. "John says you're working on your doctorate."

Alex narrowed his eyes. He seemed surprised I knew the term. "Yes, a doctorate," replied Alex. Silence. Alex didn't have much to say. If there had been a campfire, he would have pushed at it with a stick.

Finally John sprang up. "Okay. Well, I just wanted you guys to meet."

"Did you give them a key?" Alex asked.

"Not yet."

"Humpf," commented Alex. "How many keys do we have?"

John walked toward the door, waved him off, and said, "Plenty." Out on the landing he confided, "It's not that Alex doesn't trust people. I think he just envisioned a more pure experience. He's writing his anthropology thesis and I think he wanted a kind of proving ground."

"Without people?" Roberta asked.

"No, without us. Rich white kids."

"You mean," I clarified, "kids that go to Princeton." John smiled. "Besides," I said, "we're broke. We're not rich."

"Yes, we are," replied John. "Take a walk down to Tompkins Square." He smiled. "We're loaded."

Roberta asked, "So who else lives here?"

"Nobody right now. The front half of the building is pretty much trashed," John said as we stood on the landing. "The third has no flooring and the second is full of rubble from the third. The roof's bad on the fifth-floor front. The front of the fourth floor is pretty much fine. You could live there, I suppose. Or not. It needs a lot of work." In the meantime John set up a futon for Roberta in a spare room. There were plenty of spare rooms. That's all there was: rubble and spare rooms. I carried in all her things and headed back in the morning, back to my rattled mind, my spooky house, and my medicines.

The squat was thrilling. It was one huge adventure and I knew I would move. I figured in two months I'd be right, strong enough to drop the pills and sweep up Roberta and live in New York. I found an old broken coal stove back in the woods and dragged it out. It was perfect for the squat. Its body was rotted but all the castings were good—the door, base, and top. I bent some sheet metal, doubled it up with rivets, and fitted it with stove cement. I wrote well-organized, lamentably sane love letters to Roberta and eventually convinced us both: I was well.

My therapist was another matter. "David, I'm not sure New York City is the best place for you now. A squat in New York City is, well…" She trailed off, shaking her head. "You need quiet and security, David." I thanked her and never went back.

What do these doctors know, I thought, all careful and ordered and rich? They argued against excitement, curiosity, and joy. Rest comfortably, sit still, and listen to Mozart. Drink tea and nap and accept your recovery one day at a time. I'd lost my father to depression. I had lost my faith, squandered my education, lost my job, and lost Daphne. I'd lost my mind. And now, now the doctors wanted to shut out the world. I wasn't about to lose that. I gave their fucking convalescence sixty more days. If I wasn't fixed by then I'd never be fixed. I needed a project beyond my own skull. I wanted a place where I could prove useful and competent and sane. I needed New York and the squats. And mostly I needed Roberta. I missed her terribly.

I gave Nadia notice. I ate the last of my meds and let the prescriptions run out. It took a few weeks to adjust; I had trouble sleeping but pushed through. I didn't go crazy. I'd proven that madness was not in the wings. I was cured, I figured. I was fine, a little jumpy and nervous but that was all right. It was just the old jitters, and so I bought a bag of dope. I bought some flowers for my mother and drove home to Hamilton. I woke my dad. He sat at the kitchen table in his bathrobe. I told them both I was leaving, that I was moving to New York City.

"But, David, you just got home. You haven't recovered. You can't leave now and you certainly shouldn't go to New York City. What's in New York City?"

"Roberta's down there."

"You mean that nice girl we met over in Rockport?"

"Lanesville. That's right, Mom. She's working with an advocacy group down there. For the homeless."

"I liked her," Mom said. "She's very nice."

"Is it with a church?" my father asked hopefully. "What organization is she with?"

"Well . . . she's not with an organization. It's more grassroots."

There was an awkward pause. My father narrowed his eyes. "Grassroots. How do you mean, grassroots?"

"Really grassroots," I admitted, stalling. They kept watching me. "Okay, okay. I'll level with you guys. She's squatting."

"Squatting," my father said.

"Yes. There's a bunch of empty buildings down in the city and the homeless are everywhere. We'll be fixing up apartments for them."

"Like Habitat for Humanity."

"Right, Dad. It's like that. I'm a carpenter and they need me down there. I've got a place to stay and friends. Don't worry," I said, "they need me down there."

"Well, Betty Lee, I think this sounds interesting. I think we should pray about this."

"Yeah, Dad, by all means, pray. This project needs all the help it can get. That's why I'm leaving tomorrow." I had dinner and then I kissed them and said I'd be back. "I'll just be in New York," I said. "It's not like I'm going to Guatemala." No one smiled.

I was pretty pleased with myself. I'd played it just right. I was working for the common good, just like Jimmy Carter and Habitat. As far as my father was concerned, I was back on the job building the Kingdom of Heaven, that shining city on a hill. I had my Dad's blessing, and what's more, I'd told him the truth.

At its best the squatting movement was visionary, a shining intentional community covered in dust. America has a long history of utopian social experiments and the squats were rooted in that tradition. We didn't have rolling lawns and gardens like the Transcendentalists; we didn't host salons in the sitting room; we had punks instead of Shakers; but it was utopian, experimental, and brave. The Lower East Side's squats were vital and sudden and all at once past.

I was needed down there, I knew that. 537 remained a near-empty shell. It needed more people and especially more carpenters. I visited most weekends. I always had tools and sometimes some scavenged lumber or doors. When I pulled up, before I even parked, Roberta and I hauled the saws and power cords up to her room and locked them away. I met Bill on one of my first visits. Roberta and I were resting on the stoop when he walked up. He was tall, loud, and exasperated. He was dusty. We were all perpetually dusty. I was already dusty.

"Who's this?" he asked Roberta.

"That would be my boyfriend, David. David, Bill."

Bill looked me over, whistled, and shook his head. "He'll never make it." He smiled.

"We'll see," Roberta said. "Jury's out." The three of us talked for a bit about the building, the work it demanded, and all of its characters. Before long Bill commenced pacing.

"Look," he said. "I need help. I've got to move Paula over here. She'll be good for the building, don't worry. She's all right. I mean she's all right but she can't stay where she is. The fucking roof's half-caved. She doesn't get it. She just doesn't get it. It's getting cold."

"Okay," I said. "Let's just go get her." We walked over to Eighth for Paula and I felt useful and fine. I was already needed.

We stopped at C Squat, another squat plastered with broadsides. Bill hollered up at the building, calling out various names. A head full of dust in full mask and goggles appeared from an upper window. "I've come to get Paula," Bill yelled. "From next door. I'm Bill from 537." The dust mask waved, ducked inside, and returned with some keys. Bill caught them and we let ourselves in.

The building's layout was similar to 537's but they had electricity. White romex wire hung from bent nails along the stairwell, ceramic sockets were pigtailed, and bulbs illuminated the stairs. Power cords ran everywhere. The place smelled of bleach and urine. "Paula's not exactly in this building," Bill explained. "These guys started freaking her out so she moved herself next door." He looked down halls at every landing. "They say this building's full, but Christ, there's tons of space in here. They could shovel that space out, no problem." Bill was fed up with most of his fellow squatters. "They have no work ethic," he muttered. "Look at that. Wasted space. Throw up some Sheetrock and boom. Two days. Plenty of room."

I followed him back through the vacant fifth floor. He stopped at an empty window frame and pointed across the airshaft. "She's over there."

"You're kidding me." Two two-by-ten boards stretched from the windowsill over a five-story drop and into a window next door. A two-by-four ran from the top of the windows as a rail.

"It's a bit tricky, but it's safe," Bill said. He stopped in the window and appraised me. "You're a carpenter, right? Just some staging here."

"She lives over there?"

"I said it wasn't good. It's kind of a siege situation. She can pull back the planks if she feels threatened."

I scoffed. "No, she can't. She'd drop them for sure. Then what?"

"She'd have to use the fire escape. The stairs are bad and the front's blocked up. Like I say, it's not good." Bill called across, "Paula! You in there?"

A voice warbled across, a sort of muffled patrician voice. "Yes. Who is it? Who's calling?" It sounded as if Katharine Hepburn were trapped under rubble.

"It's Bill. All right, Paula? I'm coming over. Okay?"

"Oh, yes, Bill. Please do." Bill ducked through the window and out onto the boards. He turned. "I think you should wait until I get across." I hesitated and he shook his head. "You're a carpenter, right?" I nodded. Sure, I was a carpenter and I'd built plenty of staging, but this wasn't staging, just two sketchy planks shot full of knots and pushed over a death trap. Bill made it across and glanced back with encouragement. "Don't worry," he said. "She doesn't have much furniture."

The roof had indeed collapsed. Blue sky fell through broken timbers and glanced off bright plaster and red broken bricks. Paula sat in a bed made up of blankets, back in the corner where the roof remained sound. A box of pastels lay beside her and she had a large sketchbook on her lap. She had pinned bright scarves and sheets to the beams; great swoops of color covered what plaster remained. Pigeons fluttered in the corners and dust swirled through great shafts of cold sun. Bill smiled at me. It was a magnificent ruin, epic. The enormity of our project loomed all around us in the broken November light. It was London after the Blitz.

Paula sat in her bed and waved to us cheerfully. "Oh, Bill, really. There's no need for this. I'm perfectly fine." She looked fine, too, smiling amid all the wreckage. Her hair was orange and full of tangling spikes and dark roots. "Really," she said, looking toward me, "he's making a fuss over nothing." But Bill was emphatic and by the end of the day 537 had another starry-eyed tenant. We scavenged plywood, covered most of the third-floor front joists, and piled Paula's belongings there. It was a cave compared to Paula's windswept nest over on Eighth but we framed up some makeshift walls and made her place safe. It wasn't dramatic. It didn't express Paula's creativity. But Paula couldn't stay in her own art installation—not for long. None of us can.

I moved down in midwinter. I couldn't handle my own art, my poetry. I couldn't witness my astonished mind linking strange words, jumping from image to faraway meanings. I couldn't allow that. I couldn't sit in a quiet room and scratch at a notebook. I'd go crazy alone. I wasn't scared of the squats; I was scared of my mind. I could live with anarcho-punks, the dispossessed, the wild and odd. I didn't need electricity or plumbing, a lease or security. I knew the squat would save me from thinking, from my pretty games of artsy roulette, and I was right. The work was constant and demanding both physically and socially. Every day in the squats brought a crisis or a party, usually both.

Bill and I were carpenters, John was a mason, and English Steve was a plasterer and jack-of-all-trades. All of us, everyone in the building, hauled rubble. We were all makeshift plumbers and electricians and Oliver Twists. I felt needed and necessary at 537. The squats were an insane kind of wonderful circus. By contrast I was calm, logical, and competent. If I had been surrounded by accountants and manicured lawns I would have gone mad. In the squats that troubled soul Dave was just Dave, a pretty good carpenter. I avoided the self-styled leaders, the louder anarchists, and all of the Marxists. I avoided the paint-splattered Artists, our requisite radical priest, and anyone else wearing a beret. I'd preached all my manifestos out west and in hospitals. I just wanted to work.

I built a small one-room apartment for Roberta and me. I pulled the lumber from various uninhabited spaces in the building and bought the insulation and Sheetrock. We had a bed, a few chairs, and a table. I replaced half an air shaft window with plywood and cut a hole for a galvanized stovepipe. I pushed it up to the roof and wired it to the parapet. The little coal stove I salvaged heated our tiny home beautifully. Roberta and I fell in love in a small, quiet room during wartime; it was simple and safe and all that we needed.

Outside our apartment door was chaos, a hollowed-out building with half-crazy comrades and piles of rubble and hope. Bill, Paula, English Steve, Cathy—these are the friends I've kept all my life. Past the squats, past Umbrella and Foetus and Glass House and Bullet and Life, the city got cold and crack-headed and desperately sad. Beyond that was New England, the ocean and woods and my family. I called my mother weekly and she was too scared to say it out loud—that something was wrong, that my father was gone and that she was alone. I knew it, of course, I knew how deathly it was, but I was weak. I couldn't stand watch at the wake and sometimes I felt glad she was quiet, glad she couldn't ask me to stand.

I kept busy hauling buckets of water and scavenging firewood from the city. Every morning I ventured out into the icebox building with a framing hammer and stripped lathe from the walls. I'd watch my breath frost in the cold, dim rooms and feel vaguely heroic, a backwoodsman in downtown Manhattan. It was strangely gratifying—burning my house down for heat. At first it was easy; I just opened our door and tore lathe from the hall. Later on I scavenged up and down through the building with everyone else. Half-inch strips of century-old pine burn hot and fast. Our room was toasty with the teakettle steaming in just minutes. The nights, however, were long and cold and we hoarded whatever hardwood scraps we could find. I always checked the Dumpster outside a nearby furniture shop but word spread and everyone hit it and that source got dicey.

The air shaft between 537 and our sister squat, 535, was nothing more than a chimney. Stovepipes pushed through windows on both sides, some cocked and angling up the building, some belching straight out. From the roof the shaft looked positively Dickensian, dangerous and makeshift and blanketed in smoke. All of it was a flagrant and crazy code violation. The entire condemned building was a flagrant and crazy code violation and no one seemed overly concerned. The city had bigger problems than us in 1986. The squat movement was militantly anti-crack and its drug stance created unlikely and critical alliances. Squatters proved to be the lesser of two evils. The cops and the neighbors preferred squats to empty tenements left open to dealers and addicts. Punks hauling buckets of rubble were amusing and harmless compared to the alternatives.

Firemen caused greater alarm than cops. We knew the fire department could shut us down fast. I was alone on the stoop when the fire chief stepped up and flipped out his badge. "Fire chief. Listen, I'm gonna need to inspect this...this place. Do you live here?"

"Maybe," I said.

"Can you let me in?"

"No. You're a cop."

He rolled his eyes. "I'm not a cop. I'm a fireman. You guys need firemen, believe me." I sat silently and looked past him. "Listen, I don't give a rat's ass if you guys are in there. It's none of my business. I don't own the building. I'm just trying to keep you from burning down the block." I sat weighing my options. No one else was around. The chief's face darkened. "Okay? You can just let me in, we'll do a little walk-through, and that will be that. Or I can condemn this fricking firetrap—*again*—and let the city come in."

"Damn," I said, "I guess I don't have a choice."

"That's right, kid. You don't."

I felt like a Judas. I broke the squat's most fundamental law, opened the door and let the man enter. We walked into the cold dark and for once I was glad we had no electricity. He couldn't see much and if we had had electricity it would have been bootleg.

"No juice?" he asked.

"No."

"What do you use?"

"Flashlights, just flashlights," I lied pathetically. There were candles and pools of old wax all up the stairwell. I took him to my room. At least I knew our stove was properly installed—properly enough for an illegal stove in a squatted building. I opened the door and there it was, my patched-up, darling little coal stove.

The chief's jaw dropped. He looked at me and then walked over to a window. When he saw all the pipes he shook his head and began laughing softly. "You've got to be shitting me."

"I mean we do have buckets of water," I said helpfully.

He shook out a cigarette and lit it. "No you fucking don't. You don't even have plumbing. Christ." He thought for a moment. "Look, I'll tell you what. Get some fire extinguishers, for Christ's sake. Get some buckets of sand and have them on every landing." I nodded and he walked to the stairs. I hesitated. "Are you gonna let me out or what?" What? That was it? I couldn't believe it. I figured he'd return with all the right paperwork, two trucks, and some axes, but he never did. He was just curious, a sightseer.

We snaked power cords over the roof from Life Squat for our tools and occasional light. That got ridiculous fast, so we pooled our money and paid a guy named Irish Mike three hundred dollars to fix things. He came drunk but highly recommended. He jumped down the manhole out front and in ten minutes he jacked Con Ed juice right into the building. We ran wire all over the building, lit the place up like Times Square, and Con Ed never even blinked.

We never did get plumbing. There were vile, fermenting piss buckets on every floor. We took turns carrying them out and dumped them down storm drains. It was a nasty job and slackers avoided it. For the rest we strategically visited local restaurants. Eventually, a particularly brave group of volunteers cleared our building's main drain so we could manually flush toilets with buckets. We had the hydrant out front for clean water. My friend English Steve, a longtime squatter, had scored an apartment on Fourteenth. He handed out keys to everyone from 537 and we took showers there regularly, day and night.

By midsummer the building was well-established; there were actual, bona fide homeless wanting in, not just punks and politicos but dispossessed families. The building was filling up and we needed more room. So began a major drive to repair the roof and make the front of the building safe and habitable. Bill found the timbers needed for roof joists next to a Pentecostal Spanish church six blocks away.

"It's simple," he said. "There's a pile of them—ten-by-four beams. They got to be twenty-four, twenty-six feet long. They're just laying there." Five or six of us sat on the stoop and watched Bill catch his breath. He was excited.

"Are you saying we should just steal them?"

Bill grabbed at his hair. "Well, we're not going to buy them."

"All right," I said, "but where we gonna hide them?"

Bill grabbed at his hair again. "On the fucking roof, of course. Look, we build a lookout, you know, with a block and tackle and winch them right up. Seventh Street's got a block and tackle. I know it."

"What the hell is a lookout?"

"Whatever. You know. A thing we can lag the block to and stick out, over the street."

"You can't lay it on that parapet," John said. "It'll let go. I wired it in but it sways. Dangerous as hell."

Any ethical issues, any church robbery qualms, were soon trumped by our righteous cause, the Homeless—the college-educated, middle-class Homeless. We were down to the nuts and bolts of the operation now. Bill and I walked down to the church with a thirty-foot tape and the beams measured fine. We stopped at Seventh, yelled up, and got our hands on the block and tackle.

We stole the first beam just before dawn. We walked up empty Avenue A with it on our shoulders, the four of us bent and quiet like strange reverse penitents. I thought of my parents: how they prayed for me, my father's misplaced pride in his son doing the Lord's work. I started awkward, superstitious prayers in my head. First I apologized for stealing the church's wood and asked for forgiveness. Failing that, I began justifying the mission. My father taught me that nothing else mattered but the Kingdom of God. Forget money, forget career; just work toward the Kingdom. Well, this is it, God, I said, 537's all the purpose I've got. That angle failed, too, and then I just prayed we wouldn't get caught. I prayed the whole fucking rig wouldn't come down on our heads.

Three more trips and we had all the beams we needed stacked on our sidewalk. We rousted the squat. We cordoned the sidewalk and cut off the traffic like the Army Corps of Engineers. A group of onlookers formed across the street and a dozen or more people inspected our knots. We moved fast before cops showed. Four of us pulled the thick rope across the street and hauled off. Steve and John balanced the beam and kept it from swinging out into parked cars. The beam tipped and swung vertical but the rope bit into the wood and held fast. We stood in a crowd of dealers, squatters, and neighbors and pulled hand over hand fast. John and Steve appeared above the wobbly parapet, and people screamed directions in English and Spanish as they grabbed hold and swung the beam over and onto the roof. The street broke into cheers. We had them all up by ten a.m. and rebuilt the roof in three days.

By winter, small areas of the squat were almost comfortable. We found a massive potbellied stove and installed it downstairs near the front door, creating a kind of parlor. The stove was four feet across and the iron cast in an ornate Victorian design. We cut a sink into plywood counters for a common kitchen. We held our meetings around a large table and scavenged several cushioned chairs. The meetings were endlessly democratic: any ridiculous suggestion and every paranoid objection could hijack the table for hours. I felt reasonable at these meetings, even staid.

The question of James came up at one winter meeting. James was in his sixties, a dignified black man who always wore the same dark suit. His manners were impeccable. James was the calmest, most philosophical member of the squat, a grandfather figure to Roberta and me. Most mornings Roberta and I found him downstairs. We bought him coffee, he offered us cigarettes, and we sat together, quietly smoking by the stove. But James had been allowing strangers into the building and I was elected to suss out the situation, to reason with James before he was bounced.

"So, James," I started one morning. "There's been a lot of coming and going from your room. People we don't know."

He smiled. "Oh, them? Those folks are my friends, my ladies."

"Your ladies? What are they, living there?" I glanced over at Roberta, who smirked at me. "I mean, why are there so many different people coming and going?"

James's eyes narrowed. "You've seen them?"

"Not really," I admitted. "But lots of us have. It's come up at the meetings."

"Look," James said. "Those ladies are my friends. They have a little business, it's true, but it's not what you think." I looked at him expectantly. "They sell feminine items. Tampons and condoms and such. Hygiene items."

"Ah, come on, James." I sighed. "It's got to stop. You've got crackheads and who knows what coming in here. They're prostitutes."

"They're my friends," he said plaintively. "The women take care of me." James didn't do drugs, he didn't even drink, and he wasn't a pimp. He was just getting by, I figured, getting a little money for the use of his room. But it was stupid and dangerous, a complete breach of security.

"It's done now, James. It has to be. It stops now or you'll be thrown out. No drugs, no crackheads, no whores. That's the deal." For once it was me. In the lunatic squats mine was a voice of reason. I was still sick with denial and stoned on my street medicine. I hadn't transformed so much as adapted, changed my surroundings to suit my own illness, but I was listened to, respected. James stopped all the nonsense and he stayed and we were happy to have him. James was a reasonable man, and somehow I was becoming one.

The squats had three rules: no violence, no theft, and no hard drugs. The first two were easy—any transgressor met with eviction. The last rule was tricky; it smacked of moral judgment; it made us like cops. Exceptions were made. The movement had its junkies but compared to the crackheads they seemed harmless. Junkies entertain themselves quietly for hours. Our resident addict was Flowers, a black guy who kept to himself. He was useless for work and often bad-tempered but no one threw him out.

Evicting Flowers just promised a struggle and didn't seem worth it. Besides, he kept saying he was going home any day—back to South Carolina—and one day he just left.

Crack and cocaine were different. The rule was immediate expulsion, no second chances. Crack promised instant psychosis and almost immediate trouble. The radical priest sent Charles to us. "He's got a job working maintenance," the priest said. "He just needs a place. He's clean." We had our doubts but moved him onto the fourth floor. Charles wasn't clean. The man aged visibly in a matter of weeks. His cracked eyes glittered fiercely and then went sticky and dead. He moved past our rooms muttering scripture and hellfire. He knew dark scraps of my childhood: the jealous, angry God who leveled Sodom and struck Lot's wife into salt, Satan's foul pit, and six six six. Beyond his religious psychosis and crack there were questions of hygiene. Charles barbecued chicken backs on a grill in his room almost nightly. He left the bones outside his door on the slate stairway landing. "For the cats," he said. Every other night I threw burnt chicken backs into the air shaft. I slipped on the grease. It stank.

"Fucking Charles," I complained at a meeting. "He's still cooking his chicken, smokes up the whole floor. It's monoxide. I've got headaches from it. He won't answer his door anymore but I know he's in there. He could suffocate."

"So what if he chokes?" Bill said grimly. "That's his business. It's the chicken bones. They're drawing rats."

"You don't live next to him. It's nasty." I threw up my hands. "And now he's decided I'm the Devil, the fricking Antichrist." People laughed. "I'm serious. He starts screaming about the Antichrist every time he sees me."

"It's just the crack," Bill said.

"So what if it's the crack? He's psychotic. He probably got wooden stakes and is just waiting to use them. I mean the guy's dangerous."

"All right," Steve said. "Let's throw him out. We need to throw him out, that's all." He stood up.

"What?" I said, backing off. "Right now? It's past midnight. Where's he going to go?"

Steve shrugged his shoulders. "Who cares?" That was just it; no one cared. Everyone knew we were his last chance, the last safety net before the street, madhouse, and prison. None of that mattered anymore; it hadn't for weeks. Charles was crazy as hell and we were scared of him. That's the only reason he'd lasted this long.

"Look," I said. "Let's talk to him in the morning. See how it is." This plan relieved everyone. It seemed sensible but when morning came we avoided each other and, above all, avoided Charles.

A few weeks passed. Roberta was away, it was late, and I had been drinking by the big stove with Bill and English Steve. I climbed up the stairs drunk, kicked the chicken bones at Charles's door, and stopped at the floor's common toilet. Charles's door banged open and he came out screaming, "Satan, you're Satan!" I looked out from the bathroom and saw him slash at the air with a large metal crucifix. "Damien, you're Damien!" he screamed. "The Devil. The Last Days have come." He charged at me, pushing the cross in my face like some psychotic priest. "You're the fucking Antichrist!" He swung the crucifix and I caught him by the wrist and spun him into a wall. He weighed about as much as a doll. He sat for a moment, winded, the horsehair plaster falling down into his hair. I heard the others coming and zipped up my jeans. My hand was bleeding, some skin torn away by the cross. Charles jumped and bolted back into his room.

My friends and I huddled on the landing and agreed on eviction, immediate and final. I was the sane one now and I wanted the crazies gone. They had the virus; I was susceptible and I didn't want it. Whatever empathy I once had, whatever insights I claimed, disappeared. I had no compassion now. My fear and anger had boiled it off. Charles wasn't my problem. I wanted Charles out in the street, knocked out and quiet on the cold fucking pavement.

Billy banged on his door. "Okay, Charles. It's all right. The Devil's gone. We got rid of the Devil." He smiled at me and I held up my fingers like horns. "Come on, Charles. We need to talk about this. I mean, what the fuck? Dave's not Satan. He's not even Damien. How'd you get that idea? I mean think about it." Bill pulled on a Guinness. "His name is Dave, not Damien. Okay, Charles? Dave." We stood there waiting in the dark. The adrenaline was wearing off. We stood making nervous jokes and banged on Charles's door every few minutes. Someone got beer.

Then Charles stepped out fast. He'd swapped the cross for a baseball bat and ran past us and into the front swinging. "Fucking fire!" he yelled. "Fire! The Lord's flames and let's burn the fuck down. God's judgment is fire!" We stood for a moment, dumbstruck. "We need oxygen. Air for the fire and flames!" Then Charles ran at the front windows and bashed them out in a line. When he pushed his head out through the last window and started screaming out to the street, three of us pulled him down into the glass. Bill twisted an arm and kneeled on his back.

"He's out," I said. "Now." Charles started screaming again.

"Shouldn't we call someone?"

"Fuck no! He's out now."

Charles quieted when we pulled him to his feet. His arms and hands were cut and bleeding. We dragged him down to the street and a police radio squawked. We told the foot cop what happened, what the noise was, and he smiled down at Charles. "Sometimes," he said, "sometimes you just gotta kick people off the bus." He barked an address into the radio. Somewhere Charles had family—maybe a mother who took him to church, a brother or sister or someone. But I wasn't his brother. I wasn't family and I wished him good riddance. Paula ran up and gathered his things but by the time she returned the squad car was gone. She stood there with us, holding a plastic bag stuffed with cloth.

The cold was brutal that second winter and Roberta and I agreed to break up the siege. Our apartment cost nothing; I'd earned some cash and our space was secure. Roberta wanted to go down to Nicaragua and pick coffee with Sandinistas for a few months. I supported the Sandinistas but had little interest in picking their coffee. In truth, I was sick of New York's endless outrage, and Roberta's solidarity group promised more of the same. Instead, I kicked around Mexico and traveled down to Belize. I went back to the Tackle Box and claimed my computer. My novel had grown even worse in my absence. Roberta sent postcards from Nicaragua with cute, impoverished children on them. She sent me Neruda poems. I couldn't wait to get home. I got back before her, sometime in March. It was beautiful, walking from the subway stop on Fourteenth. The city even smelled good, cold and clean. Steve and a young punk were on the stoop when I arrived. Steve hugged me, ridiculed my tan, and introduced me to Misty.

"She's staying in Charles's old space."

"How is it, Steve?" I asked. "Is it okay?"

"Good, man, good. It's been smooth. Just the usual paranoia. Nothing's really happened since you've been gone. Are you back now for a while?"

I nodded. "Roberta will be back in a week or so."

"Okay, well, your room's still there. No one's in it. I think Paula may have stored some stuff in there, that's all."

Someone started yelling from deep within the building. It got closer and louder until Bill flew out, clear past the stoop, waving a three-pound sledge. "Flowers! In the air shaft. It's Flowers. We found him."

"Nah," I said. "He's in Carolina or something."

"No. He's not. He's in the air shaft. I mean I think it's him." We stared at him. "Really. Deb's been bashing out cinder blocks in the back. Her windows. There's a body out there. First we saw its hand. But now it's Flowers. He's totally fucking dead."

"Shit."

"He never went anywhere. He's been—hey, Dave, you're back—anyway, he's been frozen out there all fucking winter. Christ." Bill started pacing and working his hands, clenching and unclenching his fists. Deb came out and stood very still. She was beautiful as she stood in the door with long purply black hair and a crowbar.

"It's him," she confirmed quietly.

Bill jumped. "We've got to get him inside," he said, and started up the steps.

"What?" I said. "Are you fucking crazy? We can't move the body."

"Well, we can't just leave him there laying in the trash. I'm moving him." Steve and I reasoned with him. "What are you going to do?" asked Bill. "Call the cops?"

"Damn straight we call the cops," I said. "Nine-one-one. What do you want to do? Bury him?"

Deb said, "I think we need to call the coroner or something." Misty ran inside.

"Whatever," Bill said. "He's coming inside." Steve grabbed him by the sleeve and talked him down.

I went back in. I guess it was Flowers; his face was bloated and obscured by bricks. It was still cold and he didn't smell too bad, just a sickly sweet hint in the wet brick air. Squatters were peering down from the windows above the air shaft. Bill came in with the sledge and knocked out the remaining blocks, and then we knew it was Flowers. His arms were clutched across his chest like he had tried to keep warm.

"Well, I'm calling the cops," Deb said. "Does anyone know his real name?"

We shrugged. "Just Flowers," Steve said.

I walked out to the stoop and noticed a plainclothes cop across the street. He had to be a cop—he was wearing a trench coat and staring straight at our building. He stood, lit a cigarette, and crossed the street. Already? I thought. They knew about Flowers already? Impossible.

"Hey, pal," he said—he'd seen all the movies; he used all the language. "I'm a private eye. Here's my card." I took it and he pulled a snapshot out of his coat. "Have you ever seen this girl before?" The Misty I met had ragged black hair and torn clothes. This one had blond hair, a corsage, and a prom date with acne. The detective blew a fleck of tobacco from his tongue. "Her parents back in Ohio are looking for her. They miss her. She's their little girl. Just seventeen. Well?" I looked at the ground. He knew damn well I had just been sitting here talking to her.

"No," I said. "I've never seen her before in my life."

"Yeah, sure." He frowned momentarily and then brightened. "Hey, I hear you have a stiff over here?"

"Where'd you hear that?" He looked at me and smiled again. "Yeah, all right. So what's it to you?"

"Mind if I take a look?" He stood. "I haven't seen a stiff in a long while." And then he was in. I ran upstairs to find Misty but she was already gone, up over the roof and down through Life. The detective had his look with the rest of us and then left.

Half an hour passed and then four policemen knocked. They seemed irritable, looked at the body, and shrugged as if to say we should have buried him there, gone back to work, and saved them the trouble. Their radios hissed and cracked and it was strange to hear them.

"Okay," one of the cops said. "The coroner's office has been notified. He needs to sign a death certificate before the wagon can come. It takes a while. He's a busy man and gets backed up. We'll post a policeman here until the body is picked up." That was it. No investigation was necessary. Three of the cops left and the unlucky one stood in the back by the rank air shaft and waited. Deb got him a chair. She lit some candles. The word got around and some neighborhood friends showed up and filed past. Quite a few squatters came through, grave and curious and dry-eyed. Flowers always said he had family back in South Carolina but no one found a license or ID or letter in his room. No one knew his name. The city pulled him from the shaft about one in the morning.

When Roberta got back we drove home to Gloucester. It was high summer and we camped near the cove, along beaches and the edges of Dogtown. Every few weeks I headed back to the city for small jobs with Steve or Bill, but our time there was closing. Roberta and I gave up our room at the squat and took an apartment by Plum Cove. Paying rent was an adjustment; by January we were broke and I went back to the city for a quick little job on Wall Street, snipping tin studs and building cubicles. I slept out back on the first floor, across from Flowers's ghost. The room was used for storage, just an icebox without a stove. I found a thin, ragged electric blanket, stuffed it into my sleeping bag, and plugged it in every night.

Weeks passed and I had a dream. I heard screams and then more, and then I heard the word "fire." John the Commie's voice came across the air shaft and snapped me awake. "Come on, you guys. I'm not kidding. It's a big fire. Fire! Get the fuck up!" People were running up and down stairs, banging on doors, rousting everyone. I could smell smoke. Out on the street we tried to count heads but it was useless. No one knew who slept where anymore. Fire trucks showed and shot water up into Life's fourth floor. John the Commie and his girlfriend started screaming at the firemen, calling them fascists and pigs. He said the fire was planned, a plot against the "movement." He pulled at their hoses and tried to block them from entering.

The fire had started in Dawn's room. She was a newcomer to Life Squat but she had been on the scene for years. Everyone knew her and sympathized with her. She'd been burned out of two squats and seemed so unlucky. Now we all knew she was crazy, clearly batshit, setting fires to her life and ours. She'd gone out and left her wood stove open, surrounded it with newspaper. John the Communist lived below her and his room was drenched. "Fucking Dawn," he said, and we all joined in. I stood in the dark winter air surrounded by friends. This time we couldn't blame the city or the government, gentrification, or yuppies. We were all crazy, every one of us.

I cashed in my winnings and went home to Roberta. I was finished. It wasn't the arson. Dawn's fire woke me up all right, but it was just another crisis in a long list of good stories. It was John the C's ugly reaction, the absurd and hateful tirade he unleashed on the firemen, that finished the squats for me. I saw all the changes we'd suffered since the cops drove the homeless from Tompkins Square, the movement's slow ugly warp. Tompkins Square was a police riot—they charged the tent city on horses swinging their clubs—but their violence infected us all. The park was fenced with barbed wire and shut down for years. Freedom and humor drained from the squats and the wide-open anachro-punk scene of the squats; its makeshift beauty, its art, was supplanted by riot, faction, and rage.

———

Fifteen years later I met English Steve and Bill at Mona's, our old bar around the corner. Roberta and I see Bill regularly and Steve's family visits often—we've all moved on—but on the barstools the old stories turned maudlin. The neighborhood had changed. A handful of squats went legal and now rate as homesteads, but most were evicted and turned into co-ops. Some burned. Steve wasn't sentimental and went home, but Bill and I missed the squats, our fearful and beautiful buildings, our youth falling wide open.

We walked down to 537. Our slogans were gone for good, power-washed from the brick, the battered metal door and cinder blocks refitted with window glass and wrought iron, locks and buzzers. There was plumbing inside and light bills and such. The place almost gleamed but the stoop was the same. We sat there like war buddies returned to Europe with the rubble all gone. Bill went across to the bodega for two bottles of Guinness. We put them in brown paper bags and twisted them tight at the neck. I was in New York on business. In a few hours I would be in a warehouse buying books, but for now we were squatters. We were back on the old stoop. I pushed on the first door and it opened, and so did the next—neither lock had clicked home.

It seemed way, way too bright in the stairwell. The old hallways were serious with their identical doors, and the place didn't smell right. It smelled of floor wax and order—like a high school, like we needed a hall pass. We crept up to the penthouse and pushed through to the roof. Now the roof, the roof was impressive. The owners had improved our improvements: nothing felt spongy; the parapet no longer swayed over the street; the knee-wall surrounding the air shaft had all its bricks.

"I wonder if they left our framing," Bill said. "Our framing was good. I mean it was up to code and everything. Those beams were way beefy enough." He finished his beer. "Definitely beefy."

"Oh yeah, most definitely beefy," I slurred, and stomped the roof.

"Quit fucking making noise!" Bill screamed. "We're gonna get caught."

"Oh, yeah," I said. "Right."

The buildings burned all around like constellations. At about three a.m. Bill turned and asked, "Did you prop the door? The penthouse door?"

"You were the last one out," I said, and walked back to the door. It was locked tight. We considered our options. The fire escape was no help; it stopped at the fifth-floor windows.

"That's doable," Bill said.

"What? It's a half-story drop."

"That's not a half story, not really." I looked at him. "It's not." Bill kneeled at the parapet and hung his head and arms down toward the street. "Look," he said, waving his hands for emphasis, "if you hang from the parapet down it's maybe a four-foot drop."

"You're out of your fricking mind," I said. "I'm not hanging off that parapet. Not that one. The building's not on fire."

"Tell you what. I'll drop down, then I'll come back and unlock the door."

"No, you're not. There's no way you're doing that. You're

drunk. I'm not letting friends jump off buildings drunk. Besides," I argued, "you won't get back in from the street."

"You think the door's locked?"

"All the fucking doors are locked."

Bill considered this. "Tell you what. I'll call Steve and see if he can get in. I'll wake him up." Steve wasn't answering his phone. No one answered their phone.

I tried the door again. "I give up," I said. "We'll just have to wait until dawn and then bang on the door."

Bill never quits. "You know," he said, "the fire escape out back goes right up to the roof. All we have to do is climb over the penthouse." He stepped up on the air shaft knee-wall, stretched, and just caught the penthouse roof. "I can do it. I can pull myself up."

"Well, I can't," I protested. "You're like two feet taller than me."

"I'll pull you up," Bill promised. "You give me an arm and I'll pull you up." And then he scrambled up. He disappeared for a moment and returned triumphant. "Yup. The back escape is doable."

"Doable? You mean it comes all the way up?"

"Yup." Bill lay down, braced himself, and reached over the edge. "Come on. Don't think about it." I cursed and grabbed on to his wrist with my right hand. He pulled and I hung by the air shaft. Bill kept pulling until I found a handhold and flipped a leg up onto the roof.

We got giddy. We dropped down to the back roof and raced down the escape, whooping and hollering past the windows of young bankers and web designers, past Alex, Charles, James, and Deb Lee. We cut through a lot, scaled a fence, and sat across the street laughing until squad cars arrived. Shit.

One of the cops stepped from his car and motioned at us. "Hey, you two. Someone reported two men on the fire escape. Did you see anything?"

"What?" I asked. "On the fire escape?"

"Yeah."

"No. But two guys did come from around back. They climbed the fence there and took off."

"Which way?"

I pointed east.

"Were they black? Hispanic?"

I shrugged and said I couldn't tell. "They were wearing hoods," Bill added helpfully.

The cops headed east and we ran west. Not much has changed. We were middle-class white guys and got away clean. We weren't as young or naïve but we were still game. I slept a few hours, slugged my lithium back with hot coffee, and drove down to the warehouse. I worked all day and loaded my truck, exhausted but happy. I had hundreds of books for my shop, and much more important, I had one last, ridiculous squat story. Trespassing on an East Village rooftop was pointless, locking myself out was stupid, and swinging over the air shaft was extremely dangerous. I am the father of two small children, Mary and Hunter, who need me. Roberta and my elderly parents need me. Hanging drunk off old squats is irresponsible and even selfish. But that delicate sway, that balance between the ridiculous and the reasonable, between crazy stories and dependable bookkeeping, is something I love, a gift that I've learned from my family and from our disease. We have our adventures, our stories and visions. It beats television. It beats selling insurance.

ELEVEN

After New York and the squats Roberta planned a career. We moved to western Massachusetts in 1990. I was stubborn; I held out for a calling. She entered graduate school while I cleaned gutters and remodeled basements. I wanted to write but couldn't sit still. I wanted to teach but I was too jumpy. That's how it was, I figured. I had to keep moving. I lacked clarity and purpose. All I had was excellent taste and dashed expectations. In short, I was a dope-smoking, nail-banging cynic. But I got lucky for a guy with no vision; a poet ran off and left me with his massive used-book shop out in the woods.

"You don't want this place," Jim told me. "Let the bank have it. Trust me. It's sinking. The Bookmill is a floundering ship on a pitch-black sea. Stormy sea. A black ship pitched on a stormy sea. Something like that. Anyway, it leaks money." He took my shoulder paternally.

"Listen," I said, "I appreciate your concern, but don't worry about the shop. I don't need to make a lot of money. I think I can make this work."

He shook his head. "All right, then. Suit yourself. I'm off to make a reasonable living in Florida."

"That sounds awful," I said, and Jim threw up his hands, climbed in his Peugeot, and drove south. Once again I was surrounded by unreasonable beauty: thousands of books lining the walls of a nineteenth-century gristmill on a trout stream in the middle of nowhere. I'd been working for Jim less than two months, but a combination of luck, fiscal impropriety, and landlord panic left my penniless coworker and me owning the shop: no money down, no capital, no real estate, just good books and a banknote. It was the perfect job for me, quixotic and pure and untainted by profit. My coworker and now business partner was even a card-carrying anarchist. We hosted readings, poetry slams, and concerts— chamber, folk, punk. We hosted a ukulele festival. We added a café and a fine restaurant moved in below us. There was a waterfall just past the windows, rising trout in the pools downstream, and books everywhere.

It was peaceful. It was lovely and the checkbook usually balanced, but I stayed jittery. I was anxious, scared to answer the phone, scared of my accountant, scared of Foucault and Derrida. The only place I stood still was in trout streams, calmed by water and the rhythm of casting. And then I had dope. I had been getting stoned regularly for twelve years, every day if I could swing it. I smoked alone in the woods, at parties, at work. It helped me stand television, tie trout flies, and stay in my skin. And then it stopped working. It no longer soothed my agitated mind; worse, it jump-started my worries and pushed them toward paranoia. I withdrew. I spent whole parties contemplating bone cancer and bankruptcy. I hadn't taken lithium since the Witch House but I knew how things stood; I knew my pot was lousy medicine. I pulled a psychiatrist's name out of the phone book and made an appointment. I walked in, laid out my family's history, and walked out with a prescription.

My parents decided to sell our old house in Hamilton. It's gotten too much for your mother, our father told us. It was too much for all of us. The worst of Dad's depression had passed by then, but the disease had ruined and haunted the place. I called in a thirty-yard Dumpster and dropped it just under the living room window. I sat my mother down in the kitchen with old photo albums, left my father sorting his library, and gleefully pitched everything meaningless straight out the window. The house was bulldozed three days later, replaced by a prefab estate. Landscapers cut the oak trees and mulched thirty years' worth of leaves.

My parents moved out to Saratoga Springs, New York, to be closer to Peniel. It took two years, but I finally convinced them to move closer to us, closer to Northampton. Jonathan Edwards is buried just down the road, I said. I helped Dad find a nice apartment downtown, close to the shops. My mother got involved with a church in the neighborhood. She painted hundreds of cute watercolor cards and sold them from the bookstore. Dad began teaching at the seminary again, part-time. He shuttled back and forth to the North Shore once a month or so, and his lectures were jammed. My father, brother, and I went to Idaho and fly-fished. We drove to the Catskills and flew into remote Maine camps. Dad was happiest, I think, when he was with us and fishing.

By 1994, I had proven my bookstore could fly through the fiscal trees indefinitely. My partner and I teamed with Roberta's sister Betsy and built a second bookstore nearby. Roberta had been teaching for years. I took my lithium, wrote poems, and fished. We were pretty near broke, happy and settled. And now we wanted a family. I was still in the theoretical, advance-planning stage when Roberta began scheduling the children's arrival. We discussed Roberta's teaching career and financial concerns; we discussed midwives, home birth, and hospitals; we considered names, circumcision, and high chairs. Frankly, my family's illness was just another question, a practical concern rather than a moral quandary. We had lithium, we had knowledge and love. I had Roberta, a solid Yankee with Finnish roots whose calm, self-possessed grace had saved me. I liked my chances with Roberta from the start, and they'd only improved.

We knew the odds. My family is a textbook example of manic depression's genetic link. We could have saved Gregor Mendel a great deal of trouble. Roughly 1 percent of the general population is bipolar. Studies are ongoing, of course—and statistics vary somewhat—but if one parent is bipolar the odds of a child inheriting the disease are much greater; the percentage rises 8 to 10 percent. If both parents are bipolar, the odds are much, much greater. Five percent of the general population has suffered from major depression. If one parent has experienced major depression before age twenty, their children's chance of depression rises to 30 percent. My children, Mary and Hunter, are ten times more likely to suffer bipolar illness than their schoolmates.

I hope they've won the gene pool lottery, that they don't carry my disease, but if they do I'll be ready. I've learned my own story and I'm not afraid.

I assured Roberta that I was ready for children. I was excited, I told her. I was ready except for one little thing: Patagonia. I was obsessed with the place. Blame Bruce Chatwin, I said, blame all the rivers, the millions of trout. It's now or never, I said, and I promised I'd return in a month. Patagonia wasn't a frantic bipolar decision; it was just a prolonged adolescent decision, and Roberta has never quite forgiven me for that trip. She was already pregnant but I pretended all questions of wisdom, fairness, and timing had been settled. Roberta read *What to Expect When You're Expecting* and I studied maps and read about rivers and South American mayfly hatches. I began tying flies.

"It says here the bugs are pretty much the same," I assured Roberta. "I bet I could get away with a parachute Adams, a Wooly Bugger, and some sulphurs." She shrugged and went back to her reading. "For nymphing I'll just use a gold ribbed Hare's Ear." She ignored me. Over the weeks, Roberta evinced less and less interest in angling minutiae. It was deflating. I turned back to my tying. I picked up some notebooks, a spare reel, and a rod, and I carefully packed a month's worth of lithium into my fly vest. I felt prepared. I felt reasonable. I told myself I deserved my grand trip, that I needed it.

I knew all along Patagonia was selfish, but one of the least attractive aspects of manic-depressives—even medicated, well-adjusted manic-depressives—is their deep, nearly bottomless capacity for narcissism. They claim to be theologians and poets. They write books explaining God's own will; they write poems, throw readings, and make people listen; they write memoirs. They leave their pregnant wives alone and embark on journeys of self-discovery. A simple fishing trip is never simple.

I'd forgotten all about trout by the time I got to LaGuardia. I started to panic. We were having a baby, an actual baby. It was already real and I was skipping town for a month, maybe forever. Patagonia was a brilliant metaphor for self-destruction, the last and loneliest place. I convinced myself I'd get lost, really, really lost out in the pampas. I'd never get home. My trip was just selfish, it was self-destructive. I had planned the whole thing, I suddenly realized, just like Hart Crane. "Good-bye, everybody," he said, and he waved, stepped off the deck and into the Mexican sea. I'd gone looking for my madness and I knew I would find it. I couldn't get on that plane; I was afraid of the flying.

I called Roberta from the airport. "I'm not going," I told her. "I can't get on that plane. I'll lose it. I'll see if I can cash out the ticket or something. All right?"

"No," she said. "It's not all right. You'll regret not going. You'll feel awful." She paused and waited for me to reply. I was too busy hyperventilating. "Look, Dave, what have you got? Do you have any Xanax? Just eat some Xanax and get on the plane. Eat two; that's what they're for. You're not going to go crazy. You have to do this, now. You'll always wonder."

"Okay," I said quietly.

"Good. Now just go fishing and I'll see you when you get home." She hung up and I got on the plane. I caught a train south from Santiago as far as it went and hitchhiked to turquoise rivers. I crossed the Andes into Argentina and camped by the Malleo. I rented a car and drove it farther south, down to Esquel, and then east toward nowhere, just a small spring creek. I took my lithium with Argentine beef and red wine. I ran low on money and pan-fried my trout. I had gone south again, farther this time and still all alone, and I looked for the brink. I caught beautiful fish and I proved my return was now possible. I came home proud and happy and ready for children. Mary was born the next fall and Hunter four years later. We bought a house.

It was an old farmhouse upriver from the Bookmill. It was a young carpenter's dream and his wife's worst headache—the eternal remodel. By the time Mary was eight I was almost done with the kitchen. She and Hunter were both happy, beautiful kids. They had a barn to explore and a pond full of frogs. The bookstore was breaking even at best, but it still looked pretty handsome after ten years. I still had good books and concerts, and the Mill had a growing, albeit underground, reputation. In 2003 I decided to upgrade the Mill's café with more food, a beer and wine license, and an extensive remodel. I formed a new partnership with one of my longtime employees and his girlfriend. We took out a business loan and I tore into the carpentry. We needed the café reopened fast. I worked an intense schedule, installing counters and sinks while juggling the bookstore. Roberta took the kids out to Gloucester and I hoped to join them in a few weeks when the café reopened.

I was excited. I had a new business venture, a great family, a beautiful house. I was a success—broke, maybe, but a success. At least I wasn't a wreck. I wasn't nervous or crazy or stoned. I hadn't had a manic break or depression in years. I was steady, and so were my parents and my brother. I was just a little bipolar, I thought, or maybe I'd grown out of it. In truth, I was tired of taking my medicine, all this drug dependence. I felt addicted to lithium. It still gave me headaches. It slowed me down. I didn't need lithium if I just used common sense, if I avoided the obvious: hallucinogens, crack, civil war. I quit in late June—on the solstice, in fact—and the weather was beautiful.

I drove to the city and bought a beautiful old mahogany bar from a salvage yard, hauled it up to the mill, and cut it and fit it just right. It was perfect. I felt fine. I felt better than fine. I was efficient, productive, and decisive. I cleaned out my barn and dragged everything flammable out to the field. I built a bonfire full of broken chairs and wardrobes, pine scraps and oak pallets and saplings. There were boxes of overstocked titles and just plain dead stock in the barn. I pulled them all out and staged every bookseller's dark fantasy, a book burning. I was selective. I burned self-help and new age; I burned romance and thrillers; I burned some sociology and all the psychology. I kept the poetry.

The café still needed finishing, I knew that, but first I needed to explain my vision, describe its unfolding in the fullness of New England time. I drove to work and called my new business partners. I told them it was an emergency and demanded they rush to the mill. Bring a video camera, I said. We need documentation. I had my carpenter take a break, cleared our tools off a bench, and pushed back the tables. I scavenged the building for various props—a block and tackle, iron wheels, art books, and

ancient machinery. The bookstore had been given a beautiful
scale model of the mill, cut by a local model maker and assembled by an elderly town resident, that had made the cover of
Model Railroader; in my hurry I dropped it down the stairs. I
grabbed pine scraps from the café floor and paint, made signs,
and placed them out front.

My new partners arrived. They were clearly annoyed. "So,
Dave," Matthew asked, "what's this all about? What's going on?"
His girlfriend Sarah glowered at me.

"You'll see," I said. "It's an installation. We need the camera.
Did you bring the video camera? That's the main thing. Did you
bring it?" He held it up and nodded. Good. I needed documentation; I needed proof I was right. I ran out and gathered an ad hoc
audience of mystified customers. And then I jumped into my
dramatic presentation of the mill's epic history.

"Welcome," I said, "and thanks for coming at such short notice. The mill is at a critical juncture in its long history. One that
we all must recognize and honor. The building you stand in was
built by Alvah Stone in 1832-ish. He ground grist here. This is a
gristmill. Can anyone tell me what grist is?" No one raised a
hand. "Of course not! I'm not surprised." I looked out over my
nervous audience. They shifted anxiously; they whispered; they
weren't prepared. "Quiet, everyone!" I commanded. "Please bear
with me. I promise this will make sense." I desperately needed
it to make sense. I lined items up on the workbench just as I had
in Paul's apartment in East Palo Alto years earlier. I wanted a
well-ordered defense, a windbreak for my flickering mind. I wanted
to reassure my new partners, friends, and patrons that my free-
form business plans, my vision for the old, venerated building,

made sense. "Quiet, please." I stared down my witnesses and returned to the broken scale model. "You see, the water ran through this penstock and then into the turbines—"

"David," Sarah interrupted. "You're scaring the customers."

"No, I'm not." I looked at the small group remaining. "What? Am I scaring you?" I bullied them. "This model's scary?" My friends shook their heads unconvincingly; most left. My show wound to an inconclusive close. A friend stepped up and called the show brilliant and his girlfriend called me an artist. My rattled business partners were less impressed. They waited for me outside. "So, what did you think?" I asked. "Did you get it all on tape?"

"Yeah, Dave, we got it all on tape." Matthew looked at me quizzically. "But, I don't know. It seemed a little, well... incoherent."

"That's putting it mildly," scoffed Sarah.

I drew back. "No, it wasn't," I huffed. "It was not incoherent. It was multimedia." I stomped off. My partners lacked vision.

Later that evening I crashed their potluck and jumped from one conversation to another. I told my friend Mick the town's selectmen wanted to close down the bookstore: "The old Yankees in town hate the place. They'd rather have it empty and haunted." I harangued a pregnant woman at length about cloth diapers: "Disposable diapers are better for the environment, for all of us. I have one word," I said after talking ten minutes. "Bleach. Bleach is a killer." Afterward I returned to the mill, sat at a window overlooking the river, and waited for ghosts. They didn't show so I wrote them a letter: a sprawling historical poem on the old mill and the Sunoco station nearby. I was grappling with the Civil War when the store opened the following morning.

I knew I was fucked. I knew what was happening and I needed my family, I needed to get to Gloucester. I slipped out of the shop by a side door and drove home for some clothes, a few odds and ends. I managed the clothes and a toothbrush. I stayed focused and made it past all my books, past my music and photos. I pushed out to the truck but the barn caught me. I went in for some fishing gear and came out with a plan. I dragged out my skiff and slid it onto the bed of my truck. I decided to take my family by surprise, to approach Lane's Cove by sea with my skiff flying black flags and bones. I wanted smoke bombs and bottle rockets and considered a fireworks run to New Hampshire. Cherry bombs, roman candles, and quarter sticks—the kids would just love it.

I was lashing all my gear down when three friends pulled up beside the truck. "Where are you going, Dave?" my friend Kate asked. She's a therapist and she knew the score. She'd brought another close friend, Karen, and she brought Matthew, my business partner. All of them were obviously upset. At once I sensed they weren't thinking clearly and acted quickly. I sat them down in my kitchen and tried talking sense.

I talked over them, refusing to listen until Kate dropped the bomb and said, "Just face it, Dave. You're manic." And then I looked down. I was a cartoon; I was Wile E. Coyote run past the cliff and just hanging. I looked down and I plummeted. Poof.

"David, are you taking your lithium?" I sat frozen and finally quiet. Lost. "David?"

"Huh? What?"

"Lithium."

I looked up at Kate. I held her eye and bluffed. "Hypomanic," I said. "I'll give you hypomanic. Slightly hypomanic." I knew I couldn't bullshit her. I stood up, shirtless and scraped from hoisting my pirate skiff. "That's it," I said. "I'm not full-blown."

"Are you taking your lithium?" I shook my head. Suddenly I wanted to get better. Mania wasn't fun anymore. It wasn't creative or visionary. It was mean parody at best, a cheap chemical trick. I needed to stop and get better. I'd take whatever they gave me, I pledged silently. I'd take Trilafon or Thorazine or whatever. I just wanted to sleep.

Kate called my psychiatrist, Dr. Bryant. She made an emergency appointment for the morning. She left messages for Roberta in Gloucester. Matthew spent a sleepless night standing watch and in the morning delivered me to the doctor. His waiting room had always seemed pleasant, a few depressives, a few embarrassed neurotics, but reasonably pleasant. Apparently I was scheduled on the more hopeful days, the good-prognosis days. It was an entirely different kind of waiting room I had been squeezed into that morning. It was filled with heavily sedated, chronic patients—schizophrenics and the permanently damaged. I just sat in the chair next to Matthew, thinking: This isn't me; this isn't me; this isn't me.

Roberta returned that afternoon and relieved Matthew. At first she seemed skeptical and, quite frankly, peeved at the whole business. I hadn't been manic for years, she reasoned. It was an anxiety attack and my friends were exaggerating. David could have driven to Gloucester but no, they hauled the whole family back from the beach. It was just drama.

That defense fell apart in the driveway, as soon as she saw my eyes. I was terrified and I told her. "It's not good. I'm not well. I'm sick mostly and I think I fucked up." The kids were hungry and cranky right out of the car. I hugged them and hoped they were still happy to see me, that they weren't scared. I carried Hunter inside and bounced off the walls with him as Roberta made lunch. She was nervous and I tried to reassure her. It wasn't a crisis, not really. She was angry, too. She'd had the kids for a week straight and now she had me. The kitchen was trashed and it looked like I hadn't eaten in days. She pulled out some frozen burritos. She sliced open the packages hurriedly. I came close; she slipped and cut her thumb open. She cursed and threw the food down. She turned to the sink, flushed her hand with cold water, and the stacked dishes swirled pink. Hunter and Mary began crying.

"Dammit. It needs stitches. I've got to get stitches." She had started to panic. My fear was contagious. I tried to slow down.

"It's okay, Roberta. Stitches are not a big deal. I'm fine. I'm all right. Okay? I'm all right. Just go get some stitches. We'll be fine."

"Really? You're okay?" she asked fast.

"I'm okay," I said. I was shaking. Nothing will happen. I'm crazy but I'm really all right. "The kids will be fine. They're happy to see me."

"You stay here with the children and I'll run down to Dr. Allen's. That'll be faster than the emergency room. You'll be okay. I'll call. The food's on the counter, all right? All right, David?"

She held my shoulder and caught my eyes. "David, you'll be fine with the kids." I nodded. Of course.

Roberta rushed out of the kitchen and the three of us stood there. "Mom's going to be fine," I said. "It's not a big deal. There's nothing to worry about." Hunter latched onto my leg. I looked over at Mary. She had stopped crying and was watching me, and I wondered if she knew. "Mom's going to be fine," I repeated, stalling until I could focus. Lunch. Hunter wouldn't let go and I lurched over to the counter with him. I pushed the burritos into the microwave and pushed four seconds. It beeped and I jumped. Dammit. Four minutes. Careful, now, conservative. I'd move slowly, that's all. I knew I was sick. I wasn't right but I'd just move slowly. I pushed my mind down and stared at the ticking machine, waiting for the beep. Hunter let go and he and Mary moved into the living room. I poured out some milk. How could she do this? How could she leave me with the children? What if something happened? What if I ran off? What if I scared them? Fuck.

"Dad. Hey, Dad," Mary yelled. "Hunter just took my clay. He's throwing it."

"No, I'm not." Hunter started screaming. I charged in. Mary had her brother's arm as she peeled green bits of clay from his hand.

"Mary," I yelled angrily, "let go of your brother this instant. Goddammit. He's only four. Just share with him." I was shaking again. I stopped and sat down on the couch. Both kids stared at me. I couldn't look them in the eyes. The microwave beeped and I jumped. "Okay?" I said quietly. "Just share. Please. I can't handle this now. I just can't." I took deep breaths and sat with the children silent and watching. Hunter's screams and the bickering, Roberta's cut thumb and the microwave—all of this was sudden and loud and it lit up my head, shot me full of adrenaline and fear. My heart pounded and my mind rushed through the house.

I stood. "All right, come on, let's go out on the porch." I had to keep them happy. If I kept them happy they wouldn't scream. I wouldn't scream; I wouldn't lose it. "Mary, you bring the clay and we'll make stuff." Mary smiled and grabbed her plastic bag full of clay balls. Hunter laughed and followed her out to the porch. The kids were fine, I thought. They were happy to see me again, even now, even like this. I smiled after them. I heard them laughing just past the screen door. I was overcome with love and I started to cry. "Goddammit, Dave," I said softly. "Pull it together." I wiped my eyes and walked outside. "Okay," I said loudly, decisively. "Okay. Listen, we're going to make stuff out of clay."

Mary looked at me quizzically. "We know that, Dad. We already are." She and Hunter already had two snakes and a horse between them.

"Okay," I said again, and I sat down and crossed my legs. I concentrated and made a red car with blue wheels. I made a goat. These kids deserve better, I thought. They deserve better than a fucked-up father who yells and cannot be trusted. What was I thinking? I can't have kids. I'm too sick. My family's too sick. What if they find out? What if something happens? Roberta doesn't understand. How could she? She just left me here. I looked at little Hunter and I wanted to cry.

I brought out the phone. "I'm going to see how Mom's doing," I said. I called down to the doctor and got a recording: *"If you want to schedule an appointment, push one..."*

"Oh, goddammit," I said.

Mary looked up. "What, Dad? What's wrong?" She knew already. She knew I was wrong.

"Nothing, darling. Nothing. Keep playing. That's a nice... whatever it is."

"Elephant."

"Right.

"... *for prescription refills, press two; for referrals, press three. If this is a medical emergency, hang up and dial nine-one-one.*"

Christ. I hung up and dialed 911. "Hello, this is Officer Blaine of the State Police. This call is being recorded. How can I help—" I hung up fast. Shit. What the hell was I thinking? State troopers. They're the worst—fucking Nazis. I stepped off the front porch, away from my children. I was panicking and I didn't want them to see. Officer Blaine called back.

"Who am I speaking with?" Oh, shit. "Listen, we're sending a car out now. Hello?"

"Please don't send a car," I said. "Everything's fine."

"State your name and the reason for your call."

"David Lovelace. I'm David Lovelace. Look, everything's fine. My wife just cut herself, that's all. She's at the doctor's and I'm—"

"What doctor?"

"Dr. Allen in Amherst. Listen, I'm here with the kids—"

"Are they all right?"

"Will you fricking let me finish? They're fine, they're fine." I turned back toward the porch and found Mary right behind me. "Mary, go help your brother. I need you to help your brother." I scooted her back toward the porch, away from me. "Look, I didn't mean to call nine-one-one. I was just trying to get a hold of my wife at the doctor's. It was a mistake. Please don't send a car here."

"We already have."

"Look, it's like this. I'm bipolar. I'm, well, I'm a bit off, manic. I mean, I'm fine. But if you send a car I might lose it. Okay?" Officer Blaine waited a beat. "Hello, are you there?"

"I'm here."

I started pleading. I was terrified, standing on my summer lawn with my beautiful children and waiting for the worst—screams and guns and all of it. "Look, call the doctor. Call him now and my wife will explain." He agreed and, suddenly, he hung up.

"Is everything all right, Daddy?" Mary asked. "Are the police coming? Did you do something wrong?"

I pulled my children close and sat down on the grass. "No, darling, nothing is wrong. I'm fine. Your daddy's just fine. All of us, we're all doing fine." They both hugged me and held me and kept me from falling. Finally I said, "Mary, go get the clay and bring it out here. Let's make some more stuff."

I made a yellow dragon and then the phone rang. "David, this is Dr. Allen. What's going on up there? I just finished speaking with the State Police."

"Where's Roberta?"

"She's fine. I sent her home. Listen, she told me—"

"That I'm manic? I am. I can't have the cops—"

"They're not coming, Dave. Don't worry. Are you okay? Everything all right?"

Sure, I said, everything will be okay. I'm taking my medicine again. Thank you.

I ate my lithium and within a week or so I was level. I am fortunate to have friends with whom I can trust my history, who know how and when to intervene. That whole scary afternoon—the whole week—all of it was needless and stupid.

I called a meeting with my café partners and quit my own project. I was too humiliated and they were too scared to continue with me. It got emotional and Sarah raised her voice. "This whole thing was awful. Do you know what we did for you? Matthew had to spend the night at your house. We covered for you. Do you have any idea, any idea at all, of what you put us through?"

I did. I had a very good idea. I was out and that friendship ended. My family and I drove back to Gloucester and I went rowing and fishing. I built sand castles with Mary and Hunter, and we built fires and boiled lobsters and mussels down on the rocks. I had scared my family and friends; the episode cost me a business and a friendship, but it clarified things. I now know for certain that my mind and emotions, my fix on the real and my family's well-being, depend on just a few grams of salt. But treatment's the easy part. Without honesty, without a true family reckoning, that salt's next to worthless.

Shame fosters the denial that guarantees a return. Without treatment the episodes get worse, the cycle speeds up. Two years after my café break, my family got slammed again—the double-header with my Dad through the roof and my mom on the floor. It was easy to save my mother's life—just call 911. But once she was saved, it took all my family's compassion, every ounce, for us to recover. It took all my bipolar experience—both real and delusional—to feel my way through this horrible house of genetic mirrors, to understand and not simply react. I'm still angry; we all are. We are all still recovering.

My mother was dying; she was slipping away. It was a straightforward medical emergency, and the hospital moved fast. My father was slipping as well, but differently, strangely. He wasn't bleeding, he wasn't hurt. It wasn't his appendix or his heart that landed him in the ER. It was his brain. Bipolar disorder is a brain disease, but too often the health care system—the insurance companies, the lawyers, and even some doctors—blame the mind. To many in the ER, my father's illness was his fault, some moral weakness, something shameful. It wasn't really medical, it was emotional. It was subjective, his treatment a legal quagmire. Bipolar disorder, many insurance companies argue, cannot be covered because it cannot be proven. It won't show up in an autopsy, they say. My father wasn't dying and so the hospital sent him home, twice.

On the third day he locked his apartment door and hid. I moved back to the patio and spied on my father as he paced through trashed rooms. I began tapping on the glass door. I stood there and banged on it until my father had had enough and stepped out.

"Dad, we've got to go back," I said. "To the hospital. We can see Mom." Mom was my trump card.

He looked me square in the face and said slowly, "I am not going to the hospital. I'll see her later. I am going to church to pray for your mother." And then he took off, cutting through backyards and cul-de-sacs. I kept up with and reasoned frantically. He waved me off and I fell back and tailed him.

When we got to the church my father climbed the steps, turned, and said, "Don't come in here. You're not welcome."

"Ah, come on, Dad," I pleaded impatiently. "I'm not fooling around." He turned and opened the door. "What?" I asked angrily. "Are you claiming sanctuary or something? That doesn't work, Dad. This isn't a war." He just turned and went inside. I followed but lost him. I wandered the church until I found the pastor's office. I heard laughter, knocked, and found them both drinking coffee.

My father gestured at me proudly. "Dan, this is my son, David Lovelace."

The minister stood and assessed me. "Very pleased to meet you, David. Your father has told me a great deal about you."

"No doubt," I replied.

"Please, sit down and join us."

"I'd rather not. I'd rather take my father over to Cooley Dickinson. My mother is there."

"I'm sorry to hear that. I trust she's all right?" The minister looked toward my father and he started to speak but I cut him off fast.

"She's not. Not really. She's in the ICU," I said. "I have to take my father to the hospital."

"I'm fine, Dan," my father chimed in. "There's no reason on earth for me to go to the hospital. Betty Lee is much better now and there's nothing wrong with me."

"With you, Richard?" the minister asked. "What could be wrong with you?"

"Nothing. Nothing at all. It's my son here—"

Now the minister cut him off. "Hold on, Richard. Let's see.

David, why don't you step out and give me a few minutes with your father?"

Thirty minutes later he found me outside on the steps. "Your father seems—"

"What? Crazy?"

"Well, excited, but..."

"Crazy. He's manic. He locked me out of their apartment so I broke in and found my mother lying on the floor unconscious. She'd been there for days. He was just singing hymns and mixing protein shakes."

The minister went white. "Oh. Well. I see."

"He's off, manic. I need to get him to the hospital, get him back on lithium." I caught my breath and slowed down. "Look, I need to get help. Can you see my father home?"

"Um, yes, I suppose. I'll try."

I thanked him, ran to my truck, and sped back toward the shrink's. I called my cousin Joanna en route, the same cousin I had called from Olympia, the same cousin who had helped commit me. She said I needed a Section Twelve, a doctor's order for involuntary psychiatric commitment. No more interviews, no more bureaucrat suckers drawn in by Dad's act. I arranged an emergency meeting with Dad's psychiatrist. I told Dr. Bryant I needed the order—no more phone calls, no more recommendations. Just Section Twelve—the men in white suits.

"Of course," Bryant said nervously. "I can't believe they refused to admit him. He needs hospitalization. I spoke with the hospital and made that quite clear."

"Yeah, well, it's been ridiculous," I complained, "just stupid. I don't blame my father for not going back. I don't want to go back, that's for sure."

"I don't blame you," Bryant said sympathetically.

"Why didn't we use a Section Twelve to begin with?" It was a rhetorical question. I knew the answer: lawyers. No one wants to sign committal papers.

"A voluntary commitment is preferable, less traumatic, and two days ago he was willing. They should have admitted him immediately upon my recommendation." Bryant produced the dread Section Twelve and signed it. "Look, this will work. If they don't have beds this time we send him to Holyoke. We need him safe. Take this to the Northampton police."

"The cops?" He nodded. "That's good." The men in white coats were cops and they were the good guys. My world was a jumble.

"Yes, they'll need this and they'll call for the ambulance. This will go fast, I promise you." He shook his head in exasperation. "I can't believe they put you through this." I nodded. I was exhausted. "How is your mother?"

"Still unconscious. Still in ICU. I don't know. Her signs are better, I guess. Stable. They thought it was a stroke but the MRI showed nothing."

"Well, I'm conferring with your mother's doctor there, making sure she has the right medications. Now let's take care of your father. Take this to the police station. And don't hesitate to call if you have questions or problems."

Section Twelve worked. It summoned a squad car to my father's apartment in ten minutes. I walked up with the police, explaining my dad as fast as I could. I saw his figure dart past a window and the living room lamp switched off, then the bedroom. One of the cops rapped on the door.

No answer.

"He's in there," I said.

The cop rapped again. "Mr. Lovelace, sir. I'm Sergeant James of the Northampton Police Department. Your son..." He turned.

"David."

"Your son, David, is here, sir. He's concerned. Could you come out, sir? We'd like to speak with you." Silence.

An ambulance swung in with its lights flashing. Great, I thought, that always helps. "You're not going to need handcuffs," I said to the cops. "Really." Right then my father opened the door calmly. He even worked up a smile.

"Gentlemen, David Lovelace," he said, "welcome." He ushered us in with a grand sweep of his arm. "As you can see, everything is wonderful here." Dishes were piled on the sofa; the place reeked. "Everything is wonderful," he repeated, stalling and shrugging his shoulders. He lifted his open hands to the police. It was showtime. He'd start with the shrugs and light banter and then he'd wow them with his Presbyterian book bag of tricks.

Not this time. Not with a Section Twelve. "Yes, Mr. Lovelace, sir. Mr. Lovelace, we are bringing you to Cooley Dickinson Hospital. They'll get you checked in."

"I've already spoken with them, numerous times. I've been there for days. Everything is fine. They sent me home already." My father rose up and said deliberately, "I am not going back."

The cop touched my father's elbow lightly. "I'm afraid you

need to go back, sir." My father stood scowling. "Now, sir." And then, quite suddenly, my father just smiled, shouldered his book bag, and walked to the ambulance.

We both returned to the ER with newfound confidence. My father knew the system; he'd tied it in knots. But I was ready this time. I had Section Twelve. My father went from the ambulance straight back. No waiting room this time. The triage nurses eyed me warily. They started to whisper. I was back again. Would I threaten a social worker this time or just take a swing at an orderly? I swaggered up to their counter, glowered at the meanest, most bureaucratic nurse of the lot, and spread out my paperwork, my royal straight flush.

"Oh," the nurse said. "I see."

"Could we expedite this process now?" I said with just a trace of malice. "Perhaps my father could see a *doctor* this time? Immediately?"

The nurse didn't flinch. She simply checked the form's signatures. "Yes," she said. "Of course, Mr. Lovelace. We do have a short intake procedure, I'm afraid. I'll get someone down to talk with your father immediately." She buzzed into the back. I sat beside my father's gurney. He had his wallet out and was shuffling through business cards. He said he wanted to call his lawyer. He said the whole church was praying for me—praying bad things, he said. He told me I was manic, that I needed help, and then he turned quiet. We had him dead to rights and he knew it. When the orderly wheeled Dad toward the elevator a nurse stopped me from following.

"It's better if you just see him later. It's easier this way," the nurse told me. "Go home and get some rest." She was right, of course. I couldn't help anymore. I didn't have any questions. There was nothing left to see and I knew the drill.

I didn't go home. I took the elevator up to intensive care instead. My mother was straight ahead and laid out by machines across from the nurses' station. She was awake. Her body lay still but her eyes darted over the room and bounced from my face. "Mom," I called softly. "Hey, Mom, it's David." Her eyes stopped on me and then her face relaxed. I saw her jaw work but her mouth seemed stuck, broken. I reached for some water and watched her eyes rattle away. I called a nurse.

"Betty Lee has been conscious for five or six hours now," she said, and picked up a cup. "She's still dehydrated. She hasn't spoken, not yet." She worked a straw past my mother's pasted lips. Mom's eyes grew wide and watched the nurse as she drank. I told her I loved her, that Dad was okay. I held her small hand—a dry, translucent leaf, a thin tangle of veins.

Over the following week my mother grew stronger and was moved from intensive care. Peggy flew in from Colorado; Jonathan and his family drove from Gloucester. I briefed them in the hospital lobby. I said, "Mom almost died and she looks it. She whispers some but she's confused. She's paranoid." I told them stroke had been ruled out by the doctors but her legs were weak, the left almost paralyzed. They had run all the tests. They weren't sure what had happened and Dad couldn't help. "All he keeps saying is that she seemed more herself, that she was getting better."

"Yeah, right," Peggy said. "Sure." We had our suspicions, and sadly, they all centered on Dad: maybe he messed with her medicine, gave her too many pills or none at all. My father had stopped taking lithium—that much was horribly apparent. I thought Mom had taken too much. I'd watched her suffer lithium poisoning once and it looked like this. It's too much that will kill you, I reasoned, not too little. I was wrong.

I led the Lovelace hospital tour. First stop was Mom. She was sitting up now and had the use of her arms. "Mom," I said, "look. Peggy and Jon are here with me."

"Really?" my mom asked softly, and brightened for a moment. There were flowers, boxed chocolates, and grave kisses. Peggy smoothed her thin hair. My brother and sister smiled at Mom but their shock was apparent. She had lost a great deal of weight. Her skull was visible and her eyes sank behind her cheekbones.

I opened the chocolates and popped them while Peg and Jon leaned over the bed. "Hi, Mom. Mom, it's me, Peggy. And Jonathan's here." I thought she wouldn't speak; I knew it was hard.

"What a surprise," she whispered, and closed her eyes with the effort.

"We came to see you, Mom," Jonathan said, "to see how you're doing." My mother saw or heard something, something other than us, and her brow crumpled with fear. "You had us all worried, Mom." She started blinking, clearly agitated. She forgot us.

"Mom, hey, Mom," said Peggy. "I see you have your Bible." Peggy picked up the worn leather book, filled with notes from before we were born. "Great."

My mother put her hands to her eyes and tried to speak.

"Her glasses," I said. "Shoot. I know, Mom. I forgot. I'll go get them right now."

"Don't let them see," she whispered.

"Let who see?"

"The nurses."

"The nurses? Mom, the nurses love you. They want you to have your glasses."

"No," she said, "no."

We leaned toward her with crooked smiles and said, Mom, the nurses love you, we all love you. We were afraid; she frightened us.

My mother looked away. "Where's Richard?"

"He's around, Mom. He's close," I said, and smiled ruefully at my sister. "He'll come and see you as soon as he can." I kissed her and turned to my brother. "Listen, I'm going to go and get her glasses. Dad's upstairs on the fifth floor. I've got to go. I'll see you later tonight."

I picked up her glasses, dropped them off with a nurse, and went home. I took Django, my daughter's puppy, up into the woods along old logging roads. Afterward the two of us just lay in the sun by the barn until my children ran from the bus stop and jumped us. It was simple, this happiness, and I felt it passing.

My father had gotten high, cut my mother's lithium, and replaced it with protein shakes. Without lithium my mother's fear came to kill her, and as my father marched fearlessly—even happily—into psychosis, my mother withdrew into a stupor. By the time my father had become God's own physician—his wife's only healer—she was catatonic. Her mind had retreated to hell. She

lay on the floor for days, unable to move, but she was never coma-
tose. It's even possible that on some level she remained conscious
through the ordeal. My mother regressed to a primitive state:
mute, unable to move, literally frozen with fear. She erased herself. She fell down into the pit, closed her eyes, and drifted toward
death while my father sang hymns, while he prayed over her.

"The good news," a doctor told us, "is that it wasn't a stroke. A
stroke could have disabled her permanently. We've been hydrat-
ing her and feeding her intravenously. Now she's eating solid
food. We've got her back on her medications—lithium and
Seroquel—and that should help get her out of the woods."

"So," my sister said after the doctor had left, "that's the good
news. Dad took Mom off her meds and let her get sicker and
sicker."

"Dad was high as a kite," I countered. "You can't blame him."
And so Peggy and I played a high-stakes hand in an old, familiar
game. I defended Dad and she stood in for Mom.

"Dad made the decision to ditch all the meds before that—
before he got sick," my sister countered. "He watched her get
worse."

"So did I, Peg. I mean I drove her to Rockport like that. She
was in a stupor. I saw her like that and I didn't do a damn thing.
I went camping in Colorado, for Christ's sake."

"Nah, Dave, it wasn't just you," Jonathan said. "I was there,
too, practically the whole family. I didn't do anything. None of
us did. We let them go crazy."

"All right," Peggy said. "I'm sorry. It's pointless to blame anyone. We should just move on and see what comes next."

————

A week later my mother's doctors sent her to a nursing home for rehabilitation. She was getting stronger. She still couldn't walk, but she could sit upright and feed herself. She always recognized Roberta and me and she was happy to see us, but we spent each visit keeping her demons at bay. They always returned after we left.

"There's a boy that comes out," my mother said. "Every night."

I leaned forward. "Who do you mean, Mom?"

"A boy, a little man comes out when you leave and he helps them."

"Who?"

"The nurses. They think I'm Jewish. They think I'm a Jew."

"No, they don't," I said. She nodded slowly. "So what? What does that matter?"

"The ovens." My mother held her curled hand close to her mouth. "The boy, he comes out from under my bed and he helps them."

"No, Mom. You know that's crazy. There's no boy. And the nurses all love you. You need to stop thinking like that. It's not true."

She made a grim smile. "Yes, well... you don't know. You're not here when it's dark."

She'd been in the nursing home two weeks when Roberta and the children brought her some clothes. "So how was it?" I asked over dinner. "How's Mom?"

"She was weird," Mary said, and looked down at her plate. "She said weird things."

"Well, she's still sick, sweetheart. Don't pay attention."

"She said the nurses skinned Django, Dad. She said they had Hunter locked up in a closet." Little Hunter looked up from his plate and laughed. I felt sick.

After work I'd drive to the hospital, stand at the fifth-floor lockup, and buzz. "It's too soon," the nurses kept saying over their intercom. "Your father won't see you." My sister had flown home and my brother was back in Gloucester when Dad finally relented. I entered with trepidation but I was pleasantly surprised. The ward wasn't bad; it was fine. Not as nice, perhaps, as my ward in Beverly but better than East Palo Alto. It was bright and lacked the sick, antiseptic smell of the hospital's other floors. I saw my father before I reached the nurses' station. He was beaming.

"David! Come in." He put his hand on my shoulder and introduced me to the nurses. "This is my son, David Lovelace. He's the reason I'm here." All was forgiven, apparently, but not forgotten.

"Well, not exactly, Dad." I laughed nervously and the nurses all smiled. My father was popular. It was good to see him.

Dad pulled me toward his room. "Come on, come on. Let me introduce you to my roommate, Franklin." Franklin wasn't there. "Oh, where'd he go now?" my father muttered. "Wait here. I'll go find him." The room was small, just enough room for two single beds, two dressers and end tables. My father returned hauling a young white guy with dreadlocks. "Here he is," he said proudly. "Here's Franklin." Franklin smiled sheepishly. "We've been having great theological discussions. Isn't that right, Franklin?"

"Sure. We've been talking a lot about, um, music. And things."

"Franklin's a musician. He plays reggae."

"Really?" I said. "What instruments do you play?"

"Well, um, all of them pretty much. Like church." Franklin was sweet and vague. He was confused—I could see that already—but open and friendly, just like a kid. I wondered about his label. Was he schizophrenic or just a doped manic? In Beverly I befriended a schizophrenic girl. The nurses warned me that I shouldn't get too close. They said I would get better but that she never would. I hoped Franklin wasn't schizophrenic. I liked him already.

"Music is a spiritual practice," my father explained, "even reggae music." He leaned toward me and dropped his voice. "It's a bit one-celled, musically, but it's quite spiritual. Franklin has reminded me of that." Franklin looked positively radiant. "And, just between you and me, Franklin's also taught me that just a little marijuana can be helpful. Ritually, of course."

I smiled. "Well maybe, Dad, but I don't think now's the time to go—"

"Of course not, of course not, David." He swept his hand toward the hall. "I mean, pot's not even allowed in here."

"So. You've been talking about Rastafarianism?"

"Sure, why not?" My father smiled and shrugged.

"Hey," Franklin asked me. "You want to see Jesus Christ?"

"Sure," I said, and glanced at my father. "Who doesn't?"

He rummaged through his dresser and found what he was looking for, a shirt tie-dyed red, green, and yellow. "Here," he said, pointing at a poor silk-screened likeness. "Here he is."

"Who's that?"

"Haile Selassie. Jah. He's Jesus Christ."

"Oh. Well I suppose you—"

"And why not?" My father chimed in supportively. "You say tomato, I say tomato. *À chacun son gout.*" I laughed and I wanted to hug them both, right then. My father was sick—he wasn't thinking clearly—but he was well enough to love his odd bed-fellow, to find room in his world for Franklin, reggae, and Haile Selassie. I knew my father's reserve, his doctrinal and personal boundaries, would return, but at that moment one of my father's great gifts, his love for artists and outcasts, shone through and I loved him.

My father stood up and started gathering items from his bed, his glasses, his Bible, and his socks. "So, David, let's get out of this place. I shouldn't be locked up in here. Your mother needs me and they won't let me see her."

"Dad, she's getting better. Don't worry. You need to get better, too."

His face darkened. "I'm not leaving? You're not here to pick me up? I'm not even sick! You tricked me in here. Even the nurses know that."

"Dad, you're still a little manic. The lithium will kick in soon and you'll see." I knew my visit was over and I stepped toward the door. "Nice to meet you, Franklin," I said, and Dad pushed me out.

A few days later the hospital released him. "We can't hold him any longer against his will. We would have to bring him to court, get an order," they told me. "He'll just tie the judge into knots. I'm sorry, but we have to release him."

"Even when he's sick," I said.

"Even when he's sick. We can't hold him. The trick is to keep him on his medications. He is getting better. Incrementally."

True. The next morning, before I picked him up, Roberta and I cleaned my parents' apartment thoroughly. I threw away the foul foam rubber scraps that had cushioned my mother. I stripped her bed and threw out the sheets. Roberta washed the kitchen floor and emptied the fridge. I took all my father's papers and spider-scrawled notes to a box in the basement. I couldn't close his book on Goya. It seemed wrong so I left it propped on the living room chair, still open to the crucified Christ and my dad's marginalia. I flushed the old pills with dark satisfaction: the antipsychotics and antacids, the nameless pretty capsules, all the herbal cures and the vitamins. I placed his new prescriptions neatly in the empty bathroom cabinet. I took note of their pill counts and dosages.

When I got to the hospital, my father was in high spirits. "I'm glad," he said to the nurse while signing the paperwork, "that we've straightened out this whole mix-up." She didn't reply; she just shuffled his forms and asked him to sign.

"This is for your watch, Richard. Also your wallet and keys. And this one indicates why you were admitted."

"Whoa. Wait a minute," my father said. "Let me look at this." He picked up the sheet and it shook with his lithium tremors. "This isn't right. I'm not signing this. It says I was manic."

"Dad, you were. You still are. You're getting better but you're still not right. Just sign it. And promise that you'll take your meds. Even the Seroquel. Swear it to this nurse or you won't get out." My father looked at the uncomfortable nurse, who stared at me. "Go ahead, Dad."

"All right, fine. If that will make you happy I'll sign it. I'll humor you."

"And the meds?"

"Fine. I'll take them, although I think you should remember your place. I'm your father."

He insisted on seeing my mother straightaway and I drove him directly to the nursing home. He kissed Mom's forehead and her face lit up. She needed him. They prayed quietly until dinner. The nurse brought the tray in and my father took it and spoon-fed my mother. Afterward my father went quiet and Mom's eyes filled with tears. The three of us sat together until the nurse came to dress her for bed.

I drove my dad back to the apartment and watched him take his meds. "I'll get you some food in the morning," I said. "I can't do it now. Okay, Dad? I'll be back around breakfast."

"Oh, Dave, that won't be necessary. I've got the car keys. I'll get something on my way over to Mom's."

"Okay, Dad," I said, too tired to argue about the car. "Good night."

My mother languished in the nursing home through Christmas and on into January. The nurses tried their best for her, but the place worked on her fears. Her paranoia took root and flourished there, among the dying and confused. She couldn't recover there, not fully. She missed my father terribly; she needed him whole. Mom needed him more than level, much more than sane. She needed him honest, strong enough to learn from the crisis.

Instead his hypomania lingered and he became Mom's righteous advocate. He argued with the staff and pasted instructional Post-its all over the room, on the walls, doors, and bathroom mirror: "Remember Vitamin B! Do Not Put Glasses in Drawer!" He clipped articles on the health industry and taped them up for the nurses: tales of inefficiency, bureaucracy, pharmaceutical profits, and nursing home horrors. He observed my mother's physical therapy sessions skeptically and began interfering. I heard the complaints and spoke with him but it did no good. He was finally banned from the room when he brought in a jack-knife and whittled sharp sticks.

I became my mother's health care proxy, filling out forms in the office downstairs while Dad prayed over her bed. He missed her so much and he sat with her faithfully. He came every afternoon and stayed throughout dinner. While he stood watch I cased his apartment, checked his refrigerator, and counted his pills. He was eating pretty well; the pill counts kept dropping, but he stayed pretty high. I used to sit outside in my battered old truck and just punch at the dash. I joined a gym near my mother and pushed its machines till my pain felt simple.

My father contacted one of those swank, condolike clusters offering assisted care to the wealthy. He was excited and brought me right over. I was impressed; it was nice. The sales manager was pleasant and dressed in a pantsuit. The glossy literature explained that a one-time entrance fee was required at the time of acceptance. It was the size of a mortgage.

"As you can see, gentlemen, we do require a financial report. It's our way of making certain Pheasant Ridge is affordable."

"Of course, of course." My father waved it off. "That's understandable in this day and age. That won't be a problem. I have considerable investments in British gold sovereigns and—"

"Right," I said. "Thank you very much. You've given us plenty to consider."

My father could not be dissuaded. He kept up the pressure. He took their tours and studied their waiting list. He had found a way to save Mom. I took the sales team aside and told them the fiscal truth. They stopped answering his calls after that.

My mother was still heavily sedated; she rested in half dreams but I watched the fear move through her face like dark weather. One afternoon my father arrived looking well. He seemed almost focused and he emptied his book bag with purpose: a white sleeve of saltine crackers, one can of tomato juice drink, and *The Book of Common Prayer*, Episcopal. He announced to the nurses, who ignored him by now, that the Eucharist would be celebrated at five p.m. in room 242. All were welcome. No one came but my mother's roommate Alice, age ninety-six. She had to come; she was bedridden. Dad read beautifully from the book, his voice solemn and fearful. He made the sign of the cross over my mother and I tore open the crackers. He made it again and I gave him a coffee cup filled with Christ's blood. I found him a straw. And then I stayed back like an altar boy does. I was too young and too angry for something so holy. I left my parents still praying, got in my derelict truck, and drove home.

Weeks passed and then my father was sane. He acted appropriately and efficiently. He found a new, one-floor apartment that was perfect for Mom. He arranged all the details, worked out the lease, and stored extra furnishings. He bought new bed-spreads and blankets. He met all the social workers and signed up for health aides and meals. He had all of Peniel, all their old friends, praying for Mom. I helped him hang my mother's paintings and sort her supplies. By the time she returned it was home. Mom had visibly aged in the five months she was gone, but she was happy again. She was glad to be home where she belonged, with Richard, her husband. Now, two years later, my mother is unsteady at times but rarely needs her walker. My father drives her to the hairdresser and does all the laundry and tries his best to cook. They are devoted to each other and God. When I drop by there is opera and politics and always the Bible. They're happy, I think.

I know our disease. I deserted my family and ran from it. I denied it three times and refused it. All that drama may seem pointless and sad but it taught me. I know the empathy borne of despair; I know the fluidity of thought, the expansive, even beautiful, mind that hypomania brings, and I know this is quicksilver and precious and often it's poison. There has always existed a sort of psychic butcher who works the scales of transcendence, who weighs out the bloody cost of true art. Any list of the great artists who suffered from manic depression is both impressive and macabre: Anne Sexton, Percy Bysshe Shelley, Virginia Woolf, Vincent van Gogh, John Berryman, Paul Gauguin, Robert Schumann, Sylvia Plath, Arshile Gorky, Herman Melville, Gustav Mahler, Robert Lowell, Charles Mingus—a list full of asylums and addictions, depressions and suicides and exquisite beauty.

I know all this, but no one—not me, not the sick or their doctors, their families or priests—will ever understand this sickness, its magic and rot. My brother and I have spent years strung between its two poles and we can't explain it to our sister and wives or demark the distance between heaven and hell, between our father and mother that autumn.

My father's psychosis was murderous. He watched and he prayed while Mom slipped into darkness. He could have phoned the family but he called upon God. He swept away lithium and ascended into the clouds while my mother lay on the floor and watched him from hell. Mom was getting better, much more herself, and Dad felt great, never better. Before that, before he felt great, my father kept his demons at bay with prayer and medicine. After Hamilton, he sutured the great sucking wound made by his long sadness. He cauterized the stumps and buried the parts. He's never spoken of it, at least not to me. Once I asked him if he had lost God during those years and what it was like. He answered with shock and bluster, like such a commonplace loss was unthinkable, impossible. I've asked what bipolar illness has done to him and he waves it away like an inconvenience, one extra errand, one more prescription to fill. I fear he may never forgive himself. He may never forgive our illness.

It's difficult. I take a low dose of lithium nightly. I take an antidepressant for my darkness because prayer isn't enough. My therapist hears confession twice a month, my shrink delivers the host, and I can stand in the woods and see the world spark. Twenty-two years ago I loved my family but I started running. Now my children are growing and I cannot hide. I can't hide this disease or unmake this knowledge or swallow the whim-wham niceties, the euphemisms. Love is not enough. It takes courage to grab my father's demon, my own, or—God help me—my child's and strap it down and stop its mad jig; to sit in a row of white rooms filled with pills and clubbed dreamers and shout: stop smiling, shut up; shut up and stop laughing; you're sitting in hell. Stop preaching; stop weeping. You are a manic-depressive, always. Your life is larger than most, unimaginable. You're blessed; just admit it and take the damn pill.

ACKNOWLEDGMENTS

Thanks to my parents, my brother, and my sister for their courage and the trust they placed in this project. Thanks to Roberta and my children for humoring and supporting me through it. I want to thank Susan Shilliday for use of the cupola, Karen Chapman for her encouragement, and Dori Ostermiller for demanding new chapters. Thanks to Bill Monahan for his certainty; my agent, Byrd Leavell, for his vision; and my editor, Ben Sevier, for his clarity and insight.